# Mac OS X Lion Server

## FOR

# DUMMIES®

# Mac OS X Lion Server

## FOR

# DUMMIES®

by John Rizzo

WILEY

John Wiley & Sons, Inc.

**Mac OS X Lion Server For Dummies®**

Published by
**John Wiley & Sons, Inc.**
111 River Street
Hoboken, NJ 07030-5774

www.wiley.com

Copyright © 2011 by John Wiley & Sons, Inc., Hoboken, New Jersey

Published by John Wiley & Sons, Inc., Hoboken, New Jersey

Published simultaneously in Canada

WILEY

# About the Author

**John Rizzo** has been writing about computers for over 20 years. His work has appeared in *Macworld, Infoworld, CNET, PC Magazine,eWeek the San Francisco Chronicle,* and other publications. He's a former columnist for *MacUser, MacWeek,* and *Computer Currents.*

John is the author of a dozen books, including *Snow Leopard Server For Dummies* (John Wiley & Sons), *Mac Mini Hacks & Mods For Dummies* (John Wiley & Sons), *Moving to Windows Vista* (PeachPit), and *Mac Annoyances* (O'Reilly). He's also written several books on Mac-and-Windows cross-platform networking and other topics on Mac and Windows hardware and software.

John publishes the website MacWindows.com, which has, since 1997, has been the web's largest news and information resource devoted to helping Mac users get along in a Windows world.

John is also a member of the Board of Trustees at the San Francisco Community College District, where he promotes the use of technology to improve student learning.

# Dedication

For the students at City College and everywhere in the public education system.

# Author's Acknowledgments

I will never write another book.

That was the vow I allegedly took after writing *Snow Leopard Server For Dummies* (*SLS Dummies,* as we say in the biz). I don't recall if this is true, but family and friends claim that I say this after every book I write. I'm not sure they're correct; it doesn't sound like something I would say. Nevertheless, while going through my *SLS Dummies* notes in preparation for *Lion Server For Dummies,* I found a curious scribble next to some thoughts on Active Directory binding. It said "Note to self: Never write another book."

It may have had something to do with all the parties, movie outings, and barbeques I had to miss because I was spending weekends figuring out the best way to get DNS to work with e-mail service. Maybe it has something to do with the fact that *SLS Dummies* was my twelfth book, not counting books to which I've contributed. Which would make my next book (now *Lion Server For Dummies*) my thirteenth, which, I'm told, is unlucky.

But I'm not superstitious, and who says that I'm the author of the note in the margin? After all, it's not signed. Anyone can write a note to self. It just didn't add up.

So, ignoring my friends and family and the mysterious marginal note, I took on the *Lion Server For Dummies* project. To my surprise, it turned out to be a lot of work.

Which is why I'm very glad to have had the help of Christine, who constantly took up the slack and supported me while I was occupied with the project. Thanks to project editor Kelly Ewing for keeping things running and pointing out that you don't use a colon after the verb "to be." Dennis Cohen did a great job as technical editor and provided some nuggets of wisdom. Thanks to Kyle Looper who kept the right balance between providing ego-feeding encouragement and instilling abject fear of missing deadlines. I'd like to thank the original *Snow Leopard Server For Dummies* team at Wiley, Kyle Looper and Nicole Sholly, and also Phil Burk for his help with Active Directory. This book builds upon their work the first time around.

I also would like to thank the people at VMware and Parallels for their assistance. And I'm grateful to various developers at the Apple Developer Forums who provided the answers to several puzzles. And, thanks to the readers of MacWindows.com who have shared their knowledge and wisdom over the years. And I'm grateful to GDradio for getting me through many long, late nights and helping me stay in the zone.

Given all that, I will never write another book.

## Publisher's Acknowledgments

We're proud of this book; please send us your comments at http://dummies.custhelp.com. For other comments, please contact our Customer Care Department within the U.S. at 877-762-2974, outside the U.S. at 317-572-3993, or fax 317-572-4002.

Some of the people who helped bring this book to market include the following:

### Acquisitions and Editorial

**Project Editor:** Kelly Ewing

**Acquisitions Editor:** Kyle Looper

**Technical Editor:** Dennis Cohen

**Editorial Manager:** Jodi Jensen

**Editorial Assistant:** Amanda Graham

**Sr. Editorial Assistant:** Cherie Case

**Cover Photos:** © iStockphoto.com / Karl Dolenc; © iStockphoto.com / Nico Smit

**Cartoons:** Rich Tennant (www.the5thwave.com)

### Composition Services

**Project Coordinator:** Patrick Redmond

**Layout and Graphics:** Carl Byers, Joyce Haughey, Corrie Socolovitch

**Proofreader:** Kathy Simpson

**Indexer:** Christine Karpeles

### Publishing and Editorial for Technology Dummies

**Richard Swadley,** Vice President and Executive Group Publisher

**Andy Cummings,** Vice President and Publisher

**Mary Bednarek,** Executive Acquisitions Director

**Mary C. Corder,** Editorial Director

### Publishing for Consumer Dummies

**Kathleen Nebenhaus,** Vice President and Executive Publisher

### Composition Services

**Debbie Stailey,** Director of Composition Services

# Contents at a Glance

# Table of Contents

# Introduction

● ● ● ● ● ● ● ● ● ● ● ● ● ● ● ● ● ● ● ● ● ● ● ● ● ● ● ● ● ● ● ● ● ● ● ● ● ● ● ● ● ● ● ● ● ● ● ● ● ●

*Y*ou're about to become a magician. Soon you'll be providing your users with the illusion that they have direct access to the world of communication and information. The reality is that every connection, communication, and bit of information that the computer user sees is provided by servers — ubiquitous, imperceptible, and indefatigable.

But only if you make it so. You're going to set up Apple's Lion Server for your users, configure the wonderful services it offers, and keep it running. This book will help you do it.

## About This Book

*Mac OS X Lion Server For Dummies* takes you through the steps required to get your users doing amazing and productive things. I provide step-by-step procedures to accomplish specific tasks, such as configuring an e-mail server and setting up user accounts. In some instances, I also describe how to set up your users' Macs or Windows PCs to work with the server.

This book also introduces you to the tools that Apple provides with the server and the best ways to use them. With some of Lion Server's features, there are just too many options and network configurations to take you through every possible scenario. The book considers the most common scenarios and describes the best practices you should adopt.

I also describe the new features in Lion Server that you'll want to know about (trust me on this). I've peppered the chapters with plenty of tips and tricks that will help you become proficient.

I'm a fan of the English language, so I favor it over the technobabble found in much of computing. (Although the term *Uniform Resource Locator* may mean something specific to software engineers, *Web address* works just fine in the real world.) Where the technobabble is unavoidable, I provide explanations. You will not, however, find the word *empower* in this book. A writer can be pushed only so far.

# Conventions Used in This Book

Flip through this book, and you'll find different uses of type to point out different things. Here's what I do:

- In the step-by-step directions, the actions you perform are in bold type, **like this.** The description of what happens after the action is in normal type.

- To point out a web address, the book uses a font that looks like this: www.apple.com. You'll see the same font in the rare instances when I show you something that you need to type in a command line (in the Mac's Terminal application), such as fsck -fy, and for text that a command line returns to you in response. I also use monofont to indicate folders. For example, to indicate the Utilities folder, which is inside the Applications folder, I say /Applications/Utilities.

- In other rare cases when you need to use a menu at the top of the screen, this book uses a convention that looks like this: File⇨Get Info, which means you need to choose Get Info from the File menu. For menus that aren't at the top of the screen, such as pop-up menus, I don't use this convention. Don't worry; I almost never ask you to use menus at the top of the screen in this book, so you rarely see this.

# What You're Not to Read

When it comes down to it, you really don't have to read any of this book. Look at the pictures, hide a copy of a good mystery novel inside it to read on the subway, or use it to prop up a kitchen-table leg. As long as you buy it, I'm okay with it. (It makes a great gift, by the way.)

If you're going to read this book, you don't need to read the whole thing or to read it in any particular order. The book is organized in a logical manner from beginning to end, but it's not a narrative. Rather, it's *modular.* You need to read only the portion that applies to a specific project or technique.

If you already have Lion Server installed, you can skip Part I. And you don't have to read Part VI to accomplish any server project. Consider it the chocolate center of a Good Humor bar.

Within most of the parts, the chapters are arranged from more general to more specific. For example, if you're a Windows administrator with experience with Active Directory, you can go right to Chapter 7, which deals specifically with Macs and Microsoft networks.

If you want, you can skip the text next to the Technical Stuff icons. I won't be insulted (well, not much), but I think you'll enjoy them.

Did I mention that *Mac OX Lion Server For Dummies* makes a great gift? If so, you don't have to read this sentence.

# Foolish Assumptions

Unlike some other computer books, you won't find a lot of filler here — no dissertations that have no bearing on the task at hand. I assume that you bought this book to accomplish specific tasks using Lion Server.

You also won't find lectures on what's in the Print dialog or how to search for a file. That's because I assume that you're already a computer user. But I don't assume that you're an Apple-Certified System Administrator. I explain the alphabet soup of acronyms that you find in some of the Server's technospeak.

Don't worry if you're new to the Mac. I explain any Apple-specific knowledge that you need. Experienced Mac users can skip bits of Mac-specific material. There won't be a test on your Mac savvy at the end of the book.

Similarly, you don't need any experience with Windows if you want to support Windows clients with your Mac server. I show you what you need to know.

I don't make any assumptions about what hardware you're running. For the purposes of this book, it doesn't matter — Lion Server is scalable to most Intel-powered Macs, from mini to Xserve. I provide some guidance as to what Mac is right for you in Chapter 2.

# How This Book Is Organized

*Mac OS X Lion Server For Dummies* is organized in six parts, each with several related chapters inside. The parts are arranged in order of how you might go about using the server. But you don't have to read the book sequentially, as each part can stand alone as a sort of minibook on a topic. You don't even have to read all the sections in any particular chapter. You can use the table of contents and the index to find the information you need and quickly get your answer.

I do recommend taking a glance, at least, at Part I. You'll find some information about installing Lion Server that you won't find in Apple's documentation.

## Part 1: Getting Lion Server Up and Running

I start this part with a description of Lion Server — what it comes with, what you can do with it, and what you need to get it running. If you need advice on which Mac model to use as your server and what should be in it, look in this part. I also describe some hardware needs in the server and on the network. If you haven't already installed Lion Server, you can find step-by-step directions in Part I.

This part of the book ends with a description of server virtualization. I take you through the hows and whys of setting up a server in a virtual machine, which most people will find useful for one reason or another. If you don't know what a virtual machine is, go to Chapter 4 right now.

## Part II: Creating and Maintaining User Accounts and Directories

For networks with more than a handful of users, setting up user directories can help automate security and simplify maintenance. This part describes what you can do with a directory, including setting up user authentication and connecting your server to a bigger network.

Part II also covers the options you have for directory services, including Open Directory, which comes with Lion Server. I devote Chapter 7 to the issue of using Lion Server to connect your Macs to Microsoft Active Directory, which is common on Windows networks.

## Part III: Serving Up Files and Printers

Part III covers the meat and potatoes of servers: sharing files and printers with multiple users. File and print sharing were the first tasks for servers when personal computers came on the scene in the 1980s. Sharing is still the most common task, though other services are often wrapped around it. This part also describes limiting access to certain folders using permissions.

## Part IV: Facilitating User Collaboration

Part IV is one of the longer parts of this book. Lion Server offers an array of services that help users work with each other. Part IV covers e-mail, calendar sharing, meeting scheduling, and the sharing of contacts, as well as web-based services, from your basic website to wikis and blogs.

I describe how to set up these services and point out some of the more interesting and perhaps less obvious things you can do with them.

## Part V: Managing Clients

Client computers — the Macs and PCs on the network — can be a chore to maintain all by yourself. Fortunately, you can use your server to automate some of this work for you. This part describes how to use the tools for managing clients. You can even manage the notebook computers that float in and out of the building.

Viruses, data spies, identity thieves, and other threats are all commonplace in the electronic world that computers live in. Chapter 18 describes how to keep out the nasties and how to enable users to access the server remotely without letting in the malware.

## Part VI: The Part of Tens

I show you ten nifty things you can add to Lion Server that can make it even more useful, or at least more interesting. Part VI also delivers ten quick tips for doing even more with Lion Server.

# Icons Used in This Book

To make this book easier to use, five icons appear to the left of the text. These icons are here to help you find information as you flip through the pages. Think of them as signposts, each pointing to a different way to think about what's being said.

Here are the icons you'll find:

Tips are the best bits of the description that make the job easiest or better. They aren't always the only way to get something done, but they do point out the best way to accomplish a task. Sometimes you can reuse a tip for other tasks.

When you see this icon, I'm flagging something that you don't want to forget to do, unless you want to mess up what you're doing.

The Warning icon highlights lurking danger. With this icon, I'm telling you to pay attention to what you're doing or to what you shouldn't do.

This icon marks a general interesting fact that's a technical explanation of what's going on or why you need to do something. I didn't want to turn this book into an engineering textbook, so I kept the tech stuff short.

Readers who have extensive backgrounds with Windows but who may be new to Macs can be on the lookout for these icons. This icon points out terminology or features that PC users may not be familiar with.

# Where to Go from Here

The section "How This Book Is Organized," earlier in this Introduction, gives you a good idea as to where to begin with this book. Where you start is up to you — begin with Chapter 1, dive right into file servers in Chapter 9, or check out the tips in Chapter 19. Be sure to check out Chapter 4 to see whether you want to install Lion Server in a virtual machine. Use this book as a reference (a *For Dummies* technical encyclopedia) or read it from start to finish for the complete picture. However you use it, I won't be offended. I wrote this book so that you can find all sorts of useful information however you choose to approach it.

Occasionally, we have updates to our technology books. If this book does have technical updates, they will be posted at

`dummies.com/go/macosxlionserverfdupdates`

# Part I
# Getting Lion Server Up and Running

## The 5th Wave
By Rich Tennant

"I'm not saying I believe in anything. All I know is since it's been there, our server is running 50% faster."

# In this part . . .

*L*ion Server is an amazingly versatile and scalable solution, serving a small workgroup or acting as part of an integrated network of thousands of users. So it may not be surprising that the process of getting it up and running can involve vastly different software and hardware configurations.

This part describes the many different services available to your users and the hardware the server runs on, from the little Mac mini to the beefy Mac Pro, and how to pick the best Mac model for your use of the server.

Lion Server offers several possibilities of installation, depending on your use. This part shows you how to get ready for your installation and how to install it in different scenarios.

This part also gives you another installation option: virtualization. This technique lets you set up a test server without needing to dedicate a Mac to the purpose. Virtualization also enables you to run multiple instances of Lion Server on one Mac. You can even run Lion Server and Windows Server on the same Mac.

# Chapter 1

# Lion Server: An Overview

*I*t comes with a wide array of user services: file sharing, calendaring, contact management, web, e-mail, instant messaging, media streaming, and more. It's versatile enough to support Macs and PCs running Windows, Unix, and Linux. It even supports iPads, iPhones, and iPod touches.

It's reliable, built on the solid foundation of Unix. At the same time, it has the ease of use of a Macintosh. Anyone can set it up, get it running, and manage it. Seriously technical professionals will find tools for the kind of configuration customization that they're accustomed to.

It is Mac OS X Server.

Lion Server (also known as Mac OS X Server 10.7) is the eighth major version from Apple. Unlike Microsoft, which releases the Windows user version before the server version, Apple develops user and server versions at the same time. Lion Server looks like the copy of Lion running on users' Macs. And Mac OS X Server runs on Macs, of course — any model that Apple makes today, as well as some older models. You can use Lion Server at home, in a small business, or in a department in a large organization.

In this chapter, I describe what you can do with Lion Server, providing an overview of all the services in one place. I also point out what's new and improved and what's changed in this version and introduce you to the software tools you'll use throughout the book.

# Why You Need a Server

You've probably discovered that you can have a small network without a server. Macs and PCs can talk to each other. They can share files and printers, and you may be able to use a router to share an Internet connection.

But a server enables users to collaborate in ways that aren't possible without it. A server gives you control; it centralizes data, making it easier to manage. A server provides fast access to information and collaborative tools and provides network security.

So what's a server that does all this great stuff? *Server* refers to software, hardware, or both. Server software can be the whole package, such as Mac OS X Server, or one of its features, such as the e-mail server. The Mac that Mac OS X Server runs on is also referred to as a server. *Client* can refer to the Mac or PC sitting on a user's desk, or to a piece of user software, such as an e-mail client, that talks to server software.

## Top ten signs you know it's time to buy a server

At some point, you'll *need* to add a server. Here are the top ten signs you know it's time to buy a server:

10. **You have too many computers to go around futzing with them all.** With centralized management of client computers, you can set users' passwords and settings for network access and install software on the client computers from the server. A server doesn't eliminate messing with individual clients but can cut it down quite a bit.

9. **Users keep running out of hard drive space.** Instead of replacing or adding hard drives on multiple users' computers, put one or more hulking, huge hard drives in a server that everyone can use.

8. **Users need special software that everyone can access.** Database software, accounting software, or software specific to your line of business needs a central location.

7. **You have critical data that would cause big problems if you lost it.** Storing mission-critical files in one central location makes them easier to back up than when the files sit on user machines.

6. **Your Mac slows when other users are trying to get files off it.** Your Mac or PC should work for you, not for other users. A server frees up your computer for your work. Servers can also handle multiple users faster than a client computer.

5. **People keep changing settings on Macs, messing things up.** With a server, school computer labs and even user machines can be managed to keep or restore needed settings.

4. **People in your group need to connect to your network from home or while traveling.** Your server can provide secure, encrypted access to your organization's network, even while the user sits across the ocean sipping a cappuccino in a Wi-Fi cafe in Piazza Navona.

3. **You want to host your own websites.** Whether you or your users want to temporarily post something for your own viewing or permanently for the public, having your own web server gives you the most flexibility to host one or more sites.

2. **Your e-mail inbox fills up with messages about finding times for meetings.** A shared server-based scheduling server enables everyone to share one or more calendars. Multiple people can change details of an event or adds new ones.

1. **The number one reason that you know it's time to get a server:** You want to do *all* these things and maybe more.

## Why you need a Lion Server

Any server platform does the great things described in the preceding section. Your PC-savvy friends may be telling you to get a Windows server. You'll need it, they say, to support your PCs. For a small network, Lion Server will serve your PCs and your Macs, too. On a large network, Mac OS X will peacefully coexist with Windows servers, serving your Macs like no Windows server can.

Another friend may roll his eyes and tell you that a Linux server is the only logical choice. He'll tell you that Linux is inexpensive and reliable, and that many of the servers powering the Internet are running Linux. All true, but it takes an expert to configure and maintain a Linux server. And it still doesn't support Mac clients as well as Lion Server does.

Still not convinced? Well, you probably are because you're reading this book. But maybe your boss isn't convinced. Here are some reasons why your server should be Lion Server.

### The price is right

Windows and Linux servers can scale up to some very large networks, which Mac OS X Server isn't designed to do. But Windows servers can cost thousands of dollars more than Lion Server, and Linux costs you in terms of technical expertise.

### *Windows server versus Lion Server*

Mac OS X Server is inexpensive compared to Windows servers. Microsoft has a complicated pricing model with different configurations with multiple options. Lion Server comes in one version, with no restrictions on the number of clients.

Microsoft Windows servers not only start out at higher price points, but there's also a charge for the number of clients you have on the network. If you want to add more computers to your network, you have to write another check to Microsoft. With Mac OS X Server, there's no per-client fee. Add as many Macs, PCs, or Linux machines as the server hardware can handle.

### *Linux versus Lion Server*

A Linux server can be less expensive than Lion Server, depending on which company you get it from. But it may or may not come with the full suite of services found in Mac OS X Server. Add to that the cost of the time spent adding all the services to a Linux server and configuring it (assuming that you have sufficient Linux expertise) or paying someone else to do it, and you'll find that Lion Server is still a bargain.

## *Better service for Mac clients*

Lion Server supports Mac clients better than any other server. For example, Lion Server offers services specifically for the Apple software on your users' Macs, including Address Book and iCal (see Chapters 11 and 12, respectively). Lion Server turns these apps into groupware apps and works more smoothly for the user and the administrator than other servers and Mac clients. A server version of the Mac's Spotlight makes searching the server quick and easy.

But even for generic services, such as file sharing, Mac OS X Server serves Mac clients better than other servers. The Mac OS X Server supports any filename that the Mac supports, and it doesn't split files into two parts or leave small, empty files on the server, which are problems that can occur when Mac clients access Windows and Linux servers.

## *Service for iPads and iPhones*

Lion Server supports iOS devices — iPads, iPhones, and iPod touches — in several ways. Lion Server is the first software to provide centralized file sharing for iPads. It also provides a simple way to configure and manage iOS devices and Mac clients running Mac OS X 10.7. This includes configuring network settings setting password restrictions, as well as setting up user accounts for mail, calendar, contacts, and chat (see Chapter 16).

You can also use Lion Server to integrate devices into your network directory, as well as to define management policies for iOS devices (as you can for computers, users, and groups).

Lion Server can "push" configuration changes out to the devices using Apple Push Notification services, which you can also use to push calendar invitations and events. And the Server also optimizes wikis and blogs for viewing on iOS devices.

# The Servers in Lion Server

Lion Server isn't one server, but more than two dozen servers and tools for managing the Mac clients. Figure 1-1 lists the services available to you, as you see them in the Server Admin and the Server utilities. You turn many of them on and off with a few mouse clicks. Here's a quick look at what services you get, and what you can do with them.

**Figure 1-1:**
Lion Server
is actually
a set of
servers.

## File server

The bread and butter of a server, the file server may be all that some people need from Lion Server. File servers provide folders that everyone on the network can see. You can also limit access so that some people can't get into certain folders. Mac OS X Server provides file sharing via the Mac-native Apple Filing Protocol (AFP), which is Mac only, and Microsoft's Server Message Block (SMB), which Windows and Linux clients use. Lion Server also provides the WebDAV protocol for iPads. It's also used by Time Machine to back up Macs. (Flip to Chapter 9 for more on this topic.)

## Directory services

Mac OS X Server uses the standards-based Open Directory to store and manage the user account info and other user data that's used for all the services. You can connect the server to other directory services on the network, including Microsoft Active Directory. To keep the network secure, directory services authenticates clients that log in with the LDAP, Kerberos, and SASL standards. Chapter 5 describes what all these standards are.

Chapter 6 describes how to set up Open Directory. In Lion, Open Directory now includes a feature called Locales, which lets you specify which replica directory server a client computer will connect to based on a network location — a handy feature to keep notebook computers connected to the directory no matter where they are.

## Address Book Server

Address Book Server enables users to share both personal and group contacts with the Mac Address Book or a CardDAV-compatible client. See Chapter 11 for the scoop on Address Book Server.

## iCal Server

Users on the network can schedule events, book conference rooms, and view one another's calendars. People can send an invitation to a meeting that includes an agenda and then can accept the invitation. The iCal Server keeps track of who is inviting whom and what the group schedules are at any point in time. iCal Server works with the iCal calendar on Mac OS X, as well as with some open source software supporting the CalDAV standard. Lion Server adds a few things to iCal Server, including enabling multiple users to share To Dos. Chapter 12 describes setting up and running iCal Server.

## iChat Server

Instant messaging isn't just for mobile phones. Users of Mac OS X, Windows, and Linux (as well as iPhones and other handhelds) can have a virtual meeting by using iChat instant messaging. The server supports audio and video, as well as file transfer. Users can access persistent chat rooms that are always there. The server also stores each user's account info so that a user can iChat from any computer.

## Internet gateway and network services

Mac OS X Server can act as an *Internet gateway*, providing the computers on the network with access to the Internet while protecting the network from intruders. You can get these services in other ways, such as in a wireless router or from other servers on a larger network, but Mac OS X Server has them if you need them. These services are

- ✔ **Domain name server (DNS):** It translates a domain name, such as mycomany.com, from an IP address. DNS service is required somewhere on the network for just about all network services, including web, mail, directory services, and calendaring.

- ✔ **Network address translation (NAT):** A gateway between your private network and the public Internet. NAT allows you to have a single IP address from your Internet service provider but have all your computers connected to the Internet. This is cheaper than paying for IP addresses for each computer. With NAT, the individual IP addresses of your computers aren't visible to the outside world, but your computers can still receive e-mail and visit the web.

- ✔ **Dynamic Host Configuration Protocol (DHCP) server:** Assigns the local (private) IP addresses to your computers when you're using a NAT gateway.

- ✔ **Firewall:** Mac OS X Server comes with a firewall to protect your server from intruders. Chapter 18 describes Lion Server's firewall.

- ✔ **Virtual private network (VPN) service:** A secure method of enabling people to access your network and server via the Internet from home or on the road. The VPN service in Mac OS X Server supports several different standard methods of access.

## E-mail server

The Lion Server e-mail server has been revamped. Mail Server 3 now enables users to search the content of files attached to e-mail that is stored on the server. This search works for Microsoft Office and iWork files, PDF files, and others. Also new is the ability to provide webmail service with drag-and-drop message management.

As a full featured e-mail server, Mail Server blocks spam and e-mail that contain viruses from reaching users' desktops and can make e-mail available from a web browser. You can read more about Lion's e-mail server in Chapter 14.

## Web server

Lion Server's web server is really a package of technology, starting with the Apache web server, the most popular web server on the Internet. The web server also includes the PostgreSQL database (replacing MySQL in previous editions of the Mac OS X Server). A Perl plug-in comes loaded with the web server. The Perl programming language is used for Common Gateway Interface

(CGI) scripts for creating dynamic web pages and for functions, such as taking data that a user enters in a web-based form and moving it to the database.

But you don't need to be a programmer to take advantage of these features, as a lot of this technology is under the hood. For example, enabling users to access their e-mail from a web browser requires only a single mouse click in the Web pane of the Server app (see Figure 1-2).

**Figure 1-2:**
The Web pane of the Server app makes it easy to enable server features.

Part of the web server functionality is the automatic creation of a full-featured *wiki* — a website that users can edit from their web browser. In your organization, you can use wikis as a group collaboration tool for projects or brainstorming. Users can edit text, add hyperlinks to web pages, upload photos and documents to share, and then review the history of the changes that have been made and revert to earlier versions. Wikis automatically update to tell readers what changes other users have made.

The Wiki Server is also blogging software. Blogs in your organization are great for posting status updates and reports. Like blogs on the Internet, the Lion Server blog feature has a space at the bottom for users to post comments.

Wiki Server 3 in Lion Server has a new look and some new features, including e-mail notification, which tells a user when a page has been updated. Chapter 13 describes how to use the Wiki Server.

## Profile service for iOS and Mac OS X

Lion adds a new service called Profile Manager for creating and distributing profiles that can automatically set up iOS devices (iPads, iPod touches, and iPhones) as well as Macs. A profile can contain basic network settings and those for mail, calendar, contacts, and other things. It can also contain rules for passwords, as well as restrictions on what a user is allowed to do on the network. You can distribute profiles to devices via e-mail or have users download them from a self-service web page. You can also have Lion's Push Notification service automatically deliver updates to configuration profiles on devices.

## Podcast Producer

Podcast Producer is actually a set of software that automates the capture, creation, and distribution of video and audio. You and your users can record a lecture, training video, or student project, and Podcast Producer automatically adds, encodes, renders, and compresses titles and other elements based on your criteria. Podcast Producer automatically publishes your recording on a website or via iTunes. Windows users can also get into the action. You can read more about Podcast Producer in Chapter 15.

## Software update server

You can restrict what software updates get installed on client Macs, as well as when they get installed so that you can test updates first. The client Macs get the updates from the server instead of downloading them individually.

## NetInstall

NetInstall lets you install Mac OS X upgrades on users' Macs, requiring that their updates come from Mac OS X Server and not directly from the Internet. Because Mac OS X updates can sometimes cause incompatibilities with older software, you can test an upgrade before rolling it out on all the client Macs at the same time. NetInstall also lets you restore, from the server, a customized Mac OS X configuration to Macs that need it.

## NetBoot

NetBoot is great for a group of Macs that are available to multiple users, such as in a school computer lab or a classroom. This service enables Mac clients to boot up from the server instead of from their own hard drives. The NetBoot server can use a single disk image to boot multiple Macs. This process prevents the boot system from being altered or tampered with and makes sure that every system boots in exactly the same configuration. NetBoot also lets you update the system software of all the Macs at one time, simply by updating the disk image on the server.

## Spotlight Server

For Mac users, Spotlight is an indispensable search feature that lets you find a file almost instantaneously. Spotlight Server does the same for files on the server without bogging down server performance. Spotlight Server does this by indexing the content of the files. This server also provides advanced search features, including Boolean logic and the use of quoted phrases, and stores search criteria in the form of Smart Folders.

# Management Tools in Lion Server

In addition to providing services to client computers, Lion Server comes with a set of software for managing these servers. You can install several of the tools on any system running Mac OS X 10.7 on the network, allowing you to keep the server Mac out of sight in a secure location.

Flipping through this book, you see that I mostly describe two tools: the Server application and Server Admin. Workgroup Manager is the third most-used tool. The other tools play smaller, more specialized roles.

The Server app is included with Lion Server. You'll find it in the Applications folder. But you won't find Server Admin, Workgroup Manager, and other more advanced tools. You have to go get them yourself from Apple at this location: http://support.apple.com/downloads.

The Server app and Server Admin are both for configuring services, but you use each to configure a different set of services. The Server app generally includes the services that most people might use, such as file service, calendar, web, and wiki. Server Admin tends to include services that not everyone may use or that are aimed at infrastructure, such as DHCP, DNS, NAT, and Open Directory. The Server app is the simpler of the two, providing fewer configuration options than Server Admin.

If you have Mac server experience, these tools are a major change from earlier versions of Mac OS X Server, which had a utility called Server Preferences instead of the Server app. However, in Mac OS X Server versions 10.5 and 10.6, the two utilities presented different views of the same services, one simplified, and Server Admin with more configuration options. This is no longer the case with Lion Server, which now has the two utilities configuring different services. The lone exception is Mail, which appears in both tools.

If you're handy with Unix commands, you can still configure Lion Server via Terminal.

# The Server application

 For simpler networks, you can spend most of your server management time in the Server app (shown in Figure 1-3). The Server app offers you quick access to configuration windows for users and the services they're allowed to access.

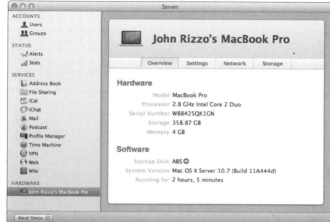

**Figure 1-3:** The Server app gives you easy access to configuring services.

The Server app enables you turn services on and off. You can assign user passwords and manage mail, calendar, and iChat servers. You can also change firewall settings and turn on remote access via a virtual private network. The Time Machine icon lets you set automated backups of server data.

### Configuring Services and Accounts with the Server app

To start up a service, click an icon under Services in the left sidebar. The pane at the right displays configuration options for that service (see Figure 1-4). Click the big switch in the upper right to turn the service on or off. It may take a few seconds for the service to start.

You can also use the Server app to create user and group accounts. (Workgroup Manager can also create user accounts and gives you more configuration options.) Click Users or Groups under Accounts in the sidebar. You can then type user and group names and passwords.

The Server app includes built-in guidance to help you configure Lion Server. Click the Next Steps button in the lower left of the Server app to expand the window at the bottom. Several new buttons appear at the bottom of the window, as shown in Figure 1-5. Clicking one displays information about your server's current setup and provides links to settings windows that will enable you to complete other tasks.

**Figure 1-4:**
The File Sharing pane of the Server app.

**Figure 1-5:**
The Next Steps button provides information about configuring your server.

For example, in Figure 1-5, the Server app tells you that the users added are local user accounts, residing only on the server Mac and not in a network directory. Clicking the Manage Network Users link in the text takes you to a screen where you can start setting up Open Directory.

### Monitoring your server and making general settings changes

The Server app provides several ways to view the status of your server. In the sidebar under Status are two items:

✔ **Alerts:** Here, you find alerts that Lion Server can send you. You're alerted to conditions of low disk space, possible virus-containing e-mail, expired SSL certificates, changes to network settings, and available software updates. You can also use this pane to designate an e-mail address where Lion Server can e-mail alerts to you.

✔ **Stats:** Stats provides live graphs of your server's processor usage, memory usage, and network traffic.

Under Hardware, you can click the name of your server to get access to four panes of information and some settings as well:

✔ **Overview:** This pane (refer to Figure 1-3) provides information about the Mac model and hardware configuration, the version of Mac OS X Server, and how long the server has been running.

✔ **Settings:** Here, you can change settings for remote login and administration, screen sharing, push notifications, and SSL certificates.

A check box called Dedicate System Resources To Server Services should always be checked. Having it uncheck can slow server performance.

✔ **Network:** This pane displays (and lets you change) the Mac's computer name and the server's hostname. It also displays the IP addresses of your network interfaces.

✔ **Storage:** This pane displays the amount of free space on any storage devices attached to the server. It also lets you change permissions for shared folders (see Chapter 9).

# *Server Admin*

Server Admin handles more complex tasks than does the Server app. Server Admin provides more options and much more fine-grained control over the services it supports. Server Admin also gives you access to services that aren't available in the Server app, such as the DNS and push notification servers, firewall, and the software update server. Figure 1-6 shows Server Admin's Overview pane. Server Admin also can keep track of multiple servers and the services they're running.

## *Configuring Services with Server Admin*

You can use Server Admin to configure and manage Lion Server's many services, including Open Directory. To get Server Admin running for the first time, follow these steps:

1. **If you're not already logged in to the server Mac, log in as the local administrator.**

2. **Open Server Admin from the `/Applications/Server` folder.**

**Figure 1-6:**
The General pane of Server Admin provides information about the server setup.

3. **Double-click the name of a server in the left column to bring up the login screen.**

   If you don't see your server, click the Add (+) button in the lower left and select Add Server from the pop-up menu.

4. **Type the hostname of the server (if not already displayed) in the Address field and then enter the administrator's username and password.**

   For best results, always enter the server's fully qualified hostname. You can also enter the server's name ending in .local, if this is what you created when you installed Lion Server because DNS wasn't running on your network. (More on DNS is in Chapter 3.)

5. **Click Connect.**

   You're now connected to the server and ready to manage its services. Click the triangle next to the server's name to view an expanded list of enabled services, as shown in Figure 1-6.

If the service you want to configure doesn't appear in the list, that means that it isn't turned on. In Server Admin, a service first needs to be turned on, and then it also needs to be started. Here's how to turn a service on:

1. **In Server Admin, click your server in the sidebar to select it.**

2. **Click the Settings icon in the toolbar and then click the Settings tab.**

3. **Select the check box next to your service (see Figure 1-7) and click the Save button in the lower right.**

   Your service should now appear in the left column under Services.

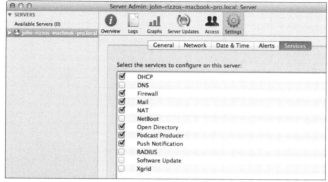

A dot next to each service in the list can be a few possible colors:

 ✔ **Clear:** Service is enabled but not running.

 ✔ **Red:** Service has an error.

 ✔ **Light green:** Infrequent, shown sometimes as a service restarts.

 ✔ **Dark green:** Service is running normally.

Typically, you want to configure settings for a service when it isn't running (with a clear dot). After you're finished with the settings, you can start the service running:

1. **Click the triangle to the left of your server to expand the list of services and then click the name of your service.**

2. **Click the Start button in the lower left of the screen.**

### Monitoring your server with Server Admin

Server Admin provides more monitoring features than the Server app. You can access them by clicking your server in the left column to select it. The General pane (refer to Figure 1-6) appears, providing information about the host Mac's hardware and software configuration and status.

The Logs icon gives you access to several types of log files for the server. The Graphs icon provides live graphs of processor usage and network traffic. The Server Update icon lists the previous updates to Mac OS X Server and lets you update from this window.

## Workgroup Manager

Workgroup Manager is a more advanced tool for setting and managing user accounts than the Server app. You can use Workgroup Manager to control aspects of users' computers. For example, you can require users to change passwords at regular intervals, create standardized preference settings for client Macs, or allow only certain applications to run. You can also use Workgroup Manager to configure certain security measures, such as blocking computers from seeing external hard drives or from burning CDs and DVDs. And you can create groups to manage settings for multiple sets of computers at once.

For more on Workgroup Manager, see Chapter 16.

## The rest of the management team

There are some other tools that you'll use less frequently than the Server app, Server Admin, and Workgroup Manager. You may never need to use them at all. In case you do, here's a rundown of what they do.

### Server Status Dashboard widget

If you're a Mac user, you're familiar with Dashboard widgets. On most Macs, hit the F4 key and up pops a calculator, the weather, and other small applets. They disappear when you click something else. Mac OS X Server has a Server Status Dashboard widget, shown in Figure 1-8, that you can use on the server or on any Mac on the network.

**Figure 1-8:**
The Server Status Dashboard widget lets you keep an eye on several server parameters.

Lion displays Dashboard widgets differently from previous versions of Mac OS X. Instead of overlaying the widgets on the screen, it switches to a different space, hiding all the current open applications. You can, however, set Dashboard to use the previous method of displaying widgets as an overlay. To do this, open System Preferences from the Dock or from the Apple menu and click Exposé & Spaces. Now uncheck Show Dashboard as a Space at the bottom of the screen.

### Podcast Composer

You can use Podcast Composer to create and edit podcast workflows. It guides you through the required steps, where you can choose titles, videos, and effects for a podcast. See Chapter 15 for more about creating podcasts and workflows with Lion Server.

### Server Monitor

Server Monitor lets you keep tabs on Apple's Xserve server hardware. Apple discontinued Xserve in early 2011, but you can still run Lion Server on it. Server Monitor can display a graph of the internal temperature of one or more Xserve(s), list warnings and failures, display the power usage, and show how much hard drive space and memory are in the Xserves on your network. You can set Server Monitor to send you an e-mail message if it detects a hardware problem in an Xserve box. (You can read more about Xserves and Lion in Chapter 3.)

If you have Lion Sever installed on another type of Mac, you won't have any use for Server Monitor. You can safely delete it.

### System Image Utility

You can use System Image Utility to create Mac OS X disk images to be used to boot Macs from the server with NetBoot or to install on multiple Macs with NetInstall. (See the "NetBoot" and "NetInstall" sections, earlier in this chapter.)

You can create a NetInstall or NetBoot disk image in two steps, or you can customize settings to include your own items in the disk image. You can also include a Boot Camp partition in a disk image if you want a client Mac to have the option of booting with Microsoft Windows.

### Xgrid Admin

Xgrid Admin is designed to monitor arrays of Macs working together as one entity. The most practical use that Apple gives is with Podcast Producer, which can use Xgrid to spread the work of processing video across multiple Macs automatically. Xgrid Admin enables you to monitor an Xgrid and to manage computing jobs that are going on.

Apple includes Xgrid Admin along with the more everyday server administration tools, almost as a dare to find out what you can do with it. If you tie together enough Macs, you can have ordinary user Macs by day and the combined power of a supercomputer by night. Stanford University uses an Xgrid of several hundred Macs to perform complex calculations related to molecular physiology and pharmacology.

You can find a very thorough description of Xgrid at `www.macresearch.org/the_xgrid_tutorials_part_i_xgrid_basics`.

## Command-line administration

If you're a deft Unix coder who likes to really get into it, you can use the Unix command-line tools that come with Mac OS X to configure and manage Lion Server. You can also use these commands from a non-Apple Unix or Linux computer on the network. But even if you aren't a Unix geek, you may come across a tip that can work around a problem by typing a couple lines of text. Some features are accessible only by command line, such as FTP and NFS file sharing.

Unix commands are accessible in the Terminal application on every Mac OS X machine. You can use one of the Unix shells that come with Terminal: bash (the default), sh, csh, tsh, and zsh. If you're managing one or more servers over a network, use ssh, or *Secure Shell.* Rest assured, though, that Unix commands aren't required to set up or manage Lion Server.

### Xsan Admin

Xsan is Apple's cluster file system for accessing terabytes of storage arrays. Xsan Admin is where you set up, configure, and monitor an Xsan system. You can find out more information about Xsan at Apple's website: www.apple.com/xsan.

# What Apple Removed from Mac OS X Server

With Mac OS X Server 10.7, Apple made a decision to simplify administration and setup. Although it added some new features, Apple removed some features as well as some configuration options. Some of the old features look like they're missing, but you can still access them via the command line if you know how to edit Unix configuration files. This change has made some long-time Mac administrators unhappy, though you may not be bothered at all.

You also don't want to spend a lot of time looking for something that isn't there. The following sections describe where you can find services, as well as the main things you'll no longer see in Lion Server.

### Services moved from Server Admin to the Server app

Settings for AFP and SMB (now combined as *file service*) and web service are now only available in the Server app. Address Book, icla, iChait, VPN, Web, and Wiki services are also now entirely in the Server app, and not in Server Admin. The drawback is that the Server app is simpler, providing far fewer configuration options than Server Admin, which means you can't do as much with them as you could in Snow Leopard Server.

### Services removed from Server Admin but not in the Server app

The missing service people complain about most is print server and management. The underlying CUPS printing engine is still there, but it's no longer in the server tools. Apple provides two ways to set up printer sharing:

- **System Preferences:** Here, you use the Print and Fax pane, as you would share a printer connected to a user's Mac. You'd have to use screen sharing to do this from another Mac.

- **The CUPS web interface:** Type **http://localhost:631/** in a web browser, and you come up with the configuration page. This page gives you some configuration options not available in System Preferences.

Neither method is completely satisfactory. For example, you no longer have any way to set quotas for printers or users. And neither method ties in with a directory. Nor are these features available from the command line — they've been eliminated. (As an editorial comment, the removal of as basic a service as print is a bit baffling. Apple has never provided a reasonable explanation as to why it removed the feature from Lion Server.)

FTP file sharing is now only available by typing Unix commands. The same is true for NFS file sharing, which used to be an alternative to AFP and SMB. NFS is still in Lion Server because it's used by NetBoot. You can still configure FTP and NFS in Terminal if you know how. But for most users, FTP and NFS file sharing is no longer an option.

More significant is the complete removal of the ability to set Mac OS X Server to act as a Primary Domain Controller for Windows climates. This feature isn't available from the command line or anywhere else. What this means is that Lion Server simply doesn't support Windows clients as well as Mac OS X Server 10.5 and 10.6. QuickTime Streaming server has also been eliminated from Lion Server.

Still, you still can do plenty with Lion Server (enough to fill this book), including the new features described in this chapter, such as Profile Manager for iOS devices.

# Chapter 2

# Choosing Server Hardware

· · · · · · · · · · · · · · · · · · · · · · · · · · · · · · · · · · · · · · · · · · · · · · ·

## In This Chapter

▶ Dissecting hardware requirements

▶ Choosing the right RAM and hard drives

▶ Selecting the right Mac for your server

▶ Considering other network hardware

· · · · · · · · · · · · · · · · · · · · · · · · · · · · · · · · · · · · · · · · · · · · · · ·

*Y*ou've chosen the software — Lion Server. Now you need to pick a Mac to run it on. You can spend anywhere from under $1,000 to over $10,000 (with storage options), and no one Mac model is best for running Lion Server. It runs on everything from a Mac mini to the now-discontinued Xserve, with varying amounts of memory and hard drive space. You can't use your old G5 Mac tower because Mac OS X 10.7 Server runs only on Intel processors.

This chapter takes you through criteria for choosing a Mac that best meets your needs as a server. By matching your anticipated uses to the available hardware, you can avoid getting an underpowered Mac server or spending too much for more than you need. If you already have a Mac in mind for use as a server, this chapter helps you decide whether it'll work for what you want to do with it.

## Criteria for Selecting Server Hardware

Before you think about processor speeds, do some planning to determine what you'll be doing with the server. Here are the two key issues: how many users access the server and what the users do with it. Neither tells the whole story by itself; you must consider both. When you have this information, your hardware options become clearer.

### Number of users

The effect of an increasing number of connected clients on server performance isn't linear. You may not notice slower service as the number of connected clients increases until you get to a tipping point, when performance suddenly slows to a crawl.

The Mac mini can handle a maximum of around 20 to 50 simultaneous client computers doing lightweight tasks. The more hardware-intensive services you run, the lower that number is. With up to ten or so users, the lower-end Macs can handle multiple tasks at once. If you add more users later, you can always add more lower-end Mac servers for other tasks. Current iMac models have faster processors and architecture than the minis, can hold more RAM, and can handle more clients.

The top-of-the-line Mac Pro can potentially handle hundreds of clients, again depending on what services you run. With the Mac Pro or an older Xserve, adding more higher-end storage or large amounts of RAM can help enlarge the client load that the server can handle. *Network capacity* (number of Ethernet cards and their speed) is also important in serving large numbers of clients.

## Type of use

The number of users doesn't tell the whole story about what Mac to use to run Lion Server. Five users accessing a database program might require beefier server hardware than ten users accessing a server-based Web site.

In Chapter 1, I describe the services that come with Lion Server. The following paragraphs describe some typical uses listed in *approximate* order of how much demand they place on your server hardware. I start with a web server, which places only light demand on hardware, and end with NetBoot, which demands a lot from your server.

### Web servers: Lightweight server use

Web servers tend to use low amounts of hardware resources. The server often caches web pages and doesn't have to access the hard drive to load web pages. Web serving also doesn't take a lot of RAM or processing power. You can run a web server on any Mac that Lion Server runs on, and you can generally run it along with other services without affecting their performances.

E-mail, DNS (domain name service), and Internet gateway functions are similarly lightweight services in terms of server hardware.

### File servers: Light on processor, big in storage

File serving is generally not an intensive use of the server hardware and doesn't use a lot of processing power. File servers primarily need a lot of storage. You can choose among a wide range of Macs for use as file servers, as long as the Mac has enough hard drive space in one or multiple hard drives. Unless you have a lot of users, file servers can run alongside other services.

File servers also need frequent backups or high levels of redundancy to pre-
serve the data.

The more users and the bigger the users' files, the more total storage you
need. Frequent movement of a lot of very large files, such as video, may
require a *storage area network (SAN),* which is storage connected directly to
a network or *RAID (Redundant Array of Individual Disks)* systems.

Backing up users' Macs and PCs to the server with a server-based backup
program is also a type of file sharing and a lightweight use of server processing power. Backing up multiple users at the same time can be a heavy use of
network bandwidth and may slow down a wireless network, but a faster Mac
server won't make a difference.

### Database server: Moving lots of data

If you install a third-party database server, it can take more resources than
file serving, especially if a lot of users are accessing the database. A database
server can require more frequent use of the hard drive and processor than
file servers, depending on the data being served and how often.

### Podcast Producer: Processor-intensive requirements

Podcast Producer or another video-related server can make heavy use of
hardware; it uses a lot of RAM, hard drive space, and processing power for
the video encoding. Video encoding is also one of the only Mac OS X Server
functions that use the graphics processor.

Apple encourages Podcast Producer to offload some of the processing to Mac
clients with the Xgrid service that comes with Lion Server. Xgrid uses spare
processing power on the clients to avoid bogging down users' Macs. The
more client Macs you can take advantage of on the network, the more video
you can process.

### Directory services: Give it what it needs

Directory services, which is supplied by Open Directory in Mac OS X Server,
can be one of the most actively used services on the network, particularly
a large network. Don't underpower a directory server, or you may slow the
whole network.

Directory servers store information about users and groups, permissions, and
configuration information for client computers; they authenticate clients and
store information that determines which clients can access which files. Running
directory services on a midsize to large network is equivalent to running multiple databases simultaneously. Fast storage is the most important directory
services requirement for any size network. A lot of memory is necessary to keep
up performance. For large networks, consider dedicating a server for directory
services and using one or more other Mac(s) for other services, such as mail.

However, directory service doesn't use a lot of CPU power. For smaller networks, running directory service along with other services should work fine.

### NetBoot: Heavy-duty server stress

NetBoot probably places more demand on the server's hardware resources than any other service in Mac OS X Server. NetBoot is where client Macs boot from the server itself instead of from their local hard drives. Even for a small network, you need a fast Mac server with multiple processors and fast hard drive storage, and lots of it.

You'll also need fast networking. Wireless networking is too slow for NetBoot, which is why it supports only Ethernet connections. A server with multiple Ethernet interfaces can prevent slowdowns. Check your Ethernet switch: You'll want 100BaseT at a minimum, and Gigabit Ethernet is better. Your network will slow to a crawl if you have an old 10BaseT switch and are using NetBoot.

With a lot of Mac clients, NetBoot may be too much for one server to handle, so the software supports load balancing on multiple Mac servers.

# Hardware Requirements for Running Lion Server

Here are the minimum requirements for running Lion Server:

- ✓ **Computer:** A Mac. Although you can hack non-Apple hardware to run the Mac OS X operating system, it violates the user license agreement.

- ✓ **Processor:** A 64-bit Intel processor. The oldest 64-bit processor found in Macs that support Lion is a Core 2 Duo. Lion won't run on Macs with an Intel Core Sole or a Core Duo, which was the first generations of Intel processors that Apple used. (Older PowerPC Macs are also not supported.)

- ✓ **RAM:** 2GB RAM base. If you're running Podcast Producer, you need an additional 512MB of RAM for each processor core. For example, if your Mac has two dual-core processors, you need 3GB minimum.

- ✓ **Hard drive space:** 8GB of free hard drive space.

The processor is, for the most part, determined by the Mac model you use. Macs with a dual-core Intel Core 2 Duo are slower than Macs with a dual-core Intel Core i3. Quad-core processors, such as the Intel Core i7, are faster yet. The Quad-Core Intel Xeon processors offered in the Mac Pro are faster than the Core i7. (Core i5s come in dual-core and quad-core models.) The Mac Pro has the option for a six-core processor. (Logic and Latin would dictate that this is a "sex-core," but the tech industry is wise enough to stay away from that one.)

The gigahertz (GHz) rating is less important than processor model and number of cores. It has meaning only when you compare two processors of the same model and same number of cores. So a 3.2 GHz Intel Core i3 is faster than a 3.06 GHz Intel Core i3.

As a general rule, use more RAM in a computer than the minimum amount of RAM required by the operating system. Some Macs can hold several dozen gigabytes of memory, which is more than most people need. See the section "Putting enough RAM in your server," later in this chapter, for more information.

For hard drive storage, you need as big a drive, or drives, as you have data to store. Hard drive storage is relatively inexpensive.

# Selecting Processor, Memory, and Hard Drives

For a server, the amount of RAM that a Mac can hold is almost as important as the processors in it. Select your Mac model for the RAM it holds as well as for the processor. The more expensive Macs hold significantly more RAM than the lower-end models.

With hard drives, you can always replace the hard drive or, in some Mac models, add hard drives.

## Selecting processors for your Mac servers

With Apple hardware, you can't choose just any processor the way you can with PCs. To get a particular type of processor, you have to select the Mac model. Within each model are some differences in clock speed. Mac Pro offers the most options in processors at purchase time, giving you a choice of one or two multicore processors.

Processors with multiple cores act as multiple processors. So two dual-core processors are equivalent to one quad-core processor. This is why processing power is sometimes described in terms of the number of cores rather than the number of processors.

You don't need a brand-new Mac for Lion Server. An older Mac is perfectly fine — as long as it has a 64-bit Intel processor. Lion won't run on the older PowerPC processors. Sometimes, the Mac's model name gives it away: A Power Mac has a PowerPC processor. All Mac Pro and MacBook models use Intel processors. Mac minis, iMacs, and Xserves, however, came in both PowerPC and Intel processor versions. When in doubt, check the About This

Mac window (see Figure 2-1), accessible from the Apple menu. This window also reveals how much memory you have in the machine.

For most Mac models, you can't upgrade a processor. You can upgrade a processor in Mac Pro, but doing so is difficult and voids the warranty. For a Mac Pro no longer under warranty, check out this website:

> www.everymac.com/systems/apple/mac_pro/faq/mac-pro-mid-2010-westmere-how-to-upgrade-processors.html

**Figure 2-1:**
The About This Mac window identifies the processor and amount of RAM.

Here, you can find information for various releases of the Mac Pro from 2008 and earlier to more modern models.

Only the Xserve has an officially upgradeable processor. Apple still has directions at its website: Go to www.apple.com/support/manuals and search for *Xserve processor.* You find PDF documents for each Xserve revision, such as *Xserve (Early 2008) DIY Procedure for Processor (Manual).*

You can't upgrade a PowerPC Mac with an Intel processor. The architecture of the machines is just too different. Don't even try.

## Putting enough RAM in your server

RAM is important for speed in the Mac OS X operating system, and this is particularly true for servers. Server applications can often run faster when you add RAM. More RAM also increases the number of simultaneous client connections that the server can handle without bogging down.

For some of the lightweight tasks that I describe in the "Type of use" section earlier in the chapter or if you have a smaller network, 4GB of RAM may be sufficient. If you're using a Mac mini or iMac on larger networks or with multiple services, add as much RAM as the machine will hold, which can be up to 16GB, depending on the model and age.

This strategy isn't always practical with the Mac Pro and Xserve because filling them to the maximum can run into hundreds or thousands of dollars — a lot of money if you don't need the RAM.

On the spare side, it's possible to achieve acceptable results with 2GB of RAM serving up to 200 users for light, occasional uses. A server with 2GB of RAM may be adequate for a small network of fewer than ten computers for file sharing.

If you've been running the server in normal use for a few hours, you can use Activity Monitor (in the server's Utility folder) to tell whether you have enough memory. At the bottom of the window, click the System Memory tab (see Figure 2-2). Look at the Page Ins and Page Outs numbers. If the size of the page outs is more than 5 to 10 percent of the page ins, the operating system has to write information from RAM to disk because it doesn't have enough RAM. This translates into slower server performance. In this case, add RAM to increase performance.

If you do need a lot of RAM, it's cheaper to buy extra RAM and install it yourself rather than buy it from Apple when you order a new Mac. The price difference is under $100 for Mac mini but can be several hundreds of dollars for Mac Pro. To find the best prices, check out Ramseeker (www.ramseeker.com), which lets you compare prices from multiple vendors — like Orbitz does with airline tickets. Just select your Mac model from a pop-up menu, and Ramseeker gives you a list of vendors and prices.

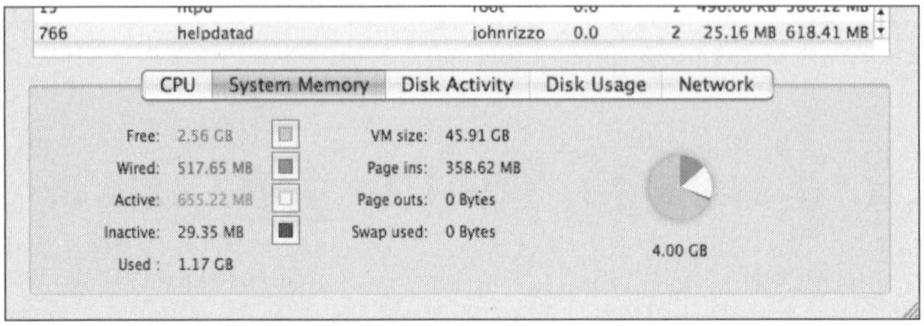

| CPU | System Memory | Disk Activity | Disk Usage | Network |

Free: 2.56 GB  □    VM size: 45.91 GB
Wired: 517.65 MB  ■    Page ins: 358.62 MB
Active: 655.22 MB  □    Page outs: 0 Bytes
Inactive: 29.35 MB  ■    Swap used: 0 Bytes
Used : 1.17 GB

4.00 GB

**Figure 2-2:**
Activity
Monitor
displays the
page ins and
page outs.

## Selecting hard drive storage

Apple gives you some hard drive choices when you buy a Mac. The drives vary in capacity, and with some models, you have a choice of rotational speed (see the following section). You can also replace the hard drive in an existing Mac with a bigger or faster drive.

You may also want to look at two other options for expanded capacity outside the Mac: NAS (network attached storage) and SAN (storage area network), which, despite the acronyms, aren't opposites. I discuss both later in this section.

### Rotational speed

*Rotational speed* is a measure of hard drive speed in revolutions per minute (rpm). This is the speed at which the platters inside the drive spin. The faster the rotational speed, the faster the drive performance.

The lowest rotational speed you'll find in a Mac that supports Lion is 5,400 rpm, which Apple used in some Mac mini and MacBook models. A speed of 5,400 rpm isn't particularly speedy for a server, so consider replacing such a drive with the next level up, 7,200 rpm. This is the fastest drive you'll see in notebooks and many desktop computers, aside from a solid state drive. A 7,200 rpm is also the standard in high-end Mac Pros and Xserves.

Apple used to offer 15,000-rpm hard drives in these two models, so if you already have one, your Mac Pro or Xserve may contain one. In some models, Apple now offers solid state drives, which are faster than even 15,000-rpm hard drives. Solid state drives have no moving parts, like USB flash drives. Solid state drives are also significantly more expensive per gigabyte than hard drives.

You can't replace a drive with a 15,000-rpm drive in lower-end Mac models because 15,000-rpm drives use a different, faster hardware interface — *serially attached SCSI (SAS)* — than slower drives. Drives of the past few years that are 7,200 rpm and slower use the Serial ATA interface. You can't plug an SAS drive into a Serial ATA connector. The Mac Pro and Xserve, however, include drive bays that accept either Serial ATA or SAS drives.

The size of a hard drive's cache is also an indication of drive performance: More is better, but sometimes it isn't noticeable.

### Drive form factor

Internal hard drives come in two form factors: 2.5 inches and 3.5 inches (the size of the disc inside the drives). The 2.5-inch drives are traditionally used in notebook computers, but some servers use them as well. Most desktop computers, including iMacs, use the 3.5-inch drive. The oddball here is the Mac mini, a desktop computer that uses a 2.5-inch hard drive.

### Server-grade/enterprise-class drives

You'll sometimes see a drive labeled with the interchangeable terms *server-grade* or *enterprise-class.* Apple uses the first term for the drive in its Time Capsule network storage product and in the drives in Xserve server hardware.

The basic feature of a server-grade or enterprise-class hard drive is a high *mean time before failure (MTBF) rating,* which represents the average working life of a drive before it needs repair. The MTBF of some server-grade drives is 1 million hours, which is 114 years! Though not a lifetime guarantee, a high MTBF reduces the chances of hard drive failure during the life of the computer. Manufacturers usually provide longer warranties for server-grade drives, and five-year warranties are common.

A high MTBF rating isn't a replacement for backing up. Any hard drive can fail at any time. A high MTBF just lowers the failure probability.

Server-grade/enterprise-class drives also feature high performance. This can include more cache, high rotational speed (such as 15,000 rpm), and faster throughput with an SAS interface. However, you don't need a server-grade drive to get high performance. A server-grade hard drive costs more than an ordinary drive.

Here are two circumstances that might cause you to replace the server Mac's drive with a server-grade model:

✔ Your network constantly (or frequently) gives the drive a workout, as it might with a large network with dozens or hundreds of users or with a heavily used database on the server.

✔ You need to keep data safe at all costs, and you can't afford the down-time that restoring data after a failure might give you.

If neither of those cases applies, you don't need to go out of your way to find a server-grade tag on a drive.

### RAID storage

The Mac Pro and Xserve contain multiple drive bays that give you the option to set up multiple drives to work together as a RAID (Redundant Array of Individual Disks) to increase performance or protect data, or both. You can also plug an external RAID box into a FireWire 800 or Thunderbolt port. Apple software supports four types of RAIDs:

- ✔ **RAID 0** isn't actually redundant, despite the name. RAID 0 uses a *striping* technique to make multiple hard drives work together as a single, fast, large hard drive. Data from a file is fragmented and written on multiple drives. When reading the file, the system can read the fragments from all the drives simultaneously, greatly increasing performance. RAID 0 also lets you create a very large single volume for storing giant files, such as video. If one of the drives in a RAID fails, all the data is lost. RAID 0 requires two hard drives minimum.

- ✔ **RAID 1** uses a *mirroring* technique to write the same data to two drives simultaneously. If one drive fails, the other drive still contains all the data. RAID 1 requires two hard drives minimum.

- ✔ **RAID 5** makes more efficient use of hard drive space than RAID 1 and has better performance. The drawback to RAID 5 is that it requires three hard drives minimum.

- ✔ **RAID 0+1** first creates a *RAID 0 striped array* — a very large volume from two hard drives, giving you the fast performance. RAID 0+1 then mirrors the first array with a second striped pair, giving you the redundancy. The drawback is that it requires at least four hard drives.

### NAS and SAN

*Network attached storage (NAS)* is a stand-alone storage device that plugs directly into the network via Ethernet or wireless (802.11 Wi-Fi). You should definitely use Ethernet for connecting a NAS device to a server. Multiple servers or computers can access a NAS device directly. The Apple Time Capsule is an example of a NAS unit, although the Time Machine software isn't well suited to backing up a server. Other NAS devices with multiple drive bays are more flexible for use with a server. NAS units are often used for backup.

Whereas a NAS can be a low-end home/office or small to medium business device, a *storage area network* (SAN) is a high-performance, high-cost investment used as primary server storage in large networks. A SAN can be a subnetwork of hard drives connected with a high-speed Fibre Channel switch. Multiple servers can access a SAN, centralizing storage on the network.

Apple offers Xsan software ($999, www.apple.com/xsan) that enables multiple desktop and server computers to directly access and share RAID storage. It can handle up to 2 petabytes, which is 2000 terabytes, or 2 million gigabytes. The iCal Server that comes with Lion Server is optimized to work with Xsan so that multiple iCal Servers can access the same SAN storage. This server *clustering* enables iCal to serve thousands of users. Lion Server's mail server is similarly optimized for Xsan. Podcast Producer can use Xsan to spread the creation of high-quality video to multiple servers all working on the same video located on the SAN.

If you want to bone up on SANs, try *Storage Area Networks For Dummies,* 2nd Edition, by Christopher Poelker and Alex Nikitin (John Wiley & Sons, Inc.).

# Choosing the Right Mac for Your Server

There are only four types of Macs to consider using as a server: Mac mini, iMac, Mac Pro, and the discontinued Xserve. Each is good for some type of network, and no size fits all. The specifications for Mac models change every year, so it's a good idea to check the Apple Web site (www.apple.com) from the Tech Specs link on each Mac's web page.

You don't need a brand-new Mac, though. A server is a good use for an older Mac, provided it has enough power for what you plan to do with it and meets the minimum requirements.

You also don't need a display monitor connected to the server. After you install Lion Server, you can run the server *headless,* using the Lion Server administration tools on another Mac on the network.

This section describes the four Macs, starting with Mac mini for lightweight tasks and ending with Xserve for large networks or heavy-duty tasks. If you haven't read how different server tasks affect the hardware, see the section "Criteria for Selecting Server Hardware," earlier in this chapter.

## Mac mini as a server

While I was writing the previous version of this book, *Snow Leopard Server For Dummies,* an internal reviewer scoffed at the idea of using a mini as a server platform, saying that it "makes no sense." I was undaunted. Several months after the book's publication, Apple came out with a special server version of the Mac mini.

I would like to believe that Apple read the book and thought, "What a great idea!" The reality is that that lots of people have been using Mac minis as servers for years. It's inexpensive, fits in small spaces, and is very quiet. You can use a single Mac mini for a small group of Macs for basic services or as a general-purpose web server. You also can use multiple Mac minis to serve larger networks. A commenter at the Apple Discussions forum once claimed that his company's data center held 500 Mac minis.

The main difference between the standard Mac mini and the server version is storage. In the latter, Apple replaces the optical DVD drive with a second hard drive, and both drives are of the faster 7200-rpm type. You can install software remotely from another Mac, or use the MacBook Air SuperDrive, a USB optical drive.

The Mac mini (see Figure 2-3), starting with the mid-2010 model, also called *unibody,* makes a *way* better server than earlier models. First, it includes an SD card slot for flash RAM from which you can quickly boot the Mac in case of an emergency. Second, it includes a removable panel for easy access to the RAM slots. And it eliminates the power brick of older models by incorporating the power supply inside the unit.

The oldest Mac mini model to support Mac OS X 10.7 Lion is the 2007 Core 2 Duo model.

### Best uses

Clearly, a Mac mini isn't going to do the work of a Mac Pro. But a Mac mini might be all the server (or servers) you need. For a network or workgroup of about 5 to 15 client computers, a single Mac mini can handle file sharing, e-mail, web services, iCal Server, DNS (domain name server), and Open Directory with Kerberos authentication. For any one of these services, a recent mini model is good for 200 users, assuming access to appropriate storage.

**Figure 2-3:** The mid-2011 Mac mini is quiet and unobtrusive and is available with two hard drives.

*Photo courtesy of Apple.*

DNS service usually works better on a server with two physical Ethernet ports. You can remedy this by buying the $29 Apple USB Ethernet Adapter to get a second Ethernet connection. It's made for the MacBook Air but works fine with a Mac mini. Keep in mind that the adapter is slower than a built-in Ethernet port. But for something like DNS, speed shouldn't matter.

You can always spread a server load over several Mac minis, as long as you don't tax the hardware. A NetBoot server isn't a good use for Mac mini. You also probably don't want to host user home directories on it.

### Pros

Using Mac minis to run Lion Server has several advantages:

- ✔ **Mac minis are cheap.** You can buy three or four for the price of a basic Mac Pro. The cost is low enough that a new mini might be worth springing for rather than using an older and slower Mac. If you find you're later adding users to your network and outgrowing your Mac mini, you can add more minis for a small investment.

- ✔ **Mac minis are small.** At just 1.4 inches high, a stack of many minis is still smaller than a toaster. You can easily mount a Mac mini on a wall or under a desk with some of the brackets made for that purpose or of your own design. You can even rack-mount Mac minis as you would other server hardware. The MX4 Rack Tray (see Figure 2-4) from Macessity ($60, www.macessity.com) holds four Mac minis and fits into a standard equipment rack.

- ✔ **Mac minis are quiet and energy efficient.** Mac minis are very quiet, able to coexist nicely in a school library or office. They don't use a lot of power or generate a lot of heat, so you won't need to use a lot of energy for cooling.

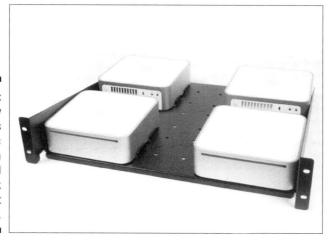

**Figure 2-4:**
This tray holds four Mac minis in a standard network equipment rack.

## Cons

Using Mac minis to run Lion Server has disadvantages as well:

✔ **Slower processor than other Macs:** The Mac mini processor is the slowest of the four Mac models you'd consider for a server, which limits its uses. Current (and recent) models meet the 64-bit requirement of Lion Server, but earlier Mac mini models might not. Check your mini's About This Mac window (refer to Figure 2-1).

✔ **Only one Ethernet port:** The Apple USB Ethernet Adapter fixes this issue, though it is slower. If multiple fast Ethernet ports are a necessity, get a Mac Pro.

✔ **Inconvenient drive replacement:** Although the newer minis make adding RAM easy, replacing a drive is still a complicated affair. The best choice is to buy the server (dual-drive) version of the mini with the largest drives Apple offers.

Contrary to popular belief, the Mac mini *is* upgradeable. After you get into the box, you can replace the drive with a bigger, faster drive.

### Upgrading Mac mini RAM and hard drive, 2010 model and later

Upgrading RAM in the newer Mac minis is easy. Here's how:

1. **Place the Mac mini upside down on a towel.**

2. **Rotate the circular panel counterclockwise a few degrees and remove it.**

   The two RAM slots are now visible.

3. **To remove a RAM module, press the tabs on either side of the module away from the center and firmly pull the module out.**

   To add a RAM module to an empty slot, insert the module.

4. **When you're finished, replace the circular panel.**

Replacing the hard drive is more tedious, and reassembling can be a bit tricky and more difficult than in older models. And once you dig out the hard drive, there's a vinyl blanket covering the hard drive that is held onto the drive by adhesive that you need to peel away and replace on the new drive. Two temperature sensors are also glued to the hard drive.

If you still want to proceed with drive replacement, you can find a number of websites with illustrated directions, though many of these are flawed in one way or another. The best YouTube video of the procedure that I've seen is at www.youtube.com/watch?v=wZy0wPniqqo.

### *Upgrading older Mac mini hard drive and RAM, pre-2010 models*

Replacing an older Mac mini's 5,400-rpm drive with a 7,200-rpm drive not only gives you faster performance, but also can triple the amount of storage. Be aware that when you do this job, the Mac mini runs hotter, and the internal fan runs more frequently.

Although the pre-2010 Mac minis are officially not user-serviceable, you can open them to upgrade RAM and the hard drive. Replacing the hard drive is actually easier than in the new models. The main thing to figure out is how to open it. Although there are no doors, once you know how to open the device, it takes less than a minute. You need a 1-inch-wide putty knife; it's helpful to bevel one side of the putty knife with some sandpaper first. Then follow these steps:

1. **Place the Mac mini upside down on a towel.**

2. **Position the knife blade where the outer casing meets the inner plastic housing and then press down firmly until the putty knife slips in about half an inch.**

3. **Push the handle of the putty knife outward and down to release the internal plastic tabs, working your way around the unit until the base is free from the cover.**

   The hard drive is located at the bottom of the internal plastic frame that also holds the DVD drive and the fan.

4. **Remove the frame by removing three small screws that hold it to the base.**

5. **Unplug the small cable for the fan.**

6. **Pull the base straight up, unplugging an interconnect board in the frame from a connector in the base.**

7. **With the frame removed, turn the mini upside down.**

   You find the hard drive attached with four screws.

8. **Upgrade the RAM.**

   You find two slots on the base, connected to the motherboard.

 For an illustrated step-by-step guide to taking apart and updating the Mac mini, see another book of mine, *Mac Mini Hacks & Mods For Dummies* (John Wiley & Sons, Inc.). The photos and directions are of the older PowerPC Mac mini, but the basic layout is the same as in the 2007–2009 Intel Mac mini models.

### *Replacing an older (pre-2010) Mac mini DVD drive with a second hard drive*

A DVD drive doesn't get a lot of use in a server, but a second internal hard drive would come in handy and would be much faster than an external

FireWire drive. Apple does this for you in the server versions of the Mac mini, but if you don't have one, you can do it yourself in an old Mac mini.

The optical drive is parallel ATA (also known as IDE), while most drives sold today are Serial ATA (SATA), which means that you need to make sure that you buy an IDE drive. They're not as high capacity as SATA but are still available.

Tom's Hardware (`www.tomshardware.com`) is a good resource for locating hard drives. Look for drives that are internal, 2.5-inch, and 7,200-rpm, and have an IDE interface.

Removing the DVD drive is easier than replacing the hard drive:

1. **Remove the Mac mini's cover, as I describe in the preceding section.**

   You don't need to remove the internal frame because the DVD drive is right at the top, held in place by four screws, two on each side.

2. **Remove the four screws holding the DVD drive in place; then remove the two screws that hold the DVD drive to a daughter card that it plugs into.**

   This is where you plug in the new IDE hard drive.

## iMac as a server

Running Lion Server on iMac isn't as common as on Mac mini. Sleek and beautiful, the all-in-one iMac sits in between the Mac mini and Mac Pro in terms of power and price. But the iMac's bright, clear display and attractive form are wasted when it's used as a server.

### Best uses

A server is a good use of an older iMac (Intel-based) that you might have sitting around. Maybe you're replacing a user's older iMac with the latest and greatest iMac or MacBook. You might buy a new iMac for a server in some situations, such as when you can make use of the display or have some multimedia use in mind.

As a server, the iMac handles the networks that the Mac mini can (which I describe in the preceding section), plus more — larger networks, more services, and possibly more internal storage. Exactly how much more depends on the iMac. Apple offers iMacs in a wide range of processor and storage options. Throw in some older models, and you're really talking about completely different computers. The highest-end iMacs rival Mac Pros in terms of speed. In fact, new top-shelf iMacs are faster than the Mac Pros of a few years ago.

### Pros

Should you decide to use iMac as a server, you'll enjoy these upsides:

✔ **Speed:** The performance is surprisingly fast. At any given time, Apple puts faster processors in the iMac than in the Mac mini. The year 2009 was the first time Apple put a quad-core processor in any Mac — even before the Mac Pro. Higher-end newer iMacs can be faster and have more storage than Mac Pros that are a few years old.

✔ **Built-in display:** A built-in display is useful if the server is sitting in your office or out in the open, and you want to use it administer and monitor the server instead of using another Mac. The display can be useful if you're using it for graphical tasks, such as with Podcast Producer.

✔ **Configuration:** The base configuration has bigger, faster hard drives than the Mac mini. (iMacs use 3.5-inch drives.) At purchase time, you can order a hard drive that's as large as the drive in the Mac Pro and the old Xserves.

✔ **Upgradeable RAM:** You can easily upgrade the RAM by removing two screws that hold a plate on the bottom.

✔ **Cost:** Cost can be thousands less than the Mac Pro, though both series have models with wide price ranges. Usually, the top-end iMac is about $500 less than the low-end Mac Pro.

### Cons

These downsides can plague you if you use the iMac as a server:

✔ **Hard drive difficult to upgrade:** Except for RAM, the iMac is really not upgradeable, even less so than the Mac mini. Although you can remove the mini's top in a minute when you know how, it's very difficult to disassemble an iMac to replace the hard drive. Reassembling it is also difficult. You can find directions if you Google *iMac take apart*, but I don't recommend it.

If you're buying an iMac for the purpose of using it as a server, consider ordering the largest drive Apple offers.

✔ **Lack of expansion:** If you need multiple drive bays or expansion slots for multiple Ethernet cards, you'll need a Mac Pro. (Like the Mac mini, the newer iMacs do include an SD card slot, however.)

✔ **Lack of second Ethernet port:** As with the Mac mini, you can add an inexpensive (and slower) USB Ethernet port.

✔ **Faster processor requires bigger display:** You have to buy the model with the bigger display to get the faster processors. At this writing, Apple wasn't offering the fastest processors with the smaller display.

## Mac Pro as a server

The Apple power workstation also includes features designed for use as a high-powered server. Up to 12 processing cores, expansion slots, multiple internal drives, and two built-in independent Ethernet connections make the Mac Pro (see Figure 2-5) well suited for running Lion Server in demanding network situations. Even older models make great servers. The Mac Pro doesn't come with a monitor, but the base configuration does include an adequate graphics card.

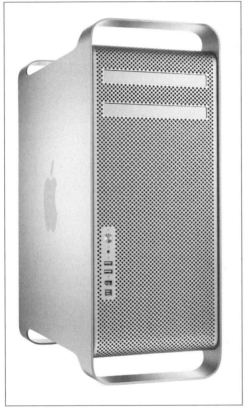

**Figure 2-5:**
A Mac
Pro tower
makes a
powerful
server.

*Photo courtesy of Apple.*

## Best uses

A Mac Pro can support file serving for hundreds of active users. For example, Mac Pro works as the file server for an entire school and also runs third-party server software and NetBoot at the same time. The Mac Pro also works for running directory services and connecting a network of Macs to a Microsoft Active Directory network. If you're using a server only for web, e-mail, DNS, and light file-sharing tasks, the Mac Pro may be more than you need.

The Mac Pro is a better choice than the Xserve in situations when the server is to be located in a workspace. The Mac Pro is quieter than the Xserve and has a form factor that fits better in a workspace.

### Pros

The Mac Pro leaves the Mac mini and the iMac in the dust as far as performance goes, and it's just about as fast as Xserve. The high points:

- **Eight processing cores minimum and a fast system architecture:** You have an optional 12 processing cores.

- **Four internal hard drive bays, one more than Xserve:** With the optional RAID card, you can use these in a RAID system.

- **Easily accessible drives that can be replaced without futzing with cables.** Just open the side door and slide them in or out.

- **Room for lots of memory:** Eight RAM slots are available.

- **Two Gigabit Ethernet ports:** This feature is designed for using the Mac Pro as a server. You can use one port to connect to the local network, and another port to connect to the Internet. This enables you to use the Mac server as a gateway, such as running the firewall, virtual private network server, or other gateway services. You can also use the two ports together, for twice the bandwidth.

- **Three extra expansion slots:** For more Ethernet ports, add Ethernet cards.

### Cons

The Mac Pro as a server also has its low points:

- **Processors aren't easily upgradeable.** Apple doesn't support upgrading the processor and doesn't provide directions. You have to pull apart the computer. The processors do sit in sockets that you can pull out. They aren't easy to get to, and you really need some hardware hacking skills.

  Other World Computing (www.macsales.com) offers an upgrade by mail service. Ship the tray that contains the Mac Pro processor, and the company upgrades it and ships it back to you.

- **Cost is more than the Mac mini or iMac.** But you also get more server power.

As with the Mac mini, Apple offers a server version of the Mac Pro. It's similar to the entry-level Mac Pro configuration but with an extra hard drive, more memory, and Lion Server preinstalled.

## Xserve as a server

Although Apple discontinued the Xserve in January 2011, a lot of fans still use it. A survey by the Enterprise Desktop Alliance showed that 65 percent of respondents planned to continue using Xserves for two or more years or until they stop functioning — which could be a while, considering the Xserve's industrial-strength design and easily replaceable parts.

If you've never seen an Xserve before, you wouldn't know that it's a Mac. The flat, horizontal body, shown in Figure 2-6, is designed to be mounted in a standard 19-inch equipment rack and to be run headless. At 30 inches long, the Xserve is a little big for a desk, but if you want to connect a display to it, you can plug in a graphics card.

Fans of the Xserve like its support of high-powered add-ons, such as internal RAIDs, with multiple, big, high-speed hard drives, including *serially attached SCSI (SAS)* drives, and eight RAM slots. The Mac Pro has all this, but the Xserve also has features to keep it running in mission-critical situations, including a redundant power supply and temperature monitor.

**Figure 2-6:**
Three
Xserves
mounted in
a rack with
a storage
array.

*Photo courtesy of Apple.*

Except for the drastically different shape, the Xserve is similar in a lot of ways to the Mac Pro. The next three sections help you decide whether you might keep your old Xserve or spring for a new Mac Pro.

### Best uses

When it was last updated in 2009, the Xserve was similarly powered to the Mac Pro. Today's Mac Pros have surpassed the Xserve, but the latter is generally good for the same uses as the Mac Pro, running multiple services for hundreds of users. You may still need additional servers to run some services for very large networks, but the Xserve is better suited than the Mac Pro to a growing network because you can easily upgrade the processors.

The Xserve is also built for mission-critical situations. If you absolutely can't afford to have any server downtime due to hardware failure, the Xserve is better than the Mac Pro. You may never have to shut down an Xserve.

These are all reasons why many owners don't easily give up their Xserves. Unlike the Mac Pro, however, the Xserve isn't well suited for sitting in the middle of an office or classroom because of the racket it can make. Xserves are designed to be located in a data center or a ventilated telecom closet.

### Pros

The Xserve has a similar set of expansion slots and high-end hardware options. But the Xserve does have some advantages over the Mac Pro:

- ✔ **Features to keep it running and reduce downtime.** Notably:

  - *An option of redundant power supply:* If one power supply fails, the other takes over. Simply pull out a power supply and replace it — without shutting down the Xserve. (Replacement power supplies are still available at `www.welovemacs.com` and `www.powermacs.com`, or you can Google *xserve power supply*.)

  - *Hot-swappable hard drives:* If a drive fails, you can pull out of Xserve without shutting it down or opening it. However, it has only three drive bays; the Mac Pro has four.

  - *Temperature measurement:* You can read the temperature from Lion Server's admin tools and set the software to send you an alarm if the Xserve gets too hot.

- ✔ **Processors that are officially user-upgradeable.** To get upgrading instructions, go to `http://support.apple.com/manuals` and search for *Xserve processor*. Manuals for the different Xserve models appear in the results.

- ✔ **A removable lid that gives you easy access to *everything* inside.**

- ✔ **Mountable in a standard 19-inch rack.**

### Cons

Disadvantages to using Xserve:

- ✔ **Discontinued:** You can no longer buy an Xserve, or parts, from Apple. However, new parts are still available if you Google around.

- ✔ **Only three hard drive bays:** The Xserve has one less than the Mac Pro. This is still a lot of storage but not enough to support an internal RAID 0+1 (as I describe in the "RAID storage" section, earlier in the chapter), as can the Mac Pro.

- ✔ **Heat:** The Xserve gets very hot and requires adequate ventilation. You'll be fine if you put it in a standard equipment rack, but think twice about stuffing it in a small, unventilated closet.

> ✔ **Form factor:** The long, flat shape is good for a rack but bad for an office or classroom setting.
>
> ✔ **Noise:** The Xserve is noisy and distracting sitting in the middle of an office or a classroom. If this is the only place for your server, consider the Mac Pro instead.

# Considering Other Network Hardware

For most of the book, I assume that you have a network. But in case you don't, here's a brief overview of what's needed for a basic network infrastructure. Many different network layouts are possible. In this section, I describe a smaller network, or a *subnetwork,* that you might plug in to a larger network.

It's best if you set up the network (or have a functioning network with DNS in place), connect your clients, and plug in the Mac server before you install Lion Server. When you run the Lion Server installer, it gathers data from the network during the setup to automate configuration. (Chapter 3 covers Lion Server installation.)

## Ethernet switches and cables

Even in today's wireless world, you need some wires for your network infrastructure. The heart of a wired network infrastructure is an *Ethernet switched hub* (or an *Ethernet switch*), a box that everything on a wired network plugs into.

Some Ethernet hubs are without switches, which aren't as fast as Ethernet switched hubs. *Plain* (unswitched) hubs aren't that common, but you don't want one if you find one. Make sure it's a switch.

You can often find Ethernet switches built into other devices, such as wireless access points, Internet routers, firewalls, and virtual private network gateways. Apple's AirPort Extreme and Time Capsule have Gigabit Ethernet switches in them.

### Ethernet speeds

Ethernet switches come in different performance levels. You want one that supports *Gigabit Ethernet* (or *1000BASE-T,* a gigabit-per-second maximum), which is the top bandwidth supported in all Mac models and many PCs. Gigabit Ethernet switches are sometimes referred to as *10/100/1000 switches* because they're backward-compatible with older, slower 100 megabits per second (Mbps) and 10 Mbps Ethernet hardware. If a switch is 10/100, it's only 100 Mbps — one tenth the bandwidth of Gigabit Ethernet.

Even faster are *10 Gigabit Ethernet* switches. You can take advantage of a 10 Gigabit switch with a 10 Gigabit Ethernet card installed in a Mac Pro.

### Ethernet ports

Ethernet switches have anywhere from 4 to 24 ports (see Figure 2-7, which shows an 8-port gigabit switch). You can also connect (daisy chain) switches together if you outgrow your current switch.

You need one of your switch's ports for your Internet connection (or for a connection to a bigger network). You need another port to plug in the server, another one for a networked printer (if it has an Ethernet port), and another port to plug in to a wireless access point if you're providing Wi-Fi connection to your network. The rest of the ports are for your client computers. Some switches also have USB ports to share a USB printer.

**Figure 2-7:**
An 8-port
Gigabit
Ethernet
switch.

If you're using the server as an Internet gateway, the Internet connection would plug directly into the server, and the server's second Ethernet port would connect to the switch.

### Cables

Ethernet cable comes in several grades. At minimum, you want Category 5e (commonly known as *Cat 5e*) cable for Gigabit Ethernet. Cat 5e cables can be used to a maximum length of about 100 meters from the switch to the computer, though interference can shorten this.

A higher grade of Ethernet cable — Cat 6 — is more immune to noise and might be considered a minimum grade for reliable use on a gigabit network. Cat 6 can also handle 10 Gigabit Ethernet (10GBASE-T), which some network devices support.

You can also connect a server to a Gigabit Ethernet switch with optical cable known as 1000Base-SX Ethernet. For this, you need a switch with an optical port and a Mac Pro or Xserve with a 1000Base-SX Ethernet card in it. The advantages of Optical Ethernet are higher performance and longer distribution due to the near-total absence of electromagnetic interference.

## Optional: Wireless equipment

If you decide to go wireless, you shouldn't go *completely* wireless. You should still use an Ethernet cable to connect the server to an Ethernet switch or wireless access point.

Although you can use the wireless AirPort card in a Mac server to connect directly to Macs and PCs on a wireless network, I don't recommend it. Doing so makes extra work for the server, and the signal strength and range aren't as good as in a wireless access point, such as Apple AirPort Extreme or many others. The lower the signal strength, the slower network traffic is.

Apple's AirPort Extreme and Time Capsule are wireless access points that contain small built-in Ethernet switches. Each supports up to 50 wireless client computers. Time Capsule also contains a hard drive. The clients on a small network can back up to the Time Capsule using the Time Capsule software that comes with Mac OS X 10.5 and later.

You don't need Apple's wireless hardware, however, because plenty of available options work. If you get a third-party wireless access point, make sure it supports the 802.11a/b/g/n standard. (The letters signify different revisions to the wireless 802.11 standard, with "g" being faster than "a" and "b," and "n" being the fastest.) All Macs built today, as well as many PCs, support 802.11n. Older Macs and PCs may support only 802.11g or 802.11b.

## UPS for your server

All networks should have an *uninterruptible power supply (UPS)* for the server. This is an external box that keeps the server running in the event of a power failure in the building. Some organizations need to keep the server running through the time of the power failure. A UPS also gives you a chance to shut down the server in an orderly fashion. Simply shutting off the power in the middle of operations can damage the data on the server, and power surges related to the power failure can damage the server hardware.

A basic UPS contains a backup battery and a surge protector. The server's power cable plugs into the UPS and runs off battery power when the building power goes out.

More sophisticated UPS units include *Automatic Voltage Regulation (AVR)*. AVR guarantees a constant level of power to the server in the event of fluctuations in delivered power, including short drops in power levels, or dips or surges that might occur before a total power outage.

One parameter to look at is the electrical load capacity, measured in volt-amps (VA). For a Mac mini or iMac, 350VA should do it. For a Mac Pro or Xserve, you can start at about 800VA. Extra drives and expansion cards draw more power and require a higher load capacity.

At the lower end, UPS boxes start at about $100 for a single outlet without AVR and can cost several hundred dollars for multiple outlets. Depending on the load capacity, a manufacturer will tell you how long the battery will run the computer — typically an hour or two at these price points, up to eight hours for units costing over $1,000.

A highly respected supplier of solid UPS systems is APC (www.apcc.com). APC offers a range of products from home/office to enterprise-class. Tripp Lite (www.tripplite.com) and Belkin (www.belkin.com) are also known for quality UPS systems.

# Chapter 3

# Installation and Setup

● ● ● ● ● ● ● ● ● ● ● ● ● ● ● ● ● ● ● ● ● ● ● ● ● ● ● ● ● ● ● ● ● ● ● ● ● ● ● ● ● ● ● ● ●

*In This Chapter*

▶ Identifying information you'll need

▶ Formatting storage

▶ Considering the differences between a new install, upgrade, and migration

▶ Performing different types of installation

▶ Checking DNS and other postconfiguration tasks

▶ Deciding when to update Lion Server

● ● ● ● ● ● ● ● ● ● ● ● ● ● ● ● ● ● ● ● ● ● ● ● ● ● ● ● ● ● ● ● ● ● ● ● ● ● ● ● ● ● ● ● ●

*T*his chapter is kind of important. Installing Lion Server is *very* different from installing previous versions of Mac OS X Server — or any other operating system you've ever installed. Frankly, it's an odd bird. Getting it wrong the first time can result in lots of wasted time later. Whether you've previously installed Mac OS X Server or this is your first foray into the world of computer servers, you really should know some things about Lion Server before double-clicking the installer.

This chapter looks at the three phases of creating a functional server: things to do to get ready, the actual installation process and its options and variations, and initial setup tasks that you perform afterward.

## A Roadmap to Installation and Setup

A little planning and knowledge of the options and pitfalls go a long way to a smooth installation of Lion Server. Here are the main decision points and tasks for installing and setting up Lion Server. This chapter is organized along these lines:

1. **Collect data about the server Mac and your network.**

2. **Decide whether you want a new installation on an erased disk drive (commonly known as a *clean install*) or an upgrade.**

3. **Download Lion from the Mac App Store and make a copy *before* installing the server software.**

4. **Decide the role of server in your network.**

   Your choices include local user accounts or shared network accounts; working alone or with other servers.

   A stand-alone server could have access to the Internet by remote secure access (VPN) only, or it could be visible to the Internet.

5. **Run the installer and, if necessary, download the server components after installing the client.**

6. **After installation, perform basic postinstallation configuration tasks, such as create a shared directory, add users, or further configure DNS.**

7. **Download the Server Admin Tools and then check DNS and Open Directory, if necessary.**

The rest of this chapter looks at the details of this road map. I start with the common point of departure for all installation and configuration routes: collecting network information.

# Prerequisites

In most chapters of the book, I include a Prerequisites section to let you know some things you might have to do in order for the setup to work. This section is no less important for installing Lion Server and doing your initial configuration.

## Collecting and understanding info

It's a good idea to gather some information about your server Mac and your network before you start installation and configuration. You may speed up your setup time by having the info in front of you. You'll also have a record of how you set up the server. And the process of gathering the information will help you understand what type of setup you need. This section describes information you may collect or later need to enter during the setup process. It also explains some of the terms that the installer software asks you about.

### Hardware ID numbers

There are two hardware identification numbers that are useful to record if your network contains multiple servers: the MAC address and the serial number. If you're using remote management software for multiple clients and server, this information may help you configure that software.

The *MAC address* doesn't refer to the Macintosh; it's the acronym for *Media Access Control*. The MAC address is a unique hardware identifier that specifies each Ethernet port or wireless network card. In general, if a Mac has two Ethernet ports, it will have two MAC addresses. (The exception is the Xserve, which has a built-in Ethernet port that has *two* MAC addresses — one used by the server's processor and the other used by the Xserve's special Lights Out Management processor.)The MAC address takes the form of a series of two-digit characters separated by colons, like this: 00:23:32:b5:d0: 43. Apple also refers to the MAC address as the *Ethernet ID*.

The *serial number* is a unique number that identifies every Mac. A Mac can have only one serial number, unlike a MAC address. All Macs list the serial number somewhere on the outside case. Many Macs also include the MAC address/Ethernet ID. The Mac Pro's serial number is written on the back side on a label located under the video ports, for example. The Xserve has a pull-out tab in the middle of the rear panel.

If you can't get to the serial number because the Mac is in a difficult-to-reach location, a Mac OS X trick has been around for many years, but even some diehard Mac fans don't know about it: Choose Apple menu⊃About This Mac. Click the Mac OS X version number twice, and it changes to the hardware serial number (see Figure 3-1).

To get the MAC address/Ethernet ID in Mac OS X 10.6 and earlier, click the More Info button to launch System Profiler. Remember that each Ethernet port and AirPort card have a MAC address, so be sure you identify the Ethernet ports that you'll use for your network. Click Network in the left pane, and the MAC address will be listed under Ethernet in the right column.

### Network ID numbers

During the installation and setup process, you may be asked for variety of numbers that identify your network and the server's role in it. You may need this information for each network port you'll use, though some of these numbers may be supplied automatically if your server is connected to the network during installation. Here's a description:

**Figure 3-1:** Click the Mac OS X version number (left) twice to reveal the hardware serial number (right).

✔ **IP address:** If you're upgrading Snow Leopard or Lion client to Lion Server, set the IP address before starting the installation. Every network port (including wireless) on a computer on the network has an IP address that identifies it to other computers. For client computers, the IP address is usually set automatically via DHCP (Dynamic Host Configuration Protocol). But servers need an IP address that never changes in order for the network to find them, so it's best to manually assign an IP address to the server, called *static* IP addressing. On a Mac, you set the IP address in the Network pane of System Preferences.

The IP address is four numbers separated by periods, such as 169.254.13.3. Each number can be from 0 through 255. See the "Rules for IP addressing" sidebar for more details on selecting IP addresses.

✔ **Subnet mask:** This number appears in the form of four numbers separated by the dots that are often 255 or 0, such as 255.255.0.0. Use a different subnet mask for each Ethernet port. The computers connected to a server's Ethernet port are on a subnet. The subnet mask limits the size of the subnet. The subnet mask can also be set automatically via DHCP.

✔ **Router:** You may need the IP address of the hardware that moves data between local subnetworks and the Internet, such as an AirPort base station. The router might also have a DHCP server that automatically assigns IP addresses to your computers. If you're setting up services that will be visible to the Internet, you may need to configure port forwarding on the router.

If you have your Mac connected to the network during installation, the installer software may detect the router and provide its IP address.

✔ **DNS servers:** Before setting up your Mac server, you need to know if you have domain name services (DNS) servers on your network or provided by your Internet service provider. Otherwise, you can disrupt your server and parts of the rest of the network. You may need to record the IP addresses of DNS servers, and you should record any domain names used. The domain name comes in the form of mycompany.com or myserver.mycompany.com. The DNS server translates domain names to IP addresses. If you configure this manually, you'll obtain the IP address of the DNS from your Internet service provider. This is one of the more important settings in getting your server to work properly.

✔ **Computer name:** The installation procedure will create a computer name, which you can change. This is a uniquely Macintosh network name that identifies Macs to other Macs, as well as Windows running Bonjour for Windows. On Mac clients, this name will appear in the Finder sidebars and in various dialogs. You can also set the computer name in the Sharing pane of System Preferences.

A Mac computer name can be 63 characters or less. Use Roman characters except for the equal sign (=), the colon (:), or the at sign (@). Spaces are okay. Users find it helpful if the name has some significance, such as *Computer Lab Server.* A computer name translates into a *local network name,* such as computer-lab-server.local. The local network name is used only on the local subnet, in addition to a DNS name of the server.

# Rules for IP addressing

When you set an IP address manually (known as *static* addressing), you need to follow some rules. An IP address takes the form of four numbers from 0 through 255, separated by periods, such as 169.254.13.3.

The total IP address range is 000.000.000.000 through 255.255.255.255, but within that, there are some ranges that are used for specific purposes, such as public and private IP addresses. A *public* IP address is one that the entire Internet can see. Every computer on the planet that the Internet can directly see has a unique public IP address. Usually, your Internet service provider provides a public IP address, either manually or automatically.

A *private* IP address is one that the Internet can't see because the computer is connected to the Internet through an Internet gateway or router. The Internet sees only the IP address of the gateway. The computers on this type of local network use private IP addresses from one of several *private* address ranges. You might give your server a private IP address if another server or hardware box is acting as the Internet gateway. (You can also have a private IP address assigned automatically through DHCP.)

There are several private address ranges. One is the range that starts with 169.254: 169.254.0.0–169.254.254.255. *Note:* For this range, the last number can be 255, but the one before it can only go as high as 254. The other two private ranges are 10.0.0.1 through 10.255.255.254 and 192.168.0.1 through 192.168.0.254.

If you manually configure the IP addresses of your Mac for a local network, you can use IP addresses from any of these ranges as long as all the Macs on the network are in the same range. They also need the same subnet mask, and *no* two computers on your local network, or *subnet*, can have the same IP address. A subnet consists of all the computers connected to one Ethernet port on the server.

## *Rethinking clean installs, updates, and reformatting options for Lion*

With any installation of a new operating system, you must decide whether to install on a freshly erased hard drive (a *clean install*) or to upgrade an existing installation. Conventional wisdom has been that a clean install gets rid of the flotsam and jetsam of configuration files and old settings that accumulate over the years and slow things down.

Because the Lion installation process is so different, you may have to rethink preconceived notions about clean installs. With Lion, Apple encourages upgrade installations and has made it more difficult (though not impossible) to do a clean install by not providing bootable DVDs — or a way for you to make one (aside from unsupported hacks). The reason for Apple's focus on upgrade installs may be a new generation of installer. Apple has indicated that Lion's installer is "smarter" than previous installers.

Apple may be right. If you're upgrading your current Mac OS X Server 10.6 to Lion Server, upgrading on the existing drive may be better than trying to migrate the server settings and data to a clean install of Lion Server using the migration assistant. This is particularly true if your old server is hosting websites or is using MySQL, which is no longer present in Lion.

You can still find good reasons to do a clean install, particularly if you're not migrating an existing server. And the Lion Server installation process is actually easier if you're installing onto a blank drive while booted from Mac OS X 10.6 or 10.7 Server. It allows you to skip the step of having to go back to the App Store to download the server components, and it further automates configuration by invoking a server setup assistant that can do things like create an Open Directory master and configure DNS. This is my favorite way to install Lion Server.

If you plan on erasing the drive, consider your storage formatting options before installing. You have three:

✔ Use a simple erase.

✔ Divide a drive into multiple partitions.

✔ Use multiple drives together in a software RAID (redundant array of independent disks).

### Planning a clean install with Lion

In most cases, the Lion installer doesn't give you the option to erase the drive or partition on which you're installing, which means you should do any erasing before you start the installation process.

But doing a clean install of Lion may mean that you will be doing *two* installations of Mac OS X. That's because to install Lion onto a blank disk or partition, you need to boot the Mac from a second drive partition, or even USB flash RAM, running Mac OS X 10.6 or 10.7. So if you don't have Mac OS X 10.6 or 10.7 on storage device that you can attach to the Mac, you will have to install it.

In order to reformat or partition a hard drive, you need to boot the Mac from another drive and run Disk Utility. I describe this process in the next section.

### Erasing or partitioning a drive

Erasing a drive in Disk Utility is similar to partitioning. Both destroy any existing data on the drive. Erasing a volume simply wipes the data off it. *Partitioning* a hard drive divides it into multiple volumes. Each volume appears as a separate hard drive to the user. You can use one partition as the startup disk containing Mac OS X Server (the operating system and services) and use another, larger partition to store the user files. If something goes wrong with the user data volume, the server can keep functioning — or at least it won't have to be re-created. This scheme also prevents the boot partition from running out of disk space because of growing user data.

Having multiple drives gives you better system performance than multiple partitions. But if have a 500 GB or larger startup disk and plan on storing user data elsewhere, you'll have a lot of wasted space if you don't partition.

One essential thing to remember about partitioning: You must use the default GUID Partition Table, not the Apple Partition Table. If you use the latter, you won't be able to boot from the drive.

You also need to choose a format. There are two formats you can use for a startup disk:

- ✔ **Mac OS Extended (Journaled):** Most people use this standard format.
- ✔ **Mac OS Extended (Case-sensitive, Journaled):** Some people who are hosting static Web sites use this format because it improves performance, with a better mapping between URLs and files.

For drives that you won't use as startup disks, you can use the nonjournaled versions of these two formats, though there isn't a compelling reason to do so.

To partition a drive, either before or during installation, do the following:

1. **Launch Disk Utility from `/Applications/Utilities`, shown in Figure 3-2.**

2. **Click the hard drive you want to partition in the left pane.**

   The drive is the leftmost item; a partition on the drive is indented.

3. **Click the Partition tab.**

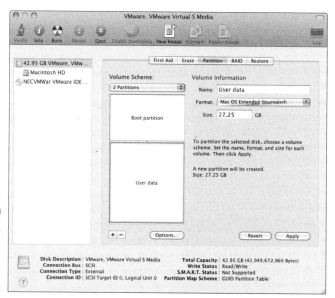

**Figure 3-2:**
Partitioning a drive with Disk Utility.

4. **In the Volume Scheme pop-up menu, choose the number of partitions you want to create.**

   The space below the pop-up menu has a number of boxes representing the partition sizes.

5. **Drag the bar that separates the boxes to resize them to the partition size (in gigabytes) that you want for each.**

6. **Click a box to select it and then type a name for it in the Name field for each partition.**

   Figure 3-2 shows that I've used the names Boot Partition and User Data.

7. **In the Format pop-up menu, make sure that Mac OS X Extended (Journaled) is selected.**

8. **At the bottom of the window, check that GUID Partition Table is selected for Partition Map Scheme.**

   If not, click the Options button and select GUID Partition Table.

9. **Click Apply.**

Erasing is simpler. Select the drive or volume from the column on the left and click the Erase tab. Choose a format from the Format pop-up menu and click the Erase button.

### Creating a software RAID

For Macs with multiple hard drives, Disk Utility can set up multiple drives to work together as a software RAID to increase performance, protect data, or both. Software RAID takes some of the computer's processing power, and it isn't as secure as a hardware RAID controller system. For example, a system crash could affect a software RAID but would not affect a hardware RAID. However, a software RAID is far less expensive and does provide the benefits of data redundancy. You can also use external FireWire drives in a RAID set.

Here's how to create a software RAID:

1. **Launch Disk Utility.**

2. **Click the RAID tab.**

3. **Drag and drop drives from the left pane into the RAID pane.**

   Use drives — *not* volumes — from the left pane. Partitions/volumes are listed under the drive name and are indented.

4. **Type a name for the RAID set in the Name field.**

5. **In the Format pop-up menu, make sure that Mac OS X Extended (Journaled) is selected.**

6. **From the RAID Type pop-up menu, choose Mirrored, Striped, or Concatenated:**

   - *Mirrored (or RAID 1)* writes the same data to two drives simultaneously. If one drive fails, the other drive still contains all the data.

   - *Striped (or RAID 0)* makes multiple hard drives of the same size work together as a single, fast, large hard drive. Data from a file is fragmented and written on multiple drives. When accessing the file, the system reads the fragments from all the drives simultaneously. If one of the drives in a RAID 0 fails, all the data is lost.

   - *Concatenated* combines multiple hard drives into one without the speed benefits of striping, but you can combine drives of different sizes. Concatenating gets really interesting when used with another RAID. For example, concatenate two FireWire drives that add up to the capacity of the internal drive and then mirror the internal drive with the concatenated FireWire drives. You can also use it to create a RAID 1+0. For example, if you have four drives, concatenate a 2-drive mirror array with a 2-drive striped array. This gives you the performance of striping with the redundancy of mirroring.

7. **Click the Create button.**

See Chapter 2 for more about the different RAID types.

# Upgrading versus Migrating

Whether you're creating your first server or upgrading or migrating an older server, you start the installation in the same place, as described in the section "Performing the Lion Server Installation, Upgrade, or Migration," later in the chapter. The differences between upgrading and migrating are significant, however.

There are also some things that aren't moved during an upgrade or a migration. But first, some basic differences:

- ✔ **A New install** is where you don't have an existing server. This includes installing on a blank drive volume and installing on top of a Snow Leopard client.

- ✔ **An Upgrade** is where you run the installer while booted from the older server, replacing an older server. If you go this route, make a backup of your older server first.

✔ **A Migration** is where the installer copies data from another server or hard drives or volumes onto the new hard disk. The old server and its data are retained intact. Migration is performed during the installation process, using a server assistant that launches when you select an option to transfer data from an existing server.

Even if you use Mac OS X Server 10.6.8, migration is your only option if the server Mac is an older model not supported by Lion Server. (See Chapter 2 for a list of supported Macs.)

All three of these installation types are highly automated, using a server assistant. You can also do a manual migration using the command-line tools. It's quite a complicated process, but Apple's manual *Lion Server Upgrading and Migrating* is available to you if you have some special needs or had a problem during an upgrade or migration process. You can find out more details in Apple's manual *Lion Server Upgrading and Migrating*, available at `http://support.apple.com/manuals`.

### Minimum requirements and location of data

New installs and upgrades both require Mac OS X Server 10.6.6 or later. Apple recommends upgrading from version 10.6.8.

You can migrate even older servers. Migration requires Mac OS X Server 10.5.8 or later.

The required location of the old server data also differs. For an upgrade, the drive or volume containing the server you're upgrading is typically installed in the server Mac. You can also do an upgrade to a FireWire or USB drive.

For a migration, you have several choices for the migration source:

✔ **A secondary drive or partition installed inside the Mac or connected via FireWire or USB.** These volumes must be mounted.

✔ **A volume on another Mac connected in Target Disk mode.** Target Disk mode is where you connect another Mac using a FireWire cable. First, connect the older Mac when it's shut off. Then start it while holding down the T key. Once the old Mac is booted in target disk mode, it will appear as a hard drive to the new Mac.

If you're migrating from a Time Machine backup, the copy of Mac OS X Server must have a static IP address configured. The new server Mac should have the same IP address at the one used in the Time Machine backup in order for DNS to be correctly configured.

### What's not moved

As I describe in Chapter 2, Lion Server doesn't include several services and features that were part of previous versions of Mac OS X Server. When you migrate or upgrade, the settings and data for these items will not be moved to Lion Server because Lion Server no longer supports them:

- ✔ Print service
- ✔ Windows Primary Domain Controller (PDC) or Backup Domain Controller (BDC)
- ✔ Wiki-based mailing list and archives
- ✔ Apache Tomcat and Apache Axis web services
- ✔ Mobile Access
- ✔ QuickTime Streaming Server (QTSS)
- ✔ NetBoot images that were created with versions of Mac OS X Server before version 10.5

The MySQL database is also not included in Lion Server; it's been replaced by PostgreSQL. However, the upgrade and migration processes will move MySQL and its data to Lion Server. You will lose a graphical user interface to manage MySQL, however, because Server Admin 10.7 no longer supports MySQL. You'll need to use the command line in the Terminal utility to manage MySQL.

Note also that an upgrade procedure will delete launch daemons located at /System/Library/LaunchDaemons. The update replaces them with newer Lion Server versions. This shouldn't be an issue unless your server includes customized launch daemons.

You can't use any of the administration tools from previous versions of Mac OS X Server. These are Server Preferences, Server Admin, Workgroup Manager, Podcast Composer, System Image Utility, and Xgrid Admin. You can download new versions separately. (The Server app replaces Server Preferences.)

### Migrating or upgrading mail

When performing an upgrade, you need to have any partitions or drives that contain the mail data and database connected and mounted to ensure the automatic installation of your mail service in Lion Server. If these items aren't available during the upgrade to Lion, you'll have to move them manually, using the command line. You'll also need to manually migrate mail data that is installed on an Xsan volume.

You can find details of a manual migration of mail in Apple's manual *Lion Server Upgrading and Migrating.*

# Performing the Lion Server Installation, Upgrade, or Migration

With Mac OS X 10.7 Lion, Apple created a very different installation process. Here are the main new aspects:

- ✔ Lion is a 4GB download and has no DVD. The server is an additional download.

- ✔ You cannot create a *bootable* disk image to make your own installer DVD.

- ✔ The Lion installer creates a small, invisible recovery partition. After installation, you can boot from this partition by holding the Option key during startup. It gives you the options of erasing the drive and downloading the whole 4GB again.

- ✔ You no longer have the option to do a remote install.

In order to run the Lion installer, you must be booted from the client or server versions of Mac OS X 10.6.8 or have Lion installed. If you have only one disk or partition, an upgrade install is your *only* choice. But a $20, 16GB USB flash drive with Snow Leopard or Lion installed on it can change that.

Another requirement is that the server Mac must be connected to the Internet during installation. The Lion Server installer downloads material during the server install process. It also gathers some information about your network during installation to further automate the setup. Also make sure any DNS or DHCP servers on your network are running.

Once you're ready, the basic installation procedure for Lion Server for most installations is as follows:

1. **Download the Lion client installer from the Mac App Store.**

   Immediately after download concludes, the installer launches.

2. **Quit the installer immediately; do not proceed.**

   If you continue with the installation now, the installer will delete itself during the process. If something goes wrong with the installation, you'll have to download the whole 4GB again.

3. **Copy the installer (which is a file called `Install Mac OS X Lion`) from the Applications folder to a DVD, USB flash device, or other storage device.**

4. **Launch the installer and proceed through the process of installing the client.**

5. **When the client installation is finished, go to the Mac App Store and download the Lion server component.**

   The server installer launches after downloading.

6. **Run the server installer.**

7. **After installation, configure the server (set up Open Directory, add users, and so on).**

The procedure is shorter if you're installing on a blank volume while booted from Snow Leopard or Lion Server. In this case, you can skip Steps 5, 6, and 7 because you'll see a setup assistant that further automates the configuration of the server to your specifications.

## *Beginning the installation process*

This section describes the first part of the Lion Server installation process for most scenarios. Here, you actually install the Lion client first. If you're upgrading the Lion client to Lion Server, skip to the section "Downloading and installing Server components from the App Store."

### *Choosing a drive*

This beginning part installs the Lion client:

1. **Launch the Install Mac OS X Lion application from the Applications folder of the volume you're booted from.**

2. **Click Continue in the first window, shown in Figure 3-3.**

3. **Click Agree in the license agreement window and then click Agree in the license agreement dialog that appears.**

4. **Choose a driver or partition on which to install Lion (see Figure 3-4).**

   The installer lets you select only drives that are either empty, formatted drives, or that have the client or server version of Mac OS X 10.6 or 10.7. If you're trying to install on a drive with an earlier version of Mac OS X installed, quit the installer and erase the drive (as described in the section "Erasing or partitioning a drive," earlier in this chapter).

5. **If you're booted from Mac OS X Server and installing to an empty drive, click the Customize button, select Server Software in the sheet that appears (see Figure 3-5), and then click OK.**

   This option shortens the installation process, and you won't have to go to the App Store. However, the Customize button is grayed out and not available if you're not booted from Mac OS X Server and installing to an empty volume.

**Figure 3-3:**
The first
window
of the Lion
installer.

**Figure 3-4:**
Select a
drive on
which to
install Lion.

6. **Click the Install button (refer to Figure 3-4).**

Time for a cup of coffee. A progress window appears, telling you that it is downloading components. The Mac restarts when this step is finished. Another dialog appears, telling you that it is installing software. The Mac restarts a second time when it's finished.

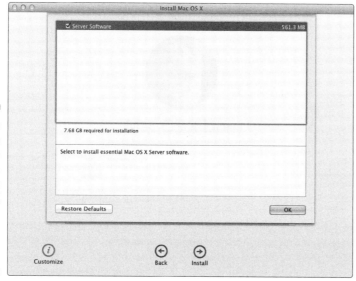

**Figure 3-5:**
This option
is available
only if you
booted from
Mac OS X
Server and
are install-
ing to an
empty drive.

The procedure now diverges. If you booted from Mac OS X Server and are installing on an empty drive volume, skip to the section "Finishing the installation for the Server-to-empty-volume scenario." Everyone else can continue to the next section.

### Registration and migration screens

Continuing on, the next set of screens asks you about registration information and migration options.

To continue setting up Lion Server, registering the software with Apple is the first task at hand. This section of the process also gives you the option to migrate configuration information and data from another server. (If you haven't started the installation process yet, follow the steps in the preceding section.) Continue the process by following these steps:

7. **In the Welcome window, select the country in which you're registering and click Continue.**

8. **In the Keyboard screen, select a country for your keyboard and click Continue.**

9. **Select one of the following items and click Continue:**

   • *Transfer the Information from an Existing Server:* Select this option to move settings and user data from another server or volume or drive installed with Mac OS X Server 10.5.8 or later. A series of screens appears in which you select a server or drive.

- *Restore from a Time Machine Backup:* The backup would have to be on a drive attached to the Mac or on a network attached storage device. The Time Machine backup must be from Mac OS X Server 10.5.8 or later and must have a static IP address configured.

- *Setup a New Server:* Select this option if you aren't migrating from another server.

10. **Enter an Apple ID and password and click Continue.**

    Use your organization's Apple ID that was used to purchase and download Lion.

11. **In the Registration screen that appears, type your name and contact information and click Continue.**

    The installer may supply info for you based on the Apple ID you entered.

12. **In the Create Your Computer Account screen (shown in Figure 3-6) that appears, enter the name and password for the first administrator account and click Continue.**

    A short name is created. This name is the local administrator account name for the server Mac. It doesn't have to be a person's name.

13. **Click Start Using Lion in the Thank You screen that appears and then log in with computer account and password you created in the preceding step.**

If you just upgraded an existing Snow Leopard Server, Lion Server is now installed and booted. If not, then the Lion client is installed and booted, which means you're not finished. Proceed to the next section to install the Server components.

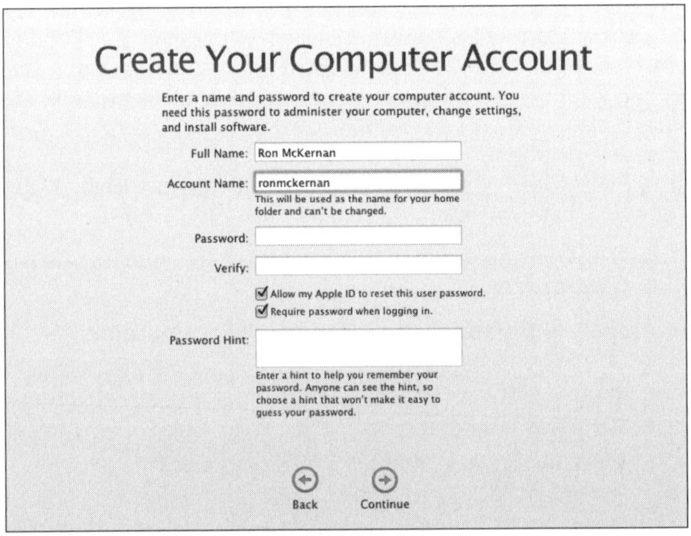

## Create Your Computer Account

Enter a name and password to create your computer account. You need this password to administer your computer, change settings, and install software.

Full Name: Ron McKernan

Account Name: ronmckernan

This will be used as the name for your home folder and can't be changed.

Password:

Verify:

☑ Allow my Apple ID to reset this user password.
☑ Require password when logging in.

Password Hint:

Enter a hint to help you remember your password. Anyone can see the hint, so choose a hint that won't make it easy to guess your password.

◀ Back      ▶ Continue

**Figure 3-6:** The Create Your Computer Account screen creates a local administrator for the server Mac.

### Downloading and installing Server components from the App Store

Follow the steps in this section if you're continuing from the preceding section or are upgrading the Lion client to a server. In either case, Lion is now installed. At this point, you need to download and install some Mac OS X Server software from the Mac App Store. I say *some* software because the 15MB you download there is only a very small part of the server software. The installer will download several hundred megabytes more. Follow these steps to convert a Lion client to Lion Server:

14. **Launch the App Store from the Dock and log in with your (or your organization's) Apple ID.**

15. **Purchase Mac OS X Server or if you've already purchased it, go to the Purchases icon in the toolbar and click the Install button.**

    After a short download, another installer launches, displaying *Welcome to Server.*

16. **Click Continue in the Welcome to Server window and then click Agree to the Software License.**

17. **Click Continue in the Install Software window (see Figure 3-7).**

    At this point, the installer begins to download server software.

18. **Enter the Mac's local administrator name and password**

    If you started in the preceding section, this is the admin name that you created in Step 12.

19. **In the Configuring Services window that appears after the download and installation of software is complete, click Finish.**

The Server app opens, with the Next Steps pane expanded at the bottom. Proceed to the next section to continue configuring Lion Server.

**Figure 3-7:**
Most of Lion's server software is downloaded after you click Continue.

## *Finishing setup in the Server: Choose a hostname, set up Open Directory*

If you upgraded a Snow Leopard Server to Lion Server or installed from a Lion Server installation to a blank second drive, you already have at least server basic settings. You don't need to read this section.

If, however, you upgraded a Snow Leopard client or a Lion client to server, you never saw the server setup assistant, and the installation process left you with a server installation that is basically unconfigured. The installer gave your Mac a .local hostname, no Open Directory master, and no DNS configured.

The Next Steps area of the Server app (shown in Figure 3-8) advises you on some of the things you can configure and enables you to launch a server setup assistant to guide you through it. Next Steps is a smart advisor, in that it gives you specific advice based on the configuration of the server. When you change settings, Next Steps changes the advice and the links.

You can see from Figure 3-8 that the installation process gave this Mac a computer name called John's Mac — not a very useful name for a server machine. That's because the installer picked a hostname based on the administrator account name that I entered. Figure 3-8 also shows the result of clicking the Configure Network button in the Next Steps pane. In this case, it tells me that the computer hostname can be seen only on my local network.

Furthermore, when I click the Add Users, Next Steps tells me that the directory is local, not shared. This means that Open Directory is not set up. Neither is DNS.

There are several ways to change these and other things. One way is to use the Server App and Next Steps to launch the server setup assistants, which automate the setup process. For example, changing the hostname can cause the setup assistant to automatically set up DNS — a nice feature.

In this example, I describe changing computer and hostnames, setting up DNS, and creating an Open Directory master. Follow these steps:

1. **In the Server app's sidebar, select your server under Hardware and click the Network tab, as shown in Figure 3-8.**

   Notice the Edit buttons next to Computer Name and Host Name. You don't need to click the first, because the Host Name Edit button brings up a server setup assistant that will let you change both.

2. **Click the Edit button next to Host Name to open the setup assistant and then click the Continue button.**

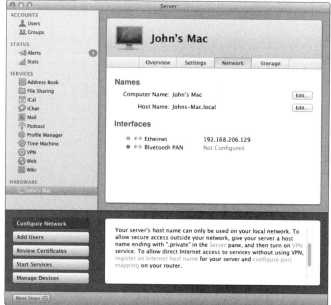

**Figure 3-8:**
After the server installation finishes, the Server app opens with Next Steps displayed.

## 3. Make a selection in the Host Name dialog and click Continue.

This dialog, shown in Figure 3-9, is one of the most important in initial setup of the server. In this example, it has appeared because the setup assistant did not find your server's IP address listed in any DNS server on your network or the Internet. What it doesn't say is if you select an option, it may set up basic DNS service on your server for you. (Such a deal!) Here are your choices:

- *Host Name for Local Network:* Leaves things the way they are, with a hostname ending in `.local` for your server. With this setting, you can't set up a network directory of accounts (described in Chapter 5) — all user accounts will be local accounts on the server Mac. Your users won't be able to connect to the server from the Internet. This setting works for a small number of users but limits what you can do with the server.

- *Host Name for Private Network:* Gives the Mac a hostname ending in `.private` (such as `server.example.private`). If you choose this option, the setup assistant turns on and configures a network directory (creates an Open Directory master). It also configures DNS lookup for the IP address and the hostname. This setup doesn't let people from the Internet access the server directly, but it does let users access the server from the Internet via a virtual private network (VPN, described in Chapter 18). The setup assistant later offers to turn on VPN for you.

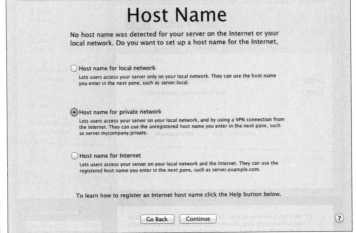

**Figure 3-9:**
This impor-
tant dialog
can result
in the
automatic
configuring
of DNS.

- *Host Name for Internet:* Enable you to set a fully qualified domain name that can identify your server on the Internet. This hostname takes the form `server.example.com`.

4. **In the Connecting to Your Mac dialog (see Figure 3-10), edit the local computer name, the hostname, and (if necessary) the IP address; then click Continue.**

   The computer name is the name that Mac and iOS devices see when they connect. You can use the Change Network button to give the Mac a fixed (static) IP address, if you haven't already.

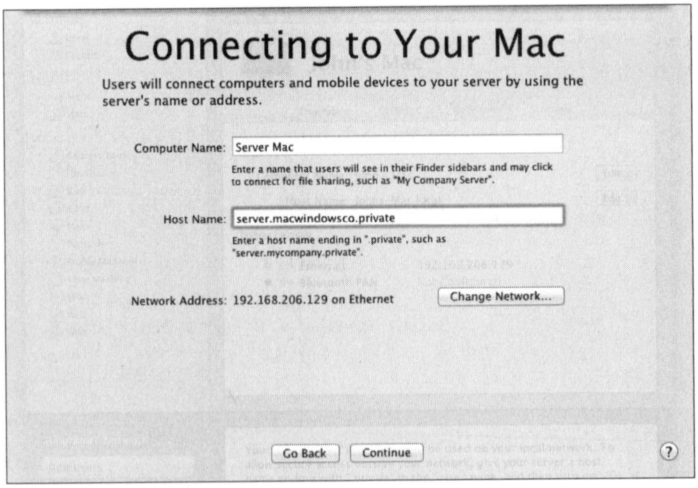

**Figure 3-10:**
The
Connecting
to Your
Mac dialog
for setting
host and
computer
names.

The Next Steps area updates to reflect the new hostname and IP address, if you changed it. It also suggests that you turn on VPN and provides a link to the VPN pane. DNS has been set up, but there's no indication of it. You have to open another application, Server Admin, to see it.

Now you can use another setup assistant to create a shared network directory of users (an Open Directory master) or import users from another directory server. Follow these steps:

1. **In the Next Steps pane of the Server app, click the Add Users button.**

    The Next Steps pane advises that your server doesn't have a shared network directory, so any users you add will be local users of the server Mac. In the text are several links that will open setup assistants.

2. **Click one of these two links to open a setup assistant:**

    • Click the Manage Network Accounts link to create a directory server on this Mac.

    • Click Connect to It to import accounts from another directory server.

    In this example, click the Manage Network Accounts link.

3. **Click Next in the Configure Users and Groups dialog.**

4. **In the Directory Administrator dialog, enter a name, short name, and password for an administrator and then click Next.**

    The default name is Directory Administrator. The default short name is diradmin, all lowercase. Spaces are not permitted in short names.

5. **In the Organization Info dialog, type a name for your department or organization and an e-mail address for the directory administrator; then click the Next button.**

6. **Review your settings in the Confirm Settings dialog and click the Set Up button.**

The assistant takes a few minutes to create an Open Directory master for you. You can now create user and group accounts.

Notice the small question mark button in the lower right of these screens. You can click it in any of the configuration screens to get help. The help that pops up is specific to the screen, and it's quite, well, helpful.

## Finishing the installation for the Server-to-empty-volume scenario

The preceding few sections describe most installation scenarios. One other scenario is installing Lion Server on an empty disk or partition while booted from

Snow Leopard Server. This type of installation gives you the advantage of a clean install while providing a more automated setup than other methods. You also don't need to go back to the App Store to download the server components.

Here's how to complete this type of installation:

1. **Follow the steps in the section "Beginning the installation process," earlier in the chapter.**

   Your Mac has rebooted, and you're looking at a Welcome window.

2. **In the Welcome window, select the country in which you're registering and click Continue.**

3. **In the Keyboard screen, select a country for your keyboard and click Continue.**

4. **In the Transfer Existing Mac Server? screen (see Figure 3-11), select one of the following buttons and click Continue:**

   • *Transfer the Information from an Existing Mac Server:* Moves settings and user data from another server or volume or drive installed with Mac OS X Server. A series of screens appears in which you select a server or drive. The new server must have the same IP address as the old server in order for DNS to continue to work without editing.

   • *Set Up a New Server:* Select this choice if you aren't migrating from another server.

5. **Enter an Apple ID and password and click Continue.**

   It's best to use your organization's Apple ID that was used to purchase and download Lion.

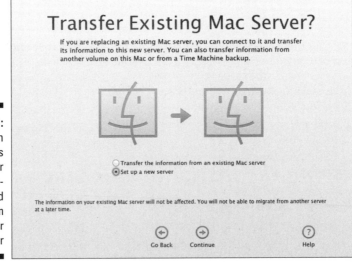

**Figure 3-11:**
This screen moves server configurations and data from another server

6. **Click the Agree button on the License Agreement screen.**

7. **In the Registration screen that appears, type your name and contact information and click Continue.**

8. **In the Administrator Account screen (see Figure 3-12) that appears, enter the name, password, and password hint for the local administrator account and click Continue.**

   If desired, select the check box called Enable Administrators to Manage This Server Remotely. This setting enables Macs installed with Apple Remote Desktop (a separate product) to remotely control the server.

9. **Type an organization name and admin e-mail address in the Organization dialog and then click Continue.**

10. **In the Time Zone dialog, select a city in your time zone from the Closest City pop-up menu and then click Continue.**

11. **In the Xsan screen (see Figure 3-13), indicate whether you'll by using the server Mac as an Xsan metadata controller or client.**

    Xsan is Apple's storage area network file system that works over a Fibre Channel interface.

12. **Make a selection in the Host Name dialog and click Continue.**

    This is essentially the same dialog as Figure 3-9 (which you didn't see if you're following these steps). This dialog appears if no hostname was detected for your server on the Internet or your local network. Basically, it did not find a DNS entry for your IP address. If you do have DNS configured somewhere, there could be a problem with DHCP. Your three choices are

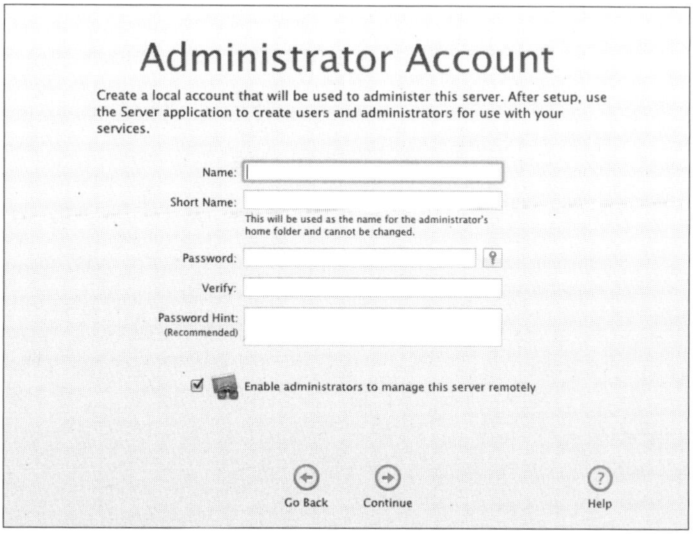

**Figure 3-12:** The Administrator Account screen.

# Administrator Account

Create a local account that will be used to administer this server. After setup, use the Server application to create users and administrators for use with your services.

Name:

Short Name:
This will be used as the name for the administrator's home folder and cannot be changed.

Password:

Verify:

Password Hint:
(Recommended)

☑ Enable administrators to manage this server remotely

Go Back    Continue    Help

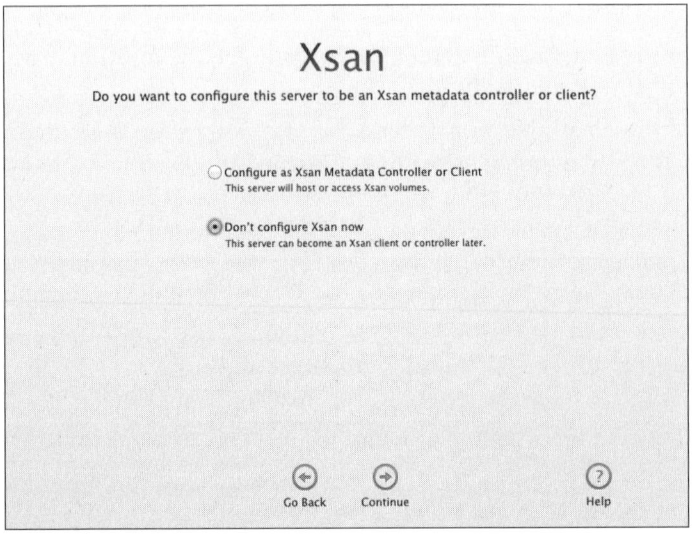

**Figure 3-13:**
The Xsan screen.

- *Host Name for Local Network:* Leaves things the way they are, with a host-name ending in `.local` for your server. With this setting, you can't set up a network directory of accounts (described in Chapter 5) — all user accounts will be local accounts on the server Mac. Your users won't be able to connect to the server from the Internet. This setting works for a small number of users but limits what you can do with the server.

  - *Host Name for Private Network:* Gives the Mac a hostname ending in `.private` (such as *server.example.*`private`). If you choose this option, the setup assistant turns on and configures a network directory (create an Open Directory master). It also configures DNS lookup for the IP address and the hostname. This setup doesn't let people from the Internet access the server directly, but it does let users access the server from the Internet via a virtual private network.

  - *Host Name for Internet:* Lets you set a fully qualified domain name that can identify your server on the Internet. This hostname takes the form *server.example.com.*

  If you choose the second or third option, the server setup assistant creates minimum DNS for you.

13. **In the Connecting to Your Mac dialog, edit the local computer name, the hostname, and, if necessary, the IP address; then click Continue.**

    The computer name is the name that Mac and iOS devices see when they connect. You can use the Change Network button to give the Mac a fixed (static) IP address, if you haven't already.

14. **In the Users and Groups screen, indicate whether you host an Open Directory server on the Mac or on another server, or if you'll be using Xsan to manage users.**

    If you select Open Directory, an Open Directory master is created for you.

15. **Click the Set Up button in the Review screen.**

The installer takes some time to implement the settings you indicated and will set up basic DNS service if appropriate. When finished, you're presented with a login screen for the server.

# Downloading the Server Administration Tools

One more important set of tools did not get downloaded from the App Store or during any of the installation procedures. This is a set of six management applications collectively known as Server Admin Tools. Download this package from Apple at `www.apple.com/support/downloads`. When you download the package and run the installer, a folder called Server installs in the Applications folder.

Included in the Server Admin Tools download are two important administration tools: Server Admin, for configuring network infrastructure services, and Workgroup Manager, for configuration and management of user accounts. I describe using these applications in almost every chapter of this book.

# Creating users and group accounts

Chapter 16 describes how to create and manage user accounts in detail, but if you're hosting a network directory on your server and want to get a quick start, you can do so with the Server app. Here's the quick-and-dirty:

1. **Launch the Server app from the Dock and log in.**

2. **Select Users from the sidebar and click the Add (+) button.**

3. **In the dialog that appears (see Figure 3-14), type a username and password and then click Done.**

That's it. Just lather, rinse, and repeat, and you'll have a directory of users in a matter of minutes. You can also create group accounts by selecting Groups in the sidebar, clicking the Add (+) button, and clicking Done. To add a user to a group, click Users in the sidebar and double-click a username. Click the Add (+) button below the Groups field and type the name of a group. Then click Done.

This is just a brief description to get you up and running. There's much you can do when creating and managing directories and user accounts. Check out the chapters in Part II and Part V of this book.

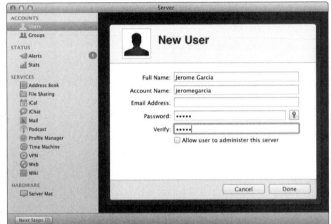

**Figure 3-14:** Creating a user account with the Server app.

# *Introducing DNS*

Domain name service (DNS) is the system that *resolves* IP addresses to domain names. For example, when you type `dummies.com` in a web browser, the DNS system tells your browser the IP address of the server hosting the site at John Wiley & Sons, Inc., allowing your computer to send a request to that host. Without DNS, you'd have to type the IP address of the Dummies website in your browser. DNS is not just for the web, though. It's used for most types of server communications on the Internet and on your local network.

If you created an Open Directory master from a setup assistant in the Server App or during some types of installation, the assistant may have done some DNS setup for you. It may be all you need, depending on your network setup and type of Internet connection. If the assistant didn't find any DNS server on your network, it configures local DNS, which enables users on your subnet to access services, but without any Internet connections. You use Server Admin to configure DNS in Lion Server manually.

If you turned on mail service, you'll need to configure DNS on your Mac if you want your e-mail to be used on the Internet. Specifically, you'll need to add a DNS entry called an *MX record*. Don't worry what that means now — I show you how to do that in Chapter 14.

DNS is a complicated subject. There are many variables and settings for different situations. In fact, I could write an entire book about DNS service. Fortunately, I don't have to because Blair Rampling and David Dalan already wrote *DNS For Dummies* (John Wiley & Sons, Inc.). It focuses on Windows and Unix servers but provides the theory and terminology about the DNS system that is common to all servers.

If your server is part of a bigger network that already has DNS servers, check with your network administrators before making changes to DNS on Lion Server. Otherwise, you may inadvertently cause problems throughout the network. Similarly, if your Internet service provider supplies your DNS service, check with them before making changes.

### Understanding DNS concepts: Zones and records

When you configured Lion Server, the server assistant may have created a *master zone with reverse lookup* and a machine record for your primary DNS name. A *DNS zone* is an organization entity that contains different types of records that relate to a domain. You could have a zone that contained IP addresses for servers in the acmehigh.edu domain, such as www.acmehigh.edu and mailserver.acmehigh.edu.

A master (primary) zone contains all the records for the zone, and it is the Internet's authority on that domain. A secondary, or slave, zone contains copies of master zone information that is stored on another server.

A DNS zone can contain several types of records. Here are the most common:

- ✔ **Machine record, also called Address (A):** This basic record holds the IP address for a domain name for a server or service.

- ✔ **Canonical name (CNAME), also called an alias:** You can use CNAMEs to resolve multiple domain names to one IP address (such as www.abc.com, ourserver.abc.com, and mail183.abc.com). For example, you might have a DNS zone with a CNAME record and an A record, as follows:

      www.abc.com.  CNAME ourserver.abc.com.

      ourserver.abc.com.  A    192.168.10.20

  In this case, when there is a lookup for www.abc.com, the IP address 192.168.10.20 is returned. (Note that a dot is always used in domain names in DNS records.)

- ✔ **Mail exchange (MX) record:** This identifies a computer as a mail server. (See Chapter 14 for more on MX records.) MX records are not created by Server Assistant during installation/configuration.

- ✔ **Service (SRV) record:** This identifies services that are hosted by one or more servers. It maps requests for the service to an IP address.

To a certain degree, Lion Server automates working with records. Server Admin asks you for information about the computer you're adding to the zone, and it creates the zone record that resolves to the computer's IP address. The focus is on the computer rather than the zone records.

Server Admin also automatically creates a reverse lookup zone when you create a master zone. A reverse lookup zone supplies a corresponding domain name when an IP address is presented by another computer.

### Using Server Admin to configure DNS zones and records

To get to the DNS settings in Server Admin, select your server in the column at the left, click the triangle next to it, and then click DNS in the list of services. Finally, click the Zones icon in the toolbar. You'll see a window such as the one in Figure 3-15. This example has a master zone with one machine record under it and a reverse lookup zone. These items were created by the server assistant during initial server setup.

**Figure 3-15:** DNS configuration in Server Admin.

The top half of the DNS Zones window lists the zones — click the triangle next to a zone to display the records in it. When you click a zone or a record, the bottom half of the window displays fields that are specific to the type of zone or record. These include zone or record names, various domain names, IP addresses, or other information. To edit one of these fields, double-click it and type the new entry.

Some fields give you a choice of using a fully qualified domain name (FQDN) or a relative domain name. If you use the former, include a period at the end for the domain name to signify that it is an FQDN.

#### Adding a zone

To add a new zone, click the Add Zone button and select Primary Zone or Secondary Zone from the drop-down menu. In the Primary Zone Name field, enter the fully qualified domain name of the primary server. In the Name Servers field, enter the server that is the "authority" for the zone. For a master zone, this is usually the server that is hosting the zone — the server you are configuring. Select the Allows Zone Transfer check box to enable secondary zones to get copies of the master zone. Click the Save button when done.

### Adding a record

To add a record to a zone, click a master zone, click the Add Record button and select a record type. The bottom half of the window changes, depending on the type of record you selected. The Machine Name field is for the hostname of the computer. An SRV record requires that you enter the service type in a special format, which you can choose from a drop-down menu, as well as the port information for the service. Click the Save button when done.

### Testing DNS

To check that DNS is properly configured, open Terminal (in /Applications/ Utilities) to access the command line and type NSLOOKUP *hostname*. If configured properly, the DNS server reports the IP address of the server. To check the reverse, type NSLOOKUP ipaddress. If configured correctly, the DNS server reports the hostname for your Mac OS X server. If either of these fails, DNS is not properly configured for your server.

# Keeping Control of Lion Server updates

The Mac's Software Update application automatically checks for updates that Apple recommends you run after you install Lion Server. Checking for updates is reasonable, and security updates are important. But I don't recommend installing any update on your brand-new Lion Server installation without doing some homework. Apple creates updates to fix problems or make improvements, but despite Apple's best intentions, system updates can also break functionality or cause conflicts with third-party software. You may want to skip an update if it's known to cause problems that would affect what you do with the server. You also need to wait for third-party software developers to catch up and release an update that is compatible with Apple's latest update.

So instead of blindly installing Apple updates, here's your homework assignment:

✔ Research what others are seeing.

✔ Configure Software Update properly.

✔ Download and test the update on another Mac or in a virtual machine (as described in Chapter 4).

## Researching the update

Check up on what other people are experiencing with the update. Then, if you decide to go for the update, test it first.

You can check websites that cover Apple software updates to see what other users are experiencing with the most recent update. If a lot of people are reporting the same problems with third-party networking or server software, you may want to hold off on the upgrade. Are people reporting that the update fixes any problems that you're seeing? Don't take Apple's word for it.

Here are three websites that report problems with Mac updates:

- **MacWindows:** My website, running since 1997, focuses on problems and solutions with Macs and PCs working together. When a new version of Mac OS X Server or a client is released, I report problems or bugs that people experience.

      www.macwindows.com

- **MacInTouch:** Ric Ford's site specializes in all things Macintosh.

      www.macintouch.com

- **Apple Discussions forums:** Click the link for Mac OS X Server 10.7 and check for problem reports.

      www.apple.com/discussions

One report of a problem doesn't usually indicate a widespread issue, but if you see the same problem reported on multiple websites, beware.

This is true for all your client Macs and Windows PCs. Don't install upgrades for them without researching first and testing the upgrade on one machine before rolling it out on all your clients.

When you do update, first perform a full backup of the server boot drive. If something breaks, you want to be able to get back to the last stable version as soon as possible.

## Configuring Software Update properly

On every Mac, Software Update is available in the Apple menu. Its preference window, however, is accessible in System Preferences by clicking the Software Update icon. As one of the final touches on your Lion Server installation, open this preferences pane and edit the settings. The default settings aren't exactly dangerous, but they are more appropriate for a client computer than for a server.

By default, Software Update is set to check for updates weekly and to download them. Don't worry, it doesn't install, download, and update; it brings up a dialog asking you if you want to install the update. To prevent this, in the Software Update Preferences window, leave the Download Important Updates Automatically check box turned off.

You might also want to deselect the Check for Updates check box so that the server isn't regularly checking for updates by itself. Best practice is to use the Check Now button to manually check for updates or simply launch Software Update. You might set up a repeating calendar reminder in iCal to remind you to check once a month or so.

If you want to update your server to a version later than what you have but earlier than the latest, you can. Apple offers older updates at its website, which you can download with a web browser. You can find updates at `www.apple.com/support/downloads`.

## Downloading and testing updates

Test an upgrade on a spare Mac or in a virtual machine before you roll it out on your server. This means downloading the upgrade on your test machine, *not* on your server.

Here's how to safely download an update:

1. **Choose Apple menu⇨Software Update.**

   Software Update automatically checks for new updates. These could be updates to the operating system (a Mac OS X 10.7.x update), updates to components (such as Java), or security updates.

   Security updates are important, but they have also been known to cause compatibility issues.

   Software Update tells you whether it found anything.

2. **If Software Update did find something, click the Show Details button to display the updates.**

   Never install an update without knowing what it is, even on a test machine.

   Software Update shows you a list of the updates it found.

3. **Select the check boxes next to the updates that you want to install.**

4. **Click the Install button.**

You can now test the update. Try replicating the kinds of things your users do. Make sure you test on Mac, Windows, and Linux clients.

# Changing Ethernet Addressing

After your initial setup, you may need to change the IP addresses of your Ethernet port(s) or change the addressing scheme from automatic (DHCP) to manual (static). You can do this in System Preferences:

1. **Open System Preferences from the Dock or the Apple menu.**

2. **Click the Network icon.**

   The Network window appears. On the left, you see a list of network ports, including AirPort.

   You can also Control-click (right-click) the System Preferences icon in the Dock and select Network from the contextual menu.

3. **Click the Ethernet port you want to configure.**

4. **Click the Configure pop-up menu and choose DHCP, Manual, or other type of addressing you'll use.**

5. **Type the IP addressing and domain name information in the appropriate fields.**

6. **Click Apply.**

After you change an IP address, you may have to update other settings, such as DNS.

# Chapter 4

# Running Servers in Virtual Machines

## In This Chapter

▶ Discovering what you can do with virtual machines

▶ Choosing virtualization software

▶ Considering hardware requirements

▶ Installing a guest OS in a virtual machine

**R**unning Lion Server on a Mac is a powerful addition to a network. Running two Lion Servers can be even more powerful. Common sense tells you that you need two Macs for that — but common sense might not know about virtualization.

Maybe you wish you could run a Windows or Linux server on a Mac. While you're wishing, how about running Windows, Linux, and Lion Server all at the same time, all on the same Mac? You can with *virtualization,* which enables you to run multiple operating systems on one computer. Each operating system is completely separate from the others, running in its own virtual machine.

Virtualization has great benefits, including easy and flexible testing of server setups before rolling them out for your users. For production servers, virtualization can save you money in hardware, add flexibility, and make for quicker disaster recovery. Virtualization has limitations as well, and for production servers, you'll want the higher-end Macs — a Mac Pro or an old Xserve — with lots of RAM.

# The Reality of Virtualization

Macs are the only computers that allow you to run Mac OS X along with Windows and Linux. Virtual machines on non-Apple PCs can't run Mac OS X. Apple doesn't permit running Mac OS X on non-Apple hardware in its user license agreement, so the virtualization software makers don't enable it.

Figure 4-1 shows a Mac running two virtual machines — Lion Server (left) and Windows 7 (right). Both are running on a Mac OS X host). In each virtual machine window, you can control that operating system as you normally would run applications, configure settings, and access the Internet. When the virtual machine is a server, users on the network access it as they would any other server. If multiple virtual machines run on a server Mac, the users see each as a separate server.

**Figure 4-1:**
Windows 7 and Lion Server running in virtual machines in Snow Leopard.

For the latest news, tips, and troubleshooting information about running virtual machines on Macs, visit MacWindows (www.macwindows.com), a website I've been running since 1997.

# How virtualization works

With virtualization, there's a host *operating system (OS)* and one or more guest OSes. The host OS (in this book, Mac OS X or Mac OS X Server) boots the real computer. On a Mac, a guest OS can be Mac OS X, Windows, Linux, or Unix. Figure 4-2 shows the relationship between the host OS and the guest OS.

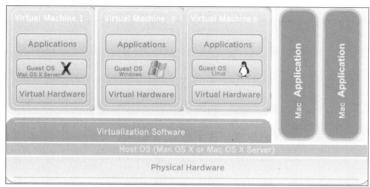

**Figure 4-2:** A diagram of how virtualization works.

Each guest OS runs in a *virtual machine,* which is a kind of a virtual reality for the guest OS. The guest OS thinks it's running on a real computer. Although real hardware's behind the scenes, the guest OS doesn't have direct control over the hard drive, graphics, and other hardware: These pieces of hardware are virtualized in the virtual machine.

For example, a virtual machine's hard drive (the boot drive) is actually a file on the host Mac. This file can be dozens of gigabytes, containing the complete guest operating system and its applications, settings, and documents. The virtual hard drive file is stored on the Mac's real hard drive, but the guest OS doesn't control the entire drive. The virtualization software creates the virtual machine and keeps the guest OS believing that it's living in a real computer — kind of like *The Matrix,* but without Keanu Reeves.

Another type of virtualization software runs directly on "bare metal," which means it doesn't use a host OS. To picture it, take Figure 4-2 and remove the Mac OS X host and the Mac applications. Eliminating the host OS decreases the complexity and uses less RAM and processing power.

# Knowing the Apple and Microsoft virtualization rules

When running guest operating systems in virtual machines, you have to abide by the software licensing agreements that Apple and Microsoft (and others) make you agree to when you install their software. Just as you can't take your $29 copy of Lion and install it on every Mac in your office, you also don't have the right to install a copy on an unlimited number of virtual machines.

### Apple's virtualization rules for Mac OS X

Apple changed its virtualization rules with Lion. The good news is that it allowed Mac OS X clients — specifically, Mac OS X 10.7 — to be run in a virtual machine. The bad news is that Apple restricted the number of versions of Lion you can run on each Mac: You cannot run more than two virtual machines containing Lion and Lion Server on one Mac. One copy of Lion or Lion Server entitles you to run it in two virtual machines per Mac, in addition to using it for the host OS.

For Mac OS X 10.5 and 10.6, you can run only the Server version, not the client, in a virtual machine. And each license entitles you to run only one copy in a virtual machine. But there's no limit on the numbers of copies you can run on one Mac. You can run three Leopard or Snow Leopard Server virtual machines running on one Mac, as long as you own two copies of Mac OS X Server and use separate serial numbers on each in order to not violate the license agreements.

You can also have a Mac mix older and newer versions of Mac OS X Server in virtual machines. In this case, you use the licensing restrictions of each version. For example, you could have one Mac running two Lion Server virtual machines and four Snow Leopard Server virtual machines. You'd have to own one copy of Lion Server and four licenses of Snow Leopard Server. Of course, your Mac can also be running virtual machines containing Windows and Linux.

For any version of Mac OS X, the virtual machine must be running on an Apple Mac. So unfortunately, you can't virtualize Mac OS X in your data center along with your Windows and Linux virtual machines.

### Microsoft's rules for Windows and others' rules for Linux

Microsoft is happy to let you run Windows Server in virtual machines on any hardware, including your Macs. But you still have to pay for the licenses. If you buy a single-license copy of Windows Server, you get to run it in one virtual machine. If, however, your organization runs a lot of Windows Server virtual machines, it may own a Microsoft Windows Server Datacenter Edition license, which includes the ability to run an unlimited number of virtual machines running Windows Server — in which case you can clone away. Check with your IT department if you work in a big organization.

The situation varies for Linux. Open source operating systems can be replicated without fees, but don't confuse them with some commercial Linux operating systems that do have license fees.

# Benefits of virtualization

The ability to run Mac and Windows servers on one Mac is not only useful, but you can also save money in hardware by consolidating multiple servers on one machine. Virtualization can also make deployment easier and more flexible. And it's convenient for testing.

## Flexibility in testing servers

Although I'm pleased that you're reading this book, I hope you aren't planning to install and configure Lion Server on your production servers without a period of testing first. Using virtual machines is a great way to test new servers. You don't have to dedicate a Mac to the task. You can run Lion Server (or Windows Server) in a virtual machine on any general-purpose Mac.

You can also use a single Mac to create multiple server configurations to test different settings, with different services turned on and different third-party applications installed. With virtual machines, you can test new versions of a server alongside the older versions in order to run comparisons. You can add Lion and Windows clients in virtual machines and have a little test network all on one Mac, not connected to your real network. To do this without virtualization, you'd have to use multiple Macs, or a Mac with multiple hard drives or partitions. You'd have to reboot the Mac every time you needed to run a different configuration.

If you're going to run your production server in a virtual machine, test it in one. After you get your test server configured and tweaked just as you like it, you can easily migrate it to a production server that you want to run in a virtual machine. You don't have to install server software and any extra applications and then configure it all over again. Just move the virtual machine files over to the server Mac.

When testing or setting up a server in a virtual machine, you can use a feature called a *snapshot*. It records the complete state of a virtual machine when you take the snapshot, including the software installed in the guest OS and the various server configurations. You can revert to a snapshot if you decide you want to go back to an earlier configuration. You can have multiple snapshots as well. Keep in mind that each one can consume several gigabytes of disk space.

### Server consolidation

Many servers use only a portion of the capabilities of the hardware's processor, RAM, and disk storage. A Mac Pro can hold 12 processor cores and 64GB of RAM, but few servers would take advantage of all this power. Info-Tech, a research firm, once estimated that most servers use 20 percent of their hardware capacity. Putting multiple servers in virtual machines on one computer takes advantage of hardware that'd be wasted. This is known as *server consolidation.*

How many servers you can consolidate with virtualization depends on how heavily they're used and how processor-intensive they are. (See Chapter 2 for types of server uses.) You can run up to a dozen virtual servers on one Mac. One Oregon school district replaced 44 computers running Mac and Windows servers with 7 Xserve computers running Parallels Server virtualization software — thus eliminating 37 computers. This move not only saved the district money in terms of hardware, but also saved money in reduced electricity and cooling costs.

Some of this cost savings from server consolidation is offset by the need for server hardware equipped with multiple fast processors and lots of RAM. You may also need multiple Ethernet cards in the server Mac to avoid a bottleneck caused by multiple servers accessing the network.

The big kibosh on server consolidation is Apple's restriction to only two Lion virtual machines. (See the section "Knowing the Apple and Microsoft virtualization rules," earlier in this chapter.) But you can run other servers, including Snow Leopard Server, in virtual machines alongside your two Lion virtual machines.

For example, you can add a virtual machine running Snow Leopard Server or a Windows or Linux server to work as a Primary Domain Controller for your Windows clients, a service that Lion Server no longer includes. You don't have to invest in additional computers.

### Faster, easier deployment and disaster recovery

You can easily clone a virtual machine and move it to another computer. This prevents you from having to run the entire server installer to create a second server to take the load off another or to run some different services on the server software. Just create a clone and adjust the settings as needed.

Running a server in a virtual machine also enables you to quickly replace it in case of a failure or data corruption. The strategy is to run the server OS and server software in the virtual machine but store the user data somewhere else, on another hard drive or other storage medium. When the server goes south, you don't need to troubleshoot, reinstall the OS, or reconfigure it: Just replace the entire virtual machine with a backup copy, and the server is back up and running.

---

## Using Boot Camp versus a virtual machine

Intel-powered Macs running Mac OS X 10.5 and later include Boot Camp software from Apple. After Boot Camp is installed, it turns the Mac into a dual-boot machine, with the ability to start up from either Mac OS X or Windows. The main benefit of Boot Camp over virtualization is that you can get somewhat better performance running Windows with Boot Camp than in a virtual machine. This makes it popular for fans of Windows games.

But for servers, Boot Camp isn't a good option. Boot Camp runs only one operating system at a time, which means that your only use for it would be to repurpose a Mac for use as a Windows server.

Another problem is that at this point, Apple doesn't officially support Windows Server with Boot Camp. Blog posts around the Internet have reported running Windows Server 2008 with Boot Camp, though it isn't a straightforward process due to driver issues. If you're interested in a weekend project, you can find some directions here: `www.harbar.net/articles/mbptb3.aspx`.

To check out Boot Camp, launch the Boot Camp Assistant, which resides in the Mac's Utilities folder inside the Applications folder. You'll also need a Microsoft Windows installation disc handy.

---

If you want to run an open source OS and server software, you can download preconfigured virtual machines for free, entirely skipping the operating system installation procedure. I describe this in the section "Virtual appliances," later in this chapter.

### Virtualizing Windows and Lion clients on Macs

Although this book is about servers, I want to mention that running Windows and Lion in virtual machines on users' computers (clients) can give you some of the same benefits of deployment and disaster recovery that I describe in the preceding section. If you have one or more Windows applications that your Mac users need to run, you have to install and configure Windows and the programs only once, in a virtual machine. You can then copy that virtual machine to all the users, provided that you have licenses for the copies of the OS.

## Virtual appliances

A *virtual appliance* is a preconfigured virtual machine, complete with operating system and applications. You don't have to install the OS or the server software on it. Just download the virtual appliance and fire it up with your virtualization software. The major virtualization companies offer free virtual appliances that contain open source operating systems, such as Ubuntu, Linux, or BSD Unix. They come preinstalled with one or more servers. You'll find virtual appliances preconfigured with DHCP and DNS servers, as well as database, mail, web, and wiki servers.

Parallels and VMware, the two major makers of virtualization software for Macs, both offer free virtual appliances at their websites. For Parallels, go to `www.parallels.com/ptn/download/va`. When you download a Parallels virtual machine, choose the Mac download. You get a virtual machine in a standard Mac DMG image file that mounts on the Desktop. Inside is an installer that automatically creates a virtual machine in Parallels Desktop or Parallels Server.

VMware offers a very large selection of virtual appliances. This includes free open source virtual appliances, such as servers configured on Ubuntu Linux, as well as commercial virtual appliances for sale from commercial developers, such as Red Hat Linux. Check them out at `www.vmware.com/ appliances`.

VMware's virtual appliances don't have Mac-specific installers, so you have to install them from within VMware Fusion. Virtual appliances from VMware work on all VMware virtualization software for Mac, Windows, and Linux.

The virtual appliances downloaded from VMware and Parallels don't work on each other's virtualization software. However, both companies supply software that converts the other company's virtual machines into their own formats.

When you start an OS from a downloaded virtual machine, the OS presents you with a login screen. You'll find a login name and password either on the website or in a readme file with the download.

# Choosing Virtualization Software

Three major companies make virtualization software for Macs: Parallels, VMware, and Oracle. In a nutshell, here are the choices:

- ✔ **Parallels Server:** Meant for serious virtualization of multiple production servers on one Mac, Parallels Server includes management software for the servers. It comes in several versions, from a $300 Mac mini edition to the $2,000 Parallels Server for Mac.

    `www.parallels.com`

- ✔ **Parallels Desktop:** This user-level, or desktop, application costs under $100. You need version 7 or later to run Lion in a virtual machine.

- ✔ **VMware Fusion:** Another user-level virtualization package, Fusion is very similar to Parallels Desktop and similarly priced. You need version 4 or later to run Lion in a virtual machine.

    `www.vmware.com`

> ✔ **Oracle VirtualBox:** This open source product is free for personal use.
> `www.virtualbox.org`

You can use the desktop versions for testing servers or for running services that don't use a lot of system resources. A desktop version won't let you assign as much of the Mac hardware to a virtual machine Parallels Server.

## Choosing a desktop virtualization package

Parallels Desktop and VMware Fusion are roughly equivalent. With each new version, one pulls slightly ahead of the other in terms of features, so at any given month, one might be ahead of the other. Both products can import virtual machines from each other, so if you decide to switch, you can move over your virtual machines. Both run Lion Server well.

One reason to use VMware Fusion is that it's compatible with its virtual machine formats that run on Windows. Parallels Desktop is compatible with Parallels' Windows products, but VMware is much more widely used in industry. So if you had a Windows server running on the Mac, you could move to a Windows server running VMware's products without having to convert the virtual machine to another format.

On the other hand, Parallels Desktop virtual machines can run in Parallels Server. So if you decided to upgrade, you could easily move a virtual machine running Lion Server, Windows, or Linux to Parallels Server. Parallels tends to be a little faster than VMware, particularly with graphics, though I haven't noticed a difference in the performance of Mac OS X Server.

VirtualBox is not quite in the same league as Fusion and Desktop. It's not as easy to install a guest OS and is just not as hassle-free as the other. The $0 price tag is a plus, but that also comes with no support unless you buy a support contract from Oracle.

## When you might use Parallels Server

Parallels Server is the only server-level virtualization software for Macs. It comes in a standard version that runs in a Mac OS X host OS. There's a Bare Metal edition as well. Parallels Server costs significantly more than the desktop version but has performance advantages over it. For example, if your Mac has four or more processor cores, Parallels Server allows you to assign up to four virtual processor cores for each machine, whereas the desktop virtualization applications support up to two cores per virtual machine. You can allocate up to 15 cores total for all virtual machines, more than the 12 possible cores in a server Mac. Parallels Server is also optimized for the Xserve and Mac Pro.

If your Mac doesn't happen to have 12 cores, a significantly less expensive Mac mini version of Parallels Server supports two CPUs and 4GB RAM for each virtual machine.

Storage is another issue. A Parallels Server virtual drive can be larger than the desktop version, up to 2 terabytes (TB — 1 terabyte equals 1,024 gigabytes). Parallels Server can support up to four 2TB drive channels per virtual machine: two SCSI storage channels and two IDE channels.

Parallels Server for Mac includes a management console application that enables you to manage multiple virtual machines. You can also use the management console to create a virtual machine template that you can use in multiple virtual machines. The software automatically creates a new IP address for each virtual machine. You can use the management console on any Mac on the network. Parallels Server 4 added a feature called Express Installation for several versions of Windows and Linux, which uses virtual machine templates to automate the creation of new virtual machines.

Another feature of Parallels Server is that it runs not as an application, but in a low-level program known as a daemon. This means that it runs in the background when the Mac boots up, even before the administrator logs in. You don't have an application to launch. This is different from the Bare Metal edition, which does not run on Mac OS X at all; the Mac boots directly from Parallels Server without a host OS.

Parallels Server for Mac also includes several tools for creating or importing virtual machines. A migration tool can move setups of physical Mac and Windows servers to virtual machines. You can also import a virtual machine from Parallels Desktop, VMware, and Microsoft formats.

I don't mean to say that you can't use VMware Fusion or Parallels Desktop to virtualize Mac OS X Server; you absolutely can. If you're not sure if you need the server version, download the 30-day trial versions of the desktop versions and do some testing to see if they'll meet your needs.

# Real and Virtual Hardware Requirements

Like any piece of software, virtualization software requires certain minimum hardware on the Mac. But the software also has *virtual* hardware requirements, which consist of settings in the virtualization software. The most important settings are those for memory and the number of processors. These settings aren't as obvious as they may seem.

To change settings, you must shut down the virtual machine from the guest OS. To get to the configuration window, you need to use the Virtual Machine menu, which appears in both VMware Fusion and Parallels Desktop. In both applications, choose Settings from this menu after you select a virtual machine. A settings window appears. Figure 4-3 shows the VMware Fusion configuration window, but the other virtualization packages have similar windows.

**Figure 4-3:**
The virtual machine hardware settings window for VMware Fusion.

The following sections describe both real and virtual hardware requirements.

## Memory

For a test machine, have a Mac with at least 4GB of RAM. You can run one virtual machine with good results, and possibly a second at the same time. For a production Mac, have at least 4GB for the host OS (Mac OS X or OS X Server), plus 2GB for each virtual machine that will be running at the same time. If you have a lot going on in the host OS or in the virtual machines, you'll want more. Installing lots of RAM isn't a problem for the Mac Pro and Xserve lines, as well as for recent iMac models.

This isn't to say that you should assign 2GB of virtual RAM for a virtual machine (which you do in the settings window of the virtualization software). The amount of RAM you specify for the virtual machine doesn't correspond to the amount of RAM the OS usually requires. This is something you should test.

Assigning RAM to a virtual machine is tricky. Assign too little RAM, and the virtual machine runs slowly. But assign too much RAM, and the host Mac OS X might not have enough, which slows down the entire Mac.

For example, on a Mac with 4GB of RAM, I find that running Lion Server in a virtual machine runs the best at VMware's default 2048MB setting — even though Lion Server requires 2GB on a real machine as a bare minimum. Increasing the RAM allocation can slow the virtual machine down. On a Mac with more real RAM, increasing the virtual machine's RAM allocation helps.

## Processors

The more virtual machines you run and the more you do with them, the more powerful processors you'll need. In addition to speed, faster processors have more processing cores. The processors in modern Macs have two cores (dual core), four cores (quad core), or six cores. In essence, a dual-core processor is two processors in one chip, and a quad core is four processors in one chip. The Mac Pro can have up to two six-core processors, for a total of twelve.

With virtualization software, you can assign one or more processing cores to any given virtual machine. Some virtualization software refers to a processing core as a *processor;* others call it a *CPU (central processing unit).* The desktop virtualization programs allow you to assign one or two cores to a virtual machine. Parallels Server allows you to assign up to 4 CPUs per virtual machine, for a total of 15 for all the virtual machines running at one time on a Mac. So if you want to put a processor-intensive service in a virtual machine, you may need Parallels Server and Mac Pro or Xserve.

Like the RAM settings, the processor settings aren't what you might expect. Sometimes on a Mac with a Core 2 Duo (two processing cores), a Lion Server virtual machine runs best by assigning it two processors. You might think that assigning two cores on a two-core Mac leaves nothing for the host OS, but that's not always the case. The best thing to do is test it for your configuration.

## Drive storage

You need enough free hard drive space for each virtual machine you run. Lion Server requires at least 20GB, but it's good to have 30GB of hard drive space available for each virtual machine.

Guest OSes can also access storage outside the virtual machine, where you might keep your user data. This could be an internal partition, a hard drive, a RAID, an external RAID array, or a SAN.

To make use of outside storage, a virtual machine maps the physical drive to a small image file. The operating system thinks the image file is the storage device, but the file points to the physical device. Virtual machines also use drive mapping to access the Mac's DVD drive. You can set the mapping to a DVD disk image, such as a DMG or an ISO file.

## Network settings

One of the reasons virtualizing server operating systems is possible is that virtual machines can act like real computers on your network. They can access the Internet through your connection, and other computers see the virtual machines as real networked computers. In fact, the host and guest operating systems can all see one another as networked computers.

Configuring networking in virtualization software is as simple as clicking a button. Three types of networking connections are available in VMware, Parallels, and VirtualBox:

- **Bridged:** This is the best choice for deploying a server on a network. The virtual machine has its own IP address and appears as a separate computer on the local Ethernet network. You can configure a static IP address if you need to.

- **Shared or NAT (network address translation):** With this setting, the Mac can access the Internet, but other computers on the local network can't see it. The virtual machine doesn't have its own IP address. (It gets its IP address from a virtual DHCP server.) This is a good choice if you're installing Lion Server in a virtual machine, for which you need an Internet connection, but don't want to expose the virtual machine to your local network.

- **Host-only:** In this configuration, only the host computer sees the virtual machine on the network, and the virtual machine sees only the host, not the Internet. The virtual machine uses a virtual private network to connect to the Mac. This is a good choice if you want to test a server without exposing it to the network or the Internet. If you have multiple guest operating systems using host-only networking, the host Mac OS X can see them all on the same network, but they can't see one another.

When you create a virtual machine and install the guest OS, one of these choices is picked for you. You can change this just before you hit the Install button or easily afterward.

# Installing an OS in a Virtual Machine

Installing an operating system in a virtual machine is similar to installing an OS on a physical computer but with a few extra steps at the beginning to create the virtual machine in which you'll install the OS.

Virtualization software won't let you use the remote Lion Server installation procedure that I describe in Chapter 3. With Parallels Server, however, you can create a virtual machine on a machine remotely from another computer on the network.

The following sections look at some of the issues with a desktop virtualization application as well as with Parallels Server.

Immediately after creating a new virtual machine, take a snapshot of the brand-new installation. In the event that you mess things up, this snapshot enables you to quickly revert to a clean, fresh install without having to reinstall the operating system. The Snapshot feature is usually available in the Virtual Machine menu of your virtualization software.

Each virtual machine can run it its own window (as in Figure 4-1) or full-screen. You can run a multiple virtual machine in full-screen mode at the same time by putting each in one of Mac OS X's Spaces. Virtualization software also includes view modes that hide the desktop of the guest OS and display only windows, enabling you to intermingle windows from the host Mac and the guest OS.

## Getting the right version of virtualization software

Older versions of virtualization software don't support Lion. Here are the versions of virtualization software that will run on Lion host OSes and those that will run inside virtual machines as guests.

Parallels Desktop 6 Build 12094 or later is required to run on a Lion host. Version 7.0 or later is required to run Lion in a virtual machine.

Parallels Server for Mac 4 Update 1 or later is required to run on a Lion host. At publishing time, the version number supporting Lion as a guest was not known.

VMware Fusion 3.1.3 and later is required to run on a Lion host. Version 4.0 or later is required to run Lion in a virtual machine. VMware Fusion 4 runs on Mac OS X 10.6.8 or later.

VirtualBox 4.0.10 or later is required to run on a Lion host. At publishing time, VirtualBox didn't support Lion Server as a guest OS. There very likely will be a version that does support Lion guests, so check `www.virtualbox.org` for updates.

## Installing Lion or Lion Server in a virtual machine

As I describe in Chapter 3, installing Lion is different from installing any other operating system, including older versions of Mac OS X. It's also very different to install in a virtual machine. With any other operating system, the standard procedure for creating virtual machines is to boot a new, empty virtual machine with a real installation DVD, or with a disk image of a DVD, and install the OS as if you were installing on a real computer. This doesn't work for Lion, which doesn't come on (or let you create) a bootable DVD or disk image (at least, not without an unsupported hack).

With Fusion 4, VMware has engineered a slick procedure for getting around the lack of an installer DVD. You simply begin to create a new virtual machine and drag the Lion installer file into the first window that appears. You need to have a copy of the Lion installer that you've previously obtained. Here's how it's done in VMware Fusion:

1. **Launch VMware Fusion and choose Window⬩Virtual Machine Library.**

   The Virtual Machine Library window appears, as shown in Figure 4-4. It displays any Mac, Windows, or Linux virtual machines you already have installed.

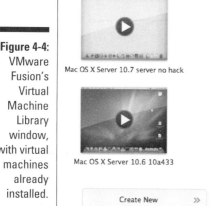

**Figure 4-4:** VMware Fusion's Virtual Machine Library window, with virtual machines already installed.

2. **Click the Create New button.**

   The Virtual Machine Assistant launches in a new window, shown in Figure 4-5.

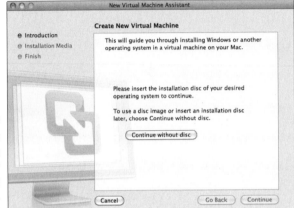

**Figure 4-5:** Drag the Lion installer file into this window.

3. **Drag the Lion installer file (Install Mac OS X Lion) from the Finder into the Virtual Machine Assistant window.**

   The Installation Media window appears, as shown in Figure 4-6. VMware Fusion treats the Lion installer as though it were a bootable DVD or a disk image. The Virtual Machine Assistant has selected Use Operating System Installation Disc or Image, and the Install Mac OS X Lion file is listed in the pop-up menu. Don't change these settings.

**Figure 4-6:** VMware Fusion now treats the Lion installer like an installer disc or disk image.

4. **Click the Continue button.**

   The Choose Operating System window (see Figure 4-7) appears, with the correct settings in place: Apple Mac OS X is selected as the operating system, and Mac OS X Server 10.7 64-bit is selected as the version.

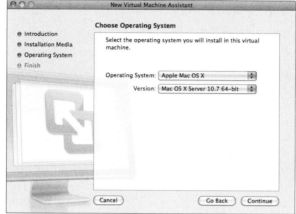

**Figure 4-7:**
Setting the operating system for the virtual machine.

5. **Click Continue and then click the Finish button in the summary screen that appears.**

6. **Give your virtual machine a name in the new dialog that appears and then click the Save button.**

   The name should be descriptive, such as Lion Mail Server Test.

7. **(Optional) Use the Where pop-up menu to change the location of the virtual machine file.**

   The virtual machine starts up, and the Lion installer launches, landing you at the Welcome screen. You can now proceed with the Lion installation, as described in Chapter 3.

If you want to change any of the settings, such the type of networking, RAM, or others, first shut the virtual machine down as you normally shut down Mac OS X, such as by choosing Apple menu⇨Shut Down inside the virtual machine. Then choose Virtual Machine⇨Settings.

# Upgrading an existing virtual machine to Lion

Upgrading an existing virtual machine containing Snow Leopard Server is a lot like upgrading a real Mac. The following steps apply to any virtualization software, including VMware Fusion, Parallels Desktop, and Parallels Server:

1. **Launch the Snow Leopard Server virtual machine and update Snow Leopard Server to version 10.6.8 if necessary.**

2. **Copy the Lion installer to the `Applications` folder in the virtual machine or download Lion from the App Store within the virtual machine.**

3. **Run the Lion Server installer and install as you would a host OS, as described in Chapter 3.**

   To update a Lion client, download the Lion Server edition from the App Store within the virtual machine, and install as you normally would.

# Installing non-Lion OSes in desktop virtualization software

For operating systems other than Lion, you can use either a bootable OS installer DVD or a disk image. Both Parallels Desktop and VMware Fusion launch an installation assistant that guides you through the setup. In either program, the assistant can recognize a Windows installation DVD.

The procedures for installing a non-Lion OS in Parallels Desktop, VMware Fusion, and VirtualBox are very similar. Here, I use Parallels Desktop as an example:

1. **Insert the operating system's install DVD, if you're using one, into the Mac.**

   If you're using a disk image, proceed to the next step.

2. **Launch Parallels Desktop.**

   The Virtual Machine Assistant opens. If it doesn't, choose File⇨New.

3. **Select your DVD drive or a drive image from the Install From pop-up menu and then click Continue.**

   If you installed a Windows installation disk, Parallels Desktop will probably recognize it. If so, enter a Windows product key in the dialog that asks for it, and click Continue.

   If you're not installing Windows, proceed to the next step.

4. **In the Integration with Mac window (see Figure 4-8), choose one of the following, and click Continue:**

   • *Like a Mac:* Hides the guest OS desktop, and applications in the guest OS float freely along with Mac OS X windows.

   • *Like a PC:* Displays the entire guest operating system in one window.

   You can always change this setting later.

**Figure 4-8:**
The
Integrate
with Mac
window
when
installing
a guest
OS with
Parallels
Desktop.

5. **In the Name and Location screen (see Figure 4-9), type a name for the virtual machine.**

6. **(Optional) To change the default location of the virtual machine data, click the Location pop-up menu and browse to a folder.**

**Figure 4-9:**
Naming a
new virtual
machine in
Parallels
Desktop.

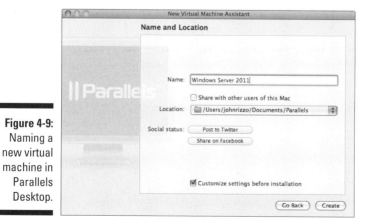

7. **(Optional) Click the Customize Settings Before Installation check box if you'd like to change settings before installing the guest OS.**

8. **Click the Create button.**

   If you clicked Customize Settings Before Installation, a settings window appears, in which you can set the number of CPUs and RAM for the virtual machine. You can do this later, but the installation process could be very slow if the settings aren't right.

The new virtual machine boots from the operating system's install DVD or disk image — within a window on your Mac. You first see a black screen, followed by the operating system's installer starting up in the virtual machine.

## Distributing services in multiple VMs

Parallels Server is designed to run many virtual machines on one high-end Mac server. When given a choice between running a bunch of services in one virtual machine (or real machine) or spreading out the services in multiple virtual machines on the same computer, choose the latter. You get overall better performance and more efficient use of the Mac hardware by cloning the virtual machine and running different services on each clone.

For example, if you run a Windows server in a virtual machine with Exchange Server, it's best to assign four CPUs to this virtual machine and dedicate it for running only Exchange: Run other Windows services in other virtual machines. You can put a Microsoft Active Directory server in another Windows virtual machine. You might be able to pair it up with lightweight services, such as DNS (domain name service). If you run Active Directory in a Windows virtual machine, it might make sense to run Open Directory in a Lion Server virtual machine on the same Mac.

Other services might be fine in a single virtual machine. Less processor-intensive services, such as web, e-mail, and file servers that have relatively few simultaneous users, probably wouldn't tax a virtual machine.

# Part II

# Creating and Maintaining User Accounts and Directories

The 5th Wave                    By Rich Tennant

AFTER INSTALLING OS X,
NED AND LORETTA SELECT THE
COMPUTER'S BACKGROUND

"Oh – I like this background much better than
the basement."

# In this part . . .

Users are the reason for servers. Keeping track of the users is the reason for much that's in Lion Server. This part focuses on maintaining shared network directories that enable multiple users and servers to communicate and network administrators to keep track of it all. I describe *user authentication,* the process in which a user connects to the computer with a name and password. The server also provides *authorization,* the process of controlling access to files and services.

The more users and computers, the bigger the user management task. Directory services enable you to manage not only user accounts but the computers themselves. Here, I describe how Mac OS X Server's Open Directory can centrally store information about the users and the computers in a single place, and in a secure manner. A shared directory also separates the user from a specific computer so that a user can log in from any computer and access her home directory.

On large networks, you may need to access other directory servers hosted on Windows servers. That's no problem for Lion Server: I describe how to use Mac OS X Server with Microsoft Active Directory.

# Chapter 5

# Controlling Access with Directories

* * * * * * * * * * * * * * * * * * * * * * * * * * * * * * * * * * * * * * *

### In This Chapter

▶ Getting familiar with account types in a directory

▶ Binding your clients and servers to directories

▶ Authenticating with LDAP and Kerberos

* * * * * * * * * * * * * * * * * * * * * * * * * * * * * * * * * * * * * * *

**T**his chapter describes the basic concepts of directory services and how they apply to Lion Server. For directions on how to create user and group accounts, see Chapter 16.

## Defining Directories

When your entire network infrastructure consists of a computer on a desk in your living room, management of your user accounts and preferences is simple and straightforward. Your account and data are stored in one physical location. Add a second computer and maybe a laptop for travel, and you now have two or three sets of user accounts, passwords, and data.

Now multiply the computers by tens, hundreds, or thousands, and you see how managing users and data becomes beyond cumbersome in a large network. The solution is to create network directory services to aid managing many computer systems and users. A *network directory* is a shared list of users, accounts, and other resources that reside on the network. From a single location, you can manage a directory of all this information for hundreds of users. A directory can reside in one server computer or can be handled by dozens of servers on a large network.

Directory services also handles the job of *authenticating* users, which confirms the identity of users logging in from a client computer. Directory services handles authentication for other services, such as e-mail or file sharing, or to the entire network, or for the entire network at once — known as *single sign-on.*

Lion Server can host a directory for your network of Mac, Windows, and Linux computers. It can also make use of a directory residing on other servers. And it can help integrate your Mac users into a Windows-based Active Directory network. Lion Server supports two directory brands: It can host the open source Open Directory and connect to Microsoft Active Directory, which are described in Chapters 6 and 7, respectively.

Electronic directories are similar to telephone books. Phone books organize people and business with their contact information and are divided into white and yellow pages. Network directories contain a hierarchical list of data that describes user accounts, attributes, and preferences, and can contain information about network resources. The data in a directory may be separated into containers associated with different physical locations, departments, or other conditions.

The structure of a directory's database — the specific types of data it stores and how it's stored — is called a *schema*. Strictly speaking, the directory consists of the schema and the data. *Directory services* is a collection of software that is the framework that shares the information among servers and clients and provides authentication.

## Local and shared directories and domains

Both client computers and servers store account data and information about the computer in a local database on each system. These databases of user information can't be distributed among multiple computers. Even if you create a network directory, each computer will still have a local database with one or more user accounts in it.

Lion Server can store the network user accounts in its local directory. You know that they're in the local directory because you see these users in System Preferences (as well as in the Server app). A local directory may work for a small network of users with a single server and few network services. But if you had multiple servers, you'd have to set up accounts on every server machine on the network, and users would find themselves using different passwords for different file servers. You also can't use Profile Manager if you don't have a shared network directory.

With a shared directory, multiple servers share the account data, and users can log on to multiple file servers using the same account and password. Users that are *bound,* or connected, with a directory can access any of the services that reside on servers that are also bound to the same directory. The use of shared directories goes much further, allowing administrators to manage clients and set password policies. It also enables servers to host home folders for computer users. A server-based home folder means that a user can log on to any computer on the network and have access to her data and settings.

Local and shared directories are also sometimes referred to as local and shared *domains.* In this context, a domain doesn't refer to registered Internet domains but is used in the sense of *spheres of influence.* A local domain has an effect on only one computer. A shared domain covers a certain area of a network of computers.

Don't get confused if you see directory domains that end in .com or .net, like Internet domains. The reason has to do with directory services' heavy reliance on DNS (domain name server, described in Chapter 2), which you see if you set up a directory in Chapter 6.

## *Account types in a directory*

In network directories, accounts come in many flavors, not just the user account:

- ✔ **Users:** This type of account is usually an individual but not necessarily unique to a single person. Several individuals who manage a server may have access to an administrator account, for example. User accounts are the most common types you encounter and manage in a directory.

- ✔ **Groups:** You can combine one or more individual user accounts to form a group account. Members of a group account get access to the same shared data or resources, such as files in a folder.

- ✔ **Computers or machines:** Specific computer systems identified in a directory are computer or machine accounts.

- ✔ **Computer or machine groups:** As with users, directories can combine several computer accounts into a group. Easily manage multiple computers with a group.

When you're ready to create a directory, the differences and benefits of various accounts become more evident. See Chapter 16 to create and manage these account types.

# Binding Clients and Servers to Directories

Any client computer that needs to communicate with the shared directory first needs to know that the directory exists. The computer also must trust the directory and the account data it contains. Servers can also connect to a directory to use the same shared accounts for services, such as file sharing and e-mail accounts.

Connecting a client or server to a directory is referred to as *binding*. A client connected to a directory is said to be *bound* to the directory.

Mac OS X Servers can bind to a variety of directories, including the native Open Directory, Microsoft Active Directory, Novel eDirectory, various OpenLDAP systems running on other Unix and Linux servers, and the legacy Unix formats. Client computers can connect to any or all of these directory services through the Mac OS X Server.

Binding comes in two types:

- **Anonymous bind:** The most common type of bind. Client or server systems connect without first authenticating to the directory. Requests for information from the directory are sent in clear text, although authentication is encrypted by default. Anonymous connections are commonly used with Mac OS X Server's Open Directory.

  You can browse directory information without first binding — most directories are configured this way — from the local network. Using anonymous binding isn't an additional security risk in a default configuration in which anyone can browse the data.

- **Authenticated bind:** Just the opposite of anonymous. A directory administrator account is required to create an authenticated bind, creating two-way trust between the client and server. Authenticated binding reduces the risk of *man-in-the-middle attacks,* in which an evildoer on your network might attempt to gather information about directory and authentication requests. Authenticated binding would be important in a high-security network environment.

  Many Microsoft Active Directory servers allow authenticated binding only. However, anonymous binding is far simpler and creates less network overhead.

To have a client running Mac OS X 10.6 and later join a shared directory, you no longer need to open Directory Access and make a number of setting changes. The connection process is consolidated in the Accounts pane (called Users & Groups in Lion) of System Preferences. See Chapter 6 for the steps to connect to an Open Directory server. Figure 5-1 shows a Mac client joining an Active Directory domain; see details on this type of connection in Chapter 7.

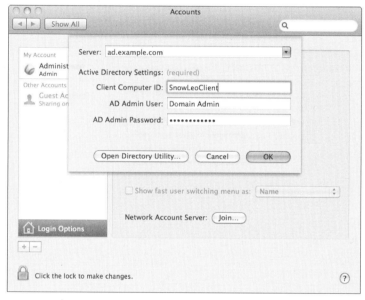

**Figure 5-1:** Join an Active Directory domain from the Accounts pane.

For advanced configuration of a Mac client, you employ the Directory Access utility, located in `/System/Library/CoreServices`. For clients running Mac OS X 10.5.x and earlier, you *must* use the Directory Access utility to bind to a shared directory.

The Users and Groups (or Accounts) pane in System Preferences shows the status of the directory with the use of a colored dot. Green indicates a good connection to the server. Red indicates an error in the link to the directory. If no connection exists, no dot is displayed.

Another location to look for the status is the login window. Click the gray text indicating the system's name in the login window, just below the Mac OS X logo, to find additional information about the system. This data includes a green or red dot and the status of network accounts. Having this knowledge can help you troubleshoot directory connections right from the login window.

# Authenticating with LDAP and Kerberos

Directory services also provide the authentication that allows users to access other services. The common authentication backbones of many prevalent directories are Lightweight Directory Access Protocol (LDAP) and Kerberos. These two technologies are built into Apple Open Directory and Microsoft Active Directory. The descriptions here just scratch the surface of LDAP and Kerberos; for more information on each technology, see www.openldap.org and http://web.mit.edu/kerberos.

Although directory services facilitate user authentication through passwords, the passwords are not usually stored in directories. That's because anyone with access to the directory can usually browse its information. In Mac OS X Server, passwords can be stored either in the Open Directory Password Server database or in a Kerberos realm, which is a kind of holding place. When authenticating, Open Directory checks with the Kerberos realm first.

In Mac OS X Server, Open Directory never even reads the passwords. Each account password is stored as encrypted value called a *shadow hash* for each user. When the user submits a password for authentication, Open Directory runs it through the hash and compares the values of the hashes. If they match, the user is authenticated. Open Directory doesn't read the actual password.

When authenticating a user, Open Directory checks the user account stored in the directory to determine whether to use Kerberos authentication, the Password Server, or other supported methods. You can change that setting for a user account in Workgroup Manager. A user account can also specify both Kerberos and Password Server. In this case, Open Directory will try Kerberos first.

## LDAP

In most modern network directories, LDAP defines how clients communicate with the directory over TCP/IP networks. Computers use LDAP to read and edit information in LDAP-compatible directories. (The LDAP Data Interchange Format, LDIF defines how data is stored in the LDAP database.)

The LDAP search base, which you see in practice in Chapter 6, tells the client where to start looking for data within the directory — usually account information.

LDAP also has a role to play with the Password Server database, mentioned in the preceding section. When you authenticate against a shared directory in Mac OS X Server, you're telling LDAP who you are, but Password Server checks your password to verify your identity. Kerberos authentication does not use the Password Server.

*Authentication* proves who you are with your username and password credentials. *Authorization* is what you can do after authentication, such as accessing file sharing or viewing your e-mail inbox. Kerberos is an authentication protocol. LDAP can be used for both authentication and authorization.

The other directories that Open Directory is compatible with are also LDAP-compatible directories. These include Active Directory, eDirectory, and others.

## Kerberos and single sign-on

If a user needs to connect to many unique services, he could send a username and password to each service, opening a path for an evildoer to intercept and crack your password. The more secure alternative is to use Kerberos *single sign-on* authentication, in which the user enters a password once and gets access to all services. With Kerberos enabled, the password is never transmitted over the network. Instead, a ticketing system issues encrypted tokens called *tickets* and authenticates you once (usually from the Mac OS X login window), and subsequent tickets allow access to other shared services.

Think of Kerberos as spending the day visiting a popular amusement park. The first thing you do when you arrive at the park is buy a pass. This pass is your Kerberos ticket granting ticket (TGT), issued by the Kerberos Key Distribution Center (KDC) when you log in to Mac OS X on a shared directory. At the park, you pay the entry fee and access the grounds all day. Users log in once and get access to the whole park.

However, the pass doesn't automatically mean that you can jump on any ride or that you get hot dogs and popcorn. You still need to queue for each ride and pay for your snacks. In Kerberos, your TGT is presented when accessing a service, such as file sharing or e-mail. The KDC creates a new service ticket that your client uses to authenticate to the service. But the user isn't presented with a login screen after that first login.

When the park closes, your pass is not good for the next day. In Kerberos, when you log out, the TGT and service tickets are destroyed. Should anyone have managed to figure out how to break in to the ticket system, TGTs are good for a set period of time only: ten hours after the login to Mac OS X Server. And the Kerberos tickets are stored in RAM, not the hard drive.

Mac OS X Server is easy to set up as a KDC; when you set it up as an Open Directory master, a KDC is set up automatically. Open Directory can also make use of another KDC running on another server, such as an Active Directory domain controller. In Mac OS X, you can view, create, and destroy TGTs by using the Ticket Viewer application, shown in Figure 5-2, found in `/System/Library/CoreServices`.

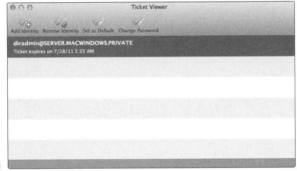

**Figure 5-2:**
Kerberos tickets in Ticket Viewer.

View TGTs and service tickets for the current user by typing `klist` in Terminal and pressing Return. Here's an example of what you might see:

```
client:~ lianabare$ klist
Default principal: lianabare@MASTER.EXAMPLE.COM
Valid Starting Expires Service Principal
06/30/11 14:24:40 06/30/11 00:24:40 krbtgt/MASTER.EXAMPLE.COM@MASTER.EXAMPLE.COM
 renew until 06/30/11 14:24:34
06/30/11 14:24:41 06/30/11 00:24:40 afpserver/fileserver.example.com@MASTER.
            EXAMPLE.COM
 renew until 06/30/11 14:24:34
06/30/11 14:24:59 06/30/11 00:24:40 http/ical.example.com@MASTER.EXAMPLE.COM
 renew until 06/30/11 14:24:34
06/30/11 14:26:27 06/30/11 00:24:40 xmpp/ichat.example.com@MASTER.EXAMPLE.COM
 renew until 06/30/11 14:24:34
```

# Chapter 6

# Setting Up Open Directory

*I*f, during the setup process, the assistant created a network directory (instead of a local one), then you've created an Open Directory master, Lion Server's shared storehouse for network user and resource information. If you haven't created an Open Directory master, you can easily create a directory using the Server app or Workgroup Manager, or both, and use Server Admin to configure the directory services. You don't have to host your own directory: Lion Server can connect to other directory servers and use their information.

This chapter describes how to set up and manage Open Directory, using the Server app for simpler tasks, and Server Admin and Workgroup Manager for more complex tasks. For more general information on network directories, see Chapter 5. For information on how to set up and manage user and group accounts, see Chapter 16.

## Determining Whether You're Running a Local or Network Directory

Before you decide on anything about Open Directory, you need to determine what Lion Server is using to store user accounts. Depending on the choices you made when you installed Lion Server, you may not be using a network directory at all. Even if you've been adding user accounts, you still may not have a network directory configured: The Server app lets you add dozens of user accounts, keeping you blissfully unaware that you're creating *local* accounts that are not shared on the network. If that occurs, it means a lot of retyping after you do create a shared Open Directory master. Here are a few ways to find out if your directory is local and you're not running Open Directory:

- ✔ **The Server App will tell you.** Expand Next Steps at the bottom of the Server app and click the Manage Users button. Next Steps lets you know whether your user accounts are local.

- ✔ **Look in System Preferences in the Dock.** Click the Users & Groups icon. If the user accounts you've added are all listed here, then you've created local accounts on the Mac, not in a shared network directory.

- ✔ **Look in Server Admin.** Enter your password (authenticate) and click the triangle next to your server in the left column. If Open Directory isn't listed here, then any accounts are you created are local.

If you upgraded to Lion Server from Snow Leopard Server running as an Open Directory master (or replica), then your updated server is also configured as an Open Directory master (or replica).

Not everyone needs to run a shared network directory. You can get away with local accounts if you're running Lion Server at home or in a small workgroup and don't need services that require a network directory, such as Profile Manager or iCal Server. You can provide file sharing just fine by using just local accounts on Lion Server, for example.

# Introducing Open Directory

Mac OS X Server's Open Directory uses several technologies: Lightweight Directory Access Protocol (LDAP), Apple's Password Server (built on the Simple Authentication and Security Layer, or SASL), Kerberos Key Distribution Center (KDC), and managed clients for Mac OS X (MCX). (Did you get all those acronyms? No? You can read more about LDAP and Kerberos in Chapter 5 and MCX in Chapter 16.)

Briefly, *LDAP* is a standard communications method for network directories, including Open Directory and Microsoft Active Directory. LDAP is commonly used in mixed networks of Windows, Mac, and Linux/Unix computers.

*Kerberos* is an authentication technology. Integration with Kerberos gives your users *single sign-on:* the ability to log in to a network only once, usually at the appropriately named login window of their computers. Your users can then access many different services in an Open Directory domain without having to type any more passwords. In fact, all the commonly used services in Mac OS X Server are *kerberized* — they're compatible with the ticket distribution system used by Kerberos — so users don't have to provide a password when signing in to access hosted services, such as Apple Mail, iChat, iCal, and shared folders on your network.

Designating Mac OS X Server as an Open Directory master creates an Open Directory domain. The directory domain can be shared to multiple servers and clients. Creating copies of your Open Directory master on other servers increases the speed and reliability of the shared domain.

Open Directory can also access other types of directory domains and the information within them. This includes other LDAP-compatible directories, including Active Directory, as well as Network Information System (NIS), a type of directory service used by some Unix servers. Open Directory can also access the local directory domains of Mac OS X Server 10.6 or later and in Mac OS X clients. And Open Directory can access BSD Unix flat files, an older but long-used directory service of Unix systems.

Lion Server provides a number of tools. You can use Server Admin to manage the Open Directory service. You can use Workgroup Manager to create and manage accounts — users, groups, machine records, and machine groups. For less technical tasks, the Server app is also an option for managing Open Directory, creating users and groups, and importing user accounts from another directory.

# Think Before You Jump: Planning for an Open Directory Deployment

You might be tempted, after you read about the benefits of a shared domain in Chapter 5, to jump right in with the instructions you find later in this chapter (in the "Creating an Open Directory master with the Server app" section) and create a shared domain. Don't give in to temptation just yet.

First, write something. Your plan is best implemented when it exists in a format that you document and reference. Collaboration is also key when you and your colleagues are simultaneously working toward implementing a shared directory.

Documentation can also save your hide if the worst happens, and you're forced to rebuild your directory. And don't forget that you might not be the only administrator of the directory — especially if you finally win the lottery and forget all about your love of Mac OS X Servers. The next administrator benefits from your documentation, too.

Open Directory relies upon other services to run properly. Domain name service and time synchronization are critical to a healthy and happy directory.

## Factors to consider for your plan

Whether you use a detailed Gantt chart, a whiteboard, or just a quick sketch on a cocktail napkin, start your Open Directory deployment with a plan. Here are some considerations to ponder prior to your deployment:

- **How many servers do you need?** For a small domain of ten or so users, you could have just one server, but consider a second for larger networks. A minimum of two Open Directory servers provides you with redundancy and failover — the ability to switch automatically to a second server in the event something goes wrong with the first.

  Two Open Directory servers can take you quite far. Apple states that Open Directory's technical limitations are

  - *LDAP records:* 200,000

  - *Simultaneous client connections:* 1,000

  Each client may open multiple connections to an Open Directory server during the initial login and when requesting additional authentication. However, a two-server Open Directory deployment handily manages several hundred clients in a local network.

- **Are you accounting for physical security?** The directory servers in your shared domain contain sensitive information, such as user passwords and permissions. Treat your Open Directory servers with the same care and caution as any of the other important data on your network.

- **Who will have responsibility for domain maintenance and backups?** When you specify an administrator to primarily manage your domain, you likely reduce mistakes and complications that result from things like ill-timed software updates and improperly made backups.

## Master, replica, and relay servers

Mac servers can play different roles in Open Directory: a master, a replica, or a relay. Another role a Mac server can have is to simply connect, or *bind,* to a directory. When planning your network, think about which you'll use.

### Open Directory masters

An *Open Directory master* is the primary Open Directory server on the network. If you have a single Mac OS X Server Mac that is hosting a shared list of users and groups, it is an Open Directory master.

# Directory authentication for Windows clients

With Lion Server, Apple removed the ability for Windows clients to authenticate through Open Directory. Previous versions of Mac OS X Server let you use Server Admin to set up your Mac server as a Windows primary domain controller (PDC). This feature created a Windows directory domain that could provide authentication for Windows clients. (You could create a PDC only on a Mac that is serving as an Open Directory master.) You also can no longer set up Mac OS X Server as backup domain controller (BCD), which is used if your network already has a PDC running on another server. Lion Server still supports SMB file sharing for Windows clients. If you have a Snow Leopard Server, you can run a PDC on it on another Mac. You must have the Open Directory Master on it, and all your users, Mac and Windows, can authenticate to it. Lion Server would bind to it under this scenario.

A master contains a read/write LDAP-compatible database and hosts the Kerberos Key Distribution Center (KDC) and the Open Directory Password Server database (described in Chapter 5). The Open Directory master is the only server that can make changes to the LDAP-compatible database. An Open Directory master is analogous to the Primary Domain Controller of Windows-based shared directory systems. (See the sidebar "Directory authentication for Windows clients.")

### Open Directory replicas

After the Open Directory master, you can add one or more Open Directory *replicas,* which are mirror servers that create a distributed directory environment with redundancy and client failover. Each Open Directory replica has a read-only copy of the LDAP directory, the Password Server database, and the Kerberos KDC that are synchronized periodically with the master and each of the other replicas. If you want to make changes to accounts in a domain, you must make them on the master server. However, password database changes, such as a user changing his password, are allowed while connected to any Open Directory server in the domain. (Passwords aren't stored in the LDAP database.) Background synchronization among all the Open Directory servers updates the changed data across the domain.

### Open Directory relays

You can deploy Open Directory servers in a topology sometimes referred to as a *tree* or a *nested approach.* Each Open Directory master can have up to 32 replica servers. Additionally, each of these replica servers can have up to 32 replicas of its own. Thus, a theoretical limit of 1,057 Open Directory servers exists for a single domain:

1 master + 32 replicas + (32×32) nested replicas

When an Open Directory replica has its own replicas, that server is an *Open Directory relay*. A relay with additional replicas might be useful in a widely distributed network of client systems.

Open Directory replicas, including relays, that connect directly to the master are *first-tier replicas*. Replicas that connect to a relay are *second-tier replicas*.

A good example of the use of an Open Directory relay is a school system with multiple school buildings spread out in a city or a county. You'd install Open Directory relay and additional replicas in each school, while the Open Directory master remains safely installed at the school system's data center away from sticky fingers, which creates a closer, faster connection to the Open Directory domain for clients in each building.

### Server connected to a directory but not hosting one

You don't need Open Directory running on every server. Another Open Directory role is to bind to an Open Directory domain instead of hosting one. You avoid the overhead of running directory services on your server, and users still get access to domain resources. You might use this option if your server is running user services, such as file sharing, e-mail, or Lion Server's wiki collaborative environment. Your services can also make use of Kerberos authentication from the bound server. To connect a server to a directory, you bind it to the domain and add it to the Kerberos realm.

Lion Server can bind to an Open Directory Master running on Mac OS X Server 10.6 Snow Leopard. In order to have Snow Leopard Server authenticate your Lion Server's users — particularly users of the wiki and podcast services — Snow Leopard Server must be running version 10.6.8 or later. A deployment of Lion and Snow Leopard Open Directory servers can't include older Mac OS X Server releases (Tiger 10.4 or Leopard 10.5, for example).

Additionally, when installing software updates on Lion Server, such as Mac OS X Server 10.7.1, 10.7.2, and so on, start with your replica servers and finish by updating on the master.

A Mac OS X Server that doesn't host or bind to a shared directory is a *stand-alone server*. This type of server has only a local database of user and group accounts, as in any Mac OS X system, and results from selecting a hostname for a local network (`hostname.local`) in the server assistant's setup.

Regardless of the Mac OS X Server Open Directory role, it always has a local database of at least one user. It's important not to confuse the local accounts, which can't be shared with other servers and clients with the accounts in the Open Directory domain. In Chapter 16, you see cues in Workgroup Manager that help differentiate which database of accounts you're working with.

After you configure an Open Directory domain, other servers and client systems utilize binding to connect and access the shared directory for authentication and authorization. Clients connect to the fastest responding Open Directory server, based on *ping response times* — the time required for a small packet of data to travel and return to the sender. If the master or any replica server fails, clients connect automatically to another Open Directory server in the domain without interruption to the user.

# Prerequisites

Before running Open Directory, you need to properly configure two aspects of your network: domain name service (DNS) and time synchronization for Kerberos.

## Checking for proper DNS setup

If, during initial setup, you configured Server Assistant so that it created an Open Directory master for you, it should have also set up DNS. If you didn't do this configuration during initial setup or have a DNS server running on another server, you'll need to ensure that DNS is configured to support Open Directory.

Properly configured DNS is critical to the configuration and normal operation of an Open Directory domain. All Open Directory servers need static IP addresses, a zone with the host domain name, and two types of records: a fully qualified DNS address (A) and pointer (PTR) records. Verify the server's DNS records prior to promoting a Mac OS X Server to either master or replica status.

In an A record, also called a *machine record,* the system's hostname is resolved to an IP address. That is, when another computer requests the IP address for a given domain name, the machine record supplies it. A pointer (PTR) record, also known as a *reverse lookup,* resolves a domain name for any given IP address. *Reverse resolution* inquires about an IP address and returns the hostname. You can find more information about hosting your own DNS and creating these records on a Mac OS X server in Chapter 3.

By default, the domain's LDAP search policy and Kerberos realm are the same as the fully qualified hostname of the Open Directory master and are generated when a server's role is changed to master. Without correct DNS records, promotion to an Open Directory master or replica will likely fail or create only a partially functional domain.

If you don't mind typing a one-line command in the Terminal utility, you can easily verify that DNS forward and reverse lookup are configured correctly. Type this, exactly:

```
sudo changeip -checkhostname
```

If forward and reverse DNS are working correctly, you see this, but with your server information:

```
Primary address = 192.168.1.69
Current HostName = ourserver.macwindowsco.com
DNS HostName = ourserver.macwindowsco.com
The names match. There is nothing to change.
dirserv:success = "success"
```

# Synchronizing time for Kerberos reliability

If you plan on using Kerberos as part of your Open Directory deployment (and why wouldn't you?), time synchronization is critical. *Time skew,* or the difference in time between the KDC and clients requesting Kerberos tickets, can be no more than five minutes. Time zones and daylight saving time aren't considered in factoring the time skew as long as the relative time between systems is the same.

In other words, if you have a client in Pacific time and a KDC in Eastern time, they both need to be set correctly for their respective time zones. Manually changing the time to match the local time but not changing the time zone causes a time difference of several hours — much more than five minutes. Open Directory compares time based on Universal Decimal Time (UDT).

It's best to set your Mac OS X Server and client systems to use a time synchronization server running the network time protocol (NTP) to avoid problems with Kerberos and single sign-on for users. The Server Assistant configured this during initial setup, but you can change it. Apple provides several publicly accessible NTP servers via the Internet, or you can run your own time server in Lion Server on a local network.

A public Internet connection isn't required, but public NTP servers often connect to trusted sources of accurate time data, such as an atomic clock. If you don't use a public server, manually adjust the time of your private time server in the Date & Time pane of System Preferences.

### Enabling time server synchronization

You can use either System Preferences or Server Admin to add or change the NTP server to automatically have the system adjust the clock. These steps set a time server on both Mac OS X clients and Mac OS X Server. Here's the procedure for System Preferences:

1. **Choose Apple menu⇨System Preferences and then click the Date & Time icon.**

2. **Under the Date & Time tab, select the Set Date & Time Automatically check box.**

3. **From the pop-up menu to the right of the check box, choose an Apple public time server or enter another time server in this field.**

   If you're not using Apple's time servers, enter the hostname or IP address of another time server (like those found at `support.ntp.org`) or a private time server on your local network.

4. **Quit System Preferences when you're done.**

Server Admin has essentially the same Date & Time pane as System Preferences. Select your server in the left column, click the Settings icon in the toolbar, and click the Date & Time tab.

### Running network time protocol in Mac OS X Server

Many servers can run the NTP service, including Mac OS X Server. If your server has Internet access, and you want to trust another NTP server for time updates, follow the steps in the preceding section to set the date and time on your NTP server. Then follow these steps to start the network time protocol:

1. **Open Server Admin and connect to the server.**

2. **Click the server's name in the left column, click the Settings icon, and then click the General tab.**

3. **Select the Network Time Server (NTP) check box and then click Save.**

4. **Follow the steps in the previous section, using your NTP server's hostname or IP address as the time server in the Date & Time pane in System Preferences or in Server Admin.**

If the time difference is greater than five minutes, Kerberos tickets can't be generated, and single sign-on fails for users.

After you properly configure and verify DNS records and hostnames for your server and set up time synchronization, proceeding with the Open Directory master configuration is a straightforward endeavor with either Server Preferences or Server Admin and its Open Directory Assistant.

# Using the Server App to Configure Open Directory

The Server app is a simplified interface for account management. Although it offers a subset of the capabilities of Server Admin, for a network that requires a simple shared domain, the Server app can quite possibly take care of everything you need.

You can do several Open Directory tasks with the Server app, depending on how you configured your server during initial installation and setup, including importing users and groups from another Open Directory server or Active Directory server and creating an Open Directory master.

The Server app is also good for adding or removing users and groups and for other user account management tasks. Chapter 16 describes those issues.

## Creating an Open Directory master with the Server app

If you didn't choose to create or import during initial installation and setup, you can create an Open Directory master with the Server app.

Open the Server app from the Dock or the Applications folder. If prompted, enter the username and password for the local administrator. To set up an Open Directory master, follow these steps:

1. **Click the Manage menu and choose Manage Network Accounts.**

   If you see only a Connect to Server item in the menu, then you haven't logged in. Select it, log in, and then choose Manage Network Accounts.

   If you already have an Open Directory master on the server, this item doesn't appear in the menu.

2. **Click the Next button in the introductory dialog that appears (see Figure 6-1).**

3. **Type a name and password for the directory administrator.**

   The default is Directory Administrator (short name diradmin).

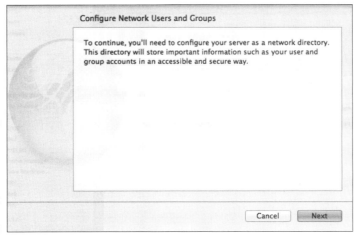

Configure Network Users and Groups

To continue, you'll need to configure your server as a network directory. This directory will store important information such as your user and group accounts in an accessible and secure way.

Cancel    Next

**Figure 6-1:**
Using the
Server app
to set up
account
management.

4. **In the next screen, enter an organization (or department) name to identify your server and then type an administrator e-mail address for users to contact.**

5. **In the Confirm Settings dialog, look over your settings, click the Back button to change settings, or click Set Up.**

If the Server app fails to create your Open Directory shared domain, DNS is a likely culprit. DNS service has to be set up before you create an Open Directory master. The Server app also doesn't allow you to change the LDAP search base path or the Kerberos realm name or to see the confirmation that these settings match the DNS server hostname.

Just because you used the Server app to create the shared domain doesn't mean you can't also use Server Admin and Workgroup Manager. After the directory is created, you can switch among the applications.

If you ever need to return a server's Open Directory role to a stand-alone server or perform other advanced management of an Open Directory master, use Server Admin. Select Open Directory in the expanded list of services, click the Settings icon in the toolbar, and click the General tab. Then click the Change button and follow the directions. You can also use Server Admin to create an Open Directory master, with more options at your disposal. I describe this in the section "Using Server Admin to Configure Open Directory," later in the chapter.

# *Importing directory information with the Server app*

You can use the Server app to import information from another directory. If you choose this option in Server Assistant during installation, the server creates an Open Directory master on your server and a connection to the other server.

If you didn't see (or select) this option during initial setup, you can still import information now. Here, I describe using the Server app, but you can also do it with Server Admin. If you don't yet have an Open Directory master, the dialog prompts you to create one, as described in the preceding section.

You can import user accounts and group accounts. When you import a group, the Server app imports all the user accounts that are members of the group.

With an Open Directory master on your server, you first use the Server app to connect to another directory and then you import a user or group. First, follow these steps to connect:

**1. Click the Manage menu and choose Connect to Directory.**

The Connect to Directory dialog appears (shown in Figure 6-2).

If you don't have an Open Directory master set up, the Configure Network Users and Groups dialog appears (refer to Figure 6-1) and takes you through the process described in the preceding section. When you're finished, the Connect to Directory dialog appears.

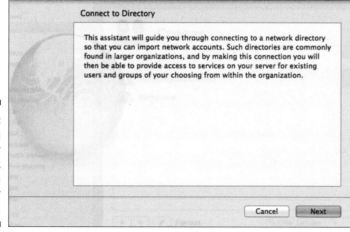

**Figure 6-2:** Connecting to another network directory in the Server app.

> **Connect to Directory**
>
> This assistant will guide you through connecting to a network directory so that you can import network accounts. Such directories are commonly found in larger organizations, and by making this connection you will then be able to provide access to services on your server for existing users and groups of your choosing from within the organization.
>
> Cancel    Next

2. **Click the Next button.**

3. **Type the IP address or domain name of an Open Directory or Microsoft Active Directory server you want to connect to and click the Next button.**

4. **Enter the name and password of a user account for a directory and then click Next.**

   If it's an Open Directory account, it can be any user. If it's an Active Directory account, the user must be an Active Directory administrator or a user account that has been designated with Add Workstations to Domain permission.

5. **In the Confirm Settings dialog, look over your settings, click the Back button to change settings, or click Set Up.**

Now that your server is connected to the other network directory, you can import users and groups:

1. **In the Server app, click either Users or Groups under Accounts in the sidebar.**

2. **Click the Add (+) button to bring up the New User (or New Group) dialog.**

3. **Click the Type pop-up menu and select Imported User from *directory* (or Imported Group from *directory*), where *directory* is the network directory you are connected to.**

   If you don't see the Type pop-up menu, Lion Server isn't connected to the other network directory.

4. **Begin typing the user or group account name you want to import, select the name when it appears, and click the Import button.**

5. **Click the Done button.**

Chapter 16 has more information about using the Server app to manager user and group accounts.

# Using Server Admin to Configure Open Directory

Although the Server app is easier to use than Server Admin, it can't change the default settings of an Open Directory domain. By using Server Admin to create and connect to domains, you have all the options available to set the LDAP search path (or policy), which defines which directory domains Open

Directory can access. You can also set the *Kerberos realm,* a database containing validation data for users, services, and sometimes servers. You also use Server Admin to set the account options for the directory administrator and to create an Open Directory replica or relay. The following section describes how you can use Server Admin to configure Open Directory.

Server Admin is located in the Server folder, inside the Applications folder. If you don't have a Server folder, then you may need to download it separately. Look for Server Admin Tools at `www.apple.com/support/downloads`.

## Working with Server Admin

You can use Server Admin to configure and manage Lion Server's support services, including Open Directory. To get Server Admin running for the first time, follow these steps:

1. **If not already logged in to the server, log in as the local administrator that you created when you installed Lion Server (see Chapter 3).**

2. **Open Server Admin from the /Applications/Server folder.**

3. **Select Choose Server⇨Add Server.**

4. **Type the hostname of the server in the Address field and then enter the administrator's username and password.**

5. **Click Connect.**

    For best results, always enter the server's fully qualified hostname. You can also enter the server's name ending in `.local`, if this is what you created with the Server Assistant when you installed Lion Server.

    You're now connected to the server and ready to manage its services.

You can click the triangle next to the server's name to view an expanded list of enabled services. A dot next to each service in the list has a few possible colors:

- ✔ *Clear:* Service is enabled but not running.

- ✔ *Red:* Service has an error.

- ✔ *Light green:* Infrequent, shown sometimes as a service restarts.

- ✔ *Dark green:* Service is running normally.

# Binding to an existing directory using Server Admin

Instead of hosting Open Directory on your server, you can have Lion Server join an existing directory domain that exists on another server. This is called *binding* the server to the directory domain. In addition to using the Server app to join the server to the domain, you can use Server Admin to properly configure your server and join the Kerberos realm, if you don't have an Open Directory master set up.

Follow these steps to bind a server to an Open Directory domain:

1. **In Server Admin, click the triangle next to your server and click Open Directory in the expanded list of services.**

2. **Click the Settings icon and then click the Change button next to the current role to launch Open Directory Assistant.**

   The Choose Directory Role screen, shown in Figure 6-3, appears.

3. **Select Connect to Another Directory, click Continue, and then click Continue again to confirm your choice.**

   Open Directory Assistant informs you that the server will be able to connect to the directory.

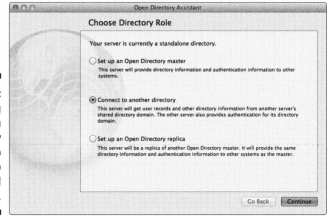

**Figure 6-3:** Changing the Open Directory role to connect to a shared domain.

4. **Click the Open Directory Utility button from Open Directory Assistant.**

5. **Click the lock icon and authenticate as the local administrator.**

   Figure 6-4 shows the service listings of Directory Utility.

6. **Select LDAPv3 from the Services tab and then click the pencil icon.**

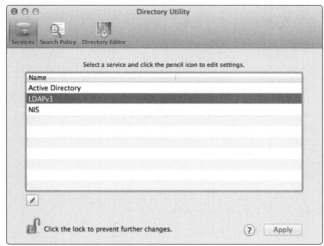

**Figure 6-4:**
Directory
Utility's
service con-
figuration.

7. **Click the New button and enter the fully qualified hostname of the Open Directory master in the Server Name or IP Address field.**

   By default, Secure Sockets Layer (SSL) is disabled.

8. **Click Edit.**

9. **Make your desired changes in the dialog that appears.**

   If desired, you can use the Security tab to enter the directory administrator username and password to create an authenticated bind. Otherwise, leave those fields blank for an anonymous binding.

10. **Click the Bind button and then click OK.**

11. **Review the configuration, click OK, and then close Directory Utility.**

After you bind a server to an Open Directory shared domain, you can configure services on the server that are available as options in Workgroup Manager. For example, if file sharing is configured on the connected server, you can now create a share point for home or group folders (see Chapter 9).

# Creating an Open Directory master using Server Admin

Follow these steps to create an Open Directory master and a shared directory domain using Server Admin:

1. **Open Server Admin on the server that will become the Open Directory master and click the server in the left column.**

2. **Click the Settings icon in the toolbar, click the Services tab, select the Open Directory check box, and click the Save button.**

   Skip this step if you previously enabled the service, and it's already listed in the server's expanded list of services.

3. **Click Open Directory in the expanded service list and observe the service's current status by clicking the Overview icon.**

   This screen shows the status of directory services. Figure 6-5 shows what you see if a server hasn't yet been configured for a shared Open Directory domain. The first line says Standalone Directory, which indicates that only a local directory is available. The items called LDAP Server, Password Server, and Kerberos all indicate Stopped. Also notice the clear dot in the expanded server list. No part of the Open Directory service is running.

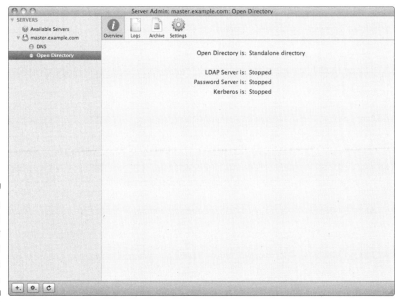

**Figure 6-5:**
The Open Directory service of a stand-alone server.

4. **Click the Settings icon in the toolbar and then click the General tab.**

5. **Next to the status Role: Standalone Directory, click the Change button.**

   The Open Directory Assistant opens and walks you through changing the server's Open Directory role. You can see the initial screen of the Open Directory Assistant in Figure 6-6.

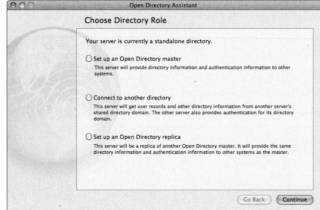

**Figure 6-6:**
The first screen of the Open Directory Assistant.

6. **Select Set Up an Open Directory Master from the three options and click the Continue button.**

   At this point, the Open Directory may alert you to a DNS problem if it detects one.

7. **View and optionally change the directory administrator name, short name, and user ID and then enter a password; click Continue when finished.**

   The directory administrator user is a critical piece of your shared domain. This user is capable of creating accounts in the directory, modifying the directory, adding and removing replica servers, serving as the Kerberos KDC administrator, and more. This administrator is just as critical to the well-being of your domain as the local administrator is to the server, so the short name and password need to be unique and difficult to guess.

   Later, after your domain is configured, you might add more directory administrators if needed. You see this option when you use Workgroup Manager in Chapter 16.

   As shown in Figure 6-7, the Name default setting is Directory Administrator, the Short Name is diradmin, and the User ID is 1000. You can modify all these default options; however, keep a record of the directory administrator's short name and User ID — information that's critical if you need to restore the shared domain from a backup archive.

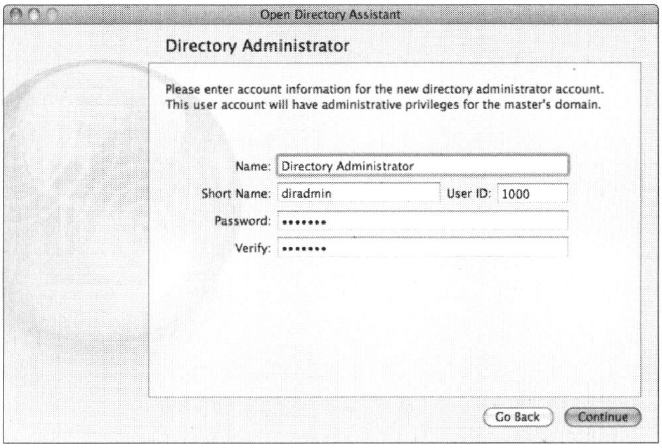

Figure 6-7:
The
Directory
Admin-
istrator
screen.

Directory administrator's default name and short name work fine in any Open Directory domain. For stronger security — making it more difficult for someone to guess your administrator's credentials — use a unique name and short name on your server.

8. **Set the Kerberos Realm name and LDAP Search Base path for the shared domain.**

   By default, the Kerberos Realm and LDAP Search Base boxes match the fully qualified hostname of your master server. Advanced users may need to modify these settings, but for most domains, the default options are perfectly acceptable. In Figure 6-8, you can see the correct Kerberos Realm and LDAP Search Base boxes, automatically populated, that match the server's `master.example.com` hostname.

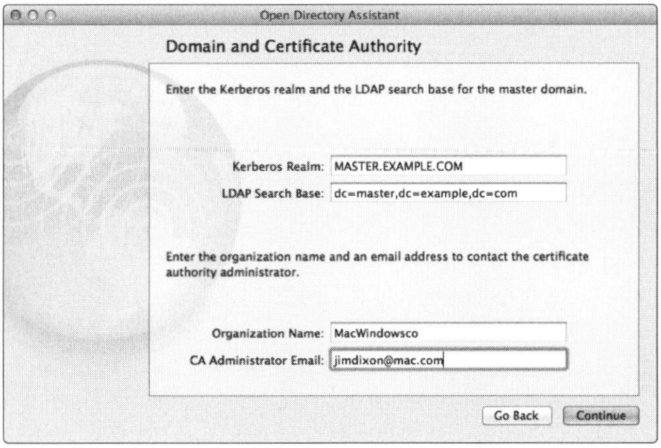

Figure 6-8:
The
Kerberos
Realm name
and LDAP
Search
Base path.

When the realm's name and search base path don't match your server's hostname, it's a good indication that something's gone wrong with your DNS settings. This is your last chance to resolve DNS problems before you continue with your shared domain. Failing to do so likely results in a domain with a broken Kerberos or LDAP, or both.

9. **Type an organization name and administrator e-mail address at the bottom of the window shown in Figure 6-8 and then click the Continue button.**

10. **Confirm your settings so far in the final screen of the Open Directory Assistant and then click the Continue button.**

    The Open Directory Assistant now processes your entries and creates the resources needed on the Open Directory master. The LDAP database, Password Server database, and Kerberos KDC are created, and their supporting background processes are started.

11. **Click the Done button after your server's been configured as an Open Directory master.**

    The Open Directory Assistant closes, returning you to Server Admin. Congratulations — you've successfully created a shared directory.

Figure 6-9 illustrates what Server Admin now shows: The Open Directory Is: Open Directory Master, and LDAP server, Password Server, and Kerberos are all Running. Also note the green dot next to Open Directory in the expanded list of services.

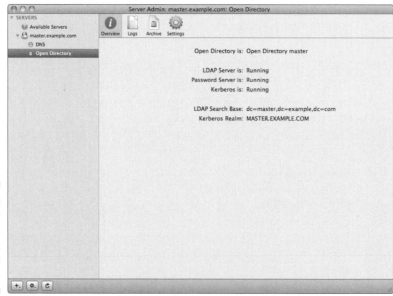

**Figure 6-9:**
Server Admin on an Open Directory master.

## *Attack of the clones: Creating Open Directory replica servers*

An Open Directory replica is essentially a clone of the Open Directory master with copies of the shared domain databases. Having one or more replicas on your network greatly helps reduce the load on any one domain server and adds peace of mind in case a server fails.

Although you can create an Open Directory master with either the Server app or Server Admin, you must use Server Admin to create a replica.

Considerations for DNS records and time synchronization are still valid for replica servers. Use the same DNS and time servers for all Open Directory servers in your shared domain. (See the sections "Checking for proper DNS setup" and "Synchronizing time for Kerberos reliability," earlier in this chapter.)

To change a server's role to a replica, follow these steps:

1. **Open Server Admin on the server that will become the Open Directory replica and connect to the server.**

2. **If Open Directory isn't enabled, select your server in the sidebar, click the Settings icon in the toolbar, click the Services tab, select the Open Directory check box, and click the Save button.**

   Skip this step if you previously enabled the service, and it's already listed in the server's expanded list of services.

3. **Click Open Directory in the expanded list of services, click Settings in the toolbar, and click the General tab.**

   The server role should be Standalone.

4. **Click the Change button.**

   As with creating a master server, this action opens the Open Directory Assistant, shown in Figure 6-10.

5. **Select Set Up an Open Directory Replica and then click the Continue button.**

6. **Enter the IP address or fully qualified hostname of the Open Directory master server, the directory administrator's short name and password, and an administrator's e-mail address; click the Continue button.**

   Figure 6-11 shows an example of these settings.

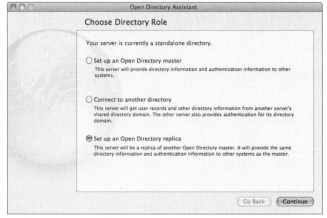

**Figure 6-10:** Creating a replica server with the Open Directory Assistant.

**Figure 6-11:** Settings in the Open Directory Assistant when creating a replica.

As a best practice, use the master's IP address on this screen. By doing so, you can avoid future problems with DNS resolution between the replica and the master; however, the fully qualified hostname also works for setting up the replica.

7. **View and verify the replica settings and then click the Continue button.**

During the replication process that follows, the master's LDAP server is temporarily stopped and its database copied to the replica. The same also happens for the Password Server database and the Kerberos realm. Although the interruptions are brief, you may want to avoid creating replica servers during times of heavy network use because users may see delays or failed logins while the databases aren't accessible during the copying process.

8. **Close the Open Directory Assistant and return to Server Admin by clicking the Done button.**

In Server Admin, you see that the role of your server has changed to a replica, and just like the master, LDAP server, Password Server, and Kerberos are all running.

You just configured your first Open Directory replica. If you followed along, you know that clients who connect to your shared domain now connect to either the master or the replica by determining which responds faster to ping requests.

Attaching a replica to another replica, which creates an Open Directory relay, is no different from creating a replica from the master. Instead of specifying the master's IP address or the hostname in Step 6 of the preceding list, you enter the IP address or the hostname of a first-tier replica. After the replication process is complete on the second-tier replica, the first-tier replica is an Open Directory relay. See the section "Master, replica, and relay servers," earlier in this chapter, for details about the roles of Open Directory.

# Backing Up and Restoring Open Directory with Archives

Open Directory contains several databases of critical information that, in heavily used domains, are constantly being accessed and modified. Open Directory includes the ability for you to easily create backup archives of the entire shared domain, including the LDAP directory, the Password Server database, and the Kerberos realm. During the archive process, which takes a matter of seconds, the open databases are closed and copied.

The downside to the Apple implementation of archiving in Server Admin is the lack of scheduling. The only way to schedule is with the command line.

Because the archive contains password information, the archive is encrypted in a disk image. Your password for the archive and the archives themselves need to be closely guarded, like any other sensitive data.

## Creating an archive in Server Admin

Start by reviewing the options for archiving and restoring Open Directory domains in Server Admin. Work on the Open Directory master — you can't create an archive from a replica server. To create an archive:

1. **Open Server Admin and connect to the Open Directory master.**

2. **Click the triangle next to the server to expand the list of services and select Open Directory.**

3. **Click the Archive icon in the toolbar.**

4. **Type a folder path or click the Choose button next to the Archive In field and select a location to save the archive.**

   You're browsing the file system of the server regardless of where you run Server Admin.

   In Figure 6-12, you can see the archive options in Server Admin, with the archive being stored in a directory on the server's local hard drive. You may want to consider storing it instead on another drive or partition, for reasons of safety.

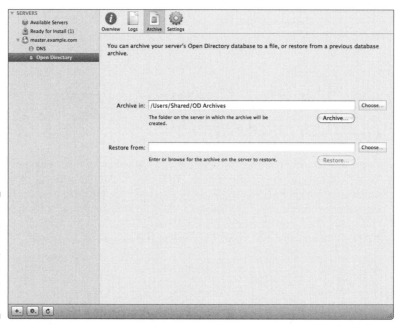

**Figure 6-12:**
Creating
an Open
Directory
archive
in Server
Admin.

5. **Click the Archive button, enter a filename and password for the archive, and then click OK.**

   Be extremely careful when you enter the archive's password. No confirmation field exists in the Server Admin interface; a mistyped password could leave you with a useless backup. After you complete the archive, you may want to verify the password by opening the archive disk image in the Finder. When you double-click the image, the Finder prompts you to enter the password you used to create the archive. Secure the image again by unmounting the disk image.

After you click OK, a progress bar indicates the archive progression.

If you haven't configured Time Machine, a dialog now appears, asking whether you want to use the another mounted hard drive to automatically back up the server's boot drive.

6. **Click Decide Later, Don't Use, Use as Backup.**

After the backup archive is created, you can look inside at the data, files, and certificates stored inside. Double-click the image to have it mount in the Finder. Figure 6-13 shows an open and mounted Open Directory archive in the Finder. Archive disk images always mount with the name `ldap_bk`.

**Figure 6-13:** An Open Directory archive mounted in the Finder.

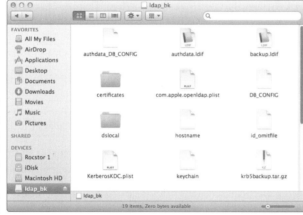

After you create the archive, it's a good idea to copy the archive to another drive, server, or location where the archive will be safely stored. Many administrators also use their backup software to make historical backups of the archives and for offsite storage.

## Restoring from an archive

In the event that your Open Directory domain becomes corrupt or you lose user records, you can restore from an archive. The process is essentially the same as the backup process, but in reverse.

Before you restore from an archive, though, be cognizant of the conditions that restoring imposes. When you restore, you're prompted to either merge or to completely restore the directory data on the server:

- ✔ **If you click the Restore button,** the data in the archive completely destroys your existing directory data; all users, passwords, and KDC data are replaced from the archive.

- ✔ **If you click the Merge button,** the data in the archive is combined with the existing domain data.

Prior to restoring an archive, if your directory is still working, you may want to create an additional archive as a precaution.

You can also restore an archive to a newly promoted Open Directory master that has no user data. However, if this is your plan, make sure that the new Open Directory administrator short name and numeric user ID match the old administrator's short name and user ID when you change the server's role from stand-alone to master.

Also realize that any Open Directory replica servers in your shared domain need to be demoted to stand-alone and then reconnected to the new master after you restore from an archive.

Figure 6-14 shows the process of restoring an archive in Server Admin, with the option to restore or merge the directory data.

**Figure 6-14:** Using Server Admin to restore from an Open Directory archive.

You can restore only from an archive that's located on the local file system of the server. If your archives are stored elsewhere, copy them to the server's hard drive. Then follow these steps to restore the archive:

1. **Open Server Admin and connect to the Open Directory master server.**

2. **Click Open Directory in Server Admin's expanded list of services and then click the Archive button.**

3. **Click the Choose button next to the Restore From field to select the location of the archive disk image or type a path.**

   The archive disk image won't appear if it is mounted in the Finder. If that's the case, eject it first by right-clicking (or Control-clicking) and choosing Eject.

4. **Click the Restore button and then enter the password for the archive (refer to Figure 6-14).**

   Server Admin processes the restoration and then enables the background directory services.

5. **Verify the directory contents by using Workgroup Manager to browse accounts and other elements of the directory.**

   See Chapter 16 for details on Workgroup Manager.

# Binding Clients to the Shared Domain

You share the directory by creating a binding between the client and the Open Directory domain. *Binding* creates a connection between the server and the client, enabling the client to read the LDAP database, send authentication requests, and interact with the Kerberos realm for service tickets. Regarding authentication, you see this interaction most frequently from the login window in Mac OS X, and most of that interaction is transparent to the user.

Any version newer than Mac OS X 10.2 can bind to Open Directory running on Lion Server. Your Mac OS X 10.7 client systems should not be bound to versions of Mac OS X Server previous to 10.7 in order to best support the newest enhancements of Mac OS X.

## Binding Mac OS X 10.6 clients

Unlike with previous versions of Mac OS X, you can bind Mac OS X 10.6 and 10.7 clients by using System Preferences. These steps are good for binding both versions of the Mac client:

1. **Select the Apple menu and choose System Preferences and then click the Users & Groups icon in Mac OS X 10.7 (or Accounts in Mac OS X 10.6).**

2. **Click Login Options.**

   If the client has never previously bound to a directory, you see a Join button next to Network Account Server at the bottom of the Login Options window. If a current binding exists, you see an Edit button.

3. **Click the Join or Edit button and enter the Open Directory master's fully qualified hostname in the Server field, as shown in Figure 6-15.**

   If you've previously enabled service discovery on your Open Directory Master server, it will be listed.

**Figure 6-15:** Joining the Open Directory master from a Mac OS X client.

4. **Click OK and, if prompted, enter the local administrator username and password, authorizing changes to the local directory structure.**

5. **(Optional) Edit the Client Computer ID and enter the directory administrator's username and password, or leave those fields blank for an anonymous binding, as shown in Figure 6-16.**

Server: master.example.com

You can enter the address of an Open Directory Server, Active Directory Domain, or Mac OS X Server.

Client Computer ID: SnowLeopardClient

User Name:

Password:

This server allows authenticated binding. You may choose to enter a name and password. You may also leave them blank to bind anonymously.

Cancel    OK

**Figure 6-16:** Options for binding to the Open Directory master.

After your client is bound to the server, the Mac OS X 10.7 Users and Groups preferences pane (or Accounts in Mac OS X 10.6) in System Preferences indicates this with a green dot and the server's hostname. You can click the Edit button to modify the settings, and you can also access Directory Utility (in `/System/Library/CoreServices`) to make more advanced changes to the directory bindings.

## *Binding Mac OS X 10.5 and earlier clients*

In previous versions of Mac OS X, you used Directory Utility, installed in the Utilities folder within the Applications folder, to bind to a network directory. To bind a Mac OS X 10.5.8 or earlier client, open Directory Utility and do the following:

1. **Click the lock icon and enter an administrator name and password.**

2. **Click the Add (+) button and select Open Directory from the pop-up menu.**

   Select Active Directory to bind to an Active Directory domain.

3. **Enter the fully qualified hostname or IP address of the server hosting the domain and click OK.**

## *Binding Windows clients*

Because Lion Server dropped the ability to act as a Primary Domain Controller (PDC) for Windows clients, Windows clients cannot authenticate to a directory hosted on Lion Server. However, you can run an Open Directory master and a PDC on a separate Mac running Mac OS X Server 10.6.8 Snow Leopard and bind Lion Server to it.

To bind Windows clients to Snow Leopard Server's directory services, you connect it to a PDC, a Windows domain. With Windows Vista and Windows 7, you can bind only the Ultimate and Business editions. You can also bind Windows XP clients. Here's how to bind them:

1. **Log in to Windows as an administrator.**

2. **Open the Control Panel from the Start menu and then double-click the System icon.**

3. **Click the Change Settings button.**

   *Note:* Skip this step for Windows XP.

4. **Click the Computer Name tab and then click the Change button.**

5. **Enter a computer name, if none exists.**

6. **Click Domain, enter the Windows domain name of the Mac OS X Server PDC, and then click the OK button.**

If you don't remember the Windows domain name, you can view it in Server Admin: Select SMB in the list of services under your server, click the Settings icon, and then click the General tab.

7. **In the dialog that appears, enter the name and password for an LDAP directory administrator and click OK.**

# Chapter 7

# Integrating Open Directory with Active Directory

*M*icrosoft Active Directory is a fact of life for most corporate networks. Sure, having a homogeneous Macintosh world would make life easier. But the reality is that most corporate and education networks are largely Microsoft territory. Fortunately, you can provide native services to Mac clients within a larger Windows network.

Apple provides every Mac with an LDAP (Lightweight Directory Access Protocol) plug-in and an Active Directory plug-in that allows a Mac to receive authentication from Active Directory. The plug-ins also enable the Mac to access information from Active Directory, allowing for single sign-on. However, the plug-ins alone don't provide the wealth of Access Directory policy features that enable administrators to set policies that enable the management of dozens or hundreds of computers at a time.

This is where Mac OS X Server comes in. Using Lion Server, you can truly integrate your Mac clients into Active Directory and provide other features.

One of the great things about Apple's implementation of Open Directory services is that your Active Directory administrator doesn't need to do anything special to support a Mac OS X server. The Mac server manages and stores the information about the Mac network and exchanges the information with Active Directory in the format that it likes. For more information about setting up an Active Directory schema, check out *Active Directory For Dummies,* 2nd Edition, by Steve Clines and Marcia Loughry (John Wiley & Sons, Inc.).

# *Doing the Directory Services Two-Step*

Directory services make a server administrator's life much easier by providing a centralized repository for information about users, groups, and computers. Using directory services, administrators can consolidate users and computing resources into groups and then apply and enforce security and permissions policies across those groups.

Windows servers use Active Directory to provide directory services on a network. Apple's Active Directory plug-in for Mac OS X allows a Mac server to maintain information about Mac clients and allows access to enforce Active Directory policies and authentication.

In an Active Directory environment, Mac servers actually provide authentication of both Open Directory and Active Directory to the Mac clients. This dual authentication role allows policies to be implemented on the Mac server for Mac clients that are nonstandard in an Active Directory environment (such as iChat services or Address Book services) while allowing Active Directory to handle the network services that are common to Windows and Mac users on the network.

The Mac server's ability to manage both Open Directory and Active Directory separately (and never the twain shall meet) is known as implementing the *magic triangle,* as shown in Figure 7-1. (The magic triangle shouldn't be confused with a percussion instrument for productions of *The Magic Flute.*) The Mac server handles the Active Directory piece of the puzzle by using the Mac's Active Directory plug-in, which sets up a special account on Active Directory that translates network requests from Mac clients into the format that Active Directory expects from Windows clients.

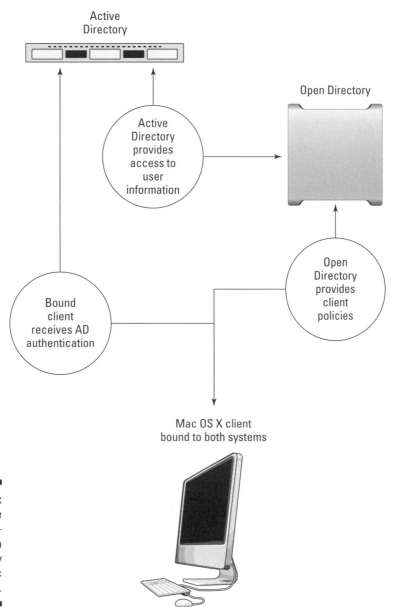

Active
Directory

Open Directory

Active Directory provides access to user information

Bound client receives AD authentication

Open Directory provides client policies

Mac OS X client bound to both systems

# Binding Your Server to Active Directory

The first step in integrating a Mac server into an Active Directory environment is to bind the Mac OS X Server to the Active Directory domain. *Binding*, in this case, means creating the link between the Mac server and Active Directory.

Prior to binding the Mac server to the Active Directory domain, you need to have ready the following information (some of which must come from your Active Directory domain administrator):

- **Mac Server credentials:** You need to have your local server administrator login and password at the ready. But you have that memorized anyway, right?

- **Domain administrator login credentials or rights:** An administrator login and password for the Active Directory domain to which the server will be bound (or having your credentials added to this administrative group in Active Directory).

- **Fully qualified domain name for the Active Directory (AD) domain:** If you don't know the fully qualified AD domain name, ask your AD administrator. Generally, the domain name is `domain.top-level-domain` — for example, `mycompany.com` in a simple structure or `NorthAmerica.BigCompany.Com` in a larger network with multiple domains.

- **The hostname or IP address of the time server used by the Active Directory domain:** The time setting for the Active Directory server must be within five minutes of the time setting for the Mac OS X Server for the binding to be successful. The easiest way to ensure that the time settings are correct is to use the same time server for all servers and clients on your network. Select the same date and time server from the Date & Time System Preferences pane.

## Checking DNS configuration

Active Directory requires that domain name services (DNS) be working properly so that the Mac OS X Lion Server hostname and IP address are linked. The linkage should work both in forward and reverse (meaning that if you check the IP, it resolves to the server's hostname; and if you check the hostname, it resolves to the correct IP address). These are stored as DNS service (SRV) records. The Mac and Windows clients must use the same DNS Server, so typically, the DNS server is running on a Windows server, not the Mac server.

To check that DNS is configured properly, open the Network Utility (located in the Utilities folder in the Applications folder). Click the Lookup tab and type the server's domain. If configured properly, the DNS server reports the IP address of the server. To check the reverse, type the IP address of the server. If configured correctly, the DNS server reports the hostname for your Mac OS X Server. If either of these methods fails, DNS isn't configured properly for your server.

You can also do the same lookup with the command line and the Terminal utility. Type NSLOOKUP *hostname.* to look up the server's IP address and NSLOOKUP *ipaddress.* to look up the server's domain name.

## Binding the server

After you have the required information in hand and have ensured that DNS is working properly (see the preceding section), you're ready to bind the server. To bind your server to an Active Directory domain, follow these steps:

1. **Launch System Preferences and click the Users & Groups icon.**

   The Users & Groups pane opens, as shown in Figure 7-2.

**Figure 7-2:** The Users & Groups pane of System Preferences.

2. **Click the lock icon (see Figure 7-2) to display a login dialog.**

3. **Enter your administrator login and password and then click OK to make changes to the Users & Groups pane.**

4. **Click the Login Options icon at the bottom left of the Users & Groups pane.**

   You see the available options, shown in Figure 7-3. This pane provides access to set network directory configuration.

**Figure 7-3:** Configure network directories by clicking the Login Options icon.

5. **Click the Edit button.**

   A sheet opens that displays all network directories that the machine has been set up to access. The first time you bind a directory, you can see only the local directory server, shown in Figure 7-4.

6. **Click the Open Directory Utility button in the sheet.**

   The Directory Utility application opens, as shown in Figure 7-5.

**Figure 7-4:** Before binding, you see only the local server in this list.

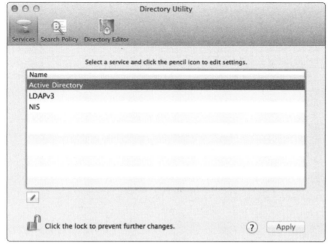

**Figure 7-5:**
The
Directory
Utility appli-
cation is
where
binding
happens.

7. **Ensure that the Services icon is selected in the toolbar.**

   Services is the default.

8. **Click the lock icon at the bottom left of the Directory Utility pane to access the login and password dialog; enter your administrator credentials again and then click OK.**

9. **Click the Active Directory line to *highlight* it.**

10. **Click the plug-in configuration button (the pencil icon, shown in Figure 7-5).**

    A sheet appears, as shown in Figure 7-6.

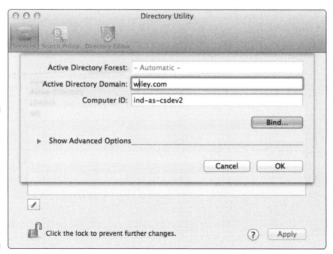

**Figure 7-6:**
Fill in the
Active
Directory
Domain text
box and
then click
Bind.

11. **Type your fully qualified Active Directory domain name in the Active Directory Domain text box.**

12. **Click the Bind button.**

    The Network Administrator Required dialog opens, as shown in Figure 7-7.

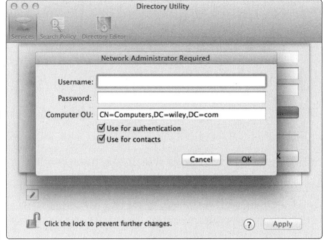

**Figure 7-7:** Enter the login credentials for a domain administrator.

13. **Enter a network domain administrator login and password and then click OK.**

    This may not be the same as the local administrator credential you entered earlier. This must be a login and password that has rights to make changes to the Active Directory domain. If you're unsure, contact your Active Directory administrator.

    The Computer OU (organizational unit) text box typically has the correct information by default. If you're unsure whether it's correct, or if this text box is blank, contact your Active Directory domain administrator for the correct organizational unit to enter.

    Another authentication dialog appears that asks for the local server administration credentials.

14. **Enter your Mac OS X Server administrator credential and password and click OK.**

    The Bind button in the Directory Utility dialog of Figure 7-6 changes to Unbind, which tells you that the binding has succeeded. The server is now bound to the Active Directory domain.

To test whether the binding is indeed successful, open a Terminal session to access the command line and type id *AD user shortname*. If the binding is successful, Active Directory returns the first 16 Active Directory groups of which the user is a member.

# Deciding Whether to Muck Around with Advanced Configuration

In some cases, Mac OS X administrators want to configure particular settings that appear in the advanced options of the Directory Utility to specify particular ways that the Mac OS X Server interacts with Active Directory. In many cases, the default settings are fine, but in some cases, particularly when the AD schema is for a large company, you may need to make some specific changes to these settings.

All the advanced options specify how the plug-in accepts information from Active Directory for the server itself. The configurations are not translated to clients and groups administered by the Mac OS X Server on the Active Directory domain.

To access the advanced options for configuring the Active Directory plug-in, follow these steps:

1. **Access the Directory Utility application by following Steps 1 through 10 in the previous section, "Binding the server."**

2. **Click the triangle next to Show Advanced Options at the bottom of the directory to expand the advanced options, as shown in Figure 7-8.**

Three tabs are available in the advanced options:

- **User Experience:** This tab lets you change some default settings for users, including changing the location of the home directory to point to an external file server rather than the hard drive on the local Mac OS X Server.

- **Mappings:** This tab allows the administrator to redirect default user and group ID settings to customized extensions in the Active Directory schema. These mappings may or may not come into play, depending upon the configuration of the Active Directory schema. Contact your Active Directory administrator for details.

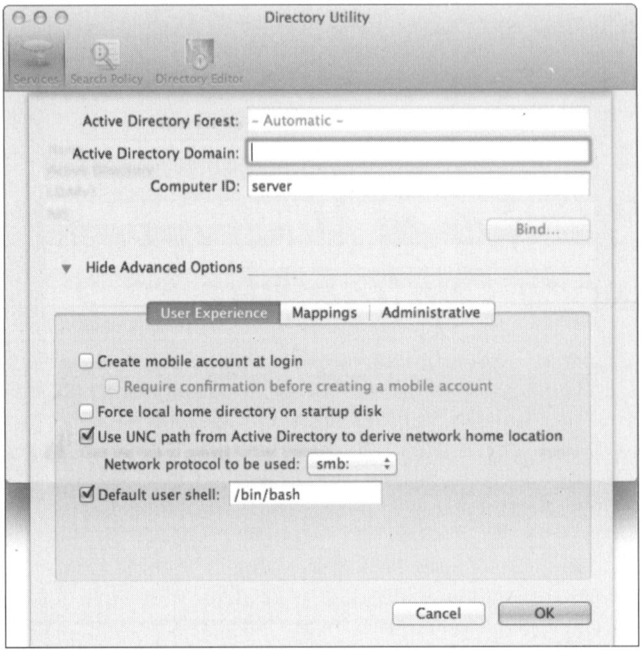

**Figure 7-8:**
Advanced
options
for Active
Directory
integration.

- **Administrative:** This tab enables the administrator to direct contact between the Mac OS X Server and Active Directory domain to a specific domain server. You can also allow domain administrators or other groups to administer without the need to log in with the server's login credentials. And you can allow the server to look up user and password information for domains administered by Active Directory that reside outside the local domain. (These domains are cryptically referred to as *other domains in the forest* in IT architecture parlance.)

# Managing User Groups with Workgroup Manager

The important thing to remember about managing users in an Active Directory environment is that you need to add the users from Active Directory to your Open Directory domain on the Mac server. Doing so is necessary because Active Directory manages the permissions and policies of the users in an Active Directory environment. Active Directory user information isn't directly translatable to a Mac client. Open Directory serves as the mechanism to implement client management policies similar to the policies that Windows clients enjoy from Active Directory.

Adding users from Active Directory is as simple as dragging and dropping users into Open Directory, which you can do with Workgroup Manager, found in `/Applications/Server`. Follow these steps:

1. **Open Workgroup Manager.**

   Workgroup Manager asks you to authenticate with your local server manager username and password to connect to the local server.

2. **Enter your local admin username and password and then click OK.**

   Workgroup Manager opens.

3. **Click the lock icon to bring up an authentication dialog to allow changes to Open Directory.**

   An authentication dialog opens.

4. **Enter the username and password for the Open Directory administrator and then click OK.**

5. **Click the Accounts icon in the toolbar (the default) and then click the Groups icon directly below the Accounts icon.**

   The window now looks similar to Figure 7-9.

**Figure 7-9:**
The Group
accounts
area of
Workgroup
Manager.

6. **Click the New Group icon in the toolbar.**

   Workgroup Manager creates a new group with a group ID (GID).

7. **Type a name for the group in the Name text box.**

   The name can include characters, numbers, and spaces. The short name is automatically created and will abide by Unix naming conventions, so you're free to name the group any way you like. You can also supply a path to an icon by entering the path in the Picture Path text box and a comment, but this isn't necessary.

8. **Click the Members tab.**

   A blank members table opens.

9. **Click the Add (+) button near the upper right, as shown in Figure 7-10, to display the Open Directory users list.**

   A drawer slides open on the right or left, listing the names of Open Directory users.

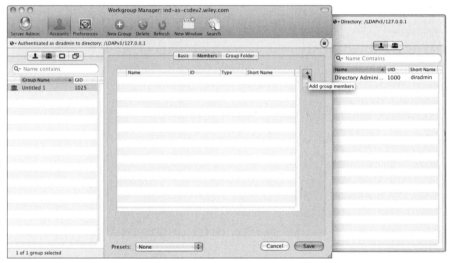

**Figure 7-10:**
Accessing
Open
Directory
users.

10. **Click the directory menu (refer to Figure 7-10) to access the Active Directory domain, as shown in Figure 7-11.**

    A list of Active Directory users for your domain is returned. All records may not appear in the list, but you can gain access to any user record in the domain via the search field.

11. **Drag the records you want to manage from the drawer list to the user list in the main window, as shown Figure 7-12.**

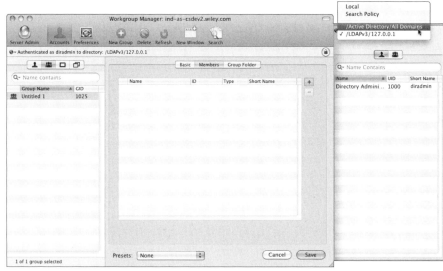

**Figure 7-11:**
Selecting
the Active
Directory
domain.

**Figure 7-12:**
Drag
records
from the
Active
Directory
domain to
the Open
Directory
domain.

**12. After you identify all records that you want to manage, click the Save button.**

At this point, Active Directory is managing authentication for the users in the groups. You can further specify user preferences under the Preferences pane (see Chapter 6).

# Configuring Single Sign-On for Mac Clients

After successfully binding the Mac server to the Active Directory domain (see the section, "Binding Your Server to Active Directory," earlier in this chapter), another step to consider is to implement Kerberos on the server. Kerberos is used by both Active Directory and Open Directory for authentication across various applications so that after a user logs in to the network, the user can access all network assets, such as file servers, for which she has permission without the need for further authentication. Doing away with the need for multiple passwords and authentications is called *single sign-on*.

Single sign-on in Active Directory works by AD's issuing a *ticket* when a user logs in to the domain. The ticket represents everything that the user can do. After you log in initially, all other authentication activities are handled automatically by the ticket.

Of course, for single sign-on to work for Mac clients on an Active Directory network, single sign-on must first be implemented in Active Directory. Single sign-on implementation in Active Directory is beyond the scope of this book.

To implement Kerberos and SSO for Mac clients in an Active Directory domain, follow these steps:

1. **Open Server Admin.**

2. **If necessary, connect to your Mac OS X Server by choosing Server⇨Connect and entering your server administrator username and password.**

3. **Click the triangle next to the server name and then select Open Directory.**

4. **Click the Settings icon in the toolbar.**

5. **Click the Kerberize button.**

   The Kerberize the Open Directory Master dialog opens (as shown in Figure 7-13) and requests authentication. The credential you enter must have administrator rights over the Kerberos domain. Contact your Active Directory administrator to gain the necessary rights.

   That's it!

Test that single sign-on is working properly by logging in as a user and attempting to access a resource to which the user has permission that's managed by Active Directory. In a working deployment, access is granted without the need to reauthenticate.

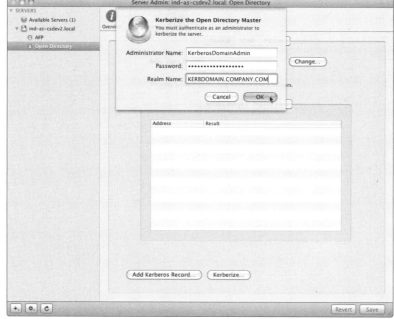

**Figure 7-13:**
The
Kerberize
the Open
Directory
Master
admin login.

# Troubleshooting and Getting Help

If you've come to this section, I can only assume that something went wrong with implementing Mac OS X Server on Active Directory. This short section provides some areas known to cause problems and some troubleshooting tips. Because every Active Directory implementation is different, trouble-shooting every possible scenario is impossible. But Apple stands behind its products and will help you figure out what's going wrong if these tips fail. The most commonly reported issues are

✓ **DNS service problems:** The Mac client must use the same DNS servers as all the Windows clients on the network. To ensure that the correct DNS server is being used, open a Terminal session, and type `dig -t SRV _ldap._tcp.yourDomainDNS.com`. If it's configured properly, you should receive, in response, the IP address of your domain server. If not, either the Mac systems are using a different DNS server than the Windows clients or DNS is set up improperly on your Mac server.

✓ **Time server issues:** If the times on the Mac server and the domain server are more than five minutes apart, you'll be unable to join the domain.

✔ **.local domain issues:** It's possible that the `.local` domain used by Bonjour may conflict with a `.local` Active Directory domain. If this is a problem, add the .local domain to the search domain settings of the Network preferences pane.

✔ **Replication issues:** In the past, binding a Mac to a large AD domain has resulted in the computer account being created on one domain and the computer account's password on another domain. If the replication interval isn't fast enough, the set password request fails, and the Mac isn't bound to the domain. Ensure that the same server is being used for both Kerberos and LDAP connections.

This book can't replicate your Active Directory schema to analyze uncommon problems (though that would be a great trick!). You can access Apple's directory support at `www.apple.com/support/macosxserver/opendirectory`.

If you're having problems, check out my MacWindows.com site. Up on the Web since 1997, MacWindows.com features lots of bug reports and tips regarding Mac integration with Active Directory, among other topics.

# Part III
# Serving Up Files and Printers

The 5th Wave                    By Rich Tennant

"...so if you have a message for someone, you write it on a piece of paper and put it on their refrigerator with these magnets. It's just until we get our printer fixed."

# In this part . . .

Meat and potatoes. For many, network file and print sharing makes up the basic work of a server. Lion Server's roots go back to file-sharing software, Apple's 1985 release of AppleShare. Apple thought it would help Mac sales to businesses by providing a central repository for files that all Mac users could access. Today, file and print sharing are only two of many functions that the server provides to users, but they still play a central role in networks. Lion Server's file and print services support client computers running any operating system with rich user and administration features and robust security.

You can easily share printers without a server, but print serving goes beyond giving users access to printers. It juggles multiple printing requests to any single printer and manages all your printers. And it provides user features, such as automatically sending a print job to a free printer rather than sitting in a queue.

But before I show you how all that works, I throw in a chapter on permissions, settings that determine who can do what to which files. Lion Server supports a set of easy-to-use permissions that you can configure in minutes. It also supports high-end, enterprise-level permissions for large and complex network situations. Use one or the other or mix and match.

# Chapter 8

# Controlling Access to Files and Folders

*In This Chapter*

▶ Working with standard POSIX permissions

▶ Setting access control list permissions

▶ Inheriting permissions

▶ Using the rules of precedence to troubleshoot permissions problems

▶ Limiting access to services with service access control lists

*I*f you're a strict egalitarian, you may be inclined to give everyone on the network complete access to everything on the server. This approach might work with a small office with a handful of users but can be confusing to users if they have to sift through numerous server folders or if they find that someone accidentally moved a needed file.

Lion Server lets you control access by users to shared folders, files, and applications. You can assign permissions to grant or limit users' ability to perform certain actions, such as opening a folder or editing a file. Lion Server has permissions for files, folders, and applications.

You assign or change these user and group entities and permissions in the Server app. In this chapter, I describe the different types of permission schemes and their options.

One more type of permission lets you control who has access to entire services, such as file sharing, iCal service, and Mail. I end the chapter with a description of how to use this type of permission.

# Owner, Group, and Others (Everyone)

In file sharing, you set permissions for three user categories: *Owner, Group,* and *Others.* There's also *Everyone,* which is similar to Others. (You can also find these user categories on users' Macs; ⌘-click or right-click any file or folder and then choose Get Info.) You can use the categories to restrict access to a certain set of users, provide different levels of access to different users, or prevent access. When you create shared folders (called *share points*), you assign permissions to these classes of users.

These user categories are hierarchical; a user gets the permissions of the highest level he's a member of. If a user is both the owner and in a group, the user gets Owner permissions.

## Owners

The owner can be a user with a local account or one with a directory domain account. By default, the owner of a file or folder is the user who created it. The owner could also be the administrator.

The owner usually has the highest level of permissions: the ability to do anything to a file, such as edit, delete, or copy it. The owner is the only entity that can change permissions for groups or for Others/Everyone. The owner can also change the owner — that is, transfer ownership to another user.

The owner doesn't have to be a person — the owner can be an entity of the operating system or the operating system itself. In the latter case, this owner is `system`, the equivalent of the Unix `root` user.

## Groups

A *group* is a collection of users that you create accounts for. When a folder on the server has permissions for a particular group, all members of the group can access the folder. In Chapter 5, I describe creating groups, which you can do with System Preferences or Workgroup Manager.

## Everyone, Others, and Guests

Everyone, Others, and Guests are similar and can be treated as one category of user. For a particular shared file or folder, they all refer to *everyone else* — users who aren't an owner or in a group. This category is given the lowest level of permissions, which may mean no access at all.

*Others* are users who are logged in to the file server but are not owners or members of a group for a particular file or folder. *Everyone* includes anonymous users who are not logged in to the file server.

Don't worry too much about it: You'll never have to choose between Others and Everyone in a dialog. They're used in different places.

You see a choice for *Guest* only in the settings for file services (not for individual share points), where you can choose to Allow Guest Access. Doing so allows anonymous users who aren't logged in to access that file service or protocol without using a password. Guests have access only to files and folders with privileges for Everyone.

# Permission Schemes: POSIX Permissions and ACLs

Lion Server offers two different types of permissions for files and folders: Portable Operating System Interface for Unix (POSIX) permissions from the Unix world and access control lists (ACLs) from the Windows world. POSIX permissions are easier to use, but ACLs give you a finer degree of control over access to files and folders. Keep in mind, however, that ACLs are more complicated to manage.

POSIX permissions allow only one owner and one group setting for a shared folder. POSIX permissions don't provide different permissions to different individual users. ACLs allow multiple individuals and multiple groups to have different permissions for a shared folder. ACLs can be useful if you have several departments in the organization that need different levels of access for the same shared folder.

Table 8-1 shows the permission types that each file-sharing protocol can use. Chapter 9 describes the file-sharing protocols in further detail, but here's the gist: Apple Filing Protocol (AFP) is the best to use for Mac clients, and Server Message Block (SMB) is the best to use for Windows clients. Lion offers the WebDAV protocol for file sharing for iOS devices (iPad, iPhone, and iPod touch).

| Table 8-1 | Permission Types Available to File-Sharing Protocols | |
|---|---|---|
| **File-Sharing Protocol** | **POSIX Permissions** | **ACL Permissions** |
| AFP | Yes | Yes |
| SMB | Yes | Yes |
| WebDAV | Yes | Yes |
| NFS | Yes (files only) | No |
| FTP | Yes | No |

Two other file sharing protocols, NFS (Network File Sharing) and FTP (File Transfer Protocol), are no longer supported from the graphical management tools (Server Admin and the Server app). Advanced administrators with knowledge of Unix can still configure file sharing from the Terminal application. I include them in Table 8-1 for the sake of comparison.

You can use the Server app to set a limited set of POSIX permissions for AFP and SMB, using only a few mouse clicks. To take advantage of the full set of permission combinations that POSIX permissions offer, or to set ACLs, use Server Admin, which enables you to set all permissions that Lion Server provides.

Standard POSIX permissions and ACLs are set in two different places in the Server app. You set standard POSIX permissions from the File Sharing pane. You set ACLs from the Hardware pane.

The following sections look more closely at POSIX permissions and ACLs.

# Standard POSIX Permissions

POSIX permissions are the standards that define how Unix interacts with applications. Among other things, POSIX permissions define a permission structure for accessing files and folders. POSIX permissions are used not only in file sharing on a network, but also on the Unix computer itself. Because Mac OS X (and, therefore, Lion Server) has Unix at its core, POSIX permissions are used on all files and folders on every user's Mac.

Because these permissions are used throughout Mac OS X, POSIX permissions are often referred to as *standard* permissions in Apple documentation and elsewhere.

For any given file, folder, or volume, standard POSIX permissions have four types of access that you can set for Owner, Group, and Others/Everyone:

- **Read and write:** Gives full access to a shared folder or file. A user can open and save files located on the server-based folder and can copy files to the folder.

- **Read-only:** A user can open the shared folder and files as well as copy a file or folder to his computer. But users with read-only access can't save changes to files that they open in the shared folder, and they can't add files to the shared folder or delete files.

- **Write-only:** Users can only copy a file into a write-only folder. They can't open the folder to see what's in it or access the files. A write-only folder on a server is sometimes referred to as a *drop folder.*

- **No access:** The user has no access to the folder or file and can't copy files to or from it.

Figure 8-1 shows these settings in the Server app. To bring up this window, click File Sharing in the left column, select a folder, and click the Edit (pencil) button. (Chapter 9 has more about configuring file sharing.)

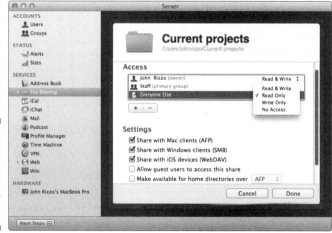

**Figure 8-1:**
Standard POSIX permissions in the Server app.

In Unix, another POSIX permission is *execute.* This permission enables a user or group to run a program. In a Unix command-line shell, the execute permissions also allows you to list the files in a directory. Execute permissions are similar to read permissions, which let you open folders to see what's inside. The execute permission isn't used in Server Admin or the Server app.

# *Propagating POSIX Permissions*

When you configure file sharing, you generally set permissions for one or more shared folders *(share points)*. Usually, users can create new files or folders and can copy files into a folder. Rather than having to set Owner and Group permissions for every new file and folder, these *child folders* and files are automatically assigned permissions based on rules.

All the file-sharing protocols can use the standard POSIX permissions behavior. The AFP and SMB protocols have another option for propagating POSIX permissions, dubbed *Inherit Permissions from Parent* or just *Inherit Permissions.* With this method, new files and folders inherit certain permissions from the *parent* folder (the folder in which the files and folders are created).

## *Standard POSIX permissions behavior*

In the standard behavior, permissions are assigned for new files and folders on a share point, regardless of what the permissions are on the parent folder. New files or folders get these permissions:

- ✔ **Owner:** The user who created the new folder or file becomes the owner and is assigned read/write permissions.
- ✔ **Group:** The new file or folder inherits the group assigned to the parent folder; however, the group is assigned read-only permissions.
- ✔ **Everyone/Other:** Is assigned read-only permissions.

Files and folders copied to the share point or duplicated don't inherit any permissions from the parent folder:

- ✔ **Owner:** The user who created the folder or file remains the owner and is assigned read/write permissions. This is just as with new files and folders.
- ✔ **Group:** Retains the group and permissions of the *original* file or folder.
- ✔ **Everyone/Other:** Retains permissions of the *original* file or folder.

These are only the default rules. Administrators can change the permissions of new or copied files and folders.

## *Inherit permissions from parent*

In addition to standard POSIX permissions behavior, the AFP and SMB protocols support a model for propagating POSIX permissions that can be more convenient. It's an *inheritance* model, in which certain permissions are inherited from the parent folder. Here's how it works:

- ✔ **Folders:** New folders, folders that are copied into the share point (parent folder), and duplicated folders inherit the Owner, Group, and Everyone permissions from the parent folder.

- ✔ **Files:** New files, files that are copied into the share point, or duplicated files. For these, the Owner inheritance is different from that for Groups and Everyone:

  - *Owner:* The owner/user who created the file or copied it to the shared folder remains the owner.

  - *Group and Other/Everyone:* The Group and Other/Everyone permissions are inherited from the parent folder. In other words, if a user copies a file or folder into a share point that uses the inheritance model, the Group permissions change. This is different from the standard POSIX permissions behavior described in the preceding section.

The standard POSIX permissions behavior and the inheritance model rules are for POSIX permissions. ACLs, described in the next section, have their own permissions propagation models.

# *Access Control Lists*

For any share point, you can also create an *access control list (ACL)* to define permissions. An ACL is a list of users and groups that have access to a share point and the permissions and inheritance settings that they have. Each entry in the list is an *access control entity (ACE)*. An ACE is a user or group and the associated permissions and inheritance settings.

Here's a simple ACL with two ACEs you might set for a share point:

|  | **Permission** | **Applies To** |
|---|---|---|
| **User:** *ronmckernan* | Read/write | This folder |
| **Group:** students | Read | This folder |

This ACL is similar to a set of POSIX permissions for a folder. There's one user and one group with read/write permissions. Applies to This Folder means no inheritance, as with POSIX permissions.

A limitation of POSIX permissions is that you can assign only one group and one user (the owner) access to a shared folder. With an ACL, you can continue to add ACEs to the list. Here, I added a teachers group with read/write privileges and a second user with write-only access:

| | *Permission* | *Applies To* |
|---|---|---|
| **User:** ronmckernan | Read/write | This folder |
| **User:** Tim Constanten | Write | This folder |
| **Group:** teachers | Read/write | This folder |
| **Group:** students | Read | This folder |

Further deviating from POSIX permissions, you can refine the ACL by setting more specific permissions, in addition to read and write and adding inheritance. Here, I've done this for the first user:

| | *Permission* | *Applies To* |
|---|---|---|
| **User:** ronmckernan | Read/create files/create folders/write extended attributes | This folder/child folders/ child files/all descendents |
| **User:** Tim Constanten | Write | This folder |
| **Group:** teachers | Read/write | This folder |
| **Group:** students | Read | This folder |

I describe these more specific ACL permissions in the next section.

## ACL permissions

ACLs provide finer shades of what read and write mean. For example, you can set write permissions to enable a group to edit files but not to create new folders. You can also enable users to edit a file but not to delete it, as shown in Figure 8-2.

Thirteen permissions are in Apple's implementation of ACLs. Figure 8-2 shows the window in the Server app where you can set ACL permissions. Here's how to access it in the Server app:

1. **Click the name of your server in the left column under Hardware.**

2. **Click the Storage tab and browse for and select a shared folder.**

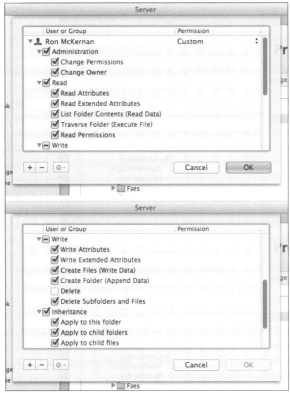

**Figure 8-2:**
The full set of ACL permissions in the Server app.

3. **Click the gear icon and select Edit Permissions from the pop-up menu.**

4. **Click the Add (+) button and start typing the name of an existing user or group.**

   The Server app finishes the name.

5. **Click the triangle to the left of the user or group name.**

   You see the 13 permissions grouped by type, as well as 4 types of inheritance.

The 13 permissions are as follows:

✔ **Administration:**

- *Change Permissions:* Users can change standard POSIX permissions even if they aren't owners.

- *Change Owner:* Users can change the file's or folder's ownership to themselves or to someone else.

✔ **Read:**

- *Read Attributes:* Users can view the file's or folder's attributes, including filename, date created, and size.

- *Read Extended Attributes:* Users can view the file's or folder's attributes, or metadata, added by third-party developers.

- *List Folder Contents (Read Data):* Users can view the folder's contents and open files.

- *Traverse Folder (Execute File):* Users can open subfolders and run programs in the folder.

- *Read Permissions:* Users can view the standard POSIX permissions of the file or folder with the Mac Finder's Get Info window (select the file or folder and choose Finder⇨Get Info) or with Terminal commands.

✔ **Write:**

- *Write Attributes:* Users can change the file's or folder's standard attributes.

- *Write Extended Attributes:* Users can change the file's or folder's other attributes.

- *Create Files (Write Data):* Users can create and edit files.

- *Create Folder (Append Data):* Users can create subfolders.

- *Delete:* Users can delete files or folders.

- *Delete Subfolders and Files:* Users can delete subfolders and files within the selected folder. You set these permissions on folders only. Files inherit permissions from the folder they're in.

You can use ACLs only on storage devices formatted in the HFS+ file system. If you want to use ACLs on a particular storage device that's formatted differently, you have to first reformat that drive in HFS+.

To take advantage of ACL permissions in Lion Server, you must use the Server app. You can't set or manage ACL permissions with Server Admin. This is the opposite of how previous versions of Mac OS X Server handled ACLs.

With this staggering array of permissions, you can easily lose track of who gets access to what and how. The best practice is to base your permission structure on group permissions. Don't set individual user permissions unless you need an exception, either with more permissive or more restrictive access. A good plan is to try to assign permissions to groups only once. Then if you need to change individuals' access, just add or remove them from groups.

## ACL inheritance

You can apply one or more of the 13 permissions to a folder. You can also set up to four types of inheritance to propagate these permissions to files in the folder and to folders within the selected folder. (Figure 8-2 shows three of the four choices for inheritance.) Each type applies to a particular level of folder hierarchy:

- ✔ **Apply to This Folder:** Applies permissions to the selected folder (the folder you're setting the permissions for).

- ✔ **Apply to Child Folders:** Applies permissions to subfolders (folders that are one level below the selected folder).

- ✔ **Apply to Child Files:** Applies permissions to the files in the selected folder.

- ✔ **Apply to All Descendants:** Applies permissions to folders and files that are inside subfolders — that is, to items that are two or more levels below the selected folder (see Figure 8-3). By itself, this setting doesn't apply to the subfolders.

**Figure 8-3:**
The ACL inheritance settings apply to different levels of folders within folders.

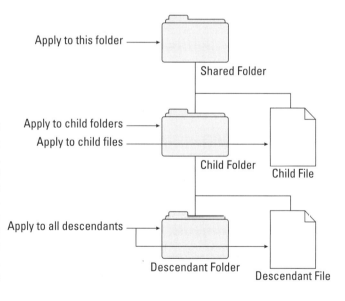

You can use the four inheritance settings in combination. If you select Applies to This Folder only, the ACL permissions settings wouldn't propagate but would apply only to the selected folder.

If you check both Applies to Child Folders and Applies to Child Files, the permissions would apply to the files and folders inside the selected folder but would not apply to the selected folder itself. Also, any folders inside the subfolders wouldn't get the permissions.

If you select Applies to This Folder and Applies to All Descendants, the permissions propagation would *skip a generation,* applying to the selected folder and to all folder levels below the first subfolder level.

## *Removing or editing inherited permissions*

You can remove all inherited permissions from an individual folder or file that is inside a folder structure with inheritance settings. Just do the following in the Server app:

1. **Click the name of your server in the sidebar under Hardware.**

2. **Click the Storage tab and browse for and select a shared folder.**

3. **Click the gear icon and select Edit Permissions from the pop-up menu.**

   A new dialog appears.

4. **Click the gear icon and choose Remove Inherited Entries from the pop-up menu, as shown in Figure 8-4; then click OK.**

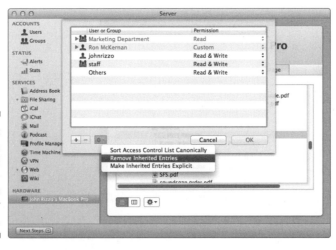

**Figure 8-4:**
Removing inherited permissions from a folder or folder.

Instead of removing all inherited ACL permissions from a nested folder or file, you can edit them, similar to the way you set them in the parent folder. (See the section "Access Control Lists," earlier in the chapter.) However, before you edit them, you need to convert them from inherited to explicit permissions.

In Figure 8-4, a choice called Make Inherited Entries Explicit converts the inherited ACL permissions to explicit entries that are set for that folder or file. Explicit permissions are described in the next section.

## Using inherited and explicit ACEs together

Permissions that you set for a file or folder are called *explicit permissions*. Permissions that are inherited from a higher-level folder are called *inherited permissions.* You can use inheritance to automatically assign ACLs together with explicit permissions.

As an example, say that you have a share point called Publications. You've assigned a Marketing group with certain ACL permissions that propagate down through all the subfolders. For two subfolders, you want to add permissions for the Art Department group. For the contents of those two subfolders, both the Marketing and Art Department groups can have permissions for the files and folders in those subfolders. Within other subfolders, only Marketing would have permissions.

Explicit permissions can also be propagated down through subfolders by inheritance settings. (Use the Propagate Permissions item in the gear icon under the permissions area.) Explicit permissions allow you to set permissions that propagate through a portion of the folder structure — useful for changing permissions for hundreds of folders and files all at once.

## Rules of Precedence

If a user complains that she can't access a certain share or save a file, look at your permission structure and the inheritance. You may have one type of inheritance unexpectedly taking precedence over another. For example, check the groups that the user belongs to and whether any Deny permissions are set. The issue is that if you have multiple sets of permissions and inheritance, only one can apply for any given shared folder and user or group. Some permissions take precedence over others.

Here are some rules that define which permissions take precedence:

- ✔ **Standard POSIX permissions apply automatically if no ACL exists for a certain file or folder.** If you don't specify any permissions to a newly created share point (and none are inherited), the default POSIX permissions and inheritance rules are applied.

- ✔ **Deny permissions take precedence.** When the server sees a Deny permission, it applies it regardless of other rules or precedence. This can unintentionally block access for a user.

✔ **ACL entries are first-come, first-served.** The order in which users and groups are listed in the ACL matters. If a user belongs to multiple groups in the list, the group listed higher takes precedence over one listed lower. So if the first entry doesn't give a user the right to delete a file even though another permission farther down in the list does, the user can't delete a file in the folder.

✔ **Mac OS X Server adds all the Allow permissions.** Mac OS X counts all the permissions that allow the user to do things and gives them to the user. If a user has one set of permissions and belongs to a group that has different permissions, she gets the Allow permissions of both.

After looking at all the ACL permissions that might apply to a user for a given folder, the server looks at the POSIX permissions for any Allow permissions that might apply. Mac OS X Server then adds them to create the access to the file for the particular user or group.

# Controlling Access to Services with SACLs

Another, even higher-level method of controlling access is *service access control lists (SACLs)*. SACLs control access to the available services, such as AFP and SMB file sharing, as well as other services such as e-mail and Address Book Server. If you set an SACL permission for a protocol, all the folders shared with that protocol get that permission.

SACLs are another layer of permissions on top of POSIX permissions and ACLs. With SACLs, you can prevent certain users and groups from having access to share points that use one or more of the protocols. Removing a user or group from a protocol's SACL prevents him from accessing share points with that protocol, including home folders.

You set SACLs using Server Admin. You can select individual services to add users and groups to or apply access to all services. You can also set administrators for individual services, or for all services.

To configure SACLs, do the following:

1. **In Server Admin, select your server listed in the left column.**

2. **Click Access in the toolbar and then click the Services tab.**

   The window in Figure 8-5 appears.

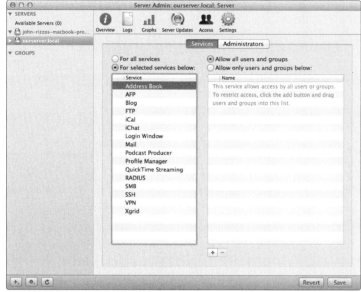

**Figure 8-5:**
Setting
SACL per-
missions
with Server
Admin.

3. **Select one of the two radio buttons on the left to restrict services:**

   • *For All Services* limits access to all services listed.

   • *For Selected Services Below* limits access for individual services.

4. **Select one of the two radio buttons on the right to choose a level of restriction for users and groups:**

   • *Allow All Users and Groups* allows access to the service(s) by all.

   • To restrict access, click *Allow Only Users and Groups Below.* Then click the Add (+) button to bring up the Users & Groups palette, and drag users and groups to the list.

5. **Click Save.**

By clicking the Administrators tab, you can also turn users and groups of users into administrators for a particular service. Drag a user and group over to the Allow to Administer or Monitor list.

The use of SACLs is optional. The default setting of each protocol's SACL is to list all users as having access to all available services. If you don't want to bother with it, just pretend it doesn't exist.

# Chapter 9

# Setting Up File Sharing

. . . . . . . . . . . . . . . . . . . . . . . . . . . . . . . . . . . . . . . . . . . . .

. . . . . . . . . . . . . . . . . . . . . . . . . . . . . . . . . . . . . . . . . . . . .

*F*or many organizations, file sharing is still the *raison d'être* for a server. It enables users to quickly and securely move files between computers sitting next to each other or in different buildings. It doesn't matter what computers an organization has because Lion Server uses the native file-sharing methods of Mac OS X, Windows, Linux/Unix — and now iPad. Apple refers to shared folders as *share points;* Microsoft calls them *shares.* But they're the same thing in Mac OS X Server.

If you have a beefy server Mac with lots of storage, you can set up file sharing so that users have their home folders on the server instead of on their Macs. Server-based home folders let them access their documents and settings from any computer.

This chapter describes setting up file sharing with the Server app. This includes setting options for file-sharing protocols and creating user permissions to control access to files and folders. Chapter 8 describes the types of permissions and how they work.

## File Sharing in Lion Server

Previous versions of Mac OS X Server used Server Admin for setting up and managing file sharing. With Lion Server, Apple stripped all file-sharing controls out of Server Admin and put it in the new Server app. The Server app provides a simple way to quickly set up file sharing and grant users and groups access. You may not need to know anything about protocols or permissions, and you don't have to understand the differences among AFP,

ACL, ACE, and other tech jargon. Although the Server app doesn't provide the level of control that previous versions of Mac OS X Server did, many of the more technical settings still exist, hidden away. Apple's approach seems to have been to keep the more complex tasks out of the way. In fact, you may never need to use them. If that's the case, congratulations — you don't have to read most of this chapter.

Unlike some other services, file sharing doesn't require much in the way of prerequisites on your network. You don't need a shared network directory; local user accounts will do. For a small network not connected to a larger network, you can do without DNS. Of course, there's nothing to prevent you from having these and other network infrastructure items, but they aren't strictly related to file sharing.

In the next section, I describe the different methods Lion Server provides for sharing files.

# Protocol Soup: AFP, SMB, and Other File-Sharing Methods

Mac OS X Server can share files using three standard *protocols* — sets of rules that the server and client use to share the files. Each protocol is known by its three-letter acronym. Because the acronyms are more widely used than the full names, acronyms are used in Mac OS X Server and in the Help system. Some services use a "secret" fourth protocol.

## File-sharing protocols 101

The different protocols are native to different operating systems, though Macs have the ability to use all these protocols. You can use multiple file-sharing protocols at the same time to support different client operating systems:

✔ **Apple Filing Protocol (AFP):** AFP is the native file-sharing protocol for Macs. It's been used in the Mac OS for years, so even your most ancient, pre-OS X Macs use it. AFP should be your first-choice file-sharing protocol for Mac clients. It can be faster than SMB, and your Mac clients will have fewer file-sharing glitches. AFP also provides Mac users with special features that the other protocols don't support, such as the ability to search server folders with Spotlight. (Users need read permissions for a share point in order to search it.) AFP also supports Kerberos authentication, access control lists, and the extended attributes of some Mac files.

AFP also provides Automatic Reconnect: When a Mac client goes into sleep mode, Mac OS X Server disconnects its AFP session. AFP can automatically reconnect to Mac clients after they wake, enabling users to resume working on open files from where they left off. Clients that wake up within a 24-hour period can reconnect automatically after waking. If the client Mac wakes after 24 hours, the user will need to log in. (This feature was editable in Snow Leopard Server, but in Lion Server, you need to use the command line to change these settings.)

Windows clients don't use AFP.

✔ **Server Message Block (SMB):** SMB is the native protocol that Windows clients use to access file servers. Many Linux and Unix clients also use SMB. Mac clients running Mac OS X 10.6 or later can also access files using SMB in Lion Server, but they get better results with AFP.

SMB is also referred to as Samba or CIFS. Samba is used in Linux, whereas CIFS (Common Internet File System) comes from the Windows world. With Lion, Apple dropped the open source Samba code and created its own SMB software. Although often used interchangeably, SMB and CIFS aren't actually the same thing, but the two technologies are often used together. Mac OS X Server's SMB service is technically SMB/CIFS.

When Mac OS X Server runs these protocols, the user can't tell that the shared files are on a Mac. To Windows clients, SMB share points hosted by Lion Server behave just as they do on a Windows server.

✔ **Web-Based Distributed Authoring and Versioning (WebDAV):** Lion Server uses WebDAV for file sharing with iPads running Apple's Pages and Numbers word-processing and spreadsheet programs, and in Apple's Keynote presentation software for iPad. It's possible that developers of other iPad apps could also make use of WebDAV as time goes on. WebDAV is based on the Hypertext Transfer Protocol (HTTP) used for the web. (Apple used WebDAV for its iDisk service.)

✔ **Network File System (NFS):** Lion Server has the ability to use NFS to host home directories, typically for Linux and Unix clients. However, you won't see anything about NFS in any of the administration tools. That's because Apple removed NFS from Server Admin and didn't include it in the Server app. Apple did, however, retain the actual server software. Lion Server uses NFS, behind the scenes, with the Podcast Producer and NetBoot services. If you know Unix commands, you can configure NFS with Terminal, share files, and create NFS home folders. For more information, see Apple's Mac OS X Command Line Administration at www.apple.com/server/docs/Command_Line.pdf.

✔ **File Transfer Protocol (FTP):** As with NFS, Apple removed the graphics user interface for FTP that was present in previous versions of Mac OS X Server. In Lion Server, FTP is available only through the command line. Unlike NFS, none of Lion Server's services uses FTP.

FTP is a different animal from AFP, SMB, and NFS. FTP volumes don't mount on a user's machine, and you can't open a document while it resides on an FTP server. A benefit of FTP is that any computer operating system can download files from an FTP server with a web browser. FTP is often used to serve files across the Internet, but it isn't secure.

If you want FTP service with a graphical user interface, you can install a third-party FTP server in Lion Server. Here are a few good FTP servers that use a graphical user interface:

- **Rumpus** from Maxum (www.maxum.com/Rumpus) is commercial FTP server software written specifically for Macs.

- **Wing FTP Server** from Wing FTP Software (www.wftpserver.com), available for Mac, Windows, and Linux, offers some security options.

- **PureFTPd Manager** (http://jeanmatthieu.free.fr/pureftpd) is a graphical front end to PureFTPd, a free command-only FTP server. Both are written specifically for Mac.

While you're at it, if you're looking for a good FTP client for users running Mac OS X, Windows, or Linux, try the free, open source FileZilla (http://filezilla-project.org). FileZilla is dependable and easy to use.

## *Security in file-sharing protocols*

The file-sharing protocols support different levels of security to protect login passwords and transmitted files from snoopers or malware that may have infected users' computers.

There are two basic levels of security in file-sharing protocols: no encryption and encryption. No encryption, or *cleartext,* sends the straight characters of a password over the network. AFP is the most secure file-sharing protocol. FTP is the least secure. This is what each protocol provides:

- **AFP** can send login passwords to the server as cleartext or with Kerberos encryption. Cleartext is disabled by default in Lion Server but can be turned on via the command line. (See http://support.apple.com/kb/HT4700 for directions.)

  If you upgraded your Snow Leopard Server to Lion Server, your Macs may not be able to authenticate via Kerberos. You can fix the problem by typing this command in Terminal:

  ```
  sudo sso_util configure -r REALM_NAME -a diradmin afp
  ```

  The realm name is usually the same as the fully qualified domain name of the Open Directory master, but in all capital letters. Restart the server when done.

✓ **SMB** supports sending passwords as cleartext or with Kerberos encryption, as well as some older Windows encryption methods. SMB does not support encryption of transmitted data, however.

✓ **WebDAV** requires a user to enter a name and password (authentication) and uses SSL encryption.

✓ **NFS** authentication always uses Kerberos but is less secure than the other protocols. NFS doesn't ask the user for a username and password. Instead, the client computer tells the server what the computer ID is. This means that anyone using that computer has access to whatever the user account has. This makes NFS authentication less secure than AFP and SMB. Like AFP, NFS file transmission can be cleartext or use Kerberos encryption.

✓ **FTP** sends all data as cleartext. It doesn't provide for encryption of passwords or data transmission. (The command line also supports FTP over `ssh`, or `sftp`, which is a secure connection.)

# Configuring File Sharing

You can use the Server app running on the server Mac or remotely from another Mac on the network. With just a few mouse clicks, you can start file service running with several folders already shared. Of course, you'll need to do more than share folders. You'll want to designate your own folders as share points, set what types of computers can access them, specify who can access the shared folders, and control what users can do. The next few sections describe how to perform these tasks.

## Logging in and turning on file sharing

If you're logging in to your server for the first time or if you're configuring it remotely, you may have to log in to the Server app before turning on file sharing. Here's how:

1. **Launch the Server app from the Dock.**

2. **If your server doesn't appear in the sidebar under Hardware, choose Manage⇨Connect to Server.**

   If your server is listed under Hardware, then you're already logged in and don't need to do anything else.

3. **Select a server from the Choose a Mac dialog and click the Continue button.**

   If you're running the Server app from your server, it will be listed as This Mac. To log in to another Mac on the network, select Other Mac.

4. **In the login dialog that appears, type a name and password and type the server's DNS name or its IP address in the Server field.**

   The username and password are those of the administrator account, which is the account you created when you installed the server.

   If you chose This Mac in Step 3, the Server app enters the hostname for you.

5. **Click the Connect button.**

   Once you're logged in, you can turn on file sharing using the Server app:

6. **Click the File Sharing icon.**

7. **If the File Sharing switch is set to Off, click it to turn it on (see Figure 9-1).**

**Figure 9-1:**
You can turn file sharing on and off by clicking the big switch.

Notice in Figure 9-1 that several share points have been created already:

- ✔ **Backups:** This appears if you've enabled Time Machine backup in the Server app. It's set for access by Macs because Time Machine is a Mac-only feature.

- ✔ **Groups:** When you create a new group in the System app's Group pane and select the Give This Group a Shared Folder check box, a shared folder is created inside the Group folder. The folder is named after the group, and the users in the group have access to their group folder.

- ✔ **Public:** This is a folder that administrators can use to distribute files to users. Members of the default Workgroup group can read and write to this shared folder. Other users can open items in the Public folder and copy items from it, but they can't put files and folders into it.

Some services will create their own share points when turned on. For example, the Shared share point in Figure 9-1 was created by Podcast Producer (activated with Server Admin). NetBoot will also create share points here when activated.

If the automatically created group folders fulfill your needs, you're finished. To share another drive, partition, or folder, read the following section.

Keep in mind that these default folders are all located on the startup drive. It's a good idea to keep shared files on another storage device, such as another partition, a second hard drive, or RAID storage. To do so, you can add a location to share, as I describe in the next section.

## Creating a share point

You can designate a folder or hard drive as a share point to enable shared access by users. Here's how:

1. **If the folder you want to share doesn't exist, create it in the Finder and give it a name.**

   You can also create a new folder from within the Server app. Select your server in the sidebar under Hardware, click the Storage tab, navigate to a folder, click the gear icon, and select New Folder. You cannot delete or move a folder from here, however.

2. **Open the Server app and click the File Sharing icon.**

3. **Click the Add (+) button (refer to Figure 9-1).**

4. **In the new dialog that appears, navigate to the folder or drive you want to share; select it, and click the Choose button.**

   After a few seconds, the new share point appears in the Share Points list in the File Sharing pane, ready for further configuration.

There's actually a second method creating a share point, but not from the Server app. You can use the Finder's Get Info box. In the Finder, select a folder and press the ⌘-I keys. Under General, select the Shared Folder check box. Here, you can also set permissions, described in the section "Using the Finder's Get Info window to set basic permissions," later in this chapter.

## Assigning file-sharing protocols to a share point

When you create a share point, it's shared automatically with the file-sharing protocols that both Mac and Windows computers can access, AFP and SMB. You can turn off either of these protocols and add WebDAV access for iPads.

I recommend turning off file-sharing protocols you're not using for any given share point. So, if you have a folder that only your Windows users access, turn off AFP for that folder.

To enable and disable file-sharing protocols for any given share point:

1. **In the Server app, click File Sharing in the sidebar.**

2. **In the Share Points list, double-click the folder you want to configure.**

   A settings pane appears for that share, as shown in Figure 9-2. The path to the shared folder is displayed at the top under the folder name.

   In Figure 9-2, because the path starts with /Volumes, you can tell that the folder resides on a drive or partition that is not the boot drive. On any Mac, the path for a nonbooted volume starts this way. The *V* is always capitalized.

**Figure 9-2:** Double-click a share in the File Sharing pane to bring up this settings window.

3. **Turn off a protocol for the share point by deselecting a check box next to Share with Mac Clients (AFP) or Share with Windows Clients (SMB).**

   Note that SMB shares not only with Windows clients, but with most Linux clients as well.

4. **To give iPads access to the folder, select Share with iOS Devices (WebDAV).**

5. **Click the check box to allow guest access if you want to permit anonymous users to access the share point without logging in.**

   This check box enables guest access for each of the protocols enabled.

6. **Click the Done button when finished.**

# Controlling User Access to Share Points

Typically, every user who has an account has read-only access to a new shared folder by default. (This access can be different, depending on your settings for inherited permissions, as described in Chapter 8.) You can use the Server app to make changes to who can access a folder and what each user can do. You can restrict access to certain users or groups or give additional people access.

You can make permissions changes for a share point in three places:

- ✔ The most obvious place is in the File Sharing pane of the Server, with the share point double-clicked (refer to Figure 9-2). Here, you can make changes to simple POSIX permissions (also known as standard permissions).

- ✔ You can also edit POSIX permissions in the Finder's Get Info window for a folder. You can even add users here.

- ✔ The least obvious place — some might say hidden — is in the pane for your server, where you can make more extensive changes to access control lists (ACLs), including setting inheritance.

Chapter 8 describes what the various permissions options are, what the terms mean, and what the options can do for you. The following sections describe how to use these three methods to change permissions.

## Using the File Sharing pane of the Server app to set basic permissions

In the File Sharing pane, you can make two types of changes to a share point's POSIX permissions:

- ✔ You can add a user or group to give them access to the folder or to block user access to the folder.

- ✔ You can set the access permission for a user or group, which appears next to the user and group names in the Access list (refer to Figure 9-2).

### Adding users and groups to the Access list

A share point you create has three default entries: Owner, Primary Group, and Everyone. You can't delete these entries. *Everyone* means everyone with a user account on the server. This differs from *Guest,* which means anyone on the network, even people without an account.

To add or remove your own users and groups using a folder's window in the File Sharing pane, follow these steps:

1. **In the File Sharing pane of the Server app, double-click a folder in the Share Points list.**

   The screen shown in Figure 9-2 appears. This time, you're working in the Access list.

2. **To add a user or group, click the Add (+) button; to delete a user or group, select it and click the Delete (-) button.**

   If you click the Add (+) button, a new field appears in the Access list.

3. **Start typing the name of a user.**

   A drop-down menu appears, listing users and groups that begin with (or are close to) the letters you've typed, as shown in Figure 9-3. Included in the list is Browse. Selecting Browse brings up a list of all users and groups, as shown in Figure 9-4.

   A quicker way to bring up the list of users and groups is to start typing the word *browse* instead of a name.

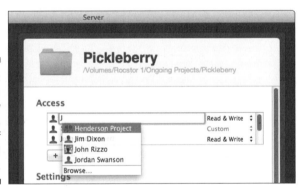

**Figure 9-3:** Start typing in the new field to bring up a list of users and groups.

4. **Select a user or group from the drop-down menu or select Browse.**

   Selecting a name adds the user or group to the Access list, giving them read and write access to the folder. Selecting Browse brings up the dialog in Figure 9-4.

5. **(Optional) If you selected Browse, select a name or add multiple users and groups by ⌘-clicking multiple names, as shown in Figure 9-4.**

   Groups are indicated with a two-headed icon.

6. **Click the OK button.**

   The users and groups you selected now appear in the Access list (refer to Figure 9-2), with full access (Read & Write permissions).

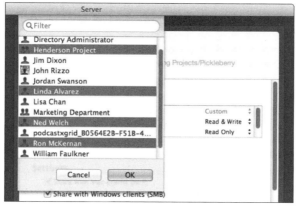

**Figure 9-4:**
You can select multiple users and groups by ⌘-clicking.

If you don't need to change the permissions of the users and groups in the list, click the Done button. To change permissions of any of the users and groups, continue on to the next section.

### Changing user and group permissions in the File Sharing pane

To change the permissions of the user and groups for a share point, make sure the window of the share point is open in the File Sharing pane of the Server app (refer to Figure 9-2).

To change the access permission for a user or group in the Access list, click the arrows to the right of the permission and select a new permission from the pop-up menu (see Figure 9-5).

For users and groups that you add to the Access list, you have three choices of permissions: Read and Write, Read Only, and Write Only. (See Chapter 8 for more information on these permissions.)

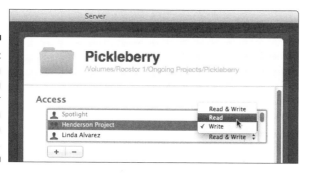

**Figure 9-5:**
Select a permission for a user or group from the pop-up menu.

For the default users and groups — Owner, Primary Group, and Everyone — you have a fourth choice, No Access. This setting is a complete ban and over- rides other settings. You can use this setting to prevent access by a user who is a member of a group that has access to the shared folder.

If you see the word *Custom* listed as a permission for a user or group, it means that the permissions are set by ACL permissions in the server's pane. (See "Configuring ACL permissions," later in this chapter, for more on config- uring ACLs.)

When you're finished making changes to permissions, click the Done button.

## Using the Finder's Get Info window to set basic permissions

You can also change a share point's user and group permissions from the Finder by using the Get Info window of the shared folder. Here, you can add and delete users and set basic POSIX permissions.

This method isn't as convenient as using the File Sharing pane of the Server app, particularly if you're configuring multiple folders. You'll have to dig through Finder windows to configure each one. But it does expose some options that more experienced administrators may find useful.

Follow these steps:

1. **In the Finder, navigate to a folder that is shared.**

2. **Click the folder to select it and press the ⌘-I keys.**

   Alternatively, you can right-click or Control-click the folder to bring up a contextual menu, where you select Get Info.

   The Get Info window appears. If you don't see a list of users and permis- sions, click the arrow next to Sharing & Permissions to expand the sec- tion of the Get Info box.

3. **To add a user, click the Add (+) button; to change the permissions of an existing user, skip to Step 6.**

   A list of users appears, as shown in Figure 9-6. On the left side are sev- eral categories of users:

   - *Users & Groups:* These are *local* user and group accounts. If you don't have a network directory, all your users are here. However, this category also displays some system accounts, which you should not alter unless you really know what you're doing.

• *Network Users and Network Groups:* These are user and group accounts in a network directory, such as Open Directory.

• *Address Book:* These are users listed in Address Book Server (see Chapter 11).

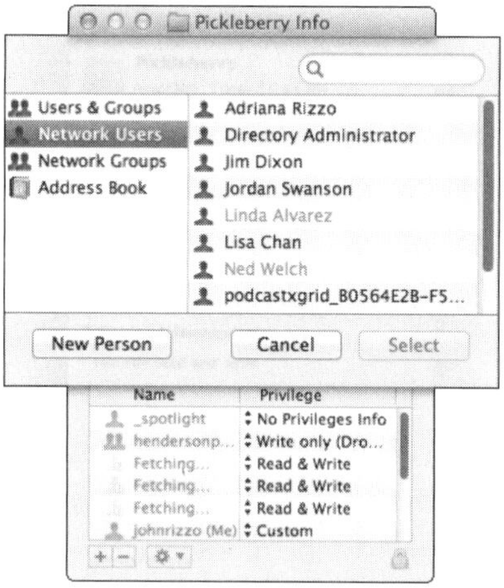

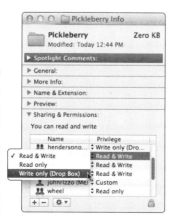

**Figure 9-6:**
Selecting user and groups to set permissions in the Finder's Get Info window.

4. **Click a category of users on the left, select a name (or multiple names by ⌘-clicking), and then click the Select button.**

   The users and/or groups you now appear in the list.

5. **To change the permissions of a user or group, click the double arrows next to the name and select an item from the pop-up menu (see Figure 9-7).**

   The changes you make here show up in the Server app's File Sharing pane.

**Figure 9-7:**
Changing user and group permissions in a folder's Get Info window.

You may see some strange-looking user or group names, such as *wheel.* These are system accounts. Do not make any changes to these accounts unless you know what you're doing. Don't touch, or you risk breaking something.

The Get Info window is available in the Finder of every Mac, not just Mac OS X Server. It exists on every version of Mac OS going back to the days when Macs were little beige boxes with built-in 9-inch screens. You can also do a Get Info on files. The Get Info windows provide useful information, including a file or folder's size, path, and a preview. You can make other changes, including setting what application will open a file. You can even share a file by selecting the Share check box.

## Configuring ACL permissions

When you first create a share point, Mac OS X Server assigns it standard POSIX permissions for Owner, Group, and Others. As described in the preceding sections, you can change the owner and group, change the permissions for all three entities, and add users. Standard POSIX permissions are easier to set than ACLs and may be all that you need.

For share points shared with AFP and/or SMB, you can also add permissions with an access control list (ACL) for a finer degree of access control. An ACL is the server's list of all permissions for all users and groups and for a share point. You add names of users and groups to the list and then use pop-up menus to assign permissions. ACLs are more complicated than POSIX permissions because they give you up to 17 choices: 13 permissions grouped by type, as well as 4 types of inheritance. I describe what they all do in Chapter 8.

With almost 100,000 possible combinations of ACL permissions, it's best to set permissions for groups and add user permissions only for exceptions.

### Setting ACL permissions for a folder

These ACL permissions settings are well hidden in the Server app. Here's how to access them in the Server app:

1. **Click the name of your server in the sidebar under Hardware.**

2. **Click the Storage tab and browse for and select a shared folder, as shown in Figure 9-8.**

3. **Click the gear icon and select Edit Permissions from the pop-up menu, shown at the bottom of Figure 9-8.**

   A list of users and groups appears.

4. **If you want to add a user or group, click the Add (+) button and start typing the name of an existing user or group.**

**Figure 9-8:**
Selecting
a shared
folder to
configure
ACL permis-
sions in the
Server app.

5. **To configure permissions, click the triangle to the left of the user or group name.**

   This exposes the first level of ACL permissions, as shown in Figure 9-9. You have four choices: Administration, Read, Write, and Inheritance (see Figure 9-9). You can make choices here. A hyphen [–] in a check box means that some, but not all, of the subordinate items for that category are selected. Selecting or deselecting a check box selects or deselects all of the subordinate items.

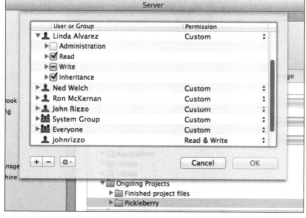

**Figure 9-9:**
The first
level of ACL
permissions.

6. **(Optional) If you want to go even deeper into ACL permissions, click the triangles next to the choices to expand them.**

   The expanded choices are shown in Figure 9-10. (I explain all ACL permission choices, including inheritance, in Chapter 8.)

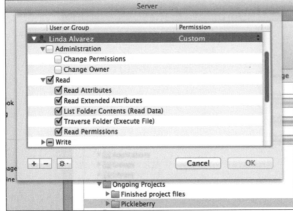

**Figure 9-10:**
The
expanded
ACL
permissions.

7. **Make any changes that you need and click OK.**

An application is a type of file that you can share. If you do, set permissions so that very few people can change permissions for shared applications. In the ACLs, under Administration, few people should have the Change Permissions and Change Owner permissions. Malware such as viruses often targets permissions in applications.

### Removing or adjusting a specific folder's inherited ACL permissions

When you use ACL inheritance settings, subfolders created inside a folder will inherit the permissions of the original folder. If you have a subfolder or file that you don't want to have those permissions, you can remove them or edit them for just that folder without changing the inheritance settings for the other subfolders.

Editing these permissions for a particular user or group is referred to as *making the inherited permissions explicit.* Removing a user's or group's permissions for a folder with inherited permissions is called *removing an ACL entry.*

The procedure for both takes you to the same permission-editing dialog described in the previous section. Open the Server app and do the following:

1. **Click the name of your server in the sidebar under Hardware.**

2. **Click the Storage tab and browse for and select the shared folder, as shown in Figure 9-8.**

3. **Click the gear icon and select Edit Permissions from the pop-up menu, as in Figure 9-8.**

   A list of users and groups with permissions appears. Permissions listed here that are inherited from a higher-level folder will be grayed out.

4. **Click the gear icon in the permissions dialog and select one of these options from the pop-up menu:**

   • *Make Inherited Entries Explicit:* When you choose this option, the formerly inherited permissions will no longer be grayed out and are editable.

   • *Remove Inherited Entries:* The grayed-out inherited permissions disappear from the list.

5. **Click the Cancel button to redo your selection or the OK button to approve.**

Chapter 8 has a thorough explanation of how inheritance works and how it can affect access.

## Propagating permissions to subfolders

With either POSIX (standard) or ACLs permissions, you can manually propagate them down through a folder hierarchy. With POSIX permissions, you can choose to propagate the Owner, Group, or Others permissions, or any combination. With ACLs, you can propagate only a folder's entire ACL, not entries for individual groups or users.

To propagate folder permissions to all the folders and files inside, open the Server app and do the following:

1. **Click the name of your server in the sidebar under Hardware.**

2. **Click the Storage tab and browse for and select the shared folder, as shown in Figure 9-8.**

3. **Click the gear icon and select Propagate Permissions from the pop-up menu.**

   The dialog shown in Figure 9-11 appears.

4. **Select the Access Control List check box to propagate ACLs and/or select the POSIX permissions in the top half of the dialog.**

5. **Click the OK button when done.**

   There is no undo here. Make sure you've selected the right permissions before clicking OK.

**Figure 9-11:**
Propagating
POSIX and
ACL permis-
sions with
the Server
app.

# Setting SACL Permissions for Limiting Access to Protocols

You can prevent specific users from accessing AFP and SMB, and/or protocol services using service access control lists (SACLs). Removing a user or group from an SACL listing for SMB, for instance, prevents that user or group from accessing *all* share points shared with SMB. You can also prevent users from accessing other services, including iCal and Profile Manager. SACLs are permissions to use a service.

For file sharing, SACLs are a way to control behavior. For example, if you want your Mac users to always use AFP to connect to the file server, you can ban them from the SMB service.

To configure SACLs, do the following:

1. **In Server Admin, select your server listed in the left column.**

2. **Click Access in the toolbar, and then click the Services tab.**

   The window in Figure 9-12 appears.

3. **Select one of the two radio buttons on the left to restrict services:**

   • *For All Services* limits access to all services listed.

   • *For Selected Services Below* limits access for individual services.

4. **Select one of the two radio buttons on the right to choose a level of restriction for users and groups:**

   • *Allow All Users and Groups* allows access to the service(s) by all.

   • To restrict access, click *Allow Only Users and Groups Below.* Select one or more services. Then click the Add (+) button to bring up the Users & Groups palette and drag users and groups to the list.

5. **Click Save.**

**Figure 9-12:**
Setting
SACL per-
missions
in Server
Admin to
restrict
access to
services.

To restrict access to services for administrators, click the Administrators tab. Here, you can also turn users and groups of users into administrators for a particular service. Drag a user and group over to the Allow to Administer or Monitor list.

# A Note on Windows Client Support

Although Windows users can access shared folders and files in Lion Server, there are features that were previously supported in Mac OS X Server (via Server Admin) that are no longer supported. If you have Snow Leopard Server 10.6.8, you can use it in concert with Lion Server to support Windows. Here are some features not supported in Lion Server:

- ✔ **Primary Domain Controller:** Enables Windows clients to authenticate directly to the Mac server. Snow Leopard Server stores the user and group information for the Windows clients, and it hosts user profiles and network home folders. Working as a Backup Domain Controller, also supported in Snow Leopard Server, is not supported in Lion Server.

- ✔ **Windows Internet Naming Service (WINS):** Enables Windows clients to find Windows servers and other Windows clients across multiple subnets. WINS resolves the Windows network computer names (called NetBIOS names) to IP addresses.

- ✔ **Windows domain browsing:** Enables Windows clients to browse for Windows servers across subnets. Snow Leopard Server makes itself appear to be a Windows server to Windows clients.

- ✔ **Domain login:** Enables Windows users to log in with the same username, password, roaming profile, and network home folder on any Windows (or Lion Server) computer that can log in to a Windows domain.

# Chapter 10

# Sharing Printers Over a Network

- - - - - - - - - - - - - - - - - - - - - - - - - - - - - - - - - - - - - - - - - - - - - - - - - - - - -

## In This Chapter

▶ Understanding printer sharing

▶ Using System Preferences and CUPS to share and manage printers

▶ Creating shared printer pools for balancing loads

▶ Keeping track of print jobs and printers

▶ Helping Mac, Windows, and Linux/Unix clients print

- - - - - - - - - - - - - - - - - - - - - - - - - - - - - - - - - - - - - - - - - - - - - - - - - - - - -

*P*rinter sharing, or print serving, is a useful feature for both users and network administrators. For users, a print server eliminates waiting for a printer when it's busy. Administrators get management tools that can keep track of how often different printers are used and who's using them, as well as keep track of print errors.

Mac OS X Server allows you to set up a shared print queue for any printer. When users hit their Print buttons, the print job doesn't go to the printer, but instead goes to the shared print queue on the server. The print server feeds print jobs in the queue to the printer one at a time. You can also schedule printing and assign priority.

That's the good news. The bad news is that with Lion Server, Apple removed the print management user interface that was part of previous versions of Mac OS X Server. What is left is the print-sharing capability that is built into every client copy of Mac OS X — which includes a print server. You don't have all the management capabilities offered by previous versions of Mac OS X, but you can still do quite a bit with a dedicated server Mac to take care of sharing printers for your users.

In this chapter, I describe using the two ways you can manage printer sharing: with System Preferences and with a web-based interface.

# Printer Sharing Features in Lion Server

The print server built into every copy of Mac OS X 10.7 client is quite capable. These are the main features:

- Printers that are accessible by users on the same local network as the server
- Print queues that are stored on the server
- Sharing of network printers, not just printers connected to the server
- Support of Windows and Linux clients
- Automatic connections to the network directory
- Printer load balancing with pooling
- Remote administration from any computer and any OS with a web browser
- Kerberos authentication for printing

Readers familiar with Mac OS X Server will notice that that Lion Server no longer supports some features found in previous versions. The most notable is the setting of print quotas for individual users and printers.

But this chapter is about all the things you *can* do with printer sharing in Lion Server and how to do it. In the following section, I go through some of the terminology you encounter when setting up shared printing.

# Print Sharing Technology and Terminology

Centralizing printing with a server enables any client to print to any printer connected to the server. Without a server, the user's computer communicates directly with the printer, and the computer and the printer both need to support the same technology. When you throw a print server into the mix, here are the two steps of communication: client to server and server to printer. The two steps don't have to use the same technology.

It starts with the printer. Lion Server supports a variety of types of printers. But in printing parlance, *printer type* can mean different things: USB, LPR (Line Printer Remote), inkjet, Ethernet, PostScript, IPP (Internet Printing Protocol), or laser printer. These sometimes cryptic terms aren't equivalent, however. We're talking apples and oranges, with some cherries and pomegranates thrown in for good measure.

## *Communicating with the printer*

Lion Server works with hundreds of new and old printer models. Here are the printer types that Mac OS X Server supports:

- ✔ **Printer technology (laser, inkjet, others):** Mac OS X Server doesn't care about how the ink's put on the paper. More exotic technologies may also work, depending on drivers and the other factors noted later in this list. Inkjet printers typically use USB to connect to the server.

- ✔ **Physical connection (USB, Ethernet, Wi-Fi, or Bluetooth):** You can share a printer that's plugged into the server Mac or a printer that connects directly to the network with its own Ethernet port.

  Ethernet printers use a print protocol to communicate with the server over the network; directly connected USB printers do not. USB printers are easier to configure in Mac OS X Server, but Ethernet printers are more convenient because you can locate them where the users are, not just where the server is located.

  You can also share a wireless printer with built-in Wi-Fi (802.11 networking) or Bluetooth. Sharing a wireless printer isn't the same, however, as connecting a USB printer to a box that puts it on the Ethernet network. Apple's Time Capsule does this, as do some wireless routers and DSL modems. For the purposes of the Mac OS X Server's print service, USB printers connected to wireless network devices are treated as Ethernet printers.

- ✔ **Page description language (PostScript, raster, or proprietary):** This is what the client uses to describe the page; the printer reads the description to re-create the page in printed form. PostScript is the most standard page-description language for Ethernet printers. Some inkjet printers also use PostScript, though many describe a page with *raster* printing, which simply defines where dots are applied on a printed page. HP's PCL (Printer Command Language), and its variant, HP-GL/2, are other common page-description languages. Proprietary page-description languages are also used for specific printers.

- ✔ **Network printing protocol:** Lion Server uses Line Printer Remote (LPR) to communicate with printers and servers. These network protocols aren't used for USB printers. In that case, the USB data transmission standards are used to move print data from server to printer.

The printing protocol that the server uses to communicate with the printer doesn't have to be the same one it uses to communicate with clients.

My old trusty LaserWriter is still kicking, but I can't use it with Lion Server. Apple dropped AppleTalk in Snow Leopard Server. You won't be able to use an older AppleTalk printer if it doesn't also support LPR.

## Communicating with the client

The print service in Mac OS X Server can communicate with user client computers with one of three network printing protocols. You set up a print queue with one more of these print protocols:

- **Internet Printing Protocol (IPP):** Mac, Windows (XP and later), and Unix/Linux clients can all use IPP to print. When Mac OS X clients print to a non-PostScript printer, they can use the printer's native driver installed on the client to have access to the printer's special features. This isn't available with LPR.

- **Line Printer Remote (LPR):** Mac, Windows (XP and later), and Unix/Linux clients can all use LPR to print.

- **Server Message Block (SMB):** Windows clients only, including older versions of Windows.

Client computers can use any of these protocols to transfer PostScript print jobs to the server. If you have a printer that uses a proprietary, non-PostScript print driver, it will use IPP to send print job data with.

A USB printer connected to the server Mac is a network printer as far as the client computers are concerned. So although a USB printer doesn't use a network printing protocol to talk to the server, the clients do use a network printing protocol to send jobs to the server. If the USB printer is a raster (non-PostScript) inkjet printer, the client computers can use any printing protocol to send a PostScript job to the server. The server converts the PostScript job to what the inkjet printer expects to receive.

# Lion's Print Management Software

Mac OS X provides two choices of software that you can use to start and manage network printer sharing. The simpler and easier of the two is System Preferences, and it may be all that you need. System Preferences is the first place you'll go to turn on print sharing. The more powerful is the web interface to the Common Unix Printing System (CUPS).

You can use either shared printers connected to the Mac, or you can share network printers. For the latter, it means hosting the print queue on the server instead of the printer. Although it is limited in abilities, you can use System Preferences to restrict usage of print sharing to certain users or groups who are in the network directory. You can also use Workgroup Manager to further limit which users and groups can access specific printers.

# Using System Preferences for printer sharing

System Preferences is the equivalent of the Control Panel in Windows. It's found in the Dock by default and accessible from the Apple menu. Found on all Macs, clients, and servers, System Preferences generally is the place for user settings on a local Mac. (It's also the place to configure local user and group accounts, if your server isn't using a shared network directory.)

To set up printer sharing, you access two areas: the Sharing pane and the Print & Scan pane, shown in Figure 10-1. I have more on System Preferences later in this chapter, in the section "Setting Up Shared Printing."

**Figure 10-1:** System Preferences has two areas, circled here, for printer sharing,

# Accessing the CUPS print engine from a browser

CUPS is actually the print engine in Mac OS X and has been since 2002. Apple adopted CUPS soon after it was created as a print system for Linux in the late 1990s. Apple became a major developer and, in 2007, purchased the CUPS code and hired the creator, Michael Sweet. Apple continues to offer the CUPS code under open source licensing, so it continues to be part of many Linux distributions.

In Mac OS X, System Preferences provides a simple front end to the CUPS printing system, and it may be all you need. Mac OS X also includes a more detailed web-based interface to CUPS that you can access by typing one of these URLs in your web browser:

      ✔ `http://127.0.0.1:631`

      ✔ `http://localhost:631`

Use these URLs if you're logged into the server Mac that is hosting the printing. If you're accessing your server from another computer, use instead a URL in this form: `http://server-ip-address:631`, where *server-ip-address* is the IP address of the server on which you have printer sharing enabled.

If you want to access CUPS from another computer (running any OS), you need to have Remote Administration enabled. Open the CUPS web portal (the first page), click the Administration tab, and select the Allow Remote Administration check box.

The web interface of CUPS allows you to add printers and do some things that you can't in System Preferences, including creating *printer pooling* (a type of load sharing) and print queues for network printers.

Figure 10-2 shows the home page of the CUPS web portal. The Online Help tabs takes you help and information pages. However, much of the help information is about the command-line interface.

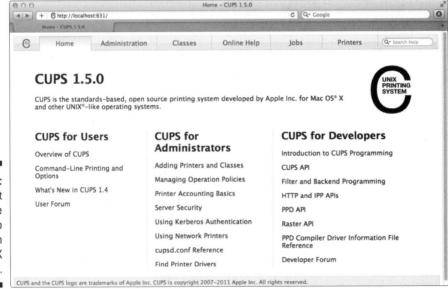

**Figure 10-2:** The first page of the CUPS web interface in Mac OS X Lion.

# Setting Up Shared Printing

This section describes how to set up print service in Mac OS XO 10.7 Lion using System Preferences and the CUPS web interface to configure print sharing. This section includes balancing the printers' workload by creating printer pools and by managing printers and print jobs. I describe how to use System Preferences and Workgroup Manager to restrict access to specific printers and to specify which printers show up in a user's list of printers.

## Before you start: Setting up your printers for print sharing

Before you configure print services in Mac OS X Server, make sure that your printers are connected to the network or plugged into the server. You also need to set up and configure your printers according to the manufacturer's directions. For network printers, it's a good idea to configure them using a static IP address so that they have a consistent location on the network.

Some printers have print serving or spooling features built in. Turn *off* these features if you want your users to go through the Mac OS X Server. Using two print queues (one in the printer and one on the Mac OS X Server) can cause users to wait longer before their documents are printed.

Some printers also come with protocols that can advertise the printer over the network, such SMB and Bonjour. You may consider turning off these features in these printers to prevent users from directly accessing the printers and avoiding the server-hosted print queues.

A good idea is to print to the printer from a Mac and a Windows PC (if you have them) before you configure printer sharing on your server. This way, you can spot any trouble that the printer may be causing.

## Turning on print sharing

You use System Preferences to turn on printer sharing:

1. **Open System Preferences and click the Sharing icon.**

2. **Select the Printer Sharing check box in the left column, as shown in Figure 10-3.**

   Printer sharing is now turned on, and you can select a printer to share (described in the next section). You may see printers listed in the lower right. If not, don't worry about it now.

**Figure 10-3:**
The Sharing
pane of
System
Preferences.

# Checking workgroup name for Windows clients

After you turn on printer sharing, check the workgroup name for your Windows clients. Mac OS X has assigned a workgroup name of Workgroup, which is the default name on all your Windows PCs. If you have an existing network set up and have changed the Windows workgroup name, you can edit it by doing the following:

1. **In System Preferences, click the Show All button and then click the Network icon.**

2. **Select the network port on which your clients reside and then click the Advanced button in the lower right.**

3. **Click the WINS tab, shown in Figure 10-4.**

4. **Type a new WINS name, if necessary, and then click the OK button (not shown in Figure 10-4).**

   The NETBIOS name is the same as the server Mac's computer name.

These settings help Windows PCs discover the server acting as a print server. Alternatively, you can install Apple's Bonjour for Windows on the PC, a free download at http://support.apple.com/kb/DL999.

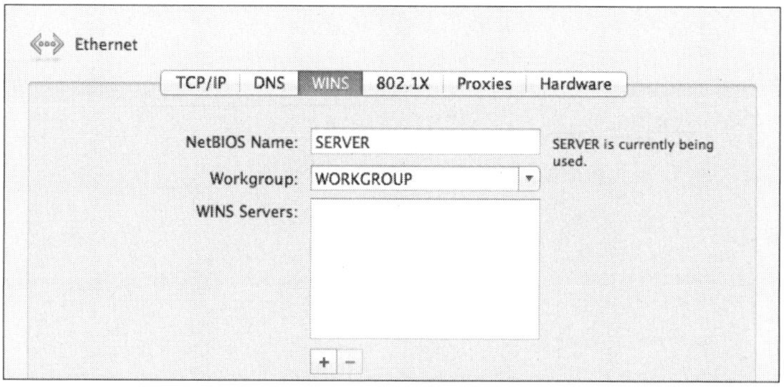

**Figure 10-4:**
You have
the option
to change
the default
settings for
Windows
clients.

## Sharing printers with System Preferences

With printer sharing turned on, you can now designate printers to share. Start with System Preferences:

1. **In the System Preference Sharing pane, make sure that Printer Sharing is selected and turned on.**

   You may see one or more printers listed in the field shown in Figure 10-3.

   If printer sharing isn't turned on, see the section "Turning on print sharing," earlier in this chapter.

2. **If a printer you want to share appears in the list, select the check box next to its name, and you're done.**

   If the printer isn't listed, proceed to the next step.

3. **If the printer you want to share doesn't appear in the list, click the Open Print & Scan Preferences button.**

   The Print & Scan pane appears, as shown in Figure 10-5.

4. **Select a printer in the Printers list and select the Share This Printer on the Network check box.**

5. **(Optional) To give the printer a new name that is more recognizable to users, click the Options & Supplies button, enter a name and location in the corresponding fields, and click OK.**

   You return to the Print & Scan pane.

If you don't see your printer in the list, it's probably an IP network printer (not attached to the Mac) and probably isn't discoverable. You can add it manually from this same Print & Scan pane. You'll need to know the printer's IP address and the print protocol that it uses.

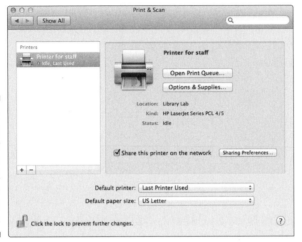

**Figure 10-5:**
Selecting
a printer
to share in
the Print &
Scan pane
of System
Preferences.

Follow these steps to add a printer that isn't appearing in the Print & Scan pane:

**1. Click the Add (+) button below the Printers list.**

The Add Printer window appears, as shown in Figure 10-6.

**Figure 10-6:**
The Add
Printer
window
with data
entered in
some of the
fields.

**2. Click the IP icon in the toolbar.**

**3. Click the Protocol pop-up menu and then select your printer's connection method: IPP, LPD, or HP Jetdirect (see Figure 10-6).**

4. **Type an IP address or a DNS name in the Address field.**

   After you type an IP address, the Mac searches the network to find the printer. If the printer is turned on and is found, the Mac adds the correct PostScript Page Description file (PPD) in the Print Using pop-up menu. Otherwise, it selects Generic PostScript Printer for you. You can also select a printer from the menu.

5. **Click the Add button.**

   The printer appears in the Printers list of the Print & Scan pane. The printer's name will be its IP address.

6. **(Optional) Give the printer a more descriptive name by clicking the Options & Supplies button in the Print & Scan pane and then typing a Name and Location; click OK.**

7. **Share the printer by selecting it in the Printers list and selecting the Share This Printer on the Network check box.**

You can also add a printer by using the CUPs web interface (see the next section).

## Using the CUPS interface to share printers

The CUPS web interface isn't quite as simple to use as System Preferences (see the preceding section), but if you're doing other work with CUPS, you can use it to designate printers to share. The CUPS web interface also provides more choices when you're manually configuring printers to add.

Here's how to designate printers to share with the CUPS web interface:

1. **Open a web browser and go to the CUPS web interface by typing one of the URLs (such as `http://localhost:631`) listed in the section "Accessing the CUPS print engine from a browser," earlier in the chapter.**

2. **Click the Administration tab.**

   The web page shown in Figure 10-7 appears.

3. **If you haven't turned on printer sharing in System Preferences, turn it on now by selecting the check box next to Share Printers Connected to this System; then click the Change Settings button.**

4. **Click the Find New Printers button.**

   A list of printers may appear if CUPS finds any.

5. **Click Add This Printer if you see your printer in the list and skip to Step 9.**

   Chances are, your printer will appear. If not, proceed to the next step.

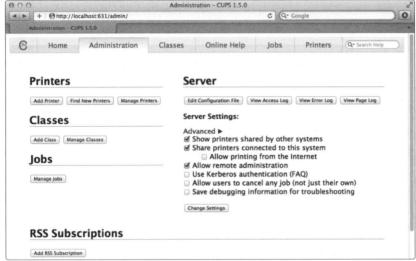

**Figure 10-7:**
The
Administra-
tion page of
the CUPS
web inter-
face.

6. **If you don't see your printer, click the Administration tab and then click the Add Printer button.**

   You may be prompted for your administrator name and password. If so, enter them and click the Log In button.

7. **Select one of ten types of printer, local, and network connections and click the Continue button.**

   Your choices include Bluetooth, fax, http, ipp (and the secure versions, https and ipps), and Windows printer via spools.

8. **If you choose a network printer connection, type the correct form of a URL identifier, using a hostname or IP address; then click the Continue button.**

9. **Type a user-friendly printer name, description, and location and click the Share This Printer check box; click the Continue button when finished.**

   The printer appears in the Printers list.

## Creating a printer pool using classes

Here is something you can do with CUPS' web interface but can't do with System Preferences: In a situation when a printer is heavily used, you may want to group two or more printers in a pool to share the load. A *printer pool* is basically a queue that contains multiple printers. When a user prints to the pool, the job gets printed to the first available printer. Often, administrators place the pooled printers next to each other so that users can easily find their printouts.

It's best to use printers of a similar model in a printer pool to ensure that printouts from the machines are the same and the printer features are consistent. If you have printers with different features, a user could select a print feature in her Print dialog that doesn't exist in one of the printers. This could lead to a situation in which a print job won't print on one of the printers in the pool.

CUPS refers to printer pools as *classes.* To set up a printer pool, you use the CUPS web interface to create a class and assign printers to it:

1. **Open a web browser and go to the CUPS web interface by typing one of the URLs (such as `http://localhost:631`) listed in the section "Accessing the CUPS print engine from a browser," earlier in the chapter.**

2. **Click the Administration tab (refer to Figure 10-7).**

3. **Click the Add Class button under the Classes heading.**

4. **Type a name, description, and location of the class (or pool).**

   The name can't include spaces, slashes, or hash marks.

5. **Select the printers you want to include in the pool from the Members list and click the Add Class button.**

   The CUPS interface now takes you to a new management page for the new class, as shown in Figure 10-8.

The management page for the class you just created is identical to the management page for an individual printer, accessible from the Printers tab. The Maintenance pop-up menu lets you manage jobs, giving you options to pause and resume all print jobs, as well as reject/accept all jobs and print a test page.

A useful option is Move All Jobs, which shifts current jobs to one printer, letting you take other printers offline without disturbing any of the printing.

The new printer class now appears in the print dialogs of users' computers. You'll also see it in the System Preferences Print & Scan pane of the user and the server, with an icon showing three printers instead of one.

**Figure 10-8:**
The CUPS management page for a printer pool.

# Restricting access to shared printers

When you first share a printer, all users on your local network can use it by default. You can restrict access to certain users and groups by using System Preferences or the CUPS web interface. System Preferences is easier to use for this purpose. After you share a printer on Lion Server, it automatically has access to the user and group accounts of your network directory, such as Open Directory; you don't need to do anything to connect the printer to the directory.

Although you can specify individual users who can access each printer or printer class (or pool), assigning groups to printer access is an easier option. You can create groups specifically for the purpose of printer access. (Use the Server app or Workgroup Manager to create groups, as described in Chapter 16.)

### Restricting printer access using System Preferences

To use System Preferences to restrict user or group access to a printer or printer class, follow these steps:

1. **Open System Preferences and click the Sharing icon to bring up the Sharing pane.**

2. **Select the Printer Sharing line in the left column.**

   Be careful not to uncheck the Printer Sharing check box.

3. **Select a printer or printer class (or pool) in the Printers list.**

   By default, the Users field displays *Everyone Can Print.*

4. **Click the Add (+) button under the Users list.**

A dialog appears, as shown in Figure 10-9, listing four categories of users in the left column:

- *Users and Groups:* These are users and groups with *local* accounts. Use this category if you don't have a network directory.

- *Network Users* and *Network Groups:* These two selections each display shared network accounts.

- *Address Book:* These are accounts listed in Address Book Server (see Chapter 11).

5. **Select a user category in the left column and one or more users or groups in the right column and then click the Select button.**

   Hold the Command key to select multiple entries.

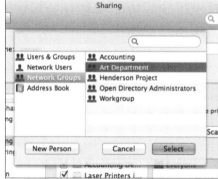

**Figure 10-9:** Selecting users or groups to access a printer.

The user or group you selected appears in the User list in the Printer Sharing pane, as shown in Figure 10-10.

6. **(Optional) Add users or groups by repeating Steps 4 and 5.**

The users and groups you add are able to access this printer or class. All other users will no longer have access. Any users you add to the Users list will need to have passwords in their directory accounts. User accounts with no password won't be able to print to a printer that has restricted use.

### Restricting printer access using the CUPS web interface

Using CUPS to restrict access to printers takes a few more clicks and requires some typing, but it does give you a little more flexibility than System Preferences provides. Follow these steps:

1. **Open a web browser and go to the CUPS web interface by typing one of the URLs (such as http://localhost:631/) listed in the section "Accessing the CUPS print engine from a browser," earlier in the chapter.**

**Figure 10-10:**
The Printer
Sharing
pane with
users and
groups
added to a
printer.

2. **Click the Printers tab (or Class tab for printer pools) and select a printer (or class).**

3. **Choose Select Allowed Users from the Administration pop-up menu.**

   A page called Allowed Users for *printername* appears.

4. **At the bottom of the page, select either Allow These Users to Print or Prevent These Users from Printing.**

   Here's the extra flexibility that you don't get with System Preferences: By using Prevent These Users from Printing, you can easily give access to everyone except for a few people or groups. The drawback is that you have to type them.

5. **Type the names of users and groups in the Users field, separating them with a comma and a space, and then click the Set Allowed Users button.**

### Restricting access with Workgroup Manager

For a different take on restricting access to printers, you can use Workgroup Manager's *managed preferences.* (See Chapter 16 for more on managed preferences.) Instead of setting which users can access a particular printer, Workgroup Manager does the opposite, letting you set which printers can be accessed by a particular user or group. Follow these steps:

1. **Open Workgroup Manager, log in if necessary, and click the Preferences icon in the toolbar.**

2. **On the left side, just below the toolbar, click the Users or Groups icon in the short tab bar.**

   It makes more sense to set allowed printers for a group.

   3. **Select one or more groups (or users) from the list on the left and click the Overview tab on the right.**

   4. **Click the printing icon.**

   5. **Click the Always radio button next to Manage, as shown in Figure 10-11.**

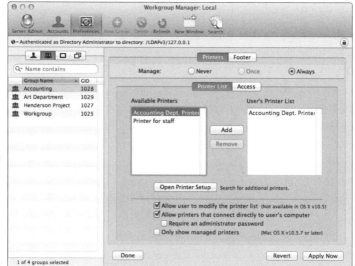

**Figure 10-11:**
Restricting
printer
access in
Workgroup
Manager.

   6. **Under the Printer List tab, select one or more printers from the Available Printers field and click the Add button.**

      *Note:* Printer pools (or classes) do not appear in Workgroup Manager and can't be used with managed preferences.

      In Figure 10-11, I've assigned the Accounting group access to the Accounting Department printer. This is the only printer users in the group will be able to print to.

   7. **(Optional) If you want require a password to access the printer, click the Access tab and select the Require an Administrator Password check box.**

      You can also select a printer and click the Make Default button to set the printer as the user's or group's default printer.

   8. **Adjust any other settings and click the Apply Now button to accept all your changes.**

# *Managing Printers and Print Jobs*

With multiple printers shared on the network, you can use either Server Preferences or the CUPS web interface to manage print jobs and printers. Print pools (classes) are treated exactly like printers. The next few sections describe some of these activities.

## *Using System Preferences to manage printers and jobs*

Designating a printer to share automatically creates a print queue on the Mac you're configuring. This is true even for network printers. The queue stores users' documents waiting to be printed and feeds them to the printer when ready.

You can see a list of the print jobs and users in the Print & Scan pane of System Preferences (refer to Figure 10-5). Select a printer or a printer class on the left and click the Open Print Queue button. Here, you can hold or delete print jobs, see a printer status message (such as Paused or Out of Paper), and view the print queue's log file.

After you click the Open Print Queue button for a selected printer or class, you also see some additional menus in the menu bar at the top of the screen. For example, the Completed Jobs item in the Jobs menu displays a list of printed jobs.

One of the most interesting tasks is moving print jobs between printers. If a print job can't wait for the queue it's in, you can move it to another printer by simply dragging and dropping it. Here's how:

1. **Open System Preferences and click the Print & Scan icon.**

2. **Select a printer that has the job to be moved and click the Open Print Queue button.**

   A separate print queue window opens. Move it to the side.

3. **In the Print & Scan pane, select the printer that you want to move the job to and click the Open Print Queue button.**

   A print queue window opens for the second printer.

4. **Drag the print job from one printer's queue window to the other.**

A pretty neat trick!

# Using the CUPS web interface to manage printers and jobs

The section "Creating a printer pool using classes," earlier in this chapter, is the most useful example of what you can do with the CUPS web interface that you can't do in System Preferences. This section describes the rest of the interface and some of the things you can do with it.

### Keep tabs on the print server with RSS

You can set up Really Simple Syndication (RSS) feeds for individual printers, printer pools, or all your printers. When something happens to the printer or jobs, CUPS creates an RSS feed to alert you. You can read the feed in any RSS reader, such as Safari or another RSS-capable web browser in any operating system, or the Mac's Mail program.

The interface isn't entirely user friendly, but these steps take the guesswork out of setting up your own feeds:

1. **Open the CUPS web interface by typing one of the URLs (such as `http://localhost:631`) listed in the section "Accessing the CUPS print engine from a browser," earlier in the chapter.**

2. **Select the Administration tab and click the Add RSS Subscription button.**

   The Add RSS Subscription page opens, as shown in Figure 10-12.

**Figure 10-12:** Creating an RSS for print server notifications with CUPS.

**3. Type a name for the RSS feed in the Name field.**

The CUPS web interface is very particular about the format of the name, and it doesn't tell you everything you need to do. If you get it wrong, it won't create a feed, and it won't tell you why. Here's what you need to know:

- The feed name must end in `.rss`.

- The feed name must not contain spaces, slashes, question marks, or hash marks.

- It's best to use simple names.

Remember this name or write it down. You need it to view your feed.

**4. Select a printer or class (pool) in the Queue field.**

CUPS won't create an RSS feed if you don't click one.

**5. Select the check boxes next to the types of job, queue, and server events.**

You may want to leave Job Created and Job Completed blank, or your RSS feed could quickly fill with non-urgent RSS articles.

**6. Edit the Maximum Events in Feed field, if desired, and then click the Add RSS Subscription button.**

To view the RSS feed in a web browser, type one of the following URLs in a web browser, replacing the items in italics with your own information:

✔ From the server Mac: `http://localhost:631/rss/`*feed-name*`.rss`

✔ From another computer: `http://`*host-domain-name*`:631/rss/`*feed-name*`.rss`

Figure 10-13 shows a feed in a web browser, logged on from another computer, with an RSS article from CUPS.

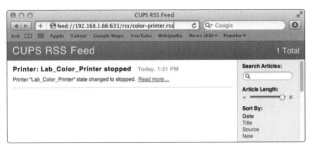

**Figure 10-13:**
An RSS feed generated by CUPS alerts you to a printer problem.

### Manage printers

Most of CUPS' printer management options appear in two pop-up menus on the page for an individual printer or class. To get there, click the Printers (or Classes) tab to get to the list of printers. Click a printer to get to its management page.

Items in the Maintenance pop-up menu (shown in Figure 10-14) are toggled — that is, when you choose Pause Printer, the item changes to Resume Printer the next time you open the menu. Items in this menu may change, depending on the type of printer and its features.

**Figure 10-14:**
The Maintenance menu on a printer's management page in CUPS.

The Administration pop-up menu contains items that take you to another page with more settings. Here are a few of them:

- ✔ **Modify Printer** is the place to go if you suspect that your printer is set up incorrectly. It takes you to the printer's configuration page, where you set the printer protocol and other items.

- ✔ **Set Default Options** includes a number of options, including print resolution, paper trays, and two-sided printing.

- ✔ **Set Allowed Users** lets you modify the users and groups that can or can't access the printer.

### Manage print jobs in the CUPS interface

You can manage print jobs from multiple places. For example, you can move jobs between printers, although not as easily as with System Preferences. Figure 10-14 shows that you can move print jobs from a printer's management page. You can also do this from the Jobs tab.

The Jobs tab lists all printing jobs sent to the queues for your shared printers. You can filter jobs with a search field and a button for completed jobs.

The entry for each job displays the status (such as Printer Not Responding or In Process). The Jobs tab also contains buttons to cancel a print job or send it to another printer (Move Job). Clicking one of these buttons brings up another window, where you choose the printer to move the job to.

To see a list of jobs for an individual printer or class only, go to the maintenance page for that printer or class. The jobs in the queue are listed at the bottom.

### View logs and edit configuration file

The Administration tab (refer to Figure 10-7) lets you view three different logs, including an error log, which is useful for troubleshooting.

Edit Configuration File brings up a field where you can edit lines. It's handy to have because you don't need to go to Terminal to edit the file. But don't even think of touching this field unless you know what you're doing.

### A note on the CUPS command line

One of the major features that the CUPS web interface provides is detailed documentation of the Unix commands that you can use in Terminal and how you can manually edit various configuration files. In fact, the Help system (accessible from the Help tab) is geared almost entirely to the text interface.

Some of the text commands, such as printing on both sides of paper, are oriented to the user. But there are many useful commands for printer servers. Notably, you use the command line to set print quotas — something you can't do anywhere else in Mac OS X. (This command is described in the help topic called Printer Accounting Basics.)

If you're interested in learning how to use text commands, the place to start is the Getting Started link, followed by the Command-Line Printing and Options link. This tutorial starts at the beginning with the print command: lP *filename*.

# Don't Forget Your Clients

You probably know how to enable your Mac and Windows clients to print. In this section, I point out a few things that are helpful to know when your clients connect to Mac OS X Server. I also mention some things you might want to remember for Mac and Windows clients.

## PPD files

It's helpful for the server and client computers to have the correct PostScript Printer Description (PPD) files for the specific network printer models.

The PPD files enable a user to choose special features, such as double-sided printing and the ability to select specific paper trays. Mac OS X Server and Mac and Windows clients come with plenty of PPD files installed.

When adding a print queue to a client computer, you or the user chooses the PPD on the client by selecting the printer model from a list. If you don't see the PPD file on the client, or if the Mac OS X server doesn't have it, check with the printer manufacturer or the software that came with the printer.

If you don't have a PPD file on the clients or the server for a network printer, the user can probably still print to that printer. Mac OS X identifies the printer as Generic PostScript Printer. Users probably won't have access to special features of that particular printer model.

## *Helping Mac clients print*

Since the earliest models, Macs have been good at printing, with easy setup and few printing errors. Today, you connect to network printers in System Preferences, in the Print & Scan pane (called Print & Fax in Mac OS X versions before 10.7). This is the same pane that you configure on the server Mac. You can also add a printer in the Print dialog of any application, in the Printer pop-up menu.

When a Mac client prints to a server's queue that's shared via IPP, the user can monitor the progress of the printing in the Print & Fax pane of System Preferences. The user can also delete a print job from the queue.

On a Mac OS X client, to add a print queue that's shared via LPR and advertised through Bonjour, do the following:

1. **Open the Print & Fax (Print & Scan in Lion) pane of System Preferences.**

2. **Click the Add (+) button and then click the Default icon in the toolbar.**

3. **Click a print queue in the list and then click the Print Using pop-up menu to select a PPD file for the printer model.**

   Usually, the correct PPD file is chosen for you. If you can't find it or don't know the printer model, choose Generic PostScript Printer.

4. **Click the Add button.**

If Bonjour isn't used with the LPR protocol, choose the protocol from the Protocol pop-up menu. You also need the IP address or the DNS name of the *server* (not the printer). You may also have to know the queue name.

## Helping Windows clients print

The best thing you can do for Windows clients to your Mac print server is install Bonjour Services for Windows. *Bonjour* is a protocol that Apple created for the advertising and discovery of computers, printers, and other services over a network. Outside of Apple, Bonjour is called ZeroConf or Multicast DNS. (It was also once called Rendezvous.) Mac OS X 10.2 and later clients have Bonjour built in, but Windows doesn't. Apple offers Bonjour for Windows as a free download at `http://support.apple.com/kb/DL999`.

After you install Bonjour in Windows, open the Bonjour Printer Wizard and select a shared printer.

Alternatively, you can use the default (non-Apple) Windows software. Most versions of Windows can send print jobs to the server with SMB. Windows XP, Vista, and Windows 7 support SMB, IPP, and LPR. To connect to print queues on Mac OS X Server, you can use the Add Printer Wizard (see Figure 10-15). To find this wizard, choose Start➪Printers and Faxes and then click Add a Printer.

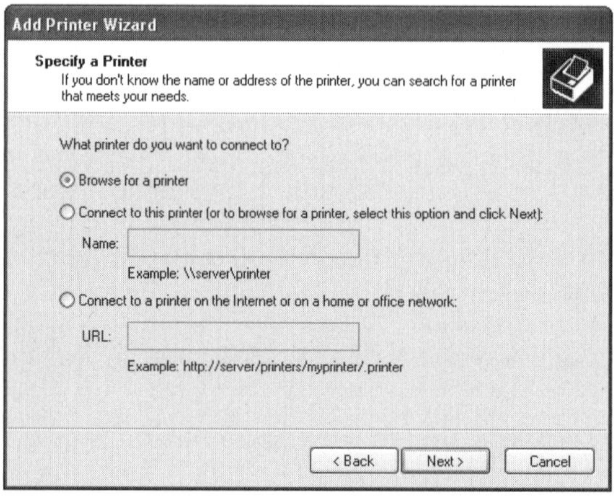

**Figure 10-15:**
The Add
Printer
Wizard in
Windows
XP.

> **Add Printer Wizard**
>
> **Specify a Printer**
> If you don't know the name or address of the printer, you can search for a printer that meets your needs.
>
> What printer do you want to connect to?
>
> ⦿ Browse for a printer
>
> ○ Connect to this printer (or to browse for a printer, select this option and click Next):
>
>    Name:
>
>    Example: \\server\printer
>
> ○ Connect to a printer on the Internet or on a home or office network:
>
>    URL:
>
>    Example: http://server/printers/myprinter/.printer
>
> [ < Back ] [ Next > ] [ Cancel ]

Here, you can either browse for a discoverable print queue or type a printer address. The latter takes this form: `\\servername\printqueuename`.

Keep in mind that the server name is actually the NetBIOS name or a Windows domain server. You can edit this name on the server Mac, which I describe in the section "Turning on print sharing," earlier in this chapter.

You can check the NetBIOS name of the Mac server with Server Admin:

1. **Click the triangle to the left of the server and then choose SMB from the list.**

2. **Click the Settings icon and then click General.**

   The Computer Name field has the NetBIOS name.

If you have trouble finding a print queue shared with SMB, check the name of the print queue. If it's longer than 15 characters, that's a problem. SMB print queue names need to be 15 characters or fewer.

## Helping Linux/Unix clients print

Linux and Unix systems that use CUPS can print to shared printers in Mac OS X. They need to be configured to send print jobs as PostScript, even if the printer hosted by your server Mac is a non-PostScript printer.

Unix/Linux users need the IP address of the network port of the server Mac. This is the port connected to the client's local subnet. You can find this port in the Server app by selecting your server in the sidebar and then selecting the Network tab. Unix/Linux users also need the queue name. You can see the queue name in the Printers tab of the CUPS web interface.

## Printing from iOS devices

iOS devices — iPads, iPhones, and iPod touches — can be enabled to print. They can print to AirPrint with some Hewlett-Packard printers. There's also a Mac application from Netputing (www.netputing.com) called AirPrint Activator 2.0 that lets iOS devices print to any shared or network printer that is visible on your wireless network. (At publishing time, AirPrint didn't yet support Lion.)

# Part IV
# Facilitating User Collaboration

The 5th Wave    By Rich Tennant

"Wow, I didn't know OS X could redirect an e-mail message like that."

# In this part . . .

In the year 1624, John Donne wrote compellingly that "no man is an island, entire of itself." Of course, Donne was talking about collaboration software, also known as *groupware:* e-mail, group scheduling and calendars, text chat, and user-editable web pages.

But Donne wrote his profound reflection *before* Apple shipped Lion Server. He didn't know about some of the stuff that other servers don't provide: a wiki-based collaborative environment, already built when you turn on Lion Server; Address Book Server, an interactive contact manager that users can safely edit without tampering with directory services; Podcast Producer, an automated video workflow system; and iChat, which adds video conferencing to instant messaging.

And Donne didn't know that he could access it all from his iPhone and iPad.

Well, I know it, and I'm sharing it with you in Part IV. It's not profound like *Meditation XVII,* but it does help you serve humankind — or at least your users — with groupware.

# Chapter 11

# Sharing Contacts with Address Book Server

**In This Chapter**

▶ Considering clients for Address Book Server

▶ Configuring Address Book Server

▶ Setting up the Mac Address Book client

▶ Setting up iOS devices to work with Address Book Server

*A*ddress Book Server enables users to share contacts in Lion Server. Address Book Server binds to a network directory, such as Open Directory or Active Directory, and then makes the contacts in the network directory available to users of Mac OS X and iOS handheld devices, as well as some Windows users. These users can search the global address list of the network's directory service. Address Book Server makes contacts available to several Mac applications, including Address Book, Mail, iCal, and iChat. (See Chapters 5 and 6 for more on directory services.) iPhone, iPod touch, and iPad users get access to Address Book Server data through the Contacts and Mail apps.

This chapter describes everything you need to know about setting up Address Book Server.

## Address Book Server and Network Directories

Supporting lots of clients is nice, but here's the key benefit to Address Book Server: It enables *users* to modify contacts and add their own contacts to the server. Changes by users usually aren't possible (or desired) in

Lightweight Directory Access Protocol (LDAP)-based directories, such as Open Directory. Users can also create their own fields for contacts, such as for Twitter names or company-specific information — an unheard-of thought with an LDAP directory. Because Address Book Server acts as kind of a gateway to the directory server, you don't need to give users write permissions to the network directory, and you don't need to modify the LDAP schema.

Address Book Server stores contacts as standard *vCards,* or electronic business cards. The cards are stored outside the Open Directory or other LDAP directory. Users can e-mail or drag vCards to the Desktop for sharing. Address Book clients connected to Address Book Server are authenticated from Open Directory and Kerberos.

# Clients for Address Book Server

Apple's Mac and iOS devices have built-in support for Address Book Server, which uses an open standard, *CardDAV,* to communicate. Like CalDAV for iCal Server, CardDAV is based on WebDAV and Hypertext Transfer Protocol (HTTP). Because these are open standards, client software for Windows can take advantage of Address Book Server.

## Mac, iPhone, iPad, and iPod touch support

Mac OS X 10.6 clients and later come with several applications that support CardDAV and work with Address Book Server. These apps include Address Book 5, which comes with Mac OS X 10.6 Snow Leopard, and Address Book 6 in the Mac OS X 10.7 Lion client.

Mail 4.0 and iChat 5.0 (and later) can access the contacts supplied by Address Book Server. In Mail 4 and 5, you configure Address Book Server connections in the Mail Preferences Composing pane. iChat 5 and 6 can locate users and groups provided by Address Book Server.

To configure the Address Book 5 and 6 client, see the section "Setting Up a User's Address Book Client," later in the chapter.

For iPads, iPhones, and iPod touches running iOS 4.0 and later, the Contacts app can display and add contacts located in Address Book Server. The section "Setting up an iPad, iPhone, or iPod touch," later in this chapter, describes how to set up your iOS devices.

## Windows clients for Address Book Server

CardDAV Windows clients that support Address Book Server are not common, but can be found. Here are two solutions:

✔ **eM Client** (www.emclient.com) is commercial software for Windows Vista and Windows 7, an all-in-one mail, contacts, and calendar application.

✔ **SOGo Connector for Thunderbird** (www.sogo.nu) is free, open source software for Windows and Linux. It's a plug-in for Thunderbird, the open source e-mail and news client from Mozilla Foundation. SOGo Connector enables Thunderbird to access CardDAV servers. Although the main piece of software you'll see at the SOGo website is the SOGo groupware server, you don't need the SOGo server to get Thunderbird to work with Address Book Server.

# Prerequisites

You don't really need to do much to your network to make Address Book Server available to users. You don't even have to alter the directory. One requirement, though, is that the Mac you run Address Book Server on needs to be configured as an Open Directory master (described in Chapter 6). This configuration is necessary because Address Book client users are provisioned in Open Directory. This means that the directory services provide the authentication and access privileges.

As an option, a DNS entry can be helpful. And as with all services, you may need port forwarding if users access the service from the Internet.

## Optional DNS

Although it's not a requirement, you can add a *service record* (SRV record) for CardDAV to a DNS server to help clients connect to the Address Book service, particularly across the Internet. The service record can be on the DNS service running in Mac OS X Server or on another server. The port number used depends on whether you're using a Secure Sockets Layer (SSL) certificate for Address Book service.

If you're using an SSL certificate, the SRV record should map `carddavs._tcp` for port 8443 of the server's hostname:

```
carddavs._tcp 86400 IN SRV 0 1 8443 our server.company.com
```

If you're not using SSL for Address Book service, add a record that maps `_carddav._tcp` for port 8008 to the server hostname. For example:

```
carddavs._tcp 86400 IN SRV 0 1 8008 server.example.com
```

If you're running DNS service in Lion Server, you can use the graphical interface of Server Admin to create an SRV record in a DNS Zone. You type **carddavs._tcp** in the Service Type field. Type **8443** or **8008** in the Port field. Chapters 3 and 14 have more about configuring DNS in Lion Server.

## Internet access through a router

If you want users to access Address Book Server from the Internet through a DSL or cable router or other Internet router, you need to configure the router for port forwarding (also called port mapping). *Port forwarding* protects your network against attacks while still permitting Address Book users on the Internet to access the server.

With port forwarding, you set the router to forward traffic from the service port numbers to your server's IP address (shown in the Server app's Hardware pane). For Address Book service, the port numbers are SSL 8443 with SSL security or 8008 without SSL. Check your router's instructions on how to configure it.

If you have an Apple router — AirPort Extreme Base Station (802.11n version) or Time Capsule — you can manage it from the Server app. You use AirPort Utility to set the device's Connection Sharing option to Share a Public IP Address. You also need to set the IPv6 mode to Tunnel by choosing Settings➪Advanced. When you're finished, the Apple router appears in the Server app's sidebar under Hardware. Click it to configure port mapping.

See Chapter 18 for more on using the Server app for port forwarding with Apple routers.

## Setting Up Address Book Server

To start Address Book Server, launch the Server app. Click the Address Book icon and then click the big switch to the On position, as shown in Figure 11-1.

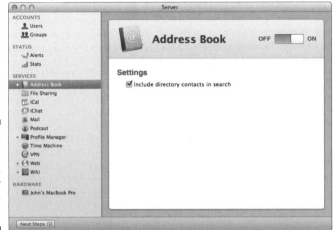

**Figure 11-1:**
Turning on
Address
Book Server
in the
Server app.

If you're familiar with Snow Leopard Server, note that Lion Server no longer uses Server Admin to manage Address Book Server. Another change is that several parameters that were available in Mac OS X Server 10.6 aren't configurable from a graphical user interface. These parameters include the location of the data store, the user quota (which is set at 100MB of Address Book data per user), and the level of detail recorded in the error log file.

To see all Address Book's settings using the command line, open the Terminal utility and type the following:

```
sudo serveradmin settings addressbook
```

If you're familiar with configuring with Unix commands, you can change most of these settings by adding a colon followed by the setting, and then the configuration value. For example, to set the SSL port number to 8443, type this:

```
sudo serveradmin settings addressbook:SSLPort = 8443
```

One thing you can't change with the command line is the location of the data store.

## Enabling user access

You can enable or disable all users or specific users from having access to Address Book Server. In the Server app, click Users in the sidebar. Click a username or select multiple users by ⌘-clicking. Now click the gear icon and select Edit Access to Services. In the Server Access dialog that appears, you can select (or deselect) Address Book and other services.

# Enabling Secure Sockets Layer (SSL) security

You can turn on SSL (Secure Sockets Layer) data encryption for Address Book and other services by specifying a digital certificate to use. I recommend always using SSL with Address Book to protect sensitive contact data.

Here's how to turn on SSL:

1. **In the Server app, click the name of your server under Hardware in the left column.**

2. **Click the Settings tab.**

3. **Click the Edit button next to SSL Certificate.**

4. **To turn on SSL for all services, click the Certificate pop-up menu and select a certificate, or select None to turn off SSL for all services.**

5. **To turn on SSL specifically for Address Book Server, click the arrows next to iCal and Address Book and select a certificate (see Figure 11-2).**

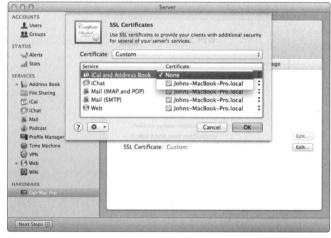

**Figure 11-2:**
Enabling SSL encryption for iCal and Address Book Services.

Lion Server comes with a self-assigned SSL certificate that you use for secure services. If you don't see a certificate, open the Next Steps panel at the bottom of the Server application, click the Review Certificates button, and follow the directions. You can use a certificate obtained from a third-party certificate authority or your company's own certificate authority.

You can find more information about SSL and certificates in Chapter 18.

## Enabling push notification

You can enable push notification to let Lion Server notify Macs and iPhones, iPod touches, and iPads of changes to data in the network Address Book. (iCal and Mail service also can use push notification.) Push notification works for clients running Mac OS X 10.6 and later and iOS 3.0 and later. Push notification uses security certificates from Apple, which you can obtain with the Server app.

To turn on push notifications, open the Server application and select your server under Hardware in the left column. Click the Settings tab and then click the check box next to Enable Apple Push Notifications (see Figure 11-3). Click the Edit button to the right.

**Figure 11-3:** Turning on push notifications.

Next, a dialog called Apple Push Notification Service Certificate appears, asking you for an Apple ID and password. You can type the ID you use for your iTunes account, though Apple recommends that you create a new Apple ID for your organization. You can follow the instructions in this dialog to create a new Apple ID, if you need it.

If you already have an Apple ID, type it and click Get Certificate. If you already have a certificate from Apple, you can also renew it here. (See Chapter 18 for more about certificates.)

## Backing up the data store

Address Book Server stores information in the form of vCards, which have filenames ending in .vcf. vCards are also created when a Mac user drags a contact from the Address Book application to the Desktop. On the server, every network Address Book Server user has a folder containing a vCard for each of the user's contacts.

The *data store* is the directory in which Address Book Server stores the vCards, one file for each contact. If you want to back up Address Book Server data, the data store is located in the directory `/var/pgsql`.

This the same data based used to store information for the iCal, Profile Manager, webmail, and wiki services. Unfortunately, Lion Server no longer provides a way to change the location of the data store, in case you wanted to store this data on a RAID, Xsan, or other storage device.

# Upgrading Contacts from Mac OS X Server Version 10.5

Mac OS X Server 10.5 didn't have Address Book Server but instead had something called Shared Contacts. Although you can't upgrade a 10.5 Server to Lion Server, you can migrate version 10.5.8 to Lion Server. (Migration is described in Chapter 3.) But before you use Lion's Server Assistant to automate the migration, you need to manually migrate the old Address Book Server's Shared Contacts. The only way to do this is from the command line within Terminal (in the `/Applications/Utilities` folder). Here's how:

1. **Log in to the server and launch Terminal.**

2. **Type the following command on one line, replacing the italics with your own information:**

```
/usr/sbin/ContactsMigrator -s /LDAPv3/serverName -d http://
        yourserverName:8800/addressbooks/groups/mygroup/addressbook/ -u
        username -p password
```

The server name is the fully qualified domain name of your Address Book Server. The username and password are those of the system administrator. Note also that in this example, 8800 is the port number; if you're using another port number (such as 8843 for SSL), type that number.

# Setting Up Users' Client Devices

You need to configure the client devices to connect to Address Book Server. In this section, I show you how to configure both Macs and iOS devices.

Setting up Windows CardDAV clients depends on the third-party software you use, so I'm not discussing that here. (See the section "Windows clients for Address Book Server," earlier in the chapter.)

You can also use Profile Manager to accomplish some client configuration tasks from the server for Lion clients and iOS devices. I describe how to do so in Chapter 16.

## Setting up a user's Address Book client

Enabling a user's Address Book (version 5 or 6) to access Address Book Server is referred to as *binding* the client to the server. After you bind, users are authenticated from Open Directory or Kerberos. To bind from the user's Address Book client in Mac OS X 10.6 and 10.7:

1. **Launch Address Book on the Mac client machine.**

2. **Click the Address Book menu and select Preferences.**

3. **Click the Accounts icon in the toolbar and then click the Add (+) button.**

   The Add Account dialog slides down, as shown in Figure 11-4.

4. **From the Account Type pop-up menu, choose CardDAV.**

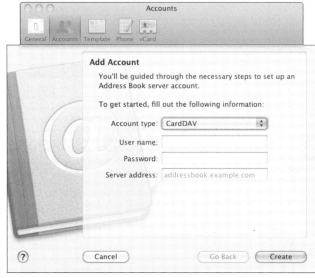

**Figure 11-4:**
Setting up a
Mac user's
Address
Book for
Address
Book
service.

5. **Type the username, password, and server hostname.**

   For example, type `ourserver.macwindowsco.com`.

6. **Click the Create button.**

   The account is now in the Accounts list at the left of the preferences window. When selected, the window displays the account information.

Figure 11-5 shows the Address Book Preferences window in Mac OS X 10.6. In the Mac OS X 10.7 client, this window is almost identical except that the Refresh Contacts menu has been renamed Fetch.

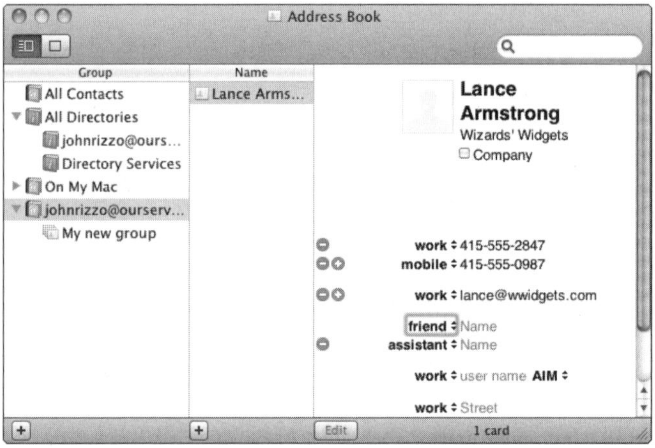

**Figure 11-5:**
The Address Book client's Preferences window shows the server binding.

If you click the Server Settings tab, you can turn on SSL for this client's connection to Address Book Server. You can also change the port number (use 8843 for SSL).

Figure 11-6 shows the Address Book 6 client in Lion. The server appears in the left page as an entry below the On My Mac area. When selected, it turns blue, and the names stored on the server are displayed on the right. The user can search the Address Book Server and Open Directory in the search field. The user can also add a new contact to the server by choosing File➪New Card.

Address Book Client 5 in Mac OS X 10.6 looks and works differently. The Address Book Server appears as a group with the user's name. The user can select it and click the Add (+) button in the Name column. The other users can now see this contact. Additionally, an All Directories group appears, with the new group (on Address Book Server) and the network directory both colored blue. You use these for searching. Click Directory Services, and you can search Open Directory from the search field.

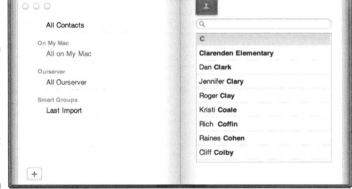

**Figure 11-6:**
Address
Book Server
appears in
the Address
Book client
in Mac OS
X 10.7.

# Setting up an iPad, iPhone, or iPod touch

To enable a device running iOS 4.0 and later to access Address Book Server, do the following:

1. **Tap the Settings app.**

2. **Tap Mail, Contacts, Calendars.**

3. **Under Accounts, tap Add Account.**

4. **Tap Other.**

5. **Under Contacts, tap Add CardDAV Account.**

6. **Type the Address Book Server's DNS name and the username and password in the appropriate fields.**

   Once connected, the Address Book Server shows up in the iOS device's Contacts app, under Groups.

# Chapter 12

# Sharing Calendars with iCal Server

- - - - - - - - - - - - - - - - - - - - - - - - - - - - - - - - - - - - - - - - - - - - - - - -

## In This Chapter

▶ Choosing clients for iCal Server

▶ Getting your network ready for iCal Server

▶ Setting up DNS

▶ Setting up calendar service

▶ Creating resources to reserve

▶ Setting up iCal clients

- - - - - - - - - - - - - - - - - - - - - - - - - - - - - - - - - - - - - - - - - - - - - - - -

*L*ion Server comes with iCal Server 3, a collaboration tool that enables users to share calendars and To Dos, schedule meetings and tasks, and include attachments. When scheduling an event, a user can check whether the people invited are available. iCal Server 3 adds the ability of users to delegate calendars. If a user delegates a calendar to others, those people can use a web browser to view the delegated calendars.

iCal Server is simple to set up. In this chapter, I describe how to get iCal Server up and running.

## iCal Server and Notifications

iCal Server works with Lion Server's push notification, which lets users (including iPhone and iPad users) instantly know about calendar changes that other users make. Notification pushes out just what's changed to clients that have subscribed to the update system (and that have been authenticated to receive updates). The server contacts clients only when new data is available.

Lion Server also provides e-mail notification of invitations to users who don't have iCal-compatible client software — or even to users who don't have calendar accounts. And with the ability to delegate calendars, users with web browsers can access iCal Server's calendar on any computer.

With, iCal Server, multiple users can update an existing event. Event attendees can add private comments to events that only they and the event organizer can see. Invitations are processed by the calendar server, freeing up the client's resources.

# Clients for iCal Server

iCal Server is based on the open CalDAV standard (Calendaring Extensions to WebDAV), which means that client calendaring applications must also be CalDAV-compatible. Not surprising, all of Apple's calendar clients for Mac and iOS (iPhone, iPad, and iPod touch) use CalDAV.

In addition to CalDAV compatibility, some calendar clients are compatible with Mac OS X Server's push notification service. These include iCal in Mac OS X 10.6 and later, and iOS 3 and later clients.

There are CalDAV clients for Windows, Linux, and older versions of Mac OS X that work with iCal Server to various degrees. The following clients support the CalDAV standard:

- ✔ **eM Client:** From E&S Software Ltd, this is a commercial messaging client for Windows. In addition to CalDAV and Google Calendar, it supports e-mail, contacts, and tasks.

    `www.emclient.com`

- ✔ **Mozilla Sunbird and Lightning:** These are two open source clients available for Mac OS X, Windows, Linux, and Unix. Sunbird is a stand-alone calendar client. Lightning is an extension for the Thunderbird e-mail client. (From the people who bring you the Firefox web browser.)

    `www.mozilla.org/projects/calendar`

- ✔ **Chandler:** From the Open Software Application Foundation, Chandler is an open source calendar and tasks program for Windows, Mac OS X, and Linux.

    `www.chandlerproject.org`

- ✔ **GNOME Evolution:** For Linux and Unix, this is an e-mail, calendar, and contact client for users of the GNOME desktop interface. Evolution requires the CalDAV plug-in to be installed.

    `http://projects.gnome.org/evolution`

Of course, the client that is glaringly missing from this list is Microsoft Outlook. Neither the Windows or Mac version supports CalDAV, and neither can be used with iCal Server. There is an open source plug-in for Outlook for

Windows — the Outlook Connector Project with Microsoft Outlook (`http://sourceforge.net/projects/otlkcon`) — but at publishing time, it hasn't been updated in over two years. Try at your own risk.

iCal Server and push notification service are based on open standards. The calendaring functionality uses CalDAV, which is based on WebDAV, which is based on Hypertext Transfer Protocol (HTTP). The push-subscriber technology uses the Extensible Messaging and Presence Protocol (XMPP), which is based on Extensible Markup Language (XML). XMMP sends a small message (like a tweet) to the client, telling it that new data exists. The client then fetches that data.

# Prerequisites

iCal Server requires a few things on your network before you can start using it:

- ✔ If a firewall is between iCal Server and your users, it needs to be configured to allow traffic on TCP port 8008 (or 8443 for Secure Sockets Layer [SSL] encryption).
- ✔ iCal Server needs directory service.
- ✔ iCal Server works best with a DNS system with full reverse lookups running on the network.

Sound simple? Maybe yes, maybe no.

## Directory service for iCal service

iCal Server must be connected to a directory server of some type on the network. This could be Open Directory running on the same server as iCal Server. You don't need to modify LDAP (Lightweight Directory Access Protocol) and Active Directory systems to designate calendar users.

Open Directory could be located on the same Mac server or on another server computer (Mac OS X 10.5 Server or later), or the directory could be another non-Apple LDAP server or Microsoft's Active Directory.

## Setting up DNS for iCal service

DNS isn't required for iCal Server, but DNS can make it work better. Clients use DNS to keep track of iCal Servers, a self-discovery feature. To enable this feature, you can create a *Service (SRV)* record in each DNS zone that has the CalDAV calendar service. The SRV record needs to be in a special format as well.

### Adding a DNS SRV record for iCal Server in Lion Server

If you're using Lion Server for your DNS service, you can use Server Admin to add an SRV record for iCal Server. You add it to the DNS zone that your server is in. If you had Open Directory created during setup, the Setup Assistant will have created Primary and Reverse Zones; in this case, you'd create the SRV record in the Primary Zone. Here's how to create the SRV record for iCal Server:

1. **In Server Admin, click the triangle to the left of your server name in the left column to expand the list of services.**

2. **Click DNS in the list of services.**

3. **Click the Zones icon in the toolbar.**

4. **Click to select the zone that the server is located in.**

   This may be the Primary Zone, as indicated in the Type column.

5. **Click the Add Record button and select Add Service (SRV) from the pop-up menu.**

   A new SRV record is created.

6. **Type the following in the fields in the bottom half of the window (see Figure 12-1):**

   - *Service Name:* Leave this field blank.

   - *Service Type:* If you aren't using SSL for iCal, type **_caldav._tcp**. If you're using SSL, type **_caldavs._tcp**.

     Be sure to include the underscores.

   - *Host:* Type your server's DNS name (include a period at the end).

   - *Port:* If you aren't using SSL for iCal, enter **8008**. Type **8443** if you're using SSL.

   - *Priority* and *Weight:* Type **0** in each field. (See the next section for an explanation of when you might use other numbers.)

   - *TXT:* Leave this field blank.

7. **Click the Save button.**

The next section describes what these terms mean. It also describes the format of the SRV record if you're using a command line to edit the zone record configuration file by hand in Lion Server or other DNS servers.

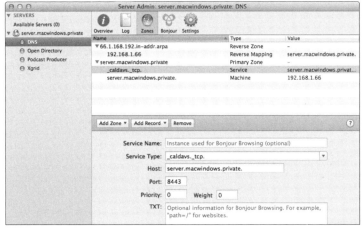

**Figure 12-1:**
Using
Server
Admin to
add a SRV
record to
DNS for iCal
Server.

### DNS SRV record format for iCal Server

On any DNS server, the SRV record needs to be in this format (on one line):

```
_caldav._tcp.example.com. 86400 IN SRV 0 0 8008 calendar.example.com.
```

The _caldav._ term is for a standard connection. If you're using a secure SSL connection, use _caldavs._ instead.

The standard port number is 8008. For SSL connections, use port 8443.

The 0 0 after SRV represent the priority and weight. These are 0 if only one CalDAV server is on the network. If multiple CalDAV servers are on the network, use numbers other than 0.

The 86400 represents the DNS time-to-live number, in seconds. 86400 is one day, but you can use another time period.

### Sample DNS zone record file for Lion Server

Because DNS for iCal can be tricky if you're editing by hand, I include a sample here. There references are to Lion Server, but you can adopt the procedure to other DNS servers. If you used Server Admin and it works, you can skip this section.

In Mac OS X Server (and some Linux/Unix servers), the DNS zone file that you edit is in the /var/named directory. The file has the form db.*domainname*, such as db.ourserver.macwindowsco.com. To access it in the Finder, choose Go➪Go to Folder and then type **/var/named**. Open the file and type your additions *after* the line that begins with $INCLUDE /var/zones/db. *Do not* delete or change this line.

This INCLUDE line inserts your additions into another similarly named file in /var/named/zone. Although you don't edit this file directly, here's a sample of the file in /var/named/zone to give you an idea of what the final looks like. This file contains the DNS entities called *A records* that are referenced in the SRV records. The text after the semicolons represents in-code comments.

```
;GUID=<GUID here>
$TTL 10800          ; default expiration time of a record
abc.com. IN SOA ns.abc.com. username.abc.com. (
     2009031903     ;Serial
     86400          ;Refresh
     3600           ;Retry
     604800         ;Expire
     345600         ;Negative caching TTL
     )
abc.com.  IN  NS    ns.abc.com.  ;ns.abc.com is the name server for abc.com
abc.com.  IN  A     10.0.0.1     ;this is the IP address of  abc.com
ns              A   10.0.0.2 ; IP address of ns.abc.com
name            CNAME ns       ;"name.abc.com" is another name for "ns.abc.
           com"
calendar     IN  A     10.0.0.12  ; the IP address for "calendar.abc.com"
                TXT    "The iCal Server that we're using"
ical         IN  CNAME calendar.abc.com. ;"ical.example.com" is another name
                for "calendar.example.com"
_caldav._tcp.abc.com.  86400 IN SRV 0 0 8008 calendar.abc.com.
```

If you have a backup server to use when the first is down, add another calendar line:

```
calendar2    IN  A     10.0.0.13
```

Then add another SRV line at the end:

```
_caldav._tcp.abc.com. 86400 IN SRV 1 0 8008 calendar2.abc.com.
```

For SSL, the CalDAV line(s) is

```
_caldavs._tcp.abc.com. 86400 IN SRV 0 0 8443 calendar.abc.com.
_caldavs._tcp.abc.com. 86400 IN SRV 1 0 8443 calendar2.abc.com.
```

# Setting Up iCal Service

Unlike previous versions of Mac OS X Server, Lion Server does not let you administer iCal Server from Server Admin; it's all done from the Server app. However, you can no longer do some things with Lion Server that you could do in previous versions of Mac OS X Server. For example, you can no longer change the location of the data store or the maximum size of an attachment to a calendar.

Here's what you can do with the Server app:

- ✔ Turn on iCal Server.
- ✔ Enable e-mail invitations.
- ✔ Enable SSL.
- ✔ Add locations and resources.
- ✔ Turn on push notification.

I describe how to do these tasks in the following sections.

## Starting iCal service

After getting your network ready, just a few mouse clicks get iCal Server running:

1. **In the Server app, click the iCal icon.**

2. **Click the big switch to the On position (see Figure 12-2).**

   You're done.

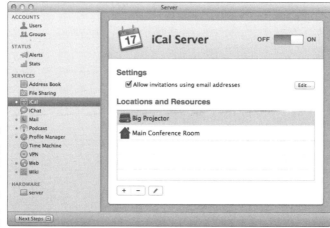

**Figure 12-2:**
The iCal Server pane of the Server app.

## Enabling e-mail notification

The Allow Invitations Using Email Addresses check box in the Server app's iCal pane enables the sending and accepting of meeting invitations by e-mail. This feature is available for users who don't have an iCal Server account, but not for those who do. Users of iCal in Mac OS X 10.6 and later use iCal client for sending and accepting invitations. Basically, the hostname of the attendee's e-mail must be different from the hostname of the iCal Server.

The way this works is that when an iCal user invites someone who is not an iCal user, the iCal Server sends an e-mail to that person. When that person responds, she sends an e-mail to the iCal Server's e-mail address. Thus, in order for the iCal Server to send and receive e-mail, it must have an e-mail account itself.

So a prerequisite for turning on iCal's e-mail notification feature is having your own e-mail server (either hosted in Lion Server or elsewhere) or e-mail with your domain, where iCal Server has an account (such as `iCalServer@ acme.com`).

Then, back on iCal Server, you have to tell it what the POP/IMAP and SMTP server information is — just as you would when setting up a user's e-mail client software. This is exactly what you do to enable iCal e-mail notification. Here's how:

1. **In the Server app's iCal Server pane, make sure that the check box next to Allow Invitations Using Email Addresses is checked.**

2. **Click the Edit button next to Allow Invitations Using Email Addresses.**

   The Configure Email Address dialog appears.

3. **Type an e-mail address that you'd like the server to use to notify users of invitations and then click Next.**

   The Server Email Address dialog appears.

4. **Enter the name of the incoming POP or IMAP mail server and the username and password and then click Next.**

5. **Enter the name of the outgoing SMTP mail server, select an authentication type (Kerberos, CRAM-MD5, or none), and enter the username and password; click Next.**

   A summary screen shows you the configuration you just entered. You can click the Back button to make a correction or click the Finish button. iCal Server will restart after you click Finish.

# *Using SSL encryption*

To enable SSL encryption with iCal Server, you simply assign an encryption certificate to the iCal service. You can use the self-signed certificate that Lion Server's setup process created (which users will have to manually accept) or a signed certificate from a certificate authority. (See Chapter 18 for more on SSL certificates.)

You can use the Server app to assign an SSL certificate to iCal server:

1. **In the Server app, under Hardware, select your server and click the Settings tab.**

2. **Click the Edit button next to SSL Certificate.**

   If your running services have different SSL settings (such as different certificates or some with No SSL assigned), you see a list of services and their SSL settings, as shown in Figure 12-3.

   If all your services have the same setting, the dialog displays only the Certificate menu, with either the word *None* or the name of the certificate. If this is the case, click the menu and select Custom to arrive at the screen in Figure 12-3.

3. **Click the arrows to the right of iCal and Address Book and select a certificate from the pop-up menu.**

4. **Click OK.**

**Figure 12-3:**
Enabling
SSL encryption for iCal
Server.

## Creating resources and locations

In addition to creating events and inviting people to them, users can reserve locations, such as meeting rooms, or resources, such as projectors or other equipment. In iCal Server, resources and locations share some of the attributes of users and groups, in that they can accept event invitations. When booking a room, iCal Server checks whether the time period is free and accepts the booking like an event invitation. Users can include resources and locations in invitations along with people they're inviting.

Resources and locations each get their own calendar. You can have iCal Server accept invitations if the resource or location is free or mark it as "busy" if it's not. You can also delegate approval of invitations so that a real user approves the use of a resource.

A third option is to have the iCal Server accept invitations automatically, while assigning a delegate to view and edit the calendar of a resource or location.

You use the Server app to add resources and locations. (Snow Leopard Server's iCal Server Utility is gone.) Follow these steps:

1. **In the iCal Server pane of the Server app, click the Add (+) button near the bottom of the window.**

2. **Click the Type menu and select Location or Resource.**

3. **Type a name for the item in the Name field.**

4. **Click the Accept Invitations menu and choose Automatically or With Delegate Approval (see Figure 12-4).**

5. **(Optional) Type the name of a user to be a delegate.**

   Delegates must be users with accounts in the network directory that the server is bound to (including Open Directory service running on your server Mac). As you type in the Delegate field, a drop-down menu appears with suggestions and a Browse command, giving you a list of all users in the directory.

   Note that you can add a delegate and still set Accept Invitations to Automatic.

6. **Click Done.**

The item you created appears in the Locations and Resources list. You can go back and edit an item in this list by selecting it and clicking the pencil icon.

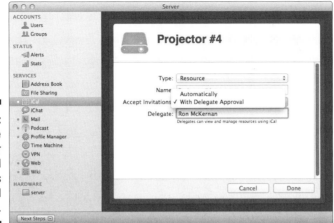

**Figure 12-4:**
Use the
Server
app to add
resources
and
locations.

# Turning on push notification

Without push notification, calendar clients will frequently ask the server if there are updates. With push notification, the client never contacts the server. The server contacts the client only when there's a new event invitation or a change. This lightens the load on the server.

Lion Server's push notification uses an SSL encryption certificate, one where Apple itself is the certificate signing authority. When you turn on push notification in Lion Server, the Server app contacts Apple's Push Notification Service to get a certificate that will be accepted by clients running Mac OS X Lion or iOS. (For other clients, you have to manually accept the certificates.)

Because Apple is the certificate signer, it requires that you use an Apple ID and password. This is the same type of ID that you use to buy songs in iTunes or software from the App Store.

It's not a good idea to use your personal Apple ID, however. Instead, your organization should have its own Apple ID. If you don't have one, the Server app can guide you through getting one.

Follow these steps to turn on push notifications:

1. **In the Server app, under Hardware, select the Lion Server that you want to run push notifications on.**

2. **Click the Settings tab.**

3. **Click the Select Enable Apple Push Notifications check box.**

4. **Type your organization's Apple ID and password and click the Get Certificate button (see Figure 12-5).**

If your organization doesn't have its own Apple ID, click the Create One Now link and follow the directions. Then enter your Apple ID in Step 4.

5. **Click the OK button.**

If you have an existing encryption certificate that has expired, click the Edit button next to Enable Apple Push Notifications. Click the Renew button and then follow the directions.

**Figure 12-5:**
To turn
on push
notification,
you need
to obtain a
certificate
from Apple.

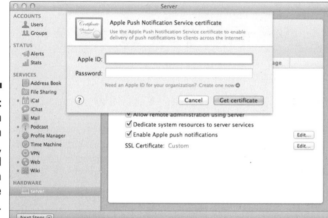

# Supporting iCal 4 Clients

Users with Mac OS X 10.6 get the iCal 4 client, which is Apple's most advanced client for iCal Server 2. This section describes how to get the client running with the server.

## Adding an iCal Server account to an iCal client

To connect the iCal 4 or 5 client (from Mac OS X 10.6 and 10.7) to the server, you add an account in the client. On the user's Mac, open iCal and do the following:

1. **Choose Preferences from the iCal menu and click the Accounts icon.**
2. **Click the Add (+) button at the bottom left of the window.**

   The Add an Account dialog slides down.
3. **In the Account Type pop-up menu, choose CalDAV.**
4. **Type a username (the short name), password, and the server address (myserver.domain.edu, for example).**
5. **Click Create.**

You can now change some of the default settings in the main Account Information tab, as shown in Figure 12-6:

**Figure 12-6:**
The Account Preferences window of the iCal 5 client.

✔ **The Description field** lists the user's domain. You can change this to something more descriptive, such as Office Calendar.

✔ **The Refresh Calendars pop-up menu** sets how the client Mac updates calendar information (including invitations) with the server. The default is Push, which means that the server contacts the client. You can change this to a time interval or manually.

## Creating another server-based calendar using an iCal client

When you create an account, which I describe in the preceding section, you'll see it when you close iCal Preferences. In Lion, the new account appears when you click the Calendars button in the upper left of iCal. In Snow Leopard, the left column of iCal has a Calendars heading. In either iCal client, there are two default calendars: Home and Work. These are local calendars. Below all this is a heading with the name of the Description field you typed in the preceding section. Below the Description field is a server-based calendar that was created and dubbed Calendar by default.

To add another server-based calendar from the iCal client, choose File⇨New Calendar⇨*server* (the name of your description field). Then enter a name for the new calendar.

## Setting a delegate using iCal client

You can set another user to be a delegate, or proxy, for one of your calendars. Delegates can be read-only delegates or read/write delegates. A *read-only delegate* can see everything that the main user can. Delegates for resources or locations can see everything about them, not just whether they're available. A *read/write delegate* can also make changes to another user's calendar.

To create a delegate:

1. **In the iCal client, choose Preferences from the iCal menu and click the Accounts icon.**

2. **Click an account to select it, and on the Delegation tab, click the Edit button.**

3. **Click the Add (+) button in the dialog that appears.**

4. **Type the account name of the user who will be the delegate.**

5. **(Optional) Select the Allow Write check box if you want the delegate to be able to edit your calendar.**

6. **Click Done.**

Delegates must have user accounts in the same authentication directory as the user.

Note that any resources or locations that you are a delegate for will show up in the Delegation tab.

# Chapter 13

# Hosting Websites and Wikis

● ● ● ● ● ● ● ● ● ● ● ● ● ● ● ● ● ● ● ● ● ● ● ● ● ● ● ● ● ● ● ● ● ● ● ● ● ● ● ● ● ● ● ● ● ●

## In This Chapter

▶ Using and managing the built-in wikis, blogs, and calendars

▶ Editing the wiki pages and enhancing navigation

▶ Hosting your own websites

● ● ● ● ● ● ● ● ● ● ● ● ● ● ● ● ● ● ● ● ● ● ● ● ● ● ● ● ● ● ● ● ● ● ● ● ● ● ● ● ● ● ● ● ● ●

*A*ny server can host a website, but Lion Server creates a complete, dynamic site for you, prebuilt. By merely turning on web and Wiki services, every user gets an automatically updated web portal called *My Page*. Users get access to a collaborative environment that includes wikis, blogs, web calendars, and mailing lists. Users can edit these with a few mouse clicks. The site uses *wiki* technology, which enables group editing of content with a web browser. Apple completely rewrote the wiki service in Lion Server, from the low-level database up to the user interface.

Mac OS X Server can also host websites for use in your organization and for publishing to the Internet. Under the hood are the powerful, industry-standard, open source Apache Web server and the PostgreSQL database. But you don't need to know anything about Apache.

This chapter doesn't tell you how to design or build a website. First, I describe the website that Lion Server creates for you. I then describe using the Server app to host your own websites and manage the web services.

## Prerequisites

Before hosting a website, you need to do a few things:

✔ If you want your website to be visible on the Internet, you need to own your domain name and register it with a domain name service, such as Network Solutions. (You can find a complete list of domain name registration services at `http://internic.net`.)

If you just want your users to access your site from the Internet, but don't need others to see it, you don't have to have a registered domain name. Instead, you can have a private domain name (in the form *server.example*.private) along with virtual private networking (VPN) configured. Your users then access your site through a secure (private) connection.

✔ Have domain name service (DNS) configured so that your domain name *resolves* (or points to) the IP address of the web server. This could be on a DNS server on your network or on the Mac server itself, if it's acting as the network's DNS server.

If DNS isn't set up, users have to enter the IP address of the server in their web browsers. (You can find some information on DNS throughout this chapter and in Chapter 3.)

✔ If you're serving content to the Internet, check your firewall. The automatically created website uses port 80 or port 443 if you're using Secure Sockets Layer (SSL) security. You can also change the defaults.

This chapter assumes that you've taken care of these things.

# The Automatically Created Website

Lion Server can set up a sophisticated wiki-based website containing collaboration tools for your user accounts. No HTML coding or design layout is required.

The built-in website is dynamically created and updated and is user-configurable. You can limit users' access to features, or you can give them the whole ball of wax. Users of Macs, Windows, Linux, and Unix can create their own pages, wikis, and blogs, and upload pictures, movies, and audio — all in a web browser, without any coding. And if users want to add some HTML code, they can — again, from the web browser.

Here's what Lion Server creates for you automatically when you have web services turned on:

✔ **A home page:** Lets users get to the web features (see Figure 13-1). To get there, just use your hostname in the form http://*server.example. net* in your browser.

✔ **A personal web page called My Page for each user account:** When a user first clicks the My Page link (see Figure 13-1), the wiki server creates a My Page for the user, to which the user can add a blog, more pages, and files. If a user wants to let others edit content, she can create a wiki. Users see a link to other users' My Page in the People page.

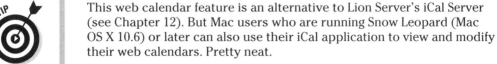

**Figure 13-1:**
The default
web home
page in Mac
OS X Server.

✔ **Blogs:** Each user can create blog entries. In an organization, people can use blogs to distribute FYI-type information rather than clogging e-mail inboxes. This information can later be linked to rather than buried in a mail folder.

✔ **Wikis:** Wikis are great for sharing documents for a work project, posting classroom notes or enabling students to work in teams, or distributing business policies. Each user and group can create a wiki. Users outside the group can have access, if you want.

✔ **Web calendar:** Individual users get their own personal calendars and also have access to shared calendars for groups. Users can choose to create multiple calendars on cither.

This web calendar feature is an alternative to Lion Server's iCal Server (see Chapter 12). But Mac users who are running Snow Leopard (Mac OS X 10.6) or later can also use their iCal application to view and modify their web calendars. Pretty neat.

✔ **Navigation links:** Get to anything from anywhere.

✔ **A Help system for the site:** Readers can see how to navigate as well as create, edit, and administer content.

✔ **Podcasts:** Users can easily subscribe to podcasts, as well as publish and delete podcasts from their web browsers.

✔ **File sharing:** Users can upload and download files or view files without downloading.

✔ **iPhone/iPad support:** Users can access and use the wiki controls from an iOS device.

iOS devices cannot edit the wiki or upload files, however. They also cannot view wiki calendars. They can subscribe to a calendar from the web browser and have the calendar appear synced in the Calendar app. iOS devices can also add tags to items to help organize items.

You get all this simply by turning on web and wiki services. You can choose to disable features you don't need or to customize the site. You can designate a group wiki as the home page. However you change it, Lion Server creates the navigation links, the autoupdates, and the relevant Help system.

Snow Leopard Server users should note that Lion Server's built-in website lacks two features found in version 10.6: the ability to host a listserv and themes. Lion Server's wiki website is significantly easier to use and manage, however.

Another change is that the wiki-based site and data for webmail, Address Book and iCal Servers, and Profile Manager are all stored in the same database, located on the server's boot drive at /var/pgsql. As of the Mac OS X Server 7.0 release, moving this database to another drive is not supported.

You don't need to choose between the preconfigured website and your own site. Lion Server can host multiple websites.

## Supported web browsers

You can access the built-in wiki-based website from anything that has a browser — Windows PCs, iPads, any version of Mac OS X, Linux and Unix PCs, iPhones, and iPod touches. However, in order to have the wiki features work at 100 percent, you need to have fairly recent web browsers. These are the officially supported browsers:

✔ Safari 5 or later for Mac OS X (10.5.8 or later), Windows (XP SP2 or later). Version 5 was released in 2010. The Safari in iOS 4 also works. www. apple.com/safari

✔ Firefox 4 or later for Windows, Mac OS X, and Linux. www.mozilla.org/ firefox

✔ Internet Explorer 9 or later for Windows. www.microsoft.com/ internetexplorer

✔ Google Chrome 1.0 and later for Windows, Mac OS X (10.5 and later), and Linux. www.google.com/chrome

## Navigating the built-in website

Clicking one of the links on the home page (refer to Figure 13-1) brings up a login screen. You can also log in by clicking the lock icon in the upper right of the page. Click the lock again to log out.

Navigation throughout all the pages of the site is best accomplished by using a pop-up navigation bar called the Service Selector, shown in Figure 13-2. To bring it up, click the Service Selector icon in the far upper left of any page. The Service Selector includes the same links as the home page, which is the leftmost link. Here are the other links:

**Figure 13-2:**
The Service
Selector.

- ✔ **Home** takes you back to Figure 13-1.

- ✔ **My Page** takes you to each user's personal My Page page. Users can edit the page, blogs, wikis, and other content here.

- ✔ **Updates** is a list of any changes everywhere on the site, such as new entries in anyone's blog, or changes to any wiki or page.

- ✔ **Wikis** lists all wikis belonging to users and groups.

- ✔ **People** lists other users' My Page pages. A user's My Page doesn't show up in People until the user makes changes to the default page.

- ✔ **Podcasts** (not shown in the figure) appears only if you're running pod-cast service (described in Chapter 15). Clicking it brings up a list of podcasts. Here, you can subscribe to a podcast, which means that new episodes appear in iTunes.

These descriptions apply to items that a user has permission to see. Items that a user doesn't have read permission for won't appear in the lists.

## Creating a new wiki and setting access

Both administrators and users can create a wiki. Just follow these steps:

1. **Bring up the Create New Wiki dialog.**

   You can bring up this dialog in one of two ways:

   • From the Server app, administrators can create a wiki from a Group's page. Click Groups in the sidebar and double-click the name of a group in the list. Then click the Create Group Wiki button.

   • From one of the web pages of the built-in website, a user can click the Add (+) button in the upper right and choose New Wiki (see Figure 13-3).

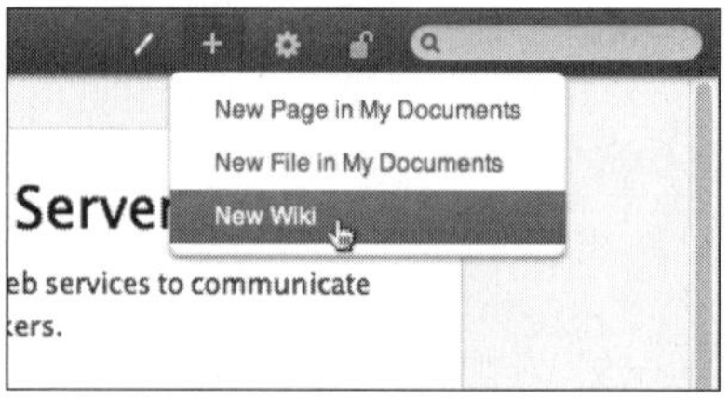

**Figure 13-3:** Creating a new wiki.

2. **In the Create a New Wiki dialog (see Figure 13-4), type a name and description for the wiki and then click Next.**

   Optionally, before clicking Next, click the Upload Image button to add a photo or image to be the icon for the wiki. A 48-x-48-pixel image is optimal, but any image will work.

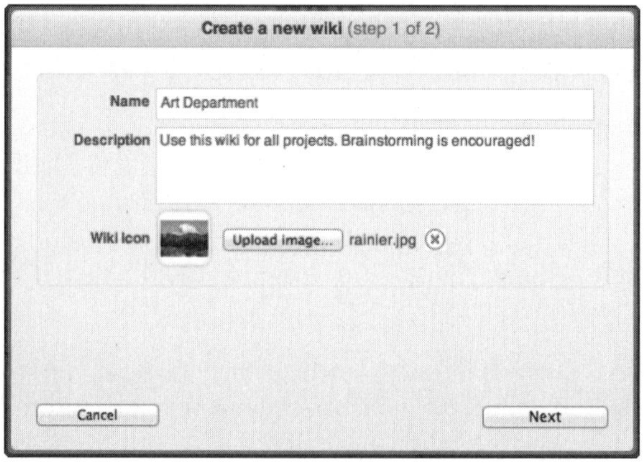

**Figure 13-4:** The Create a New Wiki dialog creates a name, description, and icon for the wiki.

3. **In the Set Wiki Access dialog, choose an access permission for each type of user.**

   By default, three items appear: you (the owner); Any Other Logged In User; and All Guests. For each, you have the following choices from the pop-up menus: Owner (can change settings), Read and Write, Read Only, and No Access. (Here, you're creating a type of access control list, used in file sharing, as described in Chapter 8.)

4. **To add another user or group, type a name in the empty field at the top, hit Return, and then choose a type of permission.**

   In Figure 13-5, I've added the name of a group account: Art Department.

**Figure 13-5:** Add users and groups and set access permissions for the new wiki.

5. **Click the Create button and then click the Go to Wiki button.**

   The home page for the new wiki appears, in editing mode.

6. **Make changes by clicking the pencil icon in the toolbar.**

You can now also create a new page for the wiki by choosing the Add (+) menu in the upper right and selecting New Page from the pop-up menu. Users who don't have write permissions for the wiki won't see this option in the menu.

## Editing wikis, blogs, and pages

Users can edit wiki pages and blogs for which they have write permissions. This includes the home page, your My Page, and other pages. You can edit from a web browser by following these steps:

1. **Navigate to the page you want to edit.**

   For a blog, click the a blog post title to bring up an individual post. You can't edit blog posts while viewing the entire blog.

2. **Click the pencil icon in the toolbar to take you into edit mode.**

   A new editing toolbar replaces the standard toolbar, as shown in Figure 13-6. Hovering over a toolbar icon brings up a description of the icon's function. Here's what's in the toolbar:

   • To edit text on the page, simply place the cursor on the page or select text and type.

   • Formatting and arranging text.

   • The curved arrow icon lets you create a link for selected text.

   • The musical notes icon inserts movies or audio.

   • The paper-clip icon lets you attach a file to the page.

**Figure 13-6:**
The editing toolbar lets you edit text, add links and photos, and more.

   • The square icon inserts a table.

   • The box icon lets you add a bit of HTML to the page's content. You can use standard HTML tags.

3. **Click the Save button on the editing toolbar when finished.**

## Using comments, tags, and notifications

Document pages have a right-side sidebar called Document Info, which contains several collaboration and navigation tools, as shown in Figure 13-7. (Wiki main pages have a truncated version. The full version is for documents that belong to wikis or My Pages.) You can expand a set of topic heads by clicking the triangles next to them. Under each topic head, you can also add content by clicking the Add (+) button to the right of each item. Click the check mark when you're done.

If you're viewing the site from an iPad, you need to be holding it in landscape mode. Only then does the Document Info sidebar appear.

**Figure 13-7:**
The
Document
Info sidebar
contains
collabora-
tion and
navigation
features.

## Tags

Expanding the Tags section lets you view and add tags that help identify it and link the page and link to related pages. Clicking a tag brings up a list of pages, blogs posts, and files that are also marked with that tag. Users can tag pages that are related for easy location and then filter pages by a tag. You might tag pages with a project name, topic, or other common identifiers.

To add a tag to the current page, click the Add (+) button and type a word. The browser will fill in the word if the tag already exists. Tags you add here are visible in other places on the site. For example, they appear in the Tags item in the toolbar, which is available on different types of pages throughout the site. That Tags toolbar item brings up a list of *all* tags used in the site, not just on the viewed page.

## Related

Expanding the Related heading displays a list of pages that have been marked as related to the current page. Click a page to go to it. To add a page to the list, click the Add (+) button and select an existing page from the pop-up menu.

### Comments

Although Figure 13-7 shows one comment, this expanded heading can show a number of comments about the current page, kind of like a mini discussion forum. Click the Add (+) button and type your comment in the thought balloon. Shorter comments tend to work better in this format, so bone up on your Twitter skills.

### History, Notifications, and Sharing

The History heading displays a list of older versions of the page, identifying the last editor and the date and time. Click one to go to that version.

Notifications are check box settings that tell the server to send you an e-mail when a change and/or comment is added to the page.

Sharing is an item that appears only if you're an owner of the page. It lets you change the user permissions, add or remove user and group access, and change read and write permissions.

## Enabling calendars and other settings

Users can administer wikis that they create as well as group wikis from a web browser within the wiki. They can turn on a group calendar, edit the wiki's name, change user access permissions, and perform other tasks.

This is all accomplished from the main wiki page of the user or group site. Click the Actions menu (gear icon) in the toolbar and choose Settings. (If you aren't an owner of the wiki, the Settings item won't appear.)

The Settings page appears with the General settings displayed, as shown in Figure 13-8. In the left sidebar are links to different types of settings. The following sections describe what these settings pages do.

**Figure 13-8:**
The Settings page for a wiki opens with the General settings.

### Turning on calendars and blogs for a wiki

A wiki can have its own web calendar. You first need to have iCal service turned on in the Server app. You also have to be an owner of a wiki. (A wiki can have more than one person designated as an owner.) You also have to be using a computer or an iPad; you can't turn on a web calendar with an iPhone or iPod touch. An iPad can use a web-based calendar, but an iPhone cannot.

To create a calendar for a wiki, go to its Services page. Click the Services item in the left column and click the Calendars check box. (If the check box is grayed out, iCal Server probably isn't running.) You can also enable a blog for this wiki by clicking the Blogs check box.

A Calendar link appears in the upper right of pages; you use it to view the shared wiki calendar and add events to it. The web calendar is also available at this URL: `http://your-domain/webcal`.

The home page of the website doesn't have a link to the web calendar. You can add one by clicking the pencil icon in the toolbar of the home page and adding a link.

Mac users can use iCal Server with the iCal software that comes with Mac OS X. One reason to use a wiki-based calendar is that it grants access to Windows and Linux users as well.

However, users of iCal, Outlook, and Google Calendar can subscribe to a wiki calendar to get a read-only view from their calendar clients. You can do this by clicking the View Calendar Settings button of a wiki calendar and choosing Add or Subscribe. (iCal users should choose Add.)

### Changing the wiki name, icon, and description

The General page lets you change three aspects that identify the wiki site:

- ✔ **Wiki icon:** Click the Upload Image button to change the default icon to any picture you might have. This icon appears in the list of wikis.
- ✔ **Wiki name:** Type a new name in the Wiki Name field. This name appears on the top of every page of this wiki site, including related calendars and blogs.
- ✔ **Wiki description:** This can be anything you like.

When you're finished, click the Save button in the lower right of the screen.

Although you make these changes from the main wiki page, they apply to all the pages related to a wiki, including blogs, calendars, and other wiki pages.

### Editing user permissions

The Permissions link on the wiki Settings page is shown in Figure 13-9. This page provides two basic functions: changing access by users and groups and defining access to comments.

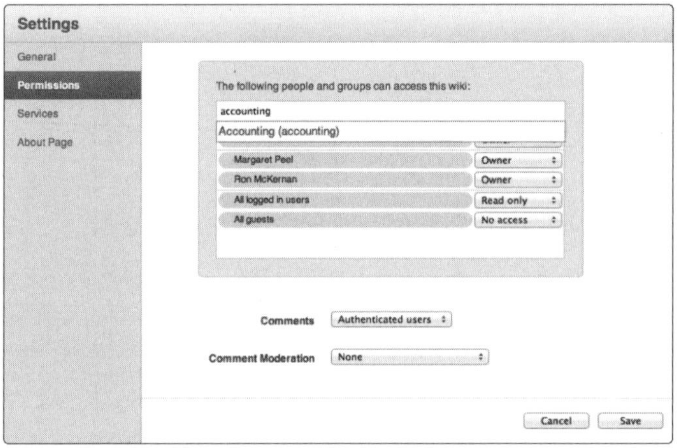

**Figure 13-9:**
Setting user and group access to a wiki.

In the top half, you have the same choices you have when you create a new wiki, and you can add new users and groups to give them access to the wiki. In Figure 13-9, I've created several owners (who are able to change these settings) and am in the process of adding a group.

At the bottom of the page, you can use the Comments pop-up menu to specify who can leave comments — only authenticated users or anyone — or to ban comments by setting this option to None. The Comment Moderation pop-up menu lets you require comments to be moderated for all commenters or just anonymous commenters. The default is no moderation.

Click the Save button in the lower right when you're finished.

### Editing the About page

The last item on the Settings page lets you edit the About page of your wiki specifically to include tags that would enable users to get to places relevant to the wiki.

# Hosting Your Own Websites

Outside the built-in website that Lion Server creates, you can host your own websites, whether they're for internal use only or being served to the

Internet. If you have a site that is for internal use, you can easily limit access to the members of a group account.

Lion Server replaced the MySQL database software with PostgreSQL (www. postgresql.org). If you're migrating a database-backed site that used MySQL (such as one from Snow Leopard Server), you'll have to make the switch.

As with other services in Lion Server, you use the Server app to configure and manage your website. To turn on web service, open the Server app and click Web in the sidebar. The window shown in Figure 13-10 appears. As with other services, you turn web services on and off with the big switch.

**Figure 13-10:** The Server app's Web pane.

If you've turned wiki services on, you'll see it listed here. It's described by your server's fully qualified domain name (*server.example.net*) along with the default location on the server hard drive (/Library/Server/ Web/Data/Sites/Default). In the lower right corner is a link called View Server Web Site. Clicking this link takes you to the server-created home page. However, if you set the default website to your own custom site, that page opens instead.

## Adding websites

With the Server app, you can host websites that you've created with other web tools and copied onto the server Mac. You can replace the built-in site with your own, or you can add one or more sites.

Replacing the default wiki-based website is easy. Just use the same host domain name as the default and be sure to assign your Mac's IP address to the new site. You don't have to change any DNS settings. If you want to run *both* the default site and your own, be sure to use a different domain name for the new site. Your DNS server will need to be configured to have the domain name resolve to the server IP address. With either option, the files for the default site stay in place and are not deleted.

You can also host multiple websites on one server, each with a different domain name. If these multiple sites share an IP address, they're called *virtual hosts.* However, if they have different IP addresses, the process is called *multihoming.*

The built-in wiki-based website by default uses Lion Server's fully qualified domain name and uses port 80. You can't change these settings. But you can use a different port number and domain name for a new site that you add.

If you want to replace the default site with your own, use the same qualified domain name and IP address as the default site and set the IP address.

To publish a custom website, either replacing the default site or adding to it, do the following:

1. **Launch the Server app and select Web from the sidebar.**

2. **Click the Add (+) button to bring up a dialog for a new website, shown in Figure 13-11.**

3. **To specify a custom location to store your website files, choose a folder where your website files will be from the Store Site Files In pop-up menu.**

   If you accept the setting Default Location, Server Preferences creates a folder for you in this location: /Library/Server/Web/Data/Sites/ CustomSitesDefault. It's safer to store web data on a hard drive or storage device other than the boot drive.

   The folder you designate will need to include a site home page — an index.html or index.php file. To view the folder contents, click the View Document Root Contents link in the dialog.

4. **In the Domain Name field, type the site's fully qualified DNS name.**

   The *fully qualified DNS name* is a unique identifier for the website. For example, two different fully qualified DNS names might be homework. abc.edu and teachers.abc.edu. You might use these two names to host both the built-in default site and your new site.

5. **From the IP Address pop-up menu, choose an IP address that people will use to access the website or choose the Any setting.**

   If you choose Any and your site has the same domain name as the default site, only the default site will be served.

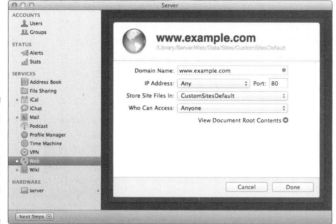

**Figure 13-11:**
Type the fully qualified DNS name for your new site.

6. **(Optional) In the Port field, change the Port number.**

   The default port setting is 80. If you're using SSL, port 443 is a good number. You can have multiple websites using the same port if you want, or you can choose a port number that isn't being used by another service. You may be able to use port 8080, which is another port that the server uses as a default. Port numbers 81–87 are generally safe to use for websites. Chapter 18 lists ports used by services.

7. **(Optional) In the Who Can Access pop-up menu, select a group account to allow only those members to visit the site or select Customize to restrict access to subfolders of the website.**

8. **Click the Done button.**

Your new site appears in the Web Sites list of the Web pane of the Server app, along with the location of its files (refer to Figure 13-10). If you want to make changes, you can edit the configuration by double-clicking it in the Web Sites list. You cannot, however, change the domain name or the location of the site files. If you need to make changes to those items, you'll need to delete the configuration and create a new one. You delete a configuration by select it from the Web Sites list and selecting the Delete (–) button.

## Using SSL security with your site

You can add Secure Sockets Layer security to a website by assigning a certificate to it. (The Server app doesn't enable you to use SSL without a certificate.) You can use a self-signed SSL certificate or use one from a certificate authority. (See Chapter 18 for more on certificates.)

If you have multiple sites configured in the Server app's Web pane, you can assign each one a different certificate or use the same one on all. You don't set certificates from the Web pane, however. You do it from the Server pane. Here's how:

1. **In the Server app, select your server in the sidebar under Hardware.**

2. **Click the Settings tab.**

   The SSL Certificate item will have one of these descriptions next to it:

   • The name of the certificate selected for all running services

   • Not Configured, if none of the running services has a certificate

   • Custom, if different services use different certificates

3. **Click the Edit button next to SSL Certificate.**

4. **Select the Custom option from the pop-up menu to expand the dialog, as shown in Figure 13-12.**

   You should see your websites listed. Figure 13-12 shows three: the default site and two others.

5. **For each website, click the double arrows next to the set and select a certificate from the pop-up menu.**

6. **Click the OK button when you're finished selecting certificates.**

**Figure 13-12:** Choosing SSL certificates for your websites.

You can go back to the Web pane and change the port numbers of sites to those used by SSL, such as 443 (instead of 80).

# Running into DNS problems

If, while you're still configuring the site, the dot next to the domain name is red (refer to Figure 13-11), you have a problem: The Server app can't resolve the DNS name to your server's IP address. To fix it, try one of these options:

- ✔ **Change the domain name to something that will resolve.** Check the spelling and form of the fully qualified domain name that you entered in the Server app and check your DNS server. You also can't have two virtual hosts with the same domain name.

- ✔ **Assign another available IP address.** You can assign another IP address if you're using both of the Ethernet cards in a Mac Pro or add more. To do so, double-click the site in the Web Sites list of the Server app and choose an IP address from the pop-up menu.

- ✔ **Check your port number to see if another service is using it.** Chapter 18 has a list of port numbers used by services.

If these solutions don't work, something may be wrong with the DNS service. If DNS is running on the same server Mac, use Server Admin to adjust Lion Server's DNS service or the DNS service.

# Web settings removed from Lion Server

If you're familiar with previous versions of Mac OS X Server, you'll notice that there is no longer any configuration of web services available in Server Admin. Apple removed the graphical interface to many of the settings for fine-tuning web service. If you know how to configure Apache and other relevant configuration files, most of these settings are still there. The locations of many files are different, however.

Although getting into the command-line configuration is a subject for another book, you may be interested in knowing what is no longer available in the server administration tools, so you'll know when to go to the command line. Here's a list of some of these items:

- ✔ **Maximum Attachment Size:** Limiting the size of files that users can upload to wiki and blog pages.

- ✔ **Logging levels:** You can't set the level of detail *(verbosity)* in the amount of logging for web services.

- ✔ **External Web Services:** Specifying calendar and mail servers other than those running on your server to deliver these services to the wiki-based calendar and webmail.

- ✔ **Web Server Aliases:** This lets you add domain-name-level aliases, such as `www.myschool.edu`.

- ✔ **URL Aliases and Redirects:** These are aliases and redirects that point to a file or folder on the web server with a path. These are more specific than web server aliases.

- ✔ **CGI Execution:** A way to turn on and off the enabling of Common Gateway Interface (CGI) scripts on your website.

- ✔ **Realms:** Previously, you could add realms to limit access to a website. A *realm* can be a collection of files or directories on the website. You could create a realm that includes a portion of a website that only a group can access. Realms are often used with WebDAV.

- ✔ **Maximum Simultaneous Connections:** The default is 1,024 connections, but you can't change it with the Server app. *Connections* doesn't refer to users; a web browser loading a single web page from your server can create multiple connections (the total number of connections for all the websites hosted on the server). If your server is accessible to the Internet, a lot of traffic can slow down the server. By lowering this number, you could prevent the server from being overburdened. Users receive a Server Is Busy message.

  On the flip side, if users are getting too many Server Is Busy messages, and your server isn't slowing, you could raise the default setting.

- ✔ **Connection Timeout:** This is the amount of time before an inactive user is disconnected from the server. The default is 300 seconds. A shorter timeout can free up resources for other users.

- ✔ **Minimum and Maximum Spare Servers:** This refers to the number of idle service processes running. Idle server processes can increase performance by being ready when users need them but can bog down the server if there are too many. If the number of spare server processes drops below this minimum number, the server creates them. After the maximum is reached, the server stops adding spare server processes.

- ✔ **Number of Servers to Start:** This is the number of spare server processes that are created at server startup. The default is 1.

- ✔ **Allow Persistent Connections:** This is on by default because it reduces network traffic. It enables a web browser to make multiple server requests over a single connection. You can also change the maximum allowed persistent connections and the timeout length.

# Chapter 14

# Running an E-Mail Server

*T*here are advantages to hosting your own e-mail server over using an outside provider. It gives you flexibility, letting you customize the e-mail options whenever you need to. If you have confidential data in your e-mail, storing your messages on your own server will give you peace of mind.

When using an outside e-mail server, such as an Internet service provider or an offsite host, users in your building who e-mail one another send traffic out through your Internet connection and back. This can slow the Internet connection in organizations with limited Internet bandwidth. Using your own e-mail server keeps internal e-mail traffic off your Internet connection.

This chapter describes setting up e-mail service with all the trimmings, including spam and virus blocking and domain name service (DNS). I also show you how to change the location of the data store — an important task if you don't want to run out of space on your boot drive.

## Prerequisites

Setting up your own e-mail service isn't rocket science, but you do need to know some things. This section describes the technologies involved and how you need to prepare your network before you set up mail service. If you're already familiar with mail protocols and DNS, you can skip ahead to the section "Setting Up Your E-Mail Server."

## Mail protocols

You can use three protocols to send and receive mail:

- Users send e-mail with the *Simple Mail Transfer Protocol (SMTP)*.
- Users receive e-mail with either the *Post Office Protocol (POP)* or the *Internet Message Access Protocol (IMAP)*.

You can set SMTP to require authentication to prevent spammers from using your server to relay spam to others.

POP and IMAP each provide benefits. You can enable both on the server (the default setting) and have different computers use different methods. The basic difference between the two is whether the user reads e-mail from the client or from the server. Each approach has different ramifications.

With POP, e-mail is downloaded to the client computer and deleted from the mail server. The client disconnects from the server as soon as the last message is downloaded. Because clients are connected to the server for only short periods, there's minimal use of the server's processor and RAM. This allows large numbers of users to access the server with minimal impact. And because e-mails are deleted from the server, POP has the advantage of using less server storage space than IMAP. All this makes POP an attractive alternative for a slower server Mac with limited RAM and hard drive space.

IMAP requires more server resources but can provide more benefits for the user. An IMAP connection to the server can last as long as the user needs, allowing the user to download content on demand. This can result in faster response times, and users can read one large message at a time without waiting for a whole batch to download.

IMAP also retains messages on the server even after they're read. It's up to the user to delete the messages from the server. This requires a lot more hard drive space than POP, as the amount of stored e-mail is growing constantly. (You can put a cap on the total amount of e-mail a user stores on the server.) IMAP permits users to have a mail folder structure on the server, which appears the same from any computers they use.

Snow Leopard Server's e-mail service uses the open source Postfix as the *mail transfer agent (MTA)* to send SMTP e-mail to the Internet. Snow Leopard Server uses the open source Dovecot for POP and IMAP e-mail.

If your users are sending e-mail to one another only, then SMTP, POP, and IMAP are all you need to configure. But if they're like most people and want to exchange e-mail with users on the Internet, you need to configure DNS.

## Where Lion Server stores mail

In case you're wondering for purposes of backup, Lion Server temporarily stores mail going to the Internet in this location: /Library/Server/Mail/Data/spool.

Incoming IMAP e-mail is stored in directories for each user, with each message stored as a separate file. The message resides in the folder /Library/Server/Mail/Data/mail.

Messages stay here until the user deletes them from the client e-mail application (or the e-mail application is set to automatically delete). You can change this location if you want to move it off the boot drive. See the section "Using Configuration Assistant to configure mail service," later in the chapter.

# Mail service and the Internet: DNS

In addition to mail protocols, a few more elements need to be in place in order to send mail to destinations on the Internet. Domain name service (DNS) helps determine who will eventually receive a sent e-mail by looking up the domain name of the e-mail recipient (the acme.com in bob@acme.com) and finding an IP address to send it to.

The DNS service can be running on your Lion Server Mac, on your ISP's server, or on another server in your organization. If you want to run DNS on your Mac for use on the Internet, your organization needs to own a registered domain name.

The DNS server uses mail exchange (MX) records to help route incoming e-mail to your server. An MX record contains a list of mail servers that handle mail for a particular domain name. MX records help other mail servers find your e-mail users.

An SMTP server sending a message looks at the domain name of the e-mail message and asks a DNS server for the corresponding IP address of an e-mail server — either the final destination server or an intermediate e-mail server on the Internet. The DNS server looks up the domain name in an MX record and then sends the IP address back to the SMTP server. The SMTP server can then send on the e-mail message. MX records can list multiple IP addresses for a given domain name, ranked in order for the SMTP server to try.

The "Configuring DNS for Use with E-Mail" section, later in this chapter, describes creating MX records.

## Relay servers

You may also need to connect your e-mail server to the Internet by specifying a *relay server,* which is another mail server that you'd forward outgoing mail to. Your Internet service provider may require that you relay e-mail to one of their servers. Or you may need to relay e-mail to another server in your organization if you have a server designated to send outgoing mail through a firewall. In this case, you wouldn't be using MX records on your server. You can specify a relay server with either the Server app or Server Admin.

Don't specify a relay server without telling the operator of the server. You may look like a spammer and could get your server blacklisted.

# Configuring DNS for Use with E-Mail

DNS service set up with mail exchange (MX) records allows mail to be sent to the correct host on your network. Whether you need to set this up depends on your situation:

> ✔ **Your Internet service provider supplies the DNS server for your network.** If this is the case, your ISP can set up and host MX records for you. All you do is let them know your Mail server's IP address and domain name.

> ✔ **Your network has DNS service running on a non-Mac server.** In this case, the server administrator creates an MX record for your Mail server that's hosted on the DNS server.

> ✔ **The DNS service is running on one of your Mac OS X Servers.** Use Server Admin to access any of these servers to create an MX record.

If you're in the last case, you actually *can* do without MX records if you really want to. To do this, you need to include the mail server's hostname in the e-mail addresses of your users. For example, with MX records configured, a user's e-mail address might look like `fred@acme.com`. Without MX records, you must include the mail server's hostname (`fred@our-server.acme.com`).

The problem is that if you ever change your mail server, you have to change all your users' e-mail addresses.

If you're going to use MX records, you also need to make sure that DNS has a *machine record,* a DNS entry that identifies your mail server on the network.

This section looks at creating an MX record on your Lion Server Mac. After that, I look at how to create a DNS machine record for the mail host. But first, make sure that DNS service is turned on.

## Don't have Server Admin? Get it. Now.

Can't find Server Admin? Apple now considers it optional, so the Lion Server installer doesn't install it — you have to go get it. And you should because you need it. Server Admin is part of the Server Admin Tools for Mac OS X Lion Server, which also includes Workgroup Manager and other tools. You'll find Server Admin Tools at `www.apple.com/support/downloads`. It's a free download, so if you don't have it, put this book down right now and go download it. Seriously. I'll wait.

## *Turning on DNS service in Lion Server*

When you installed Mac OS X, DNS service may have been configured and turned on, depending on what you told the Setup Assistant. If not, turn it on now using Server Admin. Launch it, log in if necessary, and follow these steps:

1. **In Server Admin, click your server in the upper left of the window.**

2. **Click the Settings icon in the toolbar and then select the DNS check box on the Services tab.**

3. **Click the Save button at the bottom right.**

You should now see DNS listed under your server.

## *Creating an MX record*

To create an MX record, do the following in Server Admin:

1. **Click the triangle to the left of the server running the DNS service.**

   If you don't see DNS listed, you need to turn it on.

2. **Select DNS from the list of services under the server and then click the Zones icon in the toolbar.**

3. **Select a zone from the list near the top of the window.**

   If you don't have a zone, create a primary zone with the Add Zone drop-down menu (see Figure 14-1). This is the zone on which you create the MX record.

   Click the triangle next to your zone to expand a list under it. If there's no Machine Record (A) for your Mail server, you need to add one. I describe how in the following section. You don't have to do it now; you can continue with creating an MX record.

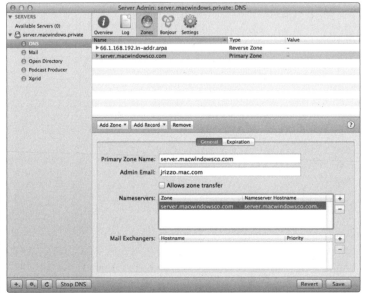

**Figure 14-1:**
Selecting a
DNS zone
in Server
Admin.

4. **With your zone selected, go to the bottom of the window and click the Add (+) button next to the Mail Exchangers box.**

 *MX* stands for *mail exchange.*

5. **Type the hostname of the Mail server in the Mail Exchangers box.**

 If you type just `mail` without the domain (see Figure 14-2), the domain (in this example, `.macwindows.com`) is added when you click the Save button.

6. **Type a priority number in the Priority column.**

 If this is your only Mail server, type `10`. If this is a backup Mail server, the priority number should be higher than that of your primary Mail server.

7. **(Optional) If you have other Mail servers for redundancy, you can add more MX records by clicking the Add (+) button.**

 Typically, the priority numbers are in multiples of 10 (10, 20, 30) to enable you to add other servers later between those numbers.

 Priority numbers tell the DNS server which Mail server to route incoming mail to. The highest priority has the lowest number, which is 10 in this example. If that server is out of commission, the mail is routed to the next priority number, 20.

8. **Click the Save button.**

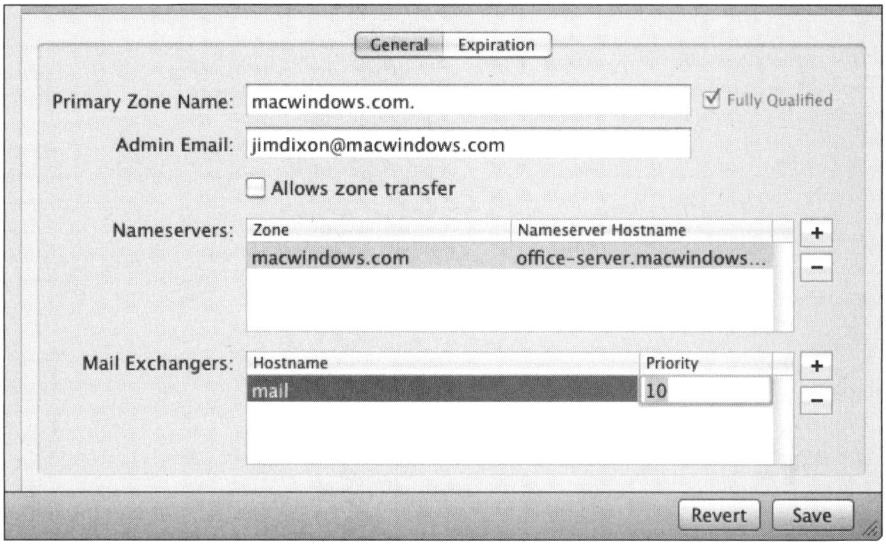

**Figure 14-2:**
The host-name and priority are essentially the MX record.

# Creating a DNS machine record for the Mail server

In addition to an MX record, the DNS zone needs to have an entry called a Machine Record (A) defined for the mail service, using the same Mail server hostname that you used in the MX record.

Start from the same DNS Zones window, shown in Figure 14-1, described in Steps 1 through 4 of the preceding section:

1. **Click the triangle to the left of the selected zone to display the list of records for that zone.**

   If you see an entry for your mail host, you're done.

   In the example in the preceding section, you want to see an entry for `mail.macwindows.com`.

2. **Click the zone to select it and choose Add Machine (A) from the Add Record pop-up menu just below the zone list, as shown in Figure 14-3.**

   A record called `newMachine` is added to the zone (see Figure 14-4).

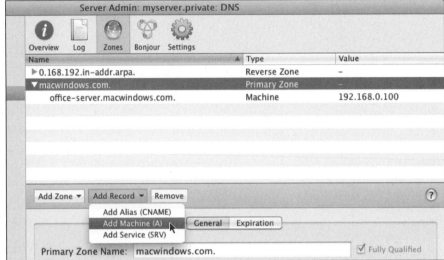

**Figure 14-3:**
The Add
Record but-
ton brings
up a pop-up
menu.

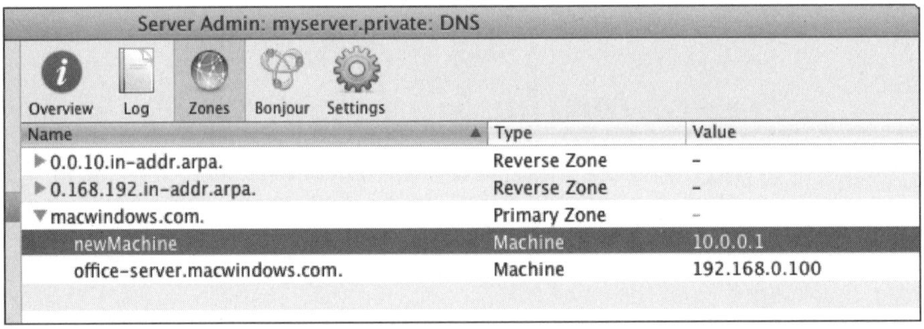

**Figure 14-4:**
The newly
created
machine
record.

3. **With the new machine record still selected, go to the Machine Name field below and type the hostname of the mail server.**

   In this example, the hostname is `mail`.

4. **Double-click the default IP address (10.0.0.1) to select it and replace it with the IP address of the Mac server.**

5. **(Optional) Enter the hardware and software information about your server in the appropriate boxes.**

6. **(Optional) Use the Comments box to include the location of the server or any other information that might identify it.**

   Figure 14-5 shows what the window looks like.

7. **Click the Save button.**

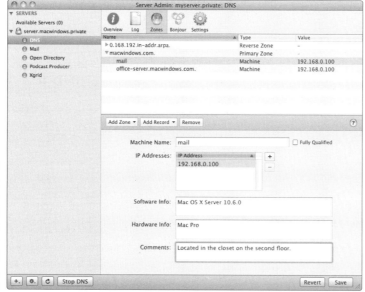

**Figure 14-5:**
The completed machine record for the Mail server.

If you like, you can add *aliases* for this server — additional names for the server that will resolve to the server's IP address. To do so, click the Add Record button and choose Add Alias (CNAME) from the pop-up menu. Then add the name for your server in the Alias Name field and add the actual hostname in the Destination field; click the Save button.

If you add an alias, you have to go back to the Mail settings:

1. **Click Mail in the left column under your server, click the Settings icon in the toolbar, click the Advanced tab, and finally, click the Hosting tab.**

2. **Click the Add (+) button and type the alias name; click Save.**

When you're finished, make sure that the DNS service is running. With DNS selected in the left column, if DNS isn't running, the button at the bottom left of the window says *Start DNS.* Click it to start.

# Setting Up Your E-Mail Server

Mail Server is unique in Lion Server in that it is the only service that is configurable from both the Server app and Server Admin. In fact, you can use *three* tools to set up and manage mail service in Lion Server. You can use one of them or all three. I recommend using two together to start with. Here are the three tools and what you can do with them:

- ✔ **The Server app:** The simplest way to get running, the Server app offers a subset of available settings, automatically configuring behind the scenes. It lets you set up a relay to an Internet service provider to send e-mail to the Internet, but doesn't enable you to create an MX record. The Server app also lets you blacklist known e-mail servers (spammers), as well as filter spam and viruses. Turning on Mail Server with the Server app turns on SMTP, POP, and IMAP protocols, but doesn't let you turn off either POP or IMAP. With the Server app, you can't see what all the settings are.

- ✔ **Server Admin:** Here is where you can see the full suite of settings. It gives you additional options for dealing with spam and lets you change settings for authentication. It also lets you set up mail lists, or *listservs,* and set maximum message sizes. You can create MX records with Server Admin, as well as configure Mail server *clustering,* in which multiple servers act as one Mail server. But Server Admin has dozens of choices in lots of screens with little help to let you know what is what.

- ✔ **Configuration Assistant:** The happy medium between the two other tools, Configuration Assistant takes you through a fairly detailed configuration with explanations of what you need to do and what the settings are.

Configuration Assistant is available only through Server Admin, however. Mail Server needs to be enabled before you can get to it. Enabling Mail Server in Server Admin is a multistep process. Enabling Mail Server in the Server app is two mouse clicks.

Therefore, I recommend a two-step method as the best way to set up mail service for the first time in Lion Server:

1. **Turn on Mail Server with the Server app.**

2. **Configure with the Configuration Assistant.**

If you later find that you need some more tweaks or you need to troubleshoot, use Server Admin.

The next few sections describe setting up initial mail service with the Server app, Server Admin, and the Configuration Assistant.

## Setting up mail with the Server app

The Server app may be all you need to set up mail service, particularly if you aren't running DNS on Lion Server. If you're using an Internet service provider that offers a relay server, a few mouse clicks may get you serving mail in no time. Here's what you do:

1. **Launch the Server app from the Dock and click the Mail icon.**

   If you don't see your server listed in the sidebar under Hardware, select Manage⟶Connect To Server, choose your server, and log in.

2. **Check the hostname next to Provide Mail For and, if you want to change it, click the Edit button and type a new DNS name.**

   The new name must be a valid, fully qualified domain name that is properly configured in DNS with your Internet service provider, a DNS hosting service, or your own network. The mail server hostname must be resolvable to an IP address with both forward and reverse DNS entries. If you change this hostname, you may have to update the DNS MX record.

3. **In the Mail pane (shown in Figure 14-6), click the switch to the On position.**

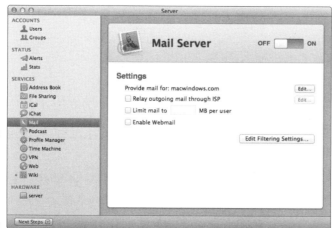

**Figure 14-6:**
Mail configuration using the Server app.

4. **If you're using an Internet service provider to relay mail to the Internet, do the following:**

   a. *Select the Relay Outgoing Mail through ISP check box.*

      The relay server could be a server in your own organization.

      A new dialog appears, as shown in Figure 14-7.

   b. *Enter an IP address or a DNS name for the relay server.*

   c. *If your ISP requires authentication for its SMTP relay, enter a username and password.*

   d. *Click OK.*

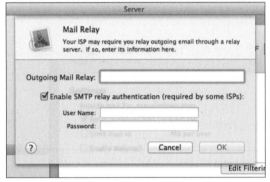

**Figure 14-7:**
Specifying
a mail relay
server in the
Server app.

The Mail Server pane has two more check boxes:

- ✔ **Limit Mail to *[blank]* MB per User:** Lets you set a quota, the maximum amount of storage space that you want to allow for each user. The default is 200MB, but you can set your own limit.

  This is the only place in Lion Server you can set this number. Server Admin has some other quota settings, but not this one.

- ✔ **Enable Webmail:** Turns on a feature that enables users to access the mail server from a web browser.

The Mail Server pane also has a button called Edit Filtering Settings for blocking spam and virus. I describe how to set up this option with both the Server app and Server Admin in the section "Blocking Spam and Other Nasty Bits," later in this chapter.

# Turning on and starting mail service with Server Admin

When you throw the On switch in the Server app, it both enables mail service and turns it on. With Server Admin, you have to enable the service and then start it running.

You can tell whether Mail is turned on and running in Server Admin by going to the left column and clicking the triangle to the left of your server to expand the list of services. If Mail isn't included in the list, it isn't enabled. If Mail appears but the circle is empty (see Figure 14-8), Mail is enabled but isn't started.

**Figure 14-8:**
Mail service
is enabled
but isn't
running.

To enable mail service with Server Admin, do the following:

1. **Select your server in the column on the left.**
2. **Click the Settings icon in the toolbar; then click the Settings tab.**
3. **Select the Mail check box and click Save.**

If you ever decide to stop using Mail Server, it's a good idea to go back here and disable it. This is the only way to do so in Lion Server.

To start the Mail service:

1. **Click the triangle to the left of your server to expand the list of services and then click Mail.**
2. **Click the Start Mail button in the lower left of the screen.**

Of course, there's much more you can do with Server Admin to configure mail service, but at this point, it's easier to do the rest of your configuration with Configuration Assistant, described in the next section.

## Using Configuration Assistant to configure mail service

Configuration Assistant is good to use if you aren't sure where to find a setting. The assistant brings up what you need to configure without you having to look for it; just click through any screens until you find what you need. And it lets you configure more settings than the Server app. Configuration Assistant also provides instructions.

Note that mail service doesn't have to be running, just enabled, as described in the preceding section. Here's how to use the Configuration Assistant:

1. **In Server Admin, click the triangle to the left of your server to expand the list of services.**

2. **Click Mail from the list and then click the toolbar's Overview icon.**

3. **Click the Configure Mail Service button in the lower right (see Figure 14-9).**

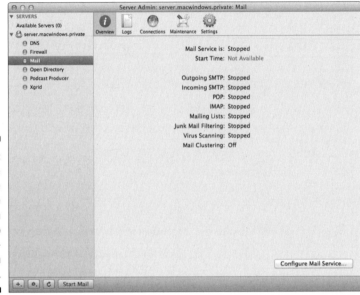

**Figure 14-9:**
The Configure Mail Service button brings up the Configuration Assistant.

4. **When the Configuration Assistant opens to an introduction screen, click the Continue button.**

5. **In the Mail Service: General window that opens (as shown in Figure 14-10), select or deselect the POP, IMAP, and SMTP protocols.**

   All are on by default.

6. **Select the Allow Incoming Mail check box to enable Internet e-mail and then type your domain name and server name.**

7. **Select the Relay Outgoing Mail through Host check box if you have an SMTP relay.**

   The Hold Outgoing Mail check box is a setting you can use for trouble-shooting or to queue mail until you solve another problem. The queued mail is sent when you deselect this setting.

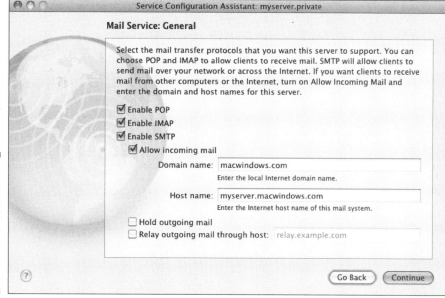

Figure 14-10:
The Mail
Service:
General
window
of Con-
figuration
Assistant.

8. **Click the Continue button.**

   The next window is Filters, for blocking spam and viruses. It is similar
   to that of the Server app. (For more on spam and virus filtering, see the
   section "Blocking Spam and Other Nasty Bits," later in this chapter.)

9. **Adjust the filter settings and click the Continue button.**

   The Security window appears, with choices for encrypting passwords.

10. **Use Kerberos and/or CRAM-MD5 for SMTP and IMAP (for POP, use
    Kerberos or APOP) and then click the Continue button.**

    See the section "Authenticating and Encrypting Mail with Server Admin,"
    later in this chapter, for more information on these settings.

11. **In the next screen that appears, change the default location for mail
    messages.**

    It's not a bad idea to keep mail data on a hard drive or partition that is
    not the boot drive, keeping the data safely away from the OS. Also, IMAP
    databases can grow in size with lots of heavy mail users or if users don't
    delete their e-mail. The default location is `/Library/Server/Mail/
    Data mail`.

12. **Click the Continue button.**

    A confirmation screen appears, listing your settings.

13. **Click the Go Back button to change your settings or click the Continue button to have your settings configured.**

    This process also starts mail service if it isn't already running.

You can come back to the Configuration Assistant any time to make changes. Or you can use the Settings window, described in the following section.

## Configuring e-mail with Server Admin's Settings window

The Configuration Assistant is a good way to get e-mail up and running, but you can also use Server Admin's Settings window to set up or make changes to mail service. This section describes the General tab, where you make or change basic e-mail server settings.

You can make a few more setting changes here that you can't make in the Configuration Assistant, including assigning a Push Notification Server and limiting the maximum number of simultaneous IMAP connections.

Here's how to use the Settings window for configuring e-mail service:

1. **In Server Admin, click the triangle to the left of your server to expand the list of services.**

2. **Click Mail in the list, click the Settings icon in the toolbar, and then click the General tab.**

    The window shown in Figure 14-11 appears.

3. **Type your domain name and hostname in the fields near the top.**

4. **Select the Enable SMTP and Allow Incoming Mail check boxes, if they're not selected already.**

5. **If your ISP or organization requires that you use a mail relay server, select the Relay Outgoing Mail through Host check box and type the domain name of the host.**

6. **If a name and password are required for the relay server, type them.**

7. **Select the Enable IMAP or Enable POP check box, or both, if they're not selected already.**

8. **Click the Save button in the lower right.**

9. **Click the Start Mail button, if Mail isn't already running.**

    Your Mail service is now configured.

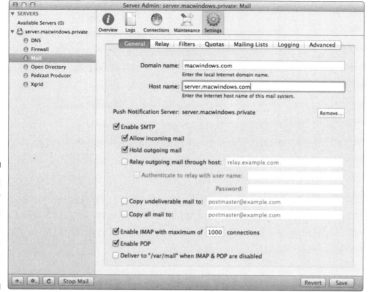

**Figure 14-11:**
Server
Admin's
Mail
Settings
window,
General tab.

A few other options are shown in Figure 14-6:

- **Push Notification Server:** This is useful for iPhone, iPad, and notebook clients. Instead of requiring the user to check for e-mail, push notification goes to the mobile device to tell it that mail has arrived. Before you select this option, you need to have the Push Notification Server turned on in the Settings tab of the Server app's Server pane.

- **Hold Outgoing Mail:** You can use this setting for troubleshooting or to queue mail while you solve another problem. Users can still send mail, but the server holds it, so mail messages won't be sent to their destinations. Queued mail is sent when you deselect this setting.

- **Allow Incoming Mail:** Block inbound messages by deselecting this option. Incoming e-mail messages are bounced back to the servers they came from.

- **Copy Undeliverable Mail To:** Selecting this option sends problem outgoing e-mail to an e-mail address, typically for an administrator.

- **Copy All Mail To:** Copies all mail to an e-mail address — something you might want to do if you want a single place to search for e-mail for all your users.

I describe some of the other settings options available in Server Admin in the next few sections.

# Authenticating and Encrypting Mail with Server Admin

Lion Server lets you require clients to encrypt passwords when they sign in to the e-mail server; it can also encrypt e-mail messages with the Secure Sockets Layer (SSL) standard. The earlier section "Using Configuration Assistant to configure mail service" describes how to do this with Configuration Assistant. This section describes Server Admin, but the concepts I describe here apply to the settings in Configuration Assistant.

Password authentication is useful if users connect to your e-mail server over the Internet from home or when traveling. Mac OS X Server offers different methods of authentication because not all mail clients support the same methods.

In Server Admin, you can find these on the Advanced tab of the Mail Settings window:

1. **In Server Admin, click the triangle to the left of your server to expand the list of services.**

2. **Click Mail from the list; then click the Settings icon in the toolbar.**

3. **Click the Advanced tab in the upper right and then click the Security tab in the second row of tabs.**

   You see the window shown in Figure 14-12.

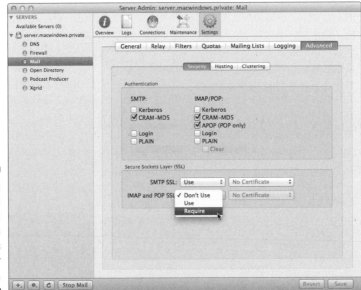

**Figure 14-12:**
Mail password protection settings in Server Admin.

Here, you can set encryption for authentication (usernames and passwords) and for e-mail messages. The following two sections describe what these settings mean and when you might use them.

## Securing mail authentication

Server Admin and the Configuration Assistant both give you options for password encryption for SMTP and IMAP/POP. Which you choose depends on what your e-mail clients support. You can choose multiple authentication methods to support multiple e-mail clients. It's a good idea to disable any authentication method that your clients aren't using. If you need only one type for all your clients, use that. Using only one type of authentication requires clients to use it.

Here's the lowdown on your choices:

- ✔ **Kerberos and CRAM-MD5** are the most secure authentication methods. To use Kerberos for mail, you need Kerberos authentication in Open Directory or on another server. Of the two, Apple recommends Kerberos.

- ✔ **APOP** is an encryption type used only for POP clients.

- ✔ **Login, Clear, and Plain** are unsecure authentication methods that send passwords unencrypted. If you choose these in addition to the more secure authentication methods, clients that don't have the more secure methods set up are allowed to log in without encryption. If you deselect these unencrypted options, these clients can't log in until they're configured for encryption.

In Server Admin, you'll find these settings in the window described in the previous section, shown in Figure 14-12. In the Configuration Assistant, you can configure these settings in the Security window.

## Securing e-mail messages with SSL

The preceding methods encrypt only passwords and usernames. You can also encrypt e-mail itself with the Secure Sockets Layer (SSL) section in the lower part of the window in Figure 14-12. For POP and IMAP, SSL encryption is between your server and your clients. For SMTP, SSL encryption is between your server and other e-mail servers.

To use SSL, click the pop-up menu for SMTP or the menu for IMAP and POP, as shown in Figure 14-12. If you choose Require, the mail service won't connect if the client or other Mail server isn't supporting SSL.

If you choose Use, SSL encryption is used if a POP or IMAP client asks for it. If a client isn't set up to request an SSL connection, the Mail service can still deliver mail to that client. The Use setting works the same with SMTP and other Mail servers: For Mail servers that don't request SSL, Lion Server's mail service sends mail unencrypted.

In the pop-up menus to the right, you can choose to select a certificate or to not use a certificate. You can use the Server app to import a certificate from a certificate authority or create a certificate-signing request and a keychain. To get there in the Server app, select your server under Hardware in the sidebar and then click the Settings tab. See Chapter 18 for information about certificates.

# Blocking Spam and Other Nasty Bits

Lion Server is integrated with several types of filtering software to keep spam and viruses from reaching users. It uses the open source spam-blocking software called SpamAssassin, which does a statistical analysis of incoming e-mail to determine whether it's probable spam. It also supports the blacklisting of certain e-mail servers, rejecting e-mail from known spammers. For this, Lion Server communicates with servers of the Spamhaus Project, an international not-for-profit organization that collects spam blacklist data. Lion Server also includes software that scans incoming messages for viruses: the open source ClamAV.

The next two sections describe how you configure filtering settings in the Server app, the Configuration Assistant, and in Server Admin. Keep in mind that all three are front ends to the same filtering software. I also describe in more detail the meanings of these settings and how you might use them effectively.

## Setting spam and virus blocking with the Server app

To access the filtering settings from the Server app, click Mail in the sidebar and then click the Edit Filtering Settings button. There are three settings, shown in Figure 14-13:

- **Enable Virus Filtering:** This option is either on or off.
- **Enable Blacklist Server Filtering:** This check box specifies a blacklist server to prevent spam from known spam servers from reaching you.

If you select this option, the default is `zen.spamhaus.org`. You can change this setting, if you like.

✓ **Enable Junk Mail Filtering:** This check box activates the slider that you can use to set the severity of filtering.

The higher you set the slider, the higher the chance that junk e-mail will be detected. Any messages that are deemed to be spam are marked JUNK and forwarded to the user. This setting also tells the Mail server to remove all e-mail messages it suspects of containing viruses and to place them in this folder: `/var/virusmails`.

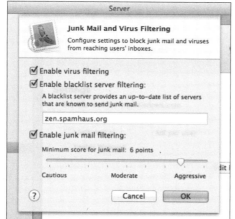

**Figure 14-13:**
Filtering settings in the Server app.

## Setting spam and virus blocking with Configuration Assistant

The Configuration Assistant is accessed from Server Admin: Select Mail in the sidebar, click the Overview tab, and click the Configure Mail Service button. The Filters screen is similar to that of the Server app, with some more detail but no access to the blacklist filtering:

✓ **Scan for Junk Mail** presents the same slider as in the Server app.

✓ **Scan Email for Viruses** includes a pop-up menu with a choice of deleting, redirecting, or bouncing infected messages.

✓ **Update the Virus Database** lets you set the number of times per day for the server to check virus databases.

## Setting spam and virus blocking with Server Admin

Using Server Admin's Mail Settings window to set spam and virus blocking gives you more choices than either the Configuration Assistant or the Server app.

Here's how to bring up the Settings window for configuring filtering:

1. **In Server Admin, click the triangle to the left of your server to expand the list of services.**

2. **Click Mail from the list; then click the Settings icon in the toolbar.**

3. **Click the Filters tab.**

   You see the window in Figure 14-14.

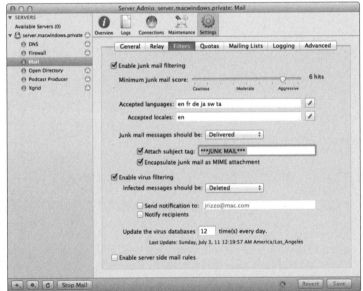

**Figure 14-14:**
Server Admin's spam and virus filter window.

The following sections describe the choices here and give some advice. Remember to click the Save button after you configure your settings.

## Statistical spam filtering

At the top of the Server Admin Filters window (refer to Figure 14-13) is the Minimum Junk Mail Score slider bar, the same one you see in Configuration Assistant and the Server app. How you set it is really a matter of philosophy.

Setting the slider toward the left (Cautious) lets more spam get through to users, where their own spam filters deal with it. Setting it toward the right (Aggressive) sends fewer junk mail messages to users but could trap more legitimate e-mail (false positives). If the server filters legitimate e-mail, users don't know about it. I tend to be conservative in setting server-based spam filtering, but it may be more secure to accept more false positives and prevent phishing e-mail from getting to users.

Lion Server's junk-mail filtering uses a statistical method known as *Bayesian filtering*. For example, instead of stopping every message with the word *loan*, it takes into consideration the context of the message and the frequency of the word used in known spam. Bayesian filtering assigns a probability that's calculated on history based on a mathematical formula. This results in high accuracy in detection and few false-positive IDs.

What you do with filtered mail can help you decide how aggressive you want to get with filtering. The Junk Mail Messages Should Be pop-up menu in Figure 14-14 gives you four choices:

- **Bounced:** Sends the message back to the sender. I don't recommend this setting because it usually doesn't help and could invite a malicious attack. With this setting, you have the option of sending a notification to an e-mail address.

- **Deleted:** Saves hard drive space but eliminates the possibility of ever retrieving false positives. This setting also gives you the option to send a notification to an e-mail address.

- **Delivered:** Delivers the message to the user with a warning in the Subject line (such as \*\*\*JUNK MAIL\*\*\*). I like this setting because it lets the user look through it for false positives. You can also encode the message as an attachment for extra security.

- **Redirected:** Sends the e-mail to another address. This could be an address for an administrator, who could look through it for false positives. The downside is that it takes a lot of hard drive space, given the flood of spam that everyone gets.

You can also block all e-mail from a known spam server. In the left column of Server Admin, under your server, click Mail, click the Settings icon in the toolbar, and then click the Relay tab. You can then type the IP addresses of one or more known spammers.

## Spam-filtering exceptions by country or language

Below the slider in the Server Admin spam and virus filter window are settings for accepted languages and locales (refer to Figure 14-14). These are exceptions to the Bayesian filtering rules. For example, the spam filter often categorizes all e-mail with nonroman typefaces as junk mail. If you routinely get legitimate e-mail in the Korean language, you can use the Accepted Locales setting to enable e-mail with a Korean country code to get through. The Accepted Languages list lets through e-mail written in different specific languages that you might receive.

Click the pencil icon to bring up a new window for selecting additional languages or locales.

## Virus filtering

The Enable Virus Filtering setting in the Server Admin spam and virus filter window (refer to Figure 14-14) looks at e-mail by using a different method from the one it uses for spam. It uses the open source ClamAV (www. clamav.net) software to keep track of known malicious e-mail viruses, worms, and other malware and is automatically updated regularly. You can set how often the virus database is updated in the Update the Virus Databases box at the bottom of the window.

You can tell the server what to do with the virus e-mail in the Infected Messages Should Be pop-up menu. You get three of the four options that are found in the junk-mail-filtering section:

- ✔ **Bounced:** I don't recommend the Bounced setting because it usually doesn't help and may invite a malicious attack.
- ✔ **Deleted:** Lets you notify the user or any e-mail address that a suspected virus has been deleted. Most people should use this setting.
- ✔ **Redirected:** Sends the suspected infected e-mail to an e-mail address.

For whatever reason, fewer viruses are written for Macs than for Windows PCs. However, your Mac e-mail server can just as easily pass malware to your Windows clients as any other server. And you don't want to risk your Mac clients' getting infected with the malware that does exist.

# Creating New User E-Mail Addresses

When you create a user account after mail service has been set up and started, Lion Server automatically creates an e-mail address based on the short name followed by the domain name — for example, ronmckernan@acme.com.

You can create additional e-mail addresses for any user. For example, you might assign `info@acme.com` to a user who's responsible for a public website.

To create an alternative e-mail address for a user, you must use Workgroup Manager to create a second short name for the user. Here's how:

1. **In Workgroup Manager, click the Accounts icon in the toolbar.**

2. **Click the globe icon below the toolbar on the left and select the account's directory domain.**

    Log in if prompted.

3. **Select the user from the list on the left.**

4. **Click the Basic tab.**

5. **Double-click the empty space in the Short Names list box, as shown in Figure 14-15, and then type an alias that you want to use in the e-mail address for the selected user.**

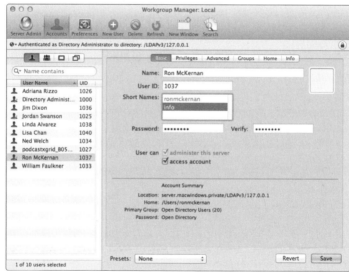

**Figure 14-15:** To create a new e-mail address for a user, create an additional short name.

If a virtual host is enabled, type the full e-mail address (for example, `info@acme.com`).

6. **Click the Save button.**

# *Setting Up a Mailing List*

Mailing lists, or *listservs,* are good ways to enable group discussions via e-mail. When a member of the listserv sends a message to the list address, it gets delivered to all the members. To create a listserv, use Server Admin:

1. **In Server Admin, click the triangle to the left of your server to expand the list of services.**

2. **Click Mail from the list; then click the Settings icon in the toolbar.**

3. **Click the Mailing Lists tab and select the Enable Mailman Mailing Lists check box.**

4. **In the new dialog that appears (see Figure 14-16), type a master password and the e-mail addresses of users who can administer the mailing lists set up on this server.**

   List administrators don't have to have access to Server Admin. They administer the list by going to this web page:

   *yourserver.yourdomain.tld*/mailman/listinfo

   In place of .tld, use .com, .edu, or another ending.

5. **Click OK and then click the Add (+) button below the Mailing Lists list box to add a mailing list.**

**Figure 14-16:**
Setting a
password
and list
administra-
tors for a
mailing list.

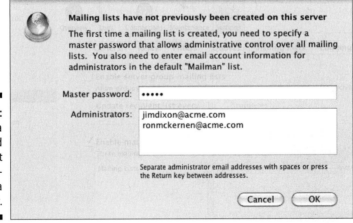

**Mailing lists have not previously been created on this server**

The first time a mailing list is created, you need to specify a master password that allows administrative control over all mailing lists. You also need to enter email account information for administrators in the default "Mailman" list.

Master password:  •••••

Administrators:  jimdixon@acme.com
ronmckernen@acme.com

Separate administrator email addresses with spaces or press the Return key between addresses.

Cancel        OK

6. **In the new dialog that appears (see Figure 14-17), type a list name and an administrator.**

7. **(Optional) Enable users to self-subscribe and choose a language.**

   Maximum Length of a Message Body is by default set to 40KB, which is a bit limiting. Keeping this low saves hard drive space.

8. **Click OK.**

   The new list appears in the main Mailing Lists pane (see Figure 14-18).

9. **Select it and click the Users & Groups button in the lower right.**

10. **When the Users & Groups window appears, drag the names of people you want to be members of the list into the main window.**

11. **Click the Save button.**

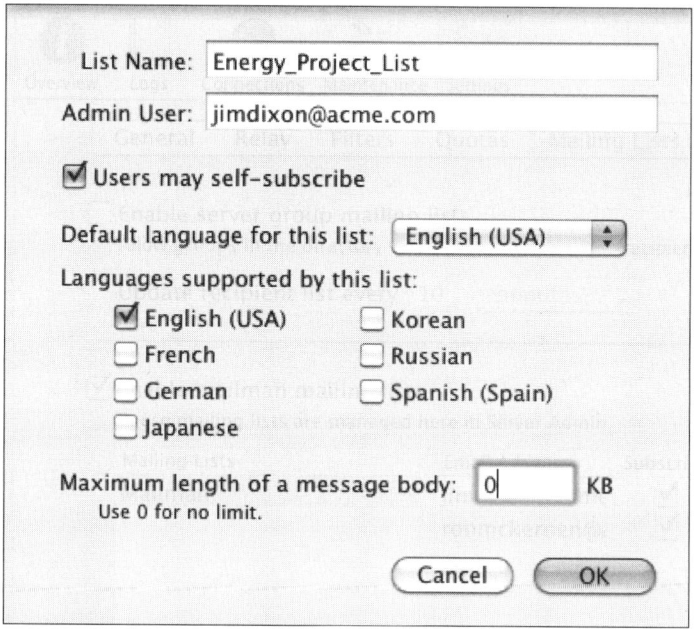

**Figure 14-17:**
Naming the
mail list and
setting how
it works.

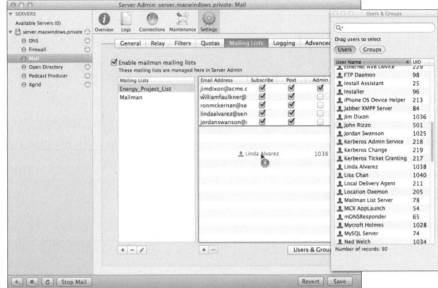

**Figure 14-18:**
Drag users
from the
list into the
main win-
dow to add
them to the
listserv.

Lion Server uses Mailman open source software to provide mailing lists. For more information about the features and roles for users, list administrators, and server administrators, check here: `www.list.org/docs.html`.

# Chapter 15

# More Collaboration: iChat and Podcast Producer

**S**ome of Lion Server's built-in goodies may not be central to everyone's mission, but can be of great value to groups that can use them. If you take a look at this chapter, you may find yourself in the latter group as I explore iChat Server and Podcast Producer.

iChat Server is a collaborative tool for brainstorming sessions, virtual meetings, video conferencing, and file sharing. One way to think of iChat Server is as a live version of the wiki tools I describe in Chapter 13, plus video and audio. iChat Server works for Mac, Windows, and Linux computers, and for iPhones, iPads, and iPod touches.

Podcast Producer has been revamped and supercharged in Lion Server. But don't let the *Pod* in *Pod*cast Producer fool you — it's not about iPods. Podcast Producer is an automated video production system that yields professional results. Use it to create training videos, classroom projects, or tech-support resources and to distribute your work automatically.

## *iChat Instant Messaging and More*

iChat Server provides instant messaging, audio and video conferencing, and file transferring; it supports Mac, Windows, and Linux clients as well as mobile phones. iChat works on a person-to-person basis and in multiuser situations.

iChat Server can also create *persistent chat rooms,* which let participants leave or log off. When they return, they can see everything that happened in their absence. Users can send chat messages to other users who are offline.

iChat also acts as a kind of automatic note-taking service because users can generate chat transcripts. On the server, you can log chat text so that the administrator can read it or forward it to a group that needs it.

Chats aren't just text, however. The server and clients support audio and video conferencing using the built-in mics and video cameras of most Macs and iOS devices.

iChat service is private and secure, using Secure Sockets Layer (SSL) encryption. Users must have accounts in (and are authenticated by) the Open Directory domain, which means they can use iChat services from any computer and still see their buddy lists, groups, and other information.

Lion Server's iChat service is compatible with a number of instant-messaging servers and clients. iChat service is based on the open standard Extensible Messaging and Presence Protocol (XMPP), also called Jabber, which is used in the Jabber and Google Talk servers. This compatibility enables iChat Server to communicate (or federate) with other XMPP servers or domains, including Google Talk, to enable users of both to interact. XMPP support also means that the server supports Jabber clients on any platform.

## Clients for iChat Server

For Macs, the iChat client application is the best to use and most trouble-free, seamlessly accessing all iChat's features. iChat Server works with older versions of the Mac iChat client as well as the latest and greatest. There are also a number of other Jabber clients for Macs as well.

For Windows, Linux, Unix, mobile phones, and iPads and iPod touches, you can use any instant-messaging client that supports XMPP or is Jabber-compatible. Instant-messaging clients often support multiple protocols. There are a lot of XMPP clients, and more are popping up all the time. If you're looking for an open source client for Mac OS X, Windows, and Linux, try Pidgen (`www.pidgin.im`) or Spark (`www.igniterealtime.org/projects/spark/index.jsp`). Trillian (`www.ceruleanstudios.com`) is a Windows commercial product with a free version and a $25 pro version.

For iOS, you need to install a Jabber-compatible client app. The $9.99 BeeJive IM with Push (from BeeJive, Inc., `www.beejive.com`) is a popular iOS app that supports multiple chat protocols, including XMPP. There are separate versions for iPhone/iPod touch and iPad. Another option is Agile Messenger HD Pro ($7.99 from Agilemobile.com, Ltd.). Agile Messenger also supports full Facebook support from within the app. Both apps work with text only, not video, and are available from the App Store.

For longer list of XMPP-compatible clients, check out `http://xmpp.org/software/clients.shtml`.

Reality check: Not all XMPP clients and servers communicate smoothly with iChat service. You may find versions of XMPP software that have some issues, and you may find some that work better than others. Do a little testing before distributing a chat client to all your users.

## Prerequisites for iChat service

Before you set up iChat service, you need to take care of several network items. Quite likely, your network already has some of these things.

### Open Directory configuration

To authenticate users, iChat uses Open Directory (or another Lightweight Directory Access Protocol [LDAP] server) bound to iChat Server. iChat Server doesn't directly access the LDAP server. iChat users must have directory accounts in a directory domain. (See Chapter 6 for information on Open Directory.)

You also need an Open Directory master if you want to enable authentication with Kerberos or to use a Kerberos domain controller on another server. If you use the latter, the Kerberos realms of the controller and iChat Server must match.

### Firewall ports

If your iChat users are crossing a firewall to get to the server, you have to open some firewall ports. This is true for any service, but iChat requires a relatively large number of firewall ports to be open. (See Chapter 18 for more on firewalls.)

### Internet routers

If you want Internet users to access iChat service on your server and you have a DSL, cable router, or other Internet router, you need to configure it for port forwarding.

### DNS configuration for some situations

You may not need to do anything to your DNS server to support iChat service. But you could optionally add DNS records in two cases:

- ✔ You're enabling server-to-server communications so that your server talks to other chat servers. DNS can help users on different servers discover each other.
- ✔ You want to provide your users with a shorter iChat address.

In either case, you'd add a service locator (SRV) record for iChat to your DNS server.

To have DNS control connections between your iChat Server and other XMPP servers, you'd add an SRV record that maps the XMPP's TCP port 5269 to your server hostname. The SRV record takes the form

```
_xmpp-server._tcp 86400 IN SRV 0 1 5269 server.mycompany.com
```

where *server.mycompany.com* is your server's full domain name.

The other SRV records enable users to have a shorter iChat address (such as bobsmith@mycompany.com) instead of using the server's full hostname (such as bobsmith@server.mycompany.com). The DNS record would look like this, specifying port 5222:

```
_xmpp-client._tcp 86400 IN SRV 0 1 5222 server.mycompany.com
```

If you're using Lion Server for your DNS service, when you create a new SRV record with Server Admin, type **xmpp-client._tcp** in the Service Type field. 0 and 1 are the Priority and Weight entries.

## Configuring iChat service

To change the default settings of iChat Server, you mostly use the Server application. If you're familiar with previous versions of Mac OS X Server, you'll notice that Apple removed some of the more advanced configuration settings from Server Admin. However, you can still make some of these changes with the Unix command-line interface using Terminal. The following sections describe how to do so.

Because Server Admin no longer lets you make some of these changes, it also doesn't let you know what the current settings for these items are. To see all of the iChat settings, including the hidden ones, type this in Terminal:

```
sudo serveradmin settings jabber
```

You must set up Open Directory before configuring iChat service. (See Chapter 6 for more on Open Directory.)

The next few sections describe the settings that you can make with the Server application.

### Turning on iChat service

In Lion Server, you administer iChat service from the Server app. This is a change from Mac OS X Server 10.6, which let you use Server Admin. To turn on iChat service, just click the iChat icon in the Server app's sidebar and click the big switch to the On position, as shown in Figure 15-1.

At this point, if you have an Apple wireless router (AirPort or Time Capsule) on the network and listed in the Server app's sidebar, a dialog may ask you whether you want to allow Internet access to iChat service. Clicking the Allow button makes iChat Server available to users on the network; clicking Don't Allow makes it unavailable. To change this setting later, select the Apple router from the Server app's sidebar. For non-Apple routers, you need to configure the router for port mapping (see Chapter 18).

### Assigning chat names for users

Users of iChat Server need to have accounts in Open Directory and need to have chat names (or Jabber names). These are in the form *shortname@ host.domain*, such as jimdixon@server.ourshcool.edu.

You can add or view the Jabber names in Workgroup Manager, which is located in the Servers folder you downloaded. Here's how:

1. **In Workgroup Manager, if you see Not Authenticated, click the lock icon at top right and log in with your Open Directory credentials.**

2. **Click the Accounts icon in the toolbar and select the Users icon on the left side.**

3. **Select a user from the list at the left and click the Info tab.**

4. **Click the Add (+) button next to the Chat field.**

   The user's short name appears in the Chat field.

5. **Click the arrows to the left of the user's short name and select Jabber, as shown in Figure 15-2.**

   The full Jabber name appears in the Chat field.

6. **(Optional) Edit the name, if desired, and click Save when you're finished.**

**Figure 15-2:**
Setting
Jabber
names in
Workgroup
Manager.

### Saving and archiving chat messages

When you click Archive All Chat Messages in the Server app, Lion Server begins saving all iChat messages that users create. It stores this information in `/Library/Server/iChat/Data/message_archives`.

If you want to store this chat archive in a different location, such as another hard drive, you need to use the command line. Unlike previous versions of Mac OS X Server, Lion Server doesn't let you change the data archive location with the administration tools. To change the location with the command line, open Terminal in the `/Applications/Utilities` folder and type the following on one line:

```
sudo serveradmin settings jabber:savedChatsLocation = "/path/message_archives"
```

where *path* is the new location you'd like to use. (If the path was on another drive, it would look something like `/Volumes/MyOther HardDrive/myfolder`.)

If you've lost track of where you set the archive, you can find it (and all of iChat Server's settings) by typing **sudo serveradmin settings jabber**. Note that these comments are case-sensitive.

### Enabling server-to-server federation

Server-to-server (S2S) communication, known as *S2S federation,* enables communications with other XMPP servers, including Google Talk, Jabber, and other iChat Servers, as long as the servers are visible to the Internet. Users of each federated server can communicate with each other.

Selecting the Enable Server-to-Server Federation check box turns on S2S (see Figure 15-3). Click the Edit button to get access to further S2S settings. In the dialog that appears, you have a choice of Allow Federation with All Domains, which lets your users connect to a user on any XMPP server, or Restrict Federation to the Following Domains. The latter choice restricts access to domains or complete server hostnames that you add with the Add (+) button. (You can have both domains and server names in this list.)

You can require S2S sessions to use encryption by selecting the Require Secure Server-to-Server Federation check box and choosing an SSL certificate. With this setting, iChat Server blocks a user from connecting to a user in another domain if the latter doesn't support encryption. The other server must also be using a public key certificate.

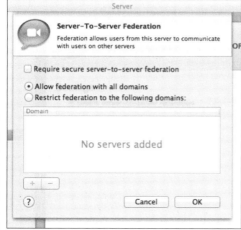

**Figure 15-3:**
Server-to-server settings for iChat Server.

If the Require Secure Server-to-Server Federation check box is grayed out, you probably don't have a certificate assigned to iChat service. You can add or change the certificate in the Server app by selecting your server in the left column and clicking the Settings tab. Next to SSL Certificate, click the Edit button and then select a certificate for iChat. (See Chapter 18 for more about certificate management.)

Finally, if you're configuring server-to-server federation, you may need to add an SRV record to your DNS server, as described in the section "Prerequisites for iChat service," earlier in this chapter.

### Turning autobuddy support on and off

With the autobuddy feature turned on, all iChat Servers in a particular group are added automatically to everyone else's buddy list. The upside is that users don't have to add buddies manually. The downside is that if users remove buddies from their list, autobuddy adds them back.

Autobuddy is turned off by default. Autobuddy is a setting that Apple removed from the graphical interface tools in Lion Server. To turn it on using Terminal, type the following:

```
sudo serveradmin settings jabber:enableAutoBuddy = yes
```

If you start autobuddy while iChat users are logged in, they can't communicate with the added buddies until the user first logs out and in again.

### Adding host domains

Lion Server can host iChat service on multiple domains. The default is a single domain, the server host. You add other hostnames for use by iChat, as long as DNS is configured to resolve the names to the iChat Server IP address.

Unlike previous versions, however, Lion Server no longer provides a way to add multiple domains using the server tool applications. You can still do this with the command-line interface. Open Terminal and type the following, all on a single line:

```
Sudo serveradmin settings jabber:hostsCommaDelimitedString="domain1.com,domain2.
          com,domain3.com"
```

Note that there is no space after the commas. Of course, substitute your real domains for *domain1.com* and so on. Include the server host in the list if it is one of the Jabber domains.

# Podcast Producer

*Podcast Producer* is an automated video and audio workflow system that you can use to create and distribute lectures, presentations, training, tech-support videos, classroom projects, and software demos. When I say *automated,* I'm not exaggerating. After Podcast Producer is set up, users can record video, send it to the server, and then wait for it to appear on a website or in iTunes's podcasting section. Educators can have Podcast Producer publish to Apple's iTunes U, part of the iTunes Store, for mass distribution to students. (For more on iTunes U, see www.apple.com/support/itunes_u.)

Podcast Producer is an assembly line: Users put in raw video, and it gets processed and published. While processing, Podcast Producer can encode video in formats for computers or iPhones or iPads. Podcast Producer automatically adds introductory and closing videos, titles, and effects; it can even add watermarks or overlays, such as logos or graphics, to the video.

What the assembly line does to the video or audio is defined in *workflows,* which are lists of tasks that the system will perform on the inputted content. You can edit default workflows, or you can create your own. The workflow also defines the encoding and output.

Because Podcast Producer is server-based, multiple users can input audio and video content over the network. The server can control access to cameras on the network. Lion Server's Xgrid service can farm out video encoding tasks to multiple Macs on the network. Podcast Producer can publish the finished video to network resources, including Lion Server's wiki-based website and its QuickTime Streaming Server.

You can take advantage of several features that help people create podcasts and workflows. Users of Windows, Linux, and older versions of Mac OS X can input content with a web browser, as can iPhone and iPad users. Users can have two video sources and place a video inside a box *(picture-in-picture)* with a canned template or one you create. A graphical workflow editor creates workflows, and the Podcast Library stores and organizes content.

## What's in Podcast Producer

Podcast Producer is a collection of software, both on the server and on users' Macs. Some of the Podcast Producer software has a user interface, and some doesn't. Knowing about the bits that you don't see is helpful in understanding what Podcast Producer does and how it does it:

- ✔ **The Podcast service:** This ties everything together; it passes authentication to the directory service that receives content from users and forwards information to where it needs to be. You use the Server app to turn the Podcast service on and off and make some configuration changes.

- ✔ **Podcast Capture application:** This is software for Mac OS X 10.6 and 10.7 clients to use to record audio and video and to send them to the server. You can record from a remote camera controlled by the server or from the built-in camera on a Mac or even from two video sources. Podcast Capture can also record what's happening on the computer screen. Podcast Capture can send QuickTime movies and audio to Podcast Producer for processing and distribution. It can also connect to the Podcast Producer Server. You can find it in the `/Applications/Utilities` folder.

- ✔ **Podcast Publisher application:** This is another application in the `/Applications/Utilities` folder found on users' Macs. New to Lion, Podcast Publisher is a more basic tool than Podcast Capture, enabling users to create basic podcasts. It can record from the Mac's built-in camera, as well as record the computer-screen activity, and import video and audio. Users can publish to a Podcast Library on Mac OS X Server.

- ✔ **Podcast Capture Web application:** This server-based technology enables users of any operating system to record video and then send it to the Podcast Producer service. The Podcast Capture Web application can't record the computer screen activity, however. You don't have to install anything on users' computers. Users simply access a web page on the server.

✓ **Podcast Composer application:** Podcast Composer is one of the server tools. You use it to create and edit workflows as it guides you through the steps needed. You can choose intro titles, intro and ending videos, watermarks, and effects, or you can add your own. You specify the workflow and the publishing and distribution method: wiki, iTunes U, or Podcast Library. Look for Podcast Composer in the `/Applications/ Server/` folder.

✓ **Podcast Library:** Podcast Library is a shared file system that holds the workflows and job submissions, as well as a set of software routines. The library stores the content submitted by users, as well as the rendered content generated by Xgrid. Podcast Library organizes all this based on information about the job that the user supplies in Podcast Capture.

Podcast Library is also a server that distributes content to the viewers — customers, employees, or students. It can send content to Wiki Server 3. Podcast Library sends out lists of updates as feeds viewable in Safari, Mail, or any RSS reader. Podcast Producer can also send Atom feeds to iTunes or iTunes U, which are visible in the iTunes Store but leave the content on your server. An Atom feed contains multiple versions of the podcast that have been encoded for different devices (computer, iPod, Apple TV, and audio-only). The viewer's device chooses what it needs.

✓ **The Xgrid service:** Xgrid does the grunt work of Podcast Producer — putting together the pieces, rendering transitions, and encoding the video. Because video encoding is a processor-and-memory-intensive task, Xgrid can send the jobs out to an Xgrid cluster that you set up, which consists of one or more Macs on the network.

The workflow that you create in Podcast Composer is actually a property list (`.plist` file) containing tasks for Xgrid to execute. The Xgrid service creates an Xgrid user that has privileges for certain files and folders. The Xgrid user is the owner of the Podcast Library shared file system.

Xgrid is actually a service apart from Podcast Library and is designed to be used for any processor-intensive task. Podcast Producer puts it to practical use for you without any heavy lifting on your part.

In the following sections, I cover some of the major points about getting Podcast Producer up and running on your server.

## Prerequisites for Podcast Producer

Podcast Producer requires a couple of things to be set on your network. First, it needs DNS reverse lookup, either on this server or on another server on the network.

If you don't mind typing a one-line command in the Terminal utility, you can verify easily that DNS forward and reverse lookup is configured correctly. Type this, exactly:

```
sudo changeip -checkhostname
```

If forward and reverse DNS are working correctly, you see this, but with your server information:

```
Primary address = 192.168.1.69
Current HostName = ourserver.macwindowsco.com
DNS HostName = ourserver.macwindowsco.com
The names match. There is nothing to change.
dirserv:success = "success"
```

The second thing Podcast Producer needs on the network is Open Directory, Active Directory, or another LDAP server to authenticate users. This requires your server Mac to be running an Open Directory master or to be bound to a Kerberized directory.

To support Active Directory with Podcast Producer, you need to edit a `.plist` file. To see how to do this, see the section "Mac OS X Server 10.5.6 or later" in the following Apple article: http://support.apple.com/kb/HT3289.

## Configuring podcast service with the Server app

The Server app gives you a basic setup, meant to be used with the simpler Podcast Publisher user app. The Server app's access to Podcast services is suitable for home use. If you're using Podcast Producer in schools or in professional settings or need the workflow tools for creating multiple podcasts, don't use the Server app; skip to the next section to configure with Server Admin.

If simple is all you need, you're in the right place. To configure Podcast service with the Server app, follow these steps:

1. **Open the Server app, click the Podcast icon in the left column, and turn the big switch to On.**

   This step activates the Podcast Library.

2. **Set user access to the Podcast content with the pop-up menu called Podcast Library Feeds Are Viewable By, as shown in Figure 15-4.**

The choices:

- *Anyone* means any computer user can access podcasts.

- *Authenticated Users* are people with accounts on Lion Server and who are logged in.

- *Podcast Owners* restricts access to users you designate as Administrators in the Administrators field. To add a user, click the Add (+) button and select a user from the list that appears.

**Figure 15-4:**
The Podcast
pane of the
Server app.

You can access the library by clicking the Manage Library link in the lower right of the Podcast pane. This opens your web browser with a list of podcasts.

In order to access the library, you need wiki service turned on. If you don't see the Manage Library link, you instead see a message telling you to Enable Wiki to Manage the Podcast Library. If you see this message, click the Wiki icon in the left column and turn on wiki service.

Once you're in the Podcast Library Wiki page, you can view podcasts, delete them, and read information about them. To make changes to the information, use Podcast Publisher (in the /Applications/Utilities folder). If you want to have other users access the page, access this URL, where *server* is the domain name of your server:

```
https://server/wiki/podcasts
```

Note that this is a *different* web page and URL from the one that Server Admin creates.

# Turning on and setting up Podcast Producer with Server Admin

Setting up and managing Podcast service with Server Admin gives you a much more robust and full-featured system than the one you can create with the Server app. This is reflected in the name: in Server Admin, it's called Podcast Producer, while the Server app calls it simply Podcast. If you want to create and use multiple workflows with multiple users, you're much better off using the Server Admin tools.

The procedure for getting Podcast Producer running is different from that for other services. You first need to turn on and configure Xgrid. The easiest way to do this is to run Setup Assistant. The Podcast Producer Setup Assistant configures the Podcast Producer settings, starts the library file system and the Xgrid service, assigns an Xgrid username, and connects to the directory.

The first thing to do is to enable Podcast service:

1. **Open Server Admin and select the server in the left column.**
2. **Click the Settings icon in the toolbar and then click the Services tab.**
3. **Make sure that the Podcast Producer check box is selected and click the Save button.**

Next, launch the Podcast Producer Setup Assistant and run through these steps:

1. **In Server Admin, click the triangle next to your server in the left column to expand the list of services.**
2. **Select Podcast Producer from the list.**
3. **Click the Overview icon in the toolbar.**
4. **Click the Configure Podcast Producer button in the lower right to launch Producer Setup Assistant.**
5. **Click through the introductory window.**

   You now have a choice between Express and Standard setup, as shown in Figure 15-5. Express automatically configures and turns on the needed services. With Standard setup, you have to type information. I recommend using Express and making changes later.
6. **Click the Express Setup option.**

   With either the Standard or Express choice, Podcast Producer Setup Assistant checks your directory to see whether a Kerberos-supported directory service exists.

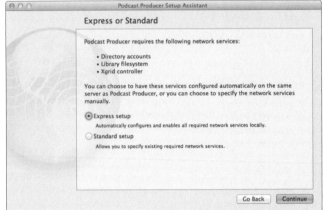

7. **Take the appropriate action in one of two screens that you may see:**

   a. *Click Continue if the assistant reports that it has found an Open Directory master on the server or if it detects that your server is bound to a kerberized directory.*

   This enables Podcast Producer to use the directory service.

   b. *If you're prompted to set up an Open Directory master or Kerberize your directory, enter a directory administrator name, short name, and password and then click the Continue button.*

8. **Click Continue in the Confirm window, which displays the settings the assistant has made.**

   Podcast Producer Assistant tells you whether the setup succeeded or failed.

9. **Click OK when you receive one of the two possible responses from the assistant:**

   a. A dialog says it succeeded.

   b. A dialog says it failed and asks whether you want to try to fix the problem or run the assistant again.

   When the process is complete, a Summary screen appears, telling you that Podcast Producer has been configured and started.

To bring back the Podcast Producer Setup Assistant later, click the Overview icon in the toolbar and then click the Configure Podcast Producer button.

Podcast Setup Assistant tells you what it is configuring while it happens. This includes turning on something called NFS file sharing. Although it was a feature of previous versions of Mac OS X Server, you won't see NFS file sharing as an option anywhere in the Lion Server administration tools. Apple removed all graphical user configuration for NFS file service, but it retained the service, which is also used with NetBoot service. NFS is still available through the command line.

## Accessing Server Admin's Podcast Library

Server Admin creates a different Podcast Library web interface from the Server app. Rather than just listing podcasts, it lists the different types of feeds that are created in a workflow, such as user feeds, workflow feeds, and keyword feeds. You get there with the URL `feed://server:8171/podcast producer/catalogs`, where `server` can be the server's IP address or full domain name. Another way to get to this is in Server Admin. Select Podcast Producer in the left column, click the Overview icon, and then click the link next to Podcast Library URL.

## Managing cameras

After Podcast Producer is set up and running, you can add cameras and restrict access to them. The cameras are plugged into Mac OS X 10.6 or later computers on the network or are built-in cameras in Macs. The process of adding the cameras to the Podcast Producer server is *binding* the Macs to the server. Binding enables these cameras to be shared remotely using the server. You bind from the Podcast Capture application on the Macs. (You can't use the Podcast Capture Web interface.)

### Binding Macs to the server and sharing cameras

To bind a Mac to the Podcast Producer server, open Podcast Capture on the Mac that has the camera you want to use and do the following:

1. **Choose the Podcast Producer server when prompted and enter a user-name and password.**

2. **Open Preferences from the Podcast Producer menu.**

3. **Click the Audio/Video icon in the toolbar.**

4. **Choose a Mac camera from the Video Source pop-up menu.**

   Make sure that you see an image from the camera in the preview area.

5. **Choose an audio source from the Microphone pop-up menu and then click the Start Sharing button.**

6. **Click the Start Sharing button in the dialog.**

7. **In the dialog that appears, type the password for your server account and click the Modify Settings button.**

8. **In the dialog that appears, enter a name for the camera, type your password once more, and click Start Sharing.**

You can do this for multiple cameras on a Mac and for multiple Macs. The cameras you add appear in Server Admin.

### Limiting access to cameras

By default, all server users have access to all cameras listed in Server Admin. For Macs used by one person, you may want to restrict access to that person. You can limit access to cameras in Server Admin:

1. **Click the triangle next to your server in the left column to expand the list of services.**

2. **Select Podcast Producer from the list and click the Cameras icon on the toolbar, as shown in Figure 15-6.**

3. **Select a camera from the list.**

4. **Select Allow Access to *Camera Name* for the Following Users and Groups.**

5. **Click the Add (+) button to add users and groups to the list.**

6. **Click the Save button.**

You can re-enable all users to access a selected camera by selecting Allow Access to *Camera Name* for All Users and Groups.

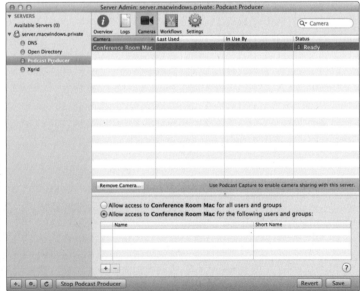

**Figure 15-6:**
Server Admin's Podcast Producer Cameras window.

## *Opening the web-based Podcast Capture*

After you set up Podcast Composer , Podcast Capture is one of the items on the home page of the built-in website, which I describe in Chapter 13. (The others are My Page, Wikis, and Blogs.) If you haven't disabled the home page, a user can get to it by typing the server's IP address or domain name in a browser's address bar. Click Podcast Capture, and you see the same interface as in the stand-alone Podcast Capture application.

# Part V
# Managing Clients

The 5th Wave                    By Rich Tennant

"No, that's not the icon for iCal. It's the icon for iCan't, the database of reasons you forgot an appointment."

# In this part . . .

The more computers you have in your organization, the more you need to manage them centrally. You can keep accounts up-to-date and keep track of notebook computers. Central enforcement of policies can prevent troubleshooting of clients.

But it's not about authoritarian control and being the big network boss. Well, okay, there is some of that. But client management also has user benefits. A server-based home folder allows a user to access a home folder from any computer. Notebook computer users can get the benefits of a directory domain even when not connected to the network.

Client management is based on directory services, which I describe in Part II. You may want to review those chapters if you haven't yet set up your directory.

In this part, I cover the concepts for managing desktop and mobile accounts and take you through the steps you need to make it all work. I start at the beginning, creating users and groups with both the Server app and Server Admin, divulging some useful tricks along the way.

In Chapter 18, I switch gears a bit, moving on to secure remote client access to the network and other security issues. This is client management in the sense of keeping control of security, which protects the client computers as well as the server. Kind of like your own airport security, but without having to take off your shoes.

# Chapter 16

# Managing Client Accounts

## In This Chapter

▶ Looking at account types and comparing the Server app and Workgroup Manager

▶ Creating, managing, and deleting accounts with the Server app and Workgroup Manager

▶ Importing and exporting accounts with Workgroup Manager

▶ Using Profile Manager to configure iPhones, iPads, and Mac clients

▶ Setting managed preferences to configure Mac OS X clients

*W*hen you install Lion Server, the Server Assistant creates a local directory of accounts containing the initial local administrator account. After the initial account, you can create more local accounts with System Preferences. This process is identical to managing accounts in Mac OS X clients.

The Server Assistant may have also created a shared directory of accounts and set up an Open Directory master, as described in Chapter 6. If your initial setup left you with only a local account, don't worry; you can still create an Open Directory shared domain. After a shared directory is created in Mac OS X Lion Server, use the Server app or Workgroup Manager to create and manage accounts. In this chapter, I describe how to use both utilities for this purpose.

Another powerful use of the server is to configure the computers of users and set policies on how they're used. You can do this in two ways, including using Profile Manager, a new tool that is launched from the Server app. You can use Profile Manager with iPads and iPhones, as well as Macs. The other method is using managed preferences in Workgroup Manager. I describe them both in this chapter.

# User, Group, and Computer Accounts

Lion Server has three types of accounts: user, group, and computer accounts. User accounts aren't necessarily individual people; more than one person may have access to a particular user account, such as a shared administrator account. A user account has a long name, a short name, a password, and a user ID (UID) number. Depending on the type of user account, you can assign other attributes, such as the user's home folder location. System processes, which are considered to be users but aren't actually people (at least, not yet), can also have user accounts.

In the local directory of the Mac OS X client, the first UID is 501. In a network Open Directory domain, the first UID is 1025. System-level users, like root (UID 0) or the directory administrator default (UID 1000), generally have lower level numbers.

A number of individual user accounts, when combined, become a group account. Group accounts have Group IDs (GID). Groups make it possible to better manage access to resources on a larger scale. In Lion Server, many collaboration services, including wikis, blogs, and shared folders, can be accessed with group accounts.

The third type of account, computer accounts, are created for computers bound to the shared directory. Putting computer accounts together creates a computer group, similar to a group of users. Workgroup Manager can handle computer accounts; the Server app does not. The importance of computer accounts and computer groups is evident in the section "Configuring Mac OS X Clients with Managed Preferences," later in this chapter.

The next section shows you everything you can do with accounts in the Server app. After that, I discuss account management in Workgroup Manager.

# The Server App versus Workgroup Manager

Lion Server has two types of functions to manage: services and accounts. The Server app tool can handle both. You can use the Server app to manage user services such as file sharing, web services, and e-mail, as well as for managing accounts. It provides a simple, well-designed interface that hides details that you may not need to bother with, but also has some hidden management features that some people may need. For more advanced management of the same database of accounts, you can use Workgroup Manager.

Apple hasn't upgraded Workgroup Manager for several releases of Mac OS X Server, and the user interface reflects this. It doesn't use standard Apple interface elements such as the gear-icon pop-up menus, making it difficult to browse around and figure things out. For managing accounts, I recommend using the Server app when possible, as it requires fewer actions to accomplish some of the same tasks.

Still, Workgroup Manager provides access to settings that aren't available in the Server app. It allows for editing the raw data in the Lightweight Directory Access Protocol (LDAP) database (see Chapter 5). In addition to managing user and group accounts, Workgroup Manager manages computer accounts and computer lists.

While both utilities also let you configure clients from the server, they use two completely different methods. You can use both methods to manage your clients. The Server app uses the Profile Manager to push settings to Mac, iPhone, and iPad clients. Workgroup Manager can set preferences settings for Mac clients in the shared directory domain and lets you define which applications users are permitted to launch. Workgroup Manager's managed preferences work with any Mac clients. Profile Manager works only on Macs running Lion, though it also supports the iPad, iPhone, and iPod touch.

After your Open Directory domain grows to a master server and one or more replica servers, connect the Server app or Workgroup Manager to the master server only. Replicas and bound servers contain read-only user databases that can't be modified by the server tools.

# Managing Accounts with the Server App

This section describes everything you can do with the Server app to manage user and group accounts, including a hidden feature and a few tricks.

## Logging in with the Server app

In Lion Server, the Server app is preconfigured to connect automatically to the server it's installed on. But you have to log in if you're running the Server app for the first time or from another Mac OS X 10.7 system, or if you've changed the hostname of the server postinstallation. To log in, perform the following in the Server app:

1. **Choose Manage⇨ Connect to Server and choose your Mac, or Other Mac for a remote Mac; click Continue.**

2. **Type the hostname of the server in the Server field and enter the administrator's username and password.**

3. **Click the Connect button.**

Once you're logged in, you'll see your server listed in the sidebar under Hardware.

For best results, always enter the server's fully qualified hostname in the Server field, usually in the form *server.example.com*. It could also be *server.private,* or *server.local* if you entered these forms when you installed Lion Server. Use of .local usually means that DNS isn't running on your network. The .local domain denotes *Bonjour* networking, Apple's zero-configuration host-to-host networking protocol. (See Chapter 3 for more on `.private` and `.local` in Lion Server.)

## Setting up and managing user accounts with the Server app

Users in Lion Server can be Mac, Windows, or Linux users. For the purposes of creating and managing accounts, Lion Server doesn't care. The accounts are attached to the person, not the computer. Multiple users could share a client computer, but each could still have his own user account.

### Creating new user accounts

To create and manage user accounts in the Server app, click Users in the sidebar to the left. For group accounts, click Groups. You see the window shown in Figure 16-1, which includes some user accounts already created.

**Figure 16-1:**
The list
of user
accounts in
the Server
app.

Whether you're using accounts stored locally on the Mac or on a shared network directory, the procedure for creating new accounts is the same. However, you do want to make sure you know what you have. If you create a bunch of local accounts when what you really wanted were Open Directory accounts, you'll have to create all the accounts again.

If you're not sure what you have, take a look at the user account icons. If you add a user and it has a globe in its icon (as in Figure 16-1), it's a shared network directory, an Open Directory domain. The first account is a local administrator account and has no globe. If you add further accounts and they don't have globes, then you haven't yet set up an Open Directory master. If you want to set up an Open Directory master, do it now. See Chapter 6 for instructions on how to do this.

When you're ready to add a user account, do the following:

1. **In the Server app, click Users in the sidebar.**

2. **Click the Add (+) button in the lower-left corner of the user list.**

3. **Enter the new user's name, as shown in Figure 16-2.**

   A short name is generated automatically, but you can edit it. Short names don't contain spaces, although they can contain punctuation, including periods, underscores, and hyphens. They're usually lowercase.

**Figure 16-2:** Adding a new user account in the app.

4. **Type an e-mail address with your own server's domain, or another.**

   If you have Mail Server running while you're creating new user accounts, the Server app automatically creates an e-mail address for the account and enter it for you in this dialog. This is a good reason to set up your e-mail service first if you're going to create a lot of accounts.

5. **Enter a password.**

   You can click the key icon next to the Password field to open the Password Assistant, which generates random passwords and tests password strength.

6. **(Optional) Select the Allow User to Administer This Server check box if you want to grant the user full administrative privileges to control services, modify accounts, change passwords, and install software on the server.**

If you don't want to give someone *full* admin rights, you can create limited administrators with Workgroup Manager, as I detail in the section "Creating user accounts with Workgroup Manager," later in this chapter.

7. **(Optional)** Change the icon for a user.

If you want, you can change the icon by clicking the user icon and selecting Edit Picture. You can import a photo, take one with the Mac's camera, or use another icon.

8. **Click the Done button.**

### Deleting user accounts

To delete a user, just click the user in the Users list on the left and then click the Delete (–) button. The Server app asks you to confirm the action. To delete multiple users at the same time, hold the ⌘ key while clicking usernames.

Unlike in Mac OS X's System Preferences, deleting a user account in the Server app doesn't delete the user's home folder or any files the user created on the server.

### Editing user accounts and joining groups

The Server app has another user account pane where you can edit some of the information you originally entered, add some new information, and add the user to groups. In the Users pane (refer to Figure 16-1), double-click a user to bring up the account's window, shown in Figure 16-3. Notice that it differs from the New User setup window.

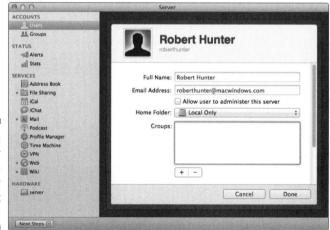

**Figure 16-3:** The Server app's basic user account pane.

There are several things you can do. You can edit the e-mail address or add one, if you haven't already. You can make the user an administrator or remove that privilege. You can set the location of a user's home folder. In the Home Folder pop-up menu, Local Only means that the home folder is on the user's computer. Other choices are home folders that you set up in the file sharing service. (Deploying home folders is described in Chapter 17.)

But there are also some things you can't do in this Users pane. Although you can edit the full name, you can't change the short name. So if I change the user's name in Figure 16-3 to John Barlow, the short name would still be `roberthunter`. Apple doesn't want people to change short names, because it can create problems if you've already done a lot of configuring of services. Although you can change the short name in this pane, there is another way to do it, which I describe in the next section.

There is also no way to add contact information besides the e-mail address. The Open Directory database can store the user's chat address(es), street address, phone numbers, and other information about him. To add this information, you have to use Workgroup Manager.

The other thing you can do in this pane is designate multiple groups that the user can be a member of. (When you edit a group account, you can designate multiple users to be a member of one group.) Here's how to add one or more groups to a user from the user's editing pane (see Figure 16-3):

1. **Click the Add (+) button below the Groups field.**

   An empty field containing the cursor appears in the Groups box. When you start typing the name of a group, a drop-down menu appears, listing groups that begin with (or are close to) the letters you've typed. But included in the list is the word *Browse.* Selecting Browse brings up a list of *all* groups.

2. **Start typing the word** browse **and hit the Return key.**

   A window lists all existing groups — easier than typing group names one at a time.

3. **In the window listing groups, select a group or ⌘-click to select multiple groups and drag them into the main window's Groups box, as shown in Figure 16-4.**

4. **Close the small window with the groups list and click the Done button in the main window.**

**Figure 16-4:**
Editing
group mem-
bership for
a user in the
Server app.

### Editing short name, UID, user alias, and other advanced options

The Server app includes an advanced settings dialog for user accounts. Apple took such great pains to hide this dialog from users that you can't get to it from any menu or button. There is only one way to get to it:

1. **In the Server app, click Users in the sidebar.**

2. **Control-click (or right-click) a user from the Users list to bring up a contextual menu.**

   You can use the gear icon to access all items in this contextual menu — *except* for the Advanced item, which is available only here.

3. **Select Advanced Options from the contextual menu.**

   The dialog shown in Figure 16-5 appears.

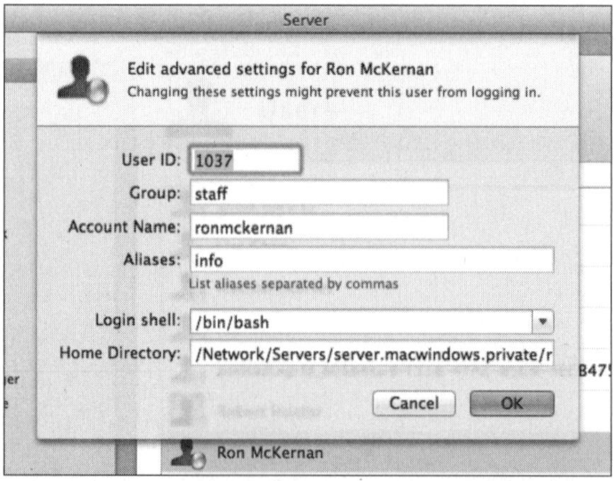

**Figure 16-5:**
The
advanced
user
account
dialog in the
Server app.

Apple hides this dialog because it contains items that should not be changed carelessly. They're most safely edited when you're first setting up your server and need to make a correction. Later changes may prevent a user from logging in or from getting access to shared folders. Here's what you can edit in this dialog:

- **User ID (UID):** The unique Unix number for an account.
- **Group:** A Unix group that all users belong to, typically called staff. This name doesn't appear in too many places. Change it at your own risk.
- **Account Name:** The short name that you can't edit in the main user window.
- **Aliases:** Additional short names you can add to enable a user to log in with, using the same password. Aliases can be useful for a shared account or for administrators in some cases. This field is not all that dangerous to edit. You can type multiple aliases separated by a comma and a space.
- **Login Shell:** The Unix shell that the user can work in if she has access to the command line. Typically, this is for administrators.
- **Home Directory:** The same home directory setting defined in the main user editing pane, but spelled out as a path here. In Figure 16-5, the path shows that this is a server-hosted home folder. Home folders on local hard drives usually are /Users/*shortname*.

### Changing passwords and setting password policy

The Server app's Users pane provides two types of password management. First, you can manually change a password for a user account. To do this, select a user from the Users list, click the gear icon, and select Reset Password from the pop-up menu. Type a new password, verify, and click the Change Password button.

The other thing you can do is create a password *policy* that applies to all user accounts. Again, click the gear icon under the Users list. This time, select Edit Global Password Policy. A dialog appears, presenting a dozen policy settings, all of which are turned off by default. You can create requirements for passwords, such the minimum number of characters. You can require that new passwords be different from previous passwords or that they be different from the account name. You can disable login after so many failed attempts or a period of inactivity, or have it expire on a certain date. Remember, though, that these policies apply to all users.

### Setting access to services (SACLs)

There is one more useful item in the gear icon's pop-up menu in the Users pane of the Server app. Select a user, click the gear icon, and choose Edit Access to Services.

This displays the services that the Server app manages (such as File, iCal, and Address Book), except for Wiki and Web. Selecting or deselecting these boxes grants or denies (respectively) a user's ability to access a service. To add or remove a user from a service that isn't listed here, use Server Admin to configure service access control lists (SACL). I describe how to do this in Chapter 9.

## *Setting up and managing group accounts with the Server app*

In the Server app, managing groups is very similar to managing user accounts, although you have fewer options to choose among for groups.

### *Creating new group accounts*

Follow these steps to create a group:

1. **In the Server app, click Groups in the sidebar.**

   Figure 16-6 illustrates the Groups pane in the Server app with group accounts already created.

**Figure 16-6:**
The Groups pane in the Server app.

2. **Click the Add (+) button in the lower-left corner under the Groups list and then enter a group name in the dialog.**

   The short name for groups is created automatically.

3. **Click the Done button.**

### *Adding members to a group*

The group you just created has no members. To add some, do the following:

1. **In the Server app, click Groups in the sidebar and double-click the name of a group in the list.**

The pane for that group appears, similar to that for a user. The bottom half is a list of users (members) belonging to the group.

**2. Click the Add (+) button below the Members field.**

An empty field containing the cursor appears below the last username. When you start typing the name of a user, a drop-down menu appears, listing members whose names begin with (or are close to) the letters you typed. Included in the list is Browse. Selecting Browse brings up a list of *all* users.

**3. Start typing the word** browse **and hit the Return key.**

A window lists all existing users — easier than typing usernames one at a time.

**4. In the window with the user list, select a user or ⌘-click to select multiple users and drag them into the main window's Members list, as shown in Figure 16-7.**

The small window with all users also includes all groups. You can add other groups as members of a group.

**Figure 16-7:**
Drag users to add them to a group in the Server app.

**5. Close the small window with the groups list and click the Done button in the main window.**

To remove a member from a group, select the user and click the Delete (–) button.

### Adding collaboration tools for a group

In the editing window for a group (refer to Figure 16-7), you can also direct Lion Server to set up collaboration tools for members of the group. In the section called Group Services, selecting these items will create them automatically:

> ✔ Selecting *Give This Group a Shared Folder* enables a shared server folder with access privileges for members of the group. File sharing services must be already running.
>
> ✔ Selecting *Make Group Members iChat Buddies* makes all group members buddies in iChat. iChat services must be already running.
>
> ✔ Clicking the *Create Group Wiki* button sets up a collaboration wiki for the group.

### Deleting a group

Deleting a group is the same process as deleting a user. Select the group from the Groups list and then click the Delete (–) button. Deleting a group removes the ability for users to connect to common collaboration resources associated with that group, including shared folders, wikis, blogs, and group calendars.

# Managing Accounts with Workgroup Manager

As Uncle Ben Parker reminds fans of *Spider-Man,* "With great power comes great responsibility." Workgroup Manager has great power for modifying the directory databases in Lion Server, so care in understanding the ability of this server tool is critical to healthy account management.

Unlike in previous versions of Mac OS X Server, Workgroup Manager is not installed with Lion Server. You must download it separately from Apple as part of the Server Admin Tools package, which also includes Server Admin. Look for it at www.apple.com/support/downloads.

You can open Workgroup Manager installed on any Mac OS X 10.7 computer connected to the same network as the Open Directory master (see Chapter 6). For the most consistent results in Workgroup Manager, connect directly to the Open Directory master. Don't connect to replica servers or any server bound to the directory. Replica servers contain read-only copies of the directory databases that are periodically synchronized from the master, so editing accounts on replicas forces directory updates on the master from the replica; instead, the master needs to update the replicas.

## Connecting to the server and authenticating to the directory

Open Workgroup Manager from the /Applications/Server folder. Workgroup Manager is preconfigured to connect to the server it's installed on. In the Workgroup Manager Connect screen, enter the address, username, and password of the local administrator created when you installed Lion Server.

If you're running Workgroup Manager from another system or you've changed the hostname of the server postinstallation:

1. **Choose Server⇨Connect and type the hostname of the server in the Server field.**

2. **Enter the administrator's username and password in the corresponding fields.**

3. **Click the Connect button.**

You could also click the Browse button to locate available servers on the network, but for the most consistent results, enter the server's fully qualified hostname, such as *server.example.com*, in the Address field.

Workgroup Manager loads the default screen, shown in Figure 16-8. In this example, a number of users have already been created.

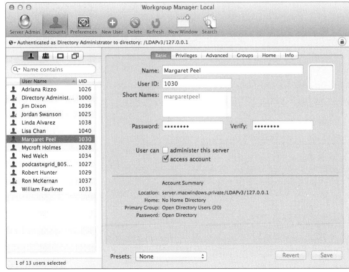

**Figure 16-8:** Workgroup Manager's default screen after connecting to a server.

Just below the toolbar is a small globe icon followed by text indicating the status of the directory you're browsing. The first time you connect to an Open Directory master, the status bar displays Viewing directory: / LDAPv3/127.0.0.1. Not authenticated. This indicates that you're browsing the shared directory on the server itself but haven't yet authenticated to modify the directory.

Clicking the globe icon allows you to change the directory you're browsing. A lock icon on the right side of this bar is used to authenticate to the directory, as I describe in the following section.

After you launch Workgroup Manager and connect, you need to authenticate to modify the directory.

1. **In Workgroup Manager, click the lock icon on the right side of the window to authenticate as the directory administrator (which you create in Chapter 6).**

2. **Enter the username and password of the directory administrator in the dialog and then click the Authenticate button.**

   The status next to the globe icon changes to `Authenticated as Directory Administrator to directory: /LDAPv3/127.0.0.1`, and the lock icon changes to an open lock.

## Creating user accounts with Workgroup Manager

Once you're connected and authenticated to the directory, you can add, remove, and modify accounts. Follow these steps to create a new user:

1. **Click the Accounts icon.**

2. **Select the Users tab just below the globe icon and then click the New User icon in the toolbar.**

   A new user is created, named Untitled 1. If Untitled 1 already exists, the new user is Untitled 2, and so on.

3. **In the Basic tab (refer to Figure 16-8), enter the username in the Name field.**

   A short name is generated automatically, based on the name.

4. **Enter a password.**

   The user ID (UID) is automatically generated based on the first available number higher than 1025 — the first UID used for regular directory accounts.

5. **Click the Save button.**

## Changing default account settings

With Workgroup Manager's Accounts icon selected in the toolbar, you can select any account from the list of users and modify its settings.

The initial short name is the only user attribute that can't be changed with Workgroup Manager. You can change it with the Server app, as described in the section "Editing short name, UID, user alias, and other advanced options," earlier in the chapter. Additional short names, or *aliases,* can be added by clicking the field below the existing short names on the Basic tab of Workgroup Manager, but some services require the user to enter the original short name.

After a user account is created and its UID is set, don't change the number for it. Permissions and access to various services are tied to the particular UID for the user; changing the UID could have unintended consequences and make it impossible for a user to access her data.

### Setting server administrators and directory administrators

By default, new user accounts aren't administrators. You can enable users to be server administrators and/or directory administrators. Server administrators can use Server Admin to modify services and settings of Lion Server. Directory administrators have privileges to change user and group settings.

To enable a user to be a server administrator:

1. **Log in to Workgroup Manager.**
2. **Click the Accounts icon in the toolbar and then click the Basic tab.**
3. **Select a user and then select the User Can Administer This Server check box to allow users to administer this server.**

To enable a user to be a directory administrator, click the Privileges tab and choose Limited or Full from the Administration Capabilities pop-up menu. For a limited administrator, you can add users or groups that the account will manage by clicking the Add (+) button on the right. A list of users and groups slides out the side of the window. Drag users and groups from the slide-out list to the User Can Administer field, as shown in Figure 16-9.

You can also set the levels of administration by selecting the Manage User Passwords, Edit Managed Preferences, Edit User Information, and Edit Group Membership check boxes for each user or group added to the limited administration list, as shown in Figure 16-9.

### Editing group membership

Continuing with the Users (head icon) tab selected on the left, you can set group membership for the selected user in the Groups tab on the right. You can see this in Figure 16-10. Near the top are fields for primary group ID and short name. By default, all new users created in Workgroup Manager are members of the primary group called Open Directory users, which has a short name of staff and a group ID (GID) of 20.

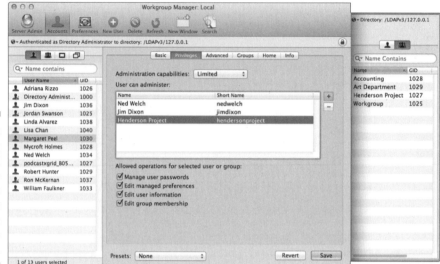

**Figure 16-9:**
Setting
limited
adminis-
tration
capabilities
of a user in
Workgroup
Manager.

When you click the Add (+) button, a Users and Groups drawer slides out of the Workgroup Manager window. Change the primary group by dragging a group from the slide-out list over one of the three fields — Primary Group ID, Short Name, or Name.

Additional group membership can be added by dragging groups to the Other Groups list.

Because groups can be members of other groups (called *nested groups*), click the Show Inherited Groups button to see additional groups that the user is a member of via nested groups.

### Setting the location of a user's home folder

With the user icon still selected on the left, the Home tab, shown in Figure 16-11, gives you various options for setting the location of a home folder:

- ✔ Select None (the default) if the user shouldn't have a home folder on the server. Select this option if the user doesn't need to log in to a home folder — useful for an account that accesses only sharing or collaboration resources.

- ✔ Select a directory (identified as a path) if you want the user to have a server-based home folder. Folders that appear here are shared folders that you previously configured as automounted home folders on this server with the Server app or on another server bound to the directory.

  Note that Figure 16-11 shows a folder shared with NFS. Although Lion Server's admin tools don't let you configure NFS shares, Podcast Producer configures its own home folder by using NFS.

✔ The Disk Quota field is an upper limit on the amount of disk space that the folder can use. It applies to all data created by a user on the volume where the home folder exists, not just on the share point where the home folder is stored.

**Figure 16-10:** User account group membership in Workgroup Manager.

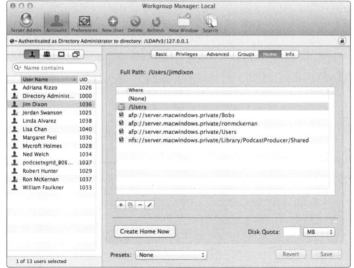

**Figure 16-11:** Setting the home folder for a user account in Workgroup Manager.

You won't use the other buttons on this page much, but here's what they do:

✔ Click the Add (+) button to add a new location for user home folders. In the dialog that appears, enter the Mac OS X Server/share point URL (this may be another server besides Lion Server), the path to the home folder, and the full path the Mac OS X client will use to access the home folder. The new location will be available to all users in the directory.

✔ If users store only their home folders on the local Mac OS X computer, set the home folder to /Users. By doing so, regardless of where the user logs in, his home folder is in the local Users folder.

  If you don't see a /Users folder in the list, and you want one, click the Add (+) button and then enter **/Users/*short name*** in the Full Path field. Leave the Mac OS X Server/Share Point URL and Path to Home Folder fields blank.

✔ Next to the Add (+) button, three additional buttons exist for managing home-folder locations. The double-window button duplicates a home-folder location. The Minus (–) button deletes a home-folder location for all users in the directory but leaves the data intact in the home folders. The pencil button allows you to edit home-folder locations.

✔ The Create Home Now button generates a new home folder at the specified location. This process doesn't overwrite an existing home folder with the same short name. The home folder is created automatically the first time a user logs in if this button isn't clicked, so creating a home folder from Workgroup Manager isn't required.

### Editing other user account settings

Workgroup Manager's User Accounts pane has a few more areas you can edit.

### The Info tab

The Info tab lets you add contact information, including street address, phone numbers, email and chat addresses, and other information about a user. Details entered in this tab become part of the account record in the user database and can be viewed by the Address Book client in Mac OS X Lion if Address Book Server (see Chapter 11) is running.

### The Advanced tab

You can find several unrelated settings here:

✔ Deselecting *Allow Simultaneous Login* prevents a user from logging into the server from more than one computer at the same time.

✔ The *Comment and Keyword fields* can help you quickly locate accounts based on similar comments or keywords.

✔ The *User Password Type pop-up menu* allows you to assign the user to a different password database. You can change from Open Directory to Crypt Password for backward compatibility with users connecting from

Mac OS X 10.1 and earlier. When managing other types of directories, such as the unshared local directory of users, another choice is Shadow Password, the standard password type for local accounts in Mac OS X.

✔ *Login Shell* selects which Unix shell environment the user has when connecting to the server from Terminal. To disallow Terminal access on the server, choose None from the pop-up menu.

## Disabling and deleting user accounts with Workgroup Manager

An alternative to immediately deleting a user account is to disable access to the account by deselecting the Access Account check box in the Basic tab of a user account. (This check box is visible in Figure 16-8.) Disabled accounts are shown in the Users list with a red X through their icons.

The more disabled accounts you have, however, the more difficult it becomes to manage a large group of users. After a while, deleting a defunct user is the best option to keep your directory tidy. To delete an account, click the Users tab just below the globe icon. Click to select a user and then click the Delete (–) button.

Files in shared and home folders created by deleted users remain on the server. However, data in Mail, iCal, Address Book, and blogs is removed from the server when the user account is deleted.

## Creating group accounts with Workgroup Manager

Although the number of options and settings is far simpler, creating a group account with Workgroup Manager is much the same as creating a user account. Group accounts contain one or more user or group accounts. Group accounts that are members of another group are *nested accounts.*

To create a new group account with Workgroup Manager, follow these steps:

1. **Click the lock icon on the right side of the Workgroup Manager window and enter the username and password of the directory administrator in the dialog; click the Authenticate button.**

2. **Select the Groups tab just below the globe icon and then click the New Group icon in the toolbar.**

   A new group is created, named Untitled 1, as shown in Figure 16-12. If Untitled 1 already exists, the new group is Untitled 2, and so on.

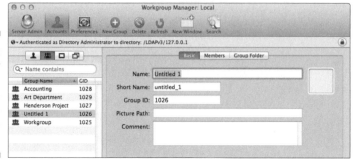

**Figure 16-12:**
A new
Untitled 1
group
created in
Workgroup
Manager.

3. **In the Basic tab, enter the group's name in the Name field.**

   A short name is generated automatically.

   The group ID (GID) is generated automatically based on the first available number higher than 1025 — the first GID used for regular directory accounts.

   The Basic tab includes a field to enter a picture path, used to set a custom picture to identify this group. You can use the Comment field for human-readable comments regarding this group account.

4. **Add users and groups to the group membership by clicking the Members tab at right (see Figure 16-13) and then the Add (+) button.**

   A users and groups drawer slides out the side of the Workgroup Manager window. Users are shown under a User icon (a single silhouetted figure) and groups under a Group icon (three silhouetted figures).

**Figure 16-13:**
Adding
users to
a group,
shown here,
is similar
to adding
groups to
a user.

5. **Drag user and group accounts (shown in Figure 16-13) to the Members tab to add them to the new group.**

   To remove a user or group, click the account name in the Members tab and then click the Delete (–) button.

Like a user account, a group can have its own automounting folder on a share point. The process is like assigning a home folder to a user (shown in Figure 16-11), except that you select Groups on the left. Where the users screen has a Home Folder tab on the right, the groups screen has a Group Folder tab. When you set the share point and folder, group members can access the shared folder as well as save and edit content, subject to permissions set for the shared folder. (See Chapter 8 for details on setting file-sharing permissions.)

When you select a share point for a group folder, you must specify an owner of the folder. Click the ellipsis (. . .) button next to the short name to select a user to be the group folder's owner. This can be a member of the group or an administrator. The owner can create, edit, or delete any file or folder in the group folder.

## *Editing and deleting group accounts with Workgroup Manager*

Although you can't change the short names of user accounts, you can modify any aspect of a group account within Workgroup Manager. Simply access an existing group account in the same way that you would for a new account. (See "Creating group accounts with Workgroup Manager," earlier in this section.)

The group ID (GID) shouldn't be changed after a group is created. The GID is tied to file permissions and resources in Lion Server; changing it may have unintended consequences, making data and resources unavailable to users.

Group accounts can't be disabled like user accounts; however, removing all members of a group effectively disables anyone from accessing the group resources. To permanently remove a group, do the following:

1. **Click the Groups tab just below the globe icon and then select the group to be deleted in the list of accounts.**

2. **Click the Delete icon in the toolbar and then confirm the deletion of the group account by clicking Delete in the dialog that appears.**

Files in shared folders created by deleted groups remain on the server. However, data such as blogs, wikis, and group calendars in other services is removed from the server when the group account is deleted.

# *Importing and exporting accounts*

Chapter 6 describes how Workgroup Manager can archive and restore the entire Open Directory domain. You can also use Workgroup Manager to import and export account records. Periodically exporting accounts can help you restore your Open Directory domain if the worst should happen and your archive won't restore the databases.

When you export user accounts from the archive process, user passwords aren't ever exported from Workgroup Manager. In addition, the Kerberos Key Distribution Center (KDC), which controls single sign-on, can't be exported.

Importing accounts can make a large influx of new users easier to manage. For example, a school may have a list of new students each fall taken from the registrar's database, manipulated, and imported into Workgroup Manager. Third-party utilities, such as Passenger from MacinMind Software (www. macinmind.com/Passenger), can help massage the raw data into a format compatible with an Open Directory domain.

To import users in Workgroup Manager, choose Server➪Import; then select a file and click the Import button. Chapter 6 describes how to import users and groups from another directory server by using the Server app.

Exporting accounts in Workgroup Manager is straightforward. Follow these steps to export a list of accounts:

1. **Click the lock icon on the right side of the Workgroup Manager window and enter the username and password of the directory administrator in the dialog; click the Authenticate button.**

2. **Depending on the type of account you plan to export, click the Users, Groups, Computers, or Computer Groups tab below the globe icon.**

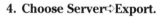

3. **Select the accounts from the list you plan to export.**

   Hold the ⌘ key to select more than one account.

4. **Choose Server➪Export.**

   A Save As dialog appears, allowing you to enter a name for the exported list of accounts and to select the location to save the file.

5. **Click the Export button.**

   Repeat this process for each type of account — users, groups, computers, and computer groups — you're exporting.

If you need to delete a number of accounts, you could also export the account lists before they're deleted. This saves you time if any account is deleted in error or needs to be added again later.

# Configuring Clients with Profile Manager

Profile Manager is one of the most useful new features introduced with Lion Server. It's an automated way to configure account settings on Macs running Lion, as well as iPad, iPhone, and iPod touch devices. Profile Manager sets up the client devices for services running on Lion Server, adding configuration information about e-mail and virtual private networks (VPN), as well as other services, including non-Apple technologies, such as Microsoft Exchange Server. You can create profiles for all users, as well for specific users, for groups, or for certain devices.

Lion Server provides three places where this happens:

- ✔ **The Server app,** where you turn on Profile Manager service. The Server app automatically pulls together basic user configuration information for client access to the services.

- ✔ **The Profile Manager web app** is where you edit the default configuration profile and create others for specific users, groups, or devices. The Profile Manager web app also pushes settings and invitations to enroll to users. The web interface is automatically created by Lion Server's web and wiki services.

- ✔ **The My Devices user web portal**, a unique web interface for each user with accounts in the shared directory. Users do two things with the web portal:

    - Download settings profiles to their Lion Macs and iOS devices.

    - Enroll devices in the Profile Manager service. Once devices are enrolled, configurations and changes to configuration will be automatically pushed to the devices. Users get another benefit as well: From the web portal, a user can remotely lock or even wipe the data from a lost Mac, iPhone, iPad, or iPod touch.

There are a few prerequisites. You need to have users' accounts in a shared directory, such as Open Directory, and you need web and wiki services turned on. It's also best to have services configured before running Profile Manager so that it can gather the data from the services.

The next few sections describe using the Profile Manager service on the server end and on the user device.

## Configuring profiles

A *configuration profile* is a small XML file that Profile Manager sends to Lion clients and iOS devices. When a Lion client or an iPod, iPhone, or iPod touch receives a configuration profile, software on the device recognizes the configuration profile file and imports the settings. There are dozens of settings that a configuration profile can create in a client device. Here are a few:

✔ Basic account info in a directory service (Open Directory, Active Directory, or LDAP)

✔ E-mail, calendar, contacts, and chat. Install user address, passwords, and server info, such as POP and SMTP servers.

✔ Microsoft Exchange Server settings for connecting to Windows servers

✔ VPN and network settings

✔ Printing preferences and restrictions

✔ Enforcement of password policies, which you can set in the Server app

✔ Restrictions, such as preventing Mac and iOS applications from launching, blocking users from making changes to System Preferences, blocking Macs from accessing external storage devices or optical discs, preventing iOS users from watching YouTube, parental controls, and much more

✔ Certificates (a configuration profile can install security certificates in a device)

✔ Custom preferences for other applications

## Configuring Profile Manager on the server

There's very little typing involved with using Profile Manager. It takes information that is already in the system, such as account names, e-mail addresses and mail server configuration data, and your server's domain name for the various services.

On the server, there are two tasks. The first is to turn on the Profile Manager service with the Server app to create the first profile (see the next section). The second task, if desired, is to use the Profile Manager to create further configuration profiles.

### Using the Server app to turn on and set up Profile Manager

If you have your services running before you turn on and set up Profile Manager, the Server app automatically creates a profile with the settings of the running services.

To turn on the Profile Manager service and have it create the first configuration profile, do the following.

1.  **Click Profile Manager in the sidebar, click the On switch, and wait for the service to start, as shown in Figure 16-14.**

2.  **Change the name of the default configuration profile, which is Settings for Everyone.**

**Figure 16-14:**
The Server
app's Profile
Manager
pane.

3. **Make sure that the Include Configuration for Services check box is selected.**

4. **If Device Management indicates Disabled, click the Configure button and follow the directions.**

   This step enables a mobile-device-management (MDM) server.

5. **Select the Include Configuration for Services check box.**

   A list of services appears. These are part of the profile.

6. **(Optional) Select the Sign Configuration Profiles check box for secure transmission of profiles.**

7. **(Optional) Select a security certificate in the dialog that appears and click the OK button.**

   Should you choose to change this later, you can click the Edit button next to Sign Configuration Profiles.

The Server app has now collected information from the accounts and the running services and has created a configuration profile for all users. It gives a default name called Settings for Everyone. You can change this name with the Edit button.

A profile is now ready, and you may be finished at this point. You can have users visit `http://server.example.com/mydevices` (using your server's domain name). To get your actual URL, you can go to the Profile Manager pane and click the arrow next to Visit User Portal. Your browser will open to the portal page, where you can copy the URL for users. If you don't need to create another profile, skip to the section "Configuring Profiles on Clients," later in the chapter.

If you'd like to edit the configuration profile or create new ones for individual users, groups, or devices, go to the Profile Manager web app, described in the next section.

### Creating additional profiles with the Profile Manager web app

You can access the Profile Manager web app from a web browser by using a URL in this form: `http://server.example.com/profilemanager`. Or, in the Server app's Profile Manager pane, click the arrow next to Open Profile Manager in the lower right. Your web browser launches and asks you to log in.

The Profile Manager web app opens, as shown in Figure 16-15. It displays the configuration profile created by the Server app, which applies to everyone, and lists the services that have settings in the profile. You can now create a profile for a subset of users that configures more items. Follow these steps:

**Figure 16-15:**
The Profile Manager web interface.

1. **Select a user or group from the left two columns.**

   If you've added devices or created groups of devices, you can select them as well.

2. **Under the Group name on the right side of the window, click the Edit button.**

   The Settings page appears.

3. **Select a setting type from the scrolling list on the left.**

   It's organized into three areas: Mac OS X and iOS, iOS only, and Mac OS X only.

4. **Select an item and click the Configure button.**

5. **Select settings options in the configuration window, like the one shown in Figure 16-16.**

6. **When you're finished with the settings in the window, click another item in the list on the left.**

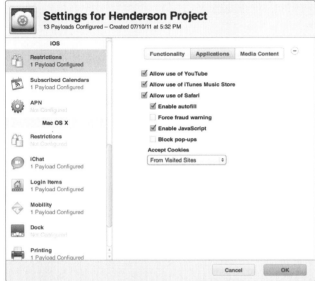

**Figure 16-16:**
A configuration profile settings window showing iOS device restrictions.

If you don't want to use anything in this settings window, *don't* click the Cancel button. Clicking Cancel will undo all the settings you've made during the current session. Instead, use the Delete (–) button.

**7. When you're finished, click the OK and Save buttons.**

The profile for this group now shows the areas that you've configured, displayed on the right side, as shown in Figure 16-17.

**Figure 16-17:**
A new, customized configuration profile for a group.

### Creating profiles for devices

For a device that has more than one person working on it, as in a school computer lab or workstations in an art department, it is more convenient to manage configuration profiles for the device instead of users. The same would be true for a user who has more than one Mac but needs different settings on each.

To create profiles for devices, just use the procedure in the preceding section, but select Devices or Device Groups in the left column (refer to Figure 16-17). If you don't have any devices listed, you can create a placeholder until a user connects with the device. Follow these steps:

1. **Click Devices in the left column.**

2. **Click the Add (+) button and select Add Placeholder from the pop-up menu.**

3. **Enter a name and serial number (or UDID, IMEI, or MEID) and click the Add button.**

   iPhones, iPads, and iPod touches have a Unique Device Identifier (UDID), which you can find in iTunes with the device plugged in to the computer. Select the device from the sidebar and then click the serial number. It will change to a UDID. iPads with 3G also have a Mobile Equipment Identity (IMEI) engraved on the back. Verizon iPhones also have Mobile Equipment Identifiers (MEID).

   The device now appears in the middle column. If you select it and click the About box, you find more information about it.

For the serial number for Macs running Lion, choose Apple menu⇨About This Mac, and click the More Info button. For iOS devices, go to Settings, click the General item, and then click About.

## Configuring profiles on clients

Once you have a configuration profile, either the one created by the Server app or your own, the users can access it from a web browser. They'll have a choice of downloading a configuration profile or enrolling the device in the mobile device management (MDM) service provided by Profile Manager. First, here's how to download a profile to have Profile Manager configure the client device:

1. **From the Lion Mac or iOS device, log in with a web browser at** *yourdomain.com*/**mydevices.**

   The My Devices page appears. Figure 16-18 shows the page on an iPhone, but it looks identical on a Mac.

**Figure 16-18:** The My Devices page, where iOS and Mac users download a configuration profile.

2. **Click the Profiles tab.**

   Clicking the Show Contents link displays what settings are in the profile.

3. **Click the Install button.**

   This step downloads a file with a filename in the form `name-of-profile.mobileconfig`. A new window opens, describing what's in the profile and asking you to approve.

4. **Inspect the window that appears for accuracy.**

   In Mac OS X 10.7, the downloaded configuration profile launches System Preferences, which displays a dialog. Click Show Profile to expand the list to get profile details, shown in Figure 16-19.

5. **Click Continue and then click the Install button.**

   On a Mac running Lion, System Preferences gets a new Profiles pane.

Installing an enrollment request is similar to downloading a profile. When a device is enrolled, the MDM service pushes configuration changes to the device, so the user no longer needs to access the web portal. (An enrollment is actually a type of configuration profile.) Enrollment also enables a user to lock or wipe the Mac or iOS device from the web portal. Here's how to enroll:

1. **After logging into the web portal, click the Devices tab, shown in Figure 16-20.**

2. **Click the Enroll button.**

**Figure 16-19:** System Preferences displaying a configuration profile request.

**Figure 16-20:** An enrollment request, which looks the same in iOS or Mac Lion.

3. **After the configuration profile file downloads and you're warned that settings will be changed, click the Install button.**

   You're asked for a password if there's an e-mail configuration in the profile.

To remotely lock or wipe a device from the admin's Profile Manager web page, choose either command from the gear icon. Users can find the commands in their My Devices page under the Devices tab.

# Configuring Mac OS X Clients with Managed Preferences

Managed Preferences for Mac OS X (MCX) is a powerful feature that allows Lion Server to manage system, user, and applications preferences on Macs connected, or bound, to an Open Directory domain. With MCX, a Mac client can automatically load predefined settings from the central server. You can also define which applications can run. If you don't want users buying items from the App Store, you can prevent the App Store from launching. If you don't want users to change preferences, you can prevent them from launching System Preferences.

You can make a lot of these same settings with Profile Manager, but only with Lion clients. With MCX, you can do this with any version of Mac OS X.

MCX can manage any preference by storing a *manifest,* one or more preference files, on the Mac. Managed preferences can be set for almost any system, user, or application preference that uses Apple's standard preference list (.plist) files. Many system and user settings are preconfigured for easy management in Workgroup Manager under the Preferences icon.

Before I get to setting up managed preferences, the next section describes how to create computer group accounts, which are very useful for applying managed preferences.

## Creating computer and computer group accounts

Managed preferences make apparent the importance of computer and computer group accounts. Specific computer and computer group preferences streamline management of Energy Saver settings, mobile accounts, and hardware-specific preferences, for example.

You don't need to create computer or computer group accounts in Workgroup Manager unless you plan on using managed preferences. You could use the list of computer and computer group accounts to help you organize and manage large deployments of Mac OS X systems, but Workgroup Manager isn't a great replacement for a simple spreadsheet or database of systems.

You could create a new computer account by selecting the Computer tab (square icon) in Workgroup Manager and then clicking the New Computer icon in the toolbar. However, you then need to type the Ethernet ID to identify the computer. It's easier to first create a computer group and then browse the list of bound computers to add the computer to the list, creating a computer account by default.

Here's how to create a computer group and add computer accounts:

1. **In Workgroup Manager, click the lock icon to authenticate as the directory administrator (which you create in Chapter 6) and enter the username and password of the directory administrator in the dialog; click the Authenticate button.**

2. **Click the Computer Groups tab (two overlapping squares) below the globe icon and then click the New Computer Group icon in the toolbar.**

   A new computer group named Untitled 1 is created. If Untitled 1 already exists, the new group is named Untitled 2, and so on. Figure 16-21 shows an example of a new computer group. Much like a group of user accounts, a computer group has Name, Short Name, Group ID (GID), and Comment fields in the Basic tab of Workgroup Manager.

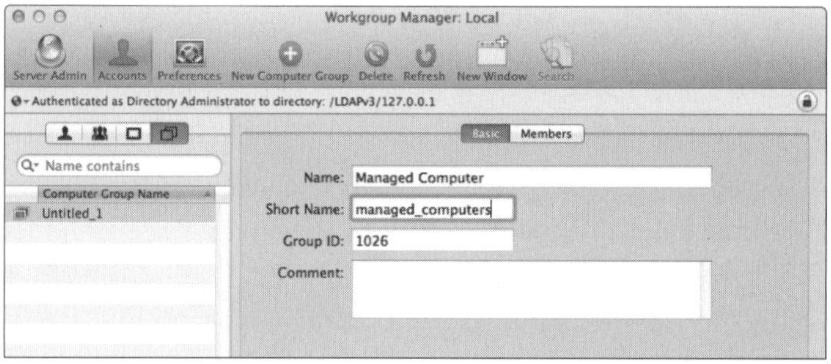

**Figure 16-21:** A new computer group created in Workgroup Manager.

3. **Enter a name for the computer group.**

   The short name is generated automatically based on the Name field. The Group ID (GID) will be created for you.

4. **Click the Members tab to add computers to the group.**

   Click the Add (+) button in the Members tab to add computers or existing computer groups to the new group or click the ellipsis (. . .) button to select computers already bound to the directory to add to the computer group.

**5. Click the Add button.**

You now have members in a computer group. Click the Computer Accounts tab (a single square) in Workgroup Manager and notice that the computer you added now has a computer account also, as shown in Figure 16-22.

**Figure 16-22:** A computer account shown in Workgroup Manager.

## *Configuring managed preferences*

In Workgroup Manager, click the Preferences icon in the toolbar to manage preferences for accounts connected to the Open Directory domain. The left side of the Preferences pane uses the same tabs (users, groups, computers, and computer groups) as the Accounts pane. Figure 16-23 shows Workgroup Manager with the Preferences icon on the toolbar selected and a computer group selected.

Note the icons on the right side of the Workgroup Manager window under the Overview tab, such as Applications, Classic, Dock, and so on. These icons represent preferences manifests that have been preset in Workgroup Manager. Some of the preset preferences icons don't apply to different types of accounts and therefore aren't displayed.

Although the Overview tab has many commonly managed preferences, nearly any preferences list in Mac OS X can be managed. Other preferences manifests can be added in the Details tab.

As an example of how to set up managed preferences, here are directions on configuring a list of applications that can be launched on Macs that belong to a computer group. Users of these Macs are prevented from launching applications not on your list. This restriction can be useful for Macs in a public place, such as a school computer lab.

**Figure 16-23:**
The Preferences screen for a computer group in Workgroup Manager.

Note that you can designate individual applications, or applications that reside in folders, such as Microsoft Office. You select those in two different places. Here's how to set allowed applications:

1. **Click the Preferences icon in the toolbar and select the Computer Group tab (two overlapping squares) above the list of accounts.**

2. **Click the Applications icon under the Overview tab.**

   The window changes to the one shown in Figure 16-18. For applications the reside in folders (such as Microsoft Office), click the Folders tab instead.

3. **Select Always from the Manage options and then select the Restrict Which Applications Are Allowed to Launch check box.**

4. **Click the Add (+) button and select the applications from the list the appears; click the Add button in the dialog.**

   The list of applications that appears includes those that are installed on your server Mac. Any application you want to permit users to launch must be also installed on the server.

   If you are in the Folders tab, when you allow an application residing in a folder to be launched (such as Office), you also allow helper applications to run. You can manually deselect the helper apps to disallow them.

5. **Click the Apply Now button to save your settings.**

   If you get a message asking you to digitally sign applications, click the Sign button if you want to enable the server to identify apps on the Macs.

   Figure 16-24 shows the result of these steps so far: a list of applications allowed to launch in the Managed Computers computer group.

6. **Click the Done button to return to the Overview tab.**

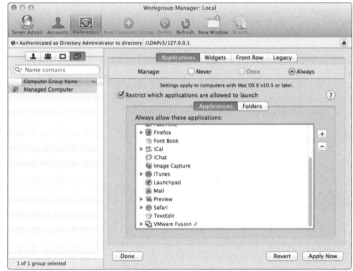

**Figure 16-24:** Managed preferences controlling the applications allowed to launch.

You can also manage other preferences from the Overview tab. In Figure 16-23, earlier in this chapter, the mouse-pointer icon next to the icons for Applications, Dock, Finder, Media Access, and Network indicates that these items all have some managed preferences configured.

If you now click the Details tab, you can view precise information about each preferences manifest, as shown in Figure 16-25.

The Details tab allows you to edit the preferences manifests by clicking an item in the list and then clicking the pencil icon below the list. A new pane opens to show the details of the preferences, as shown in Figure 16-26 for the Dock settings. This is also where you can find the option for the Often setting of a managed preference.

With the Details tab, you can import preferences from other applications or sources. Click the Add (+) button to add those preferences files (in the .plist format) to Workgroup Manager.

You can also set managed preferences for user, group, or computer accounts from their respective tabs above the list of accounts.

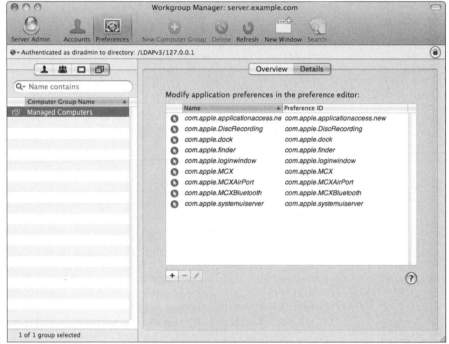

**Figure 16-25:**
Specific
details
for each
managed
preferences
manifest.

**Figure 16-26:**
A prefer-
ences
manifest
for Dock
settings
shown in
Workgroup
Manager.

# Inheriting, combining, and overriding preferences

You can set managed preferences for all types of accounts in an Open Directory domain: users, groups, computers, and computer groups. A group with managed preferences is referred to as a *workgroup*. Managed preferences can't be controlled for computers that aren't bound to the domain, but users in the domain also can't log in at those computers with directory accounts until they're bound.

Because managed preferences can be applied to all types of accounts, you have a specific hierarchy for inheritance, combining, and overriding preferences. Some settings, such as controlling which items are opened at login, are cumulative because no one particular setting overrides another — any number of items can be opened at login.

Some settings are inherited from workgroups to the user level or from within nested workgroups. Settings with only one ultimate outcome — such as the position of the Dock onscreen — use an order of priority to override the same setting for different account levels. The prioritization of conflicting preferences to override the same setting also applies for inheritance. The order of inheritance and overriding preferences is

- ✔ Workgroup (the least specific level)
- ✔ Computer group
- ✔ Computer
- ✔ User (the most specific level)

For example, a preference set at the workgroup level can't override the same preference set for the computer group, computer, or user level. In this sense, a preference set for the user always wins when overriding other levels.

However, setting preferences at the user level can be time-consuming and complicated to manage. Managing at the workgroup or computer-group level saves time and energy, and making your life a little easier is one of the reasons you bought this book.

# Enforcing managed preferences

You can set managed preferences with four different restrictions:

- ✔ **Always:** The preference is enforced continuously. Users can't change the preference.
- ✔ **Once:** The directory sets the preference one time. The user is then free to change the setting.

✔ **Often:** The Often setting isn't present in Workgroup Manager's Overview tab for preferences management, but it can be set within the raw preferences manifests with the Details tab.

Often sets the preference when the user logs in. During the user session, the preference can be changed, but it's reset on subsequent logins to the managed setting.

✔ **Never:** Effectively, Never means preferences management for that setting is disabled, and the user can set whatever preferences are desired.

These settings appear when you select the Preferences icon, select an account, select the Overview tab, and then select a preferences icon. This is described in the "Configuring managed preferences" section, earlier in this chapter.

# Chapter 17

# Creating Mobile Accounts for Notebooks

*Y*ou've had enough sitting at your desk, and it's time to get out of the office, but how do you take your data with you when you go home? What if you need to make a presentation at a client's office out of town? Do you drag your entire network infrastructure with you? Imagine the airline luggage fees.

In this chapter, you determine the best method for managing client computers that aren't tied down. Most frequently, these are notebook computers. Instead of having user home folders stored only on a server volume or only on the client computer, mobility settings offer a combination of these two choices. Lion Server lets you create mobile home folders for Mac, Windows, and Linux clients. (This is in addition to all the mobile configuration features of Profile Manager, which I describe in Chapter 16.)

With mobile accounts, domain information such as mobile preferences and user account data, as well as user data, is all updated when the user connects to the network. Mobile accounts can also have a portable home folder synchronized between a server volume and the internal hard drive. I examine the options in this chapter, and you see how to create a mobile account and a server-based home folder, which you then turn into a portable home folder.

Later in this chapter, I describe how to create and manage mobile accounts and home-folder synchronization in Workgroup Manager.

# Connecting Workgroup Manager to a Shared Domain

As with several of the topics in this book, you need to know the basics of Workgroup Manager. You can run Workgroup Manager from any network-connected system or directly on an Open Directory server. (Remember, you have to download Workgroup Manager as part of the Server Admin Tools package, available at `www.apple.com/support/downloads`.) Follow these steps to launch and connect to the directory in Workgroup Manager:

1. **Launch the Workgroup Manager application from `/Applications/Server` on your client system.**

2. **Choose Server⇨Connect.**

3. **Enter the IP address or hostname of the directory server in the Address field of the dialog that appears.**

4. **Authenticate as the server's local administrator by typing in the Username and Password fields.**

5. **Click the Connect button.**

6. **Choose the shared directory domain from the pop-up menu just above the list of users in Workgroup Manager.**

   If this is strictly an Open Directory domain and you're working directly on the Open Directory server, choose `/LDAPv3/127.0.0.1`. If you're working on a connected system, choose `/LDAPv3/your hostname or IP address`. If you're using Active Directory, choose `/Active Directory/Your Domain` from the list. Other choices are possible, depending on your directory configuration.

7. **Click the lock icon to the right of the Shared Directory pop-up menu and authenticate as the directory administrator that you created as part of the directory configuration.**

You're now ready to manage the users, groups, and computers in the directory domain. Figure 17-1 shows Workgroup Manager logged in to an Open Directory master server and shared domain, with a user account selected.

**Figure 17-1:**
Workgroup
Manager
connected
to an Open
Directory
master.

# *The Nightmare of Networked Notebooks*

When a notebook user takes his notebook to another location, in or out of the office, what happens to the user's authentication information and data when he disconnects from the network? How can the user continue to log in to his notebook and access his documents and other data away from the network directory and file sharing? The answer is the mobile account.

Unlike other accounts, a *mobile account* caches the user's account credentials on the local hard drive. User data could be stored on the local hard drive or a network volume, but the local hard drive makes the most logical sense in this configuration.

To make it even better, you can configure a mobile account to have a portable home folder. Building on the mobile account, a user's home folder is synchronized between a server volume and the local drive. Synchronization occurs at login and at predetermined intervals. The directory administrator configures the intervals.

This choice gives a notebook user freedom of movement while maintaining her data on the server and local drive.

Here are also some other options for accounts and home folders that can be used for notebook clients:

✔ **External account:** Like a mobile account, but the user's account data can be stored on any volume connected to the client, including an external USB or FireWire hard drive, or a USB flash drive. That volume can be removed and connected to another Mac OS X system. The user can log in with the account credentials stored on the external volume.

✔ **External account with portable home folder:** The combination of an external account and portable home folder, both stored on an external volume attached to the client.

One of the most flexible choices, this option allows a user to synchronize a home folder to a portable drive and take it to another computer and have full access to his data. It's also the most unsecured option because the portable drive can be easily lost or stolen.

Other users besides notebook users can benefit from external and mobile accounts and portable home folders. Regular network accounts can be used interchangeably with mobile accounts and portable home folders, with significantly less impact on network activity. Synchronizing users' home folders provides redundancy in the event of a hardware failure.

Creating portable home folders sets up a two-way mirror of files between the server and the local hard drive. Never combine regular network home folders with portable home folders: Data loss is a likely outcome. The portable home folder client tracks changes and performs the sync operation by comparing the files between the server and the local drive. If a file has previously changed on the server and the portable home folder process wasn't aware of the change, the local file will be overwritten back to the server.

Set a master password on each computer in the Security pane of System Preferences. You can also require a master password be set when a mobile account logs in to a managed computer.

# Planning and Deploying Mobile Accounts

Just as you've seen with other services in Mac OS X Server, planning before you decide on deploying mobile accounts and portable home folders saves you from wasting time and energy.

Here's the basic planning and deployment process: First, decide the type of account you'll use to manage mobility settings. Then examine the options for mobile accounts and portable home folders that I describe in the preceding section. Next, configure directory and file-sharing services on your servers. Finalize connections by binding clients to the directory and log in to mobile accounts, creating portable home folders as necessary.

## Simplifying mobile management with computer and group accounts

As I discuss in Chapter 16, accounts come in different types: user, group, computer (or machine), and computer groups. Managing mobility options is possible for any of the account types or combinations thereof. But for simplicity, with multiple accounts needing mobility and portability settings, group and computer group accounts are the best choices.

Manage your notebook systems with computer groups. When users of multiple systems always need a particular setting, such as mobility, creating a group of those systems makes your job easier.

When managing desktop systems with mobile accounts and portable homes, unless you're managing only a few user accounts, also use groups and computer groups. You probably will separate your notebook and desktop systems into separate computer groups.

To create a computer group, you need one or more clients bound to a shared directory, as described in Chapter 6. After the clients are bound, use Workgroup Manager to create a computer group by following the directions in Chapter 16.

If you decide to manage settings based on a group of users instead of a group of computers, create a user group instead. You can use either the Server app or Workgroup Manager to create a user group, as I describe in Chapter 16.

You can designate a group to be a member of another group. Adding groups to groups creates *nested groups.* This technique can save you time when managing large numbers of user accounts. It also facilitates the inheritance of permissions and managed settings, which I discuss in Chapters 8 and 16, respectively.

You can manage a group or computer group by clicking Workgroup Manager's Preferences icon in the toolbar, which I describe in Chapter 16, and the mobility settings, which I examine through the rest of this chapter.

## Configuring mobility settings

To get started with mobility, the user needs an account in a shared directory. Directory information, including the Lightweight Directory Access Protocol (LDAP) account and password data, is cached from the shared directory to the local system. By itself, a mobile account doesn't include any documents or data from the user's home folder.

When a mobile account is enabled, the user can log out and log in again without being attached to the network where the account data resides. After returning to the network and reconnecting to the directory, the local cached authentication data is resynchronized, and any updates to the LDAP or password data are cached again on the local system. You can also have a mobile account expire if it goes unused.

Any standard Open Directory network account can become a mobile account. Mobility settings can be configured for the account itself, a group that the account is a member of, a computer where a user can log in, or a group of computers where users can log in.

If, as the directory administrator, you set mobility in more than one of these locations, rules of inheritance and precedence for client preferences take effect.

Here's an example of how to configure the mobility settings for a computer group. To set up the mobile account, do the following:

1. **Open Workgroup Manager and connect to the shared directory.**

2. **In Workgroup Manager, click the Accounts icon in the toolbar and then click the Computer Groups tab above the list of accounts.**

   The Computer Groups tab is the icon represented by two overlapping squares, the fourth tab following the Users tab, Groups tab, and Computers tab.

   If your planning leads you to manage individual user accounts, groups of users, or individual computers, select that account instead of the computer group in Workgroup Manager.

3. **Click the Preferences icon in the toolbar.**

   The right side of Workgroup Manager displays the icons for the various managed preferences.

   In Figure 17-2, note the small, dark gray circle enclosing a mouse pointer next to the Mobility icon. This indicates that the preferences are being managed for the selected account.

4. **Click the Mobility icon.**

5. **Select the Account Creation tab and then click the Creation subtab.**

6. **By default, Manage is set to Never; select Always.**

   Preferences can be managed never, once, or always in Workgroup Manager. Once isn't an available option for some mobility settings. Figure 17-3 shows the mobile Account Creation settings for a computer group.

**Figure 17-2:**
Managed preferences of a computer group in Workgroup Manager.

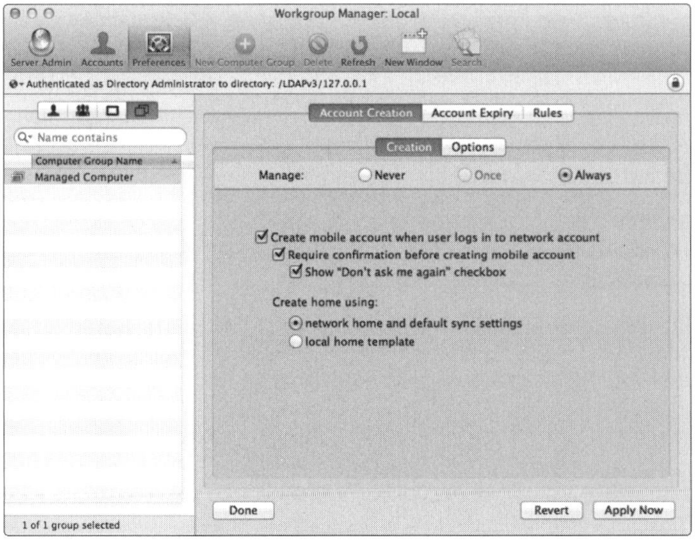

**Figure 17-3:**
Mobile Account Creation settings in Workgroup Manager.

7. **Select the Create Mobile Account When User Logs in to Network Account check box.**

   Selecting this option creates the mobile account on the local hard drive of a Mac OS X system.

8. **(Optional) Deselect the Require Confirmation Before Creating Mobile Account check box to keep the user from having to confirm mobile account creation.**

   (Optional) Deselect the Show "Don't Ask Me Again" check box to prevent the user from having to confirm again when she logs in to a managed computer.

9. **(Optional) Choose how a new home folder is created by selecting Network Home and Default Sync Settings or Local Home Template.**

   The first option uses a network volume and creates either a network home or a portable home, depending on the sync settings in the Rules tab. The second choice (Local Home Template) uses the default home folder settings on the local hard drive.

10. **Click the Apply Now button to save the settings.**

11. **(Optional) Click the Options subtab under the Account Creation tab.**

   Here, you have choices for creating a FileVault-encrypted home folder and deciding where the users' home folders will be created. Click Always to manage these settings. Enable FileVault by selecting the Encrypt Contents with FileVault check box.

12. **(Optional) If using FileVault, under the Options subtab, select either the Use Computer Master Password, If Available or the Require Computer Master Password check box.**

   You select the second choice if you want to require and verify a valid master password on the local system.

   A master password is the critical fail-safe for encrypted FileVault home folders. It provides the ability to restore access to an encrypted account if the user forgets his password.

   The remaining choices under the Options subtab set where the home folder is stored. By default, On Startup Volume is selected. The other choices are At Path, with a field to enter the specific location in the file system where the home folder will be stored; and User Chooses, with a pop-up menu. The pop-up menu choices are Any Volume, Any Internal Volume, and Any External Volume. By choosing Any Volume or Any External Volume, the user can create an external account.

13. **After making any changes, click the Apply Now button to save your settings.**

Two more tabs are in the mobility settings after Account Creation. The second tab is Account Expiry. The settings on this tab control when mobile accounts will expire on the mobile computer, as shown in Figure 17-4 for a computer group. In other words, the cached account on the local hard drive will be deleted when it expires.

Your security policies may require accounts to be deleted if users don't connect periodically to the shared directory. But be careful with this setting. If an account goes unused for the period set by the expiry settings, the mobile account's home folder is deleted, and the user can't log in while away from the network.

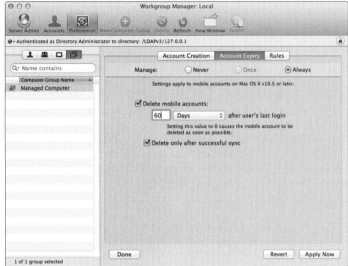

**Figure 17-4:**
Account-
expiration
settings in
Workgroup
Manager.

Select the Delete Mobile Accounts check box and set the time frame for when the account will be deleted to have a mobile account deleted after that time frame. Select the Delete Only After Successful Sync check box if you want to be certain that a mobile account is synchronized to the server before deletion occurs.

The third tab of mobility preferences is the Rules tab. Here's where you configure the settings for portable home folders, which I detail in the following section.

# Creating Server-Based Home Folders and Deploying Mobile Home Folders

Of course the account itself isn't terribly useful without the user's data. The answer is to use compatible file-sharing services on the network to create a portable home folder. To do so, you need an automountable share point configured in the directory for user home folders so that it appears to the user without intervention by the user. An automountable share point must have a network mount record in the directory domain.

Although synchronization of the user's home folder provides hardware redundancy — the user's account is easily synchronized with another system if a hard drive fails or another problem develops — synchronization isn't a replacement for a good backup strategy. Changes in files on the local system — for example, files that are modified, deleted, or corrupted on the local system — are synchronized to the server's volume. Similarly, if a problem exists on the server, the file changes get synchronized back to the local hard drive.

The next section describes creating a home folder that is located on the network. After that, I describe configuring the *mobile* home folder.

## Creating server-based home folders

Any Open Directory user can have a home folder on the server. On a Mac, the *home* folder is the directory that's named after the user. This folder contains all of a user's data, settings, bookmarks, and so on. When you locate users' home folders on the server, they log in to a Mac and authenticate to the server. Users then can log in to different computers and still get the same access to their home folders.

When you create home folders for your users, take care to select the correct file-sharing protocol. For Mac clients, the home folder must be shared with the AFP protocol. (Don't use SMB for a Mac home folder.) Home folders for Windows clients must use SMB. Linux clients use SMB.

Server-based home folders can put a heavy burden on the server and take a lot of storage, but you can assign a limit to the size of the folder. Follow these steps to create a home folder on the server:

1. **In the Server app, share the /Users directory, select Make Available for Home Directories, and click Done.**

2. **In Workgroup Manager, click the Accounts button, select a user, and then click the Home tab.**

3. **In the list of share points, select the Users folder (or other folder).**

   If you don't see it, click the Refresh icon in the toolbar.

4. **Click the Create Home Now button.**

5. **Click the Save button.**

   Workgroup Manager creates a home folder with the user's short name (for example, /Users/ronmckernan).

If you go to the Finder and look inside the new home folder, you'll see that Workgroup Manager has created the hierarchy of folders that a home folder contains to store a user's files and settings, including Documents, Library (which includes Preferences), Desktop, Downloads, and Pictures and Music.

(In Lion, the Library folder in a user's home folder is now invisible, so you'll have to go to the Finder's Go menu, choose Connect to Folder, and type ~/ **Library**.)

## Configuring the mobile home folder

Your server should already be bound to the shared directory or configured as an Open Directory master or replica, as I describe in Chapter 6.

After the binding and the share point are ready, use Workgroup Manager to set the network home folder and enable portable home synchronization. Here's how:

1. **Open Workgroup Manager and connect to the shared directory.**

2. **In Workgroup Manager, click the Accounts icon and then click the Users tab above the list of accounts.**

   The Users tab is the icon represented by the single silhouetted figure — the leftmost tab.

3. **In the list of accounts under the tabs, click a user's name and then click the Home tab on the right side of the Workgroup Manager window.**

4. **Click the share point you previously created for user home folders and then click the Save button.**

   You've set the location where the home folder will be stored on the network, as shown in Figure 17-5.

**Figure 17-5:**
Setting a user's network home folder in Workgroup Manager.

5. **Select the Computer Groups tab and then click the name of a group you want to use.**

   See the section "Simplifying mobile management with computer and group accounts," earlier in this chapter.

6. **Click the Preferences icon and then click the Mobility icon.**

   If you haven't yet, you need to set up account creation, as I outline in the section "Configuring mobility settings," earlier in this chapter.

7. **Click the Rules tab.**

   Here's where you have a multitude of options for the portable home folders.

   The second subtab, Preferences Sync, controls synchronization of preference files from the user's home folder. You come back to this in just a minute.

8. **Click the Home Sync subtab.**

9. **Select Once or Always to set sync settings for each login or always, respectively, and then decide the intervals for sync by selecting one or more of the check boxes:**

   - *At Login:* Sync occurs when the user logs in to her account. The user sees a progress bar while the sync is in progress.

   - *At Logout:* Sync occurs when the user logs out of her account. The user sees the same progress bar.

   - *In the Background:* An automatic sync occurs without any user notification.

   - *Manually:* Sync is triggered by the user from the user's account in the Accounts pane of System Preferences or by the user's selecting Sync Now from the Home Sync status menu when she is logged in.

   Figure 17-6 shows the options for home-folder synchronization.

10. **(Optional) Set the list of sync locations.**

    Below the four options for when sync occurs are the locations that will sync. By default, these include the user's home folder, indicated by the tilde (~) sign. Add locations to sync by clicking the plus (+) button and then typing the path in the new field. Select any location, and click the minus (–) button to remove that sync path. Click the ellipsis (. . .) button to open a new window, and select a location in the file system to sync.

11. **(Optional) Set the list of locations that won't synchronize in the Skip Items That Match Any of the Following area.**

    By default, several locations in the user's home folder are skipped when sync occurs. Generally, these locations are unnecessary because they contain inconsequential files. The same plus, minus, and ellipsis buttons apply to this list.

**Figure 17-6:**
Home folder synchronization settings in Workgroup Manager.

12. **(Optional) Select the Merge with User's Settings check box to combine the synchronization settings a user can set in the System Preferences Users & Groups pane (called the Account pane in versions of Mac OS X before Lion).**

13. **Click the Preferences Sync subtab.**

    The settings in Preferences Sync are similar to those in Home Sync but affect only preferences files. This tab is configured the same way as Home Sync (refer to Steps 9 through 11).

14. **(Optional) Click the Options subtab.**

    To modify the background sync interval from its 20-minute default or to change the default for the Home Sync status menu, select Once or Always. Then modify the background interval and, if desired, deselect the Show Status in Menu Bar check box. See Figure 17-7 to view the additional options available when you're using a computer group.

15. **Click the Apply Now button to save the settings.**

Maintaining regular backups of the server volume and the local hard drive remains a critical part of your network deployment. Easier backup of just the server volume, if the portable home folders regularly and reliably sync to the server, is a side benefit of synchronizing home folders. An always-on backup system for laptops should still be part of your backup strategy, especially for road warriors whose systems are more susceptible to a bad fall or to evildoers looking to steal a fancy Mac laptop.

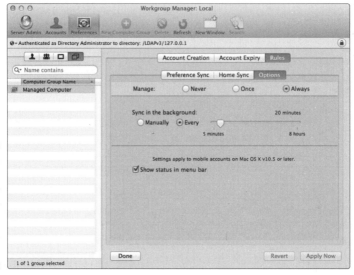

**Figure 17-7:**
Additional options for home-folder sync in Workgroup Manager.

## Putting sync to work on the client

After the services have been configured and managed preferences set, the client needs to connect to the directory and file sharing, and a user will log in to his account. During login and logout, if sync has been enabled at this time, the user sees a window with a scrolling bar indicating the synchronization status. In Figure 17-8, you see an example of this window on a Mac. This window is also displayed if a user triggers a manual sync.

**Figure 17-8:**
Home folder sync at login, at logout, and during manual sync.

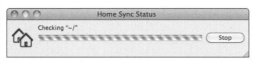

If you selected the options to have the user confirm the creation of the mobile account in the section "Configuring mobility settings," earlier in this chapter, the user confirms the mobile account. From then on, the account is much the same as a local account. The following are the two differences a user sees:

✔ **The addition of the Home Sync status menu (shown in Figure 17-9) is indicated by an icon depicting two overlapping houses to the left of the clock and other menu extras in the menu bar.**

This menu displays the current status of home synchronization with the network home-folder server. The user sees the date and time of the last sync and can choose Sync Home Now to manually sync her home folder with the server.

The two house icons in the menu-bar icon alternate between the normal black outline and a gray version of each house when the background sync process is running.

✔ **In the Users & Groups pane of System Preferences, a mobile tag is added under the user's name in the list of accounts.** A mobile account in System Preferences is shown in Figure 17-10. The user also sees an additional button under the Password tab: Mobile Account Settings.

This user is running Mac OS X 10.6, which is supported along with Mac OS X 10.7 and 10.5.

**Figure 17-9:**
The Home Sync status menu for a portable home folder.

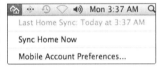

**Figure 17-10:**
A mobile Mac user's account settings in System Preferences.

Clicking this button displays choices for the background sync interval, the folders that are synced, and whether the Home Sync status menu is displayed. These settings, however, may be overridden by the managed preferences in the Mobility settings of Workgroup Manager.

# Chapter 18

# Keeping Your Server Secure

. . . . . . . . . . . . . . . . . . . . . . . . . . . . . . . . . . . . . . . . . . . . . . . .

## In This Chapter

▶ Setting up firewalls

▶ Configuring Internet routers for port forwarding

▶ Creating and using SSL certificates

▶ Setting up virtual private networks

. . . . . . . . . . . . . . . . . . . . . . . . . . . . . . . . . . . . . . . . . . . . . . . .

*O*ne aspect of managing clients is using server security to keep clients from compromising the network. Lion Server comes with tools to prevent snooping, malware, and malicious attacks. In other chapters, I describe password encryption with authentication, Secure Sockets Layer (SSL) data encryption, the use of secure certificates, and spam and virus blockers for individual services, including file sharing, e-mail, and the web.

This chapter looks at overall issues, including using the firewall to guard access to the network and using and creating secure certificates for encryption. It ends with configuring a virtual private network to give offsite users secure access to the local network. You use the Server application to create and import certificates and set up a virtual private network. You use Server Admin to configure a firewall.

## Configuring a Firewall

A *firewall* blocks certain types of incoming traffic from the Internet while allowing outgoing traffic to the Internet. If you're running a firewall, your job is to configure it to allow incoming traffic in response to outgoing traffic from your users. For example, if your users try to access a website, you want traffic from web servers to reach the users.

If your network already has a firewall on another server or a router or other security gateway appliance, you may not need to run Lion Server's firewall. You do need to run a firewall on your Mac server if it's acting as an Internet gateway, with the Mac in between the Internet connection and the local network. You also need to run a firewall on the server if your Internet connection goes directly into a wireless router, and the router doesn't have a firewall built in or running on it. In this case, the server needs to be connected to the router via Ethernet.

Regardless of whether you're running a firewall on Lion Server or somewhere else, the next few sections provide useful information.

## Port numbers used by Lion Server services

A firewall blocks incoming traffic through software ports (settings identified by port numbers) and by port type: TCP (Transmission Control Protocol) and UDP (User Datagram Protocol). A port can be *open,* which allows traffic to come through, or *closed,* which blocks traffic. Each service has a standard port associated with it. For example, the default port for IMAP e-mail is TCP port 143. When used with SSL encryption, the default IMAP port is TCP 993. Some services have a range of ports. Web service defaults to TCP 8080, but has a range of TCP 8000–8999 that you can use.

If you're configuring a firewall that's not on Lion Server, take a look at Table 18-1, which lists the default port numbers used by Lion Server. You also use these port numbers if you're doing port forwarding for an Internet router. Of course, a firewall on Lion Server also uses these numbers, but Server Admin lists Lion's services by name, as well as the numbers, so all you need to do is select them.

Apple has a more extensive list of ports that Apple networking software uses here: http://support.apple.com/kb/TS1629.

In earlier chapters, I describe changing some of the default ports for e-mail, iCal, and other services. You can also set these ports all at once by using the Server app.

### Table 18-1 TCP and UDP Port Numbers for Lion Server Services

| *Service* | *Port Number* | *Port Type* |
| --- | --- | --- |
| Address Book Server | 8008 | TCP |
| Address Book Server with SSL | 8443 | TCP |
| File-sharing AFP | 548 | TCP |
| File-sharing SMB | 139 | TCP |
| iCal Server | 8008 | TCP |
| iCal Server with SSL | 8443 | TCP |
| iChat Server | 5222 | TCP |
| iChat Server with SSL | 5223 | TCP |

| Service | Port Number | Port Type |
|---|---|---|
| iChat server-to-server | 5269 | TCP |
| iChat Server file transfer | 7777 | TCP |
| iChat local | 5678 | UDP |
| iChat audio/video RTP and RTCP | 16384–16403 | UDP |
| Mail, SMTP standard | 25 | TCP |
| Mail service SMTP submission | 587 | TCP |
| Mail service IMAP | 143 | TCP |
| Mail clients IMAP with SSL | 993 | TCP |
| Mail service POP3 | 110 | TCP |
| Mail clients POP3 with SSL | 995 | TCP |
| Profile Manager services | Same as web HTTP, HTTPS | TCP |
| Remote login SSH (Secure Shell) | 22 | TCP |
| Screen sharing (VNC) | 5900 | TCP |
| VPN L2TP | 1701 | UDP |
| VPN L2TP IKE NAT Traversal | 4500 | UDP |
| VPN L2TP ISAKMP/IKE | 500 | UDP |
| VPN L2TP ESP (firewall only) | IP protocol 50 | n/a |
| VPN PPTP | 1723 | TCP |
| Web service HTTP | | TCP |
| Web service HTTPS | | TCP |
| Web service custom website | | TCP |
| Wiki, web calendar, webmail | Same as web HTTP, HTTPS | TCP |

# Firewalls, network routers, and NAT

If you're using a network router (such as a DSL or cable router) that provides the Internet connection, network address translation (NAT), and a firewall, you have two options for configuring the router. (You use the router's software, often accessed through a Web browser.) Your options are

✔ **Run the firewall on the server.** In this case, on your router, you have to make the server the router's default host. This setting, which you make on the router, tells the router to send all incoming connect requests to the server.

✔ **Run the firewall on the router.** Here, you need to configure *port forwarding* (or *port mapping*) on the router. Port forwarding means you set the router to forward traffic from the service port numbers to your server's IP address (shown in the Server Preferences Information pane).

In addition to the firewall, you can run NAT service on Lion Server. I describe how to do this in the section "Hosting NAT on Lion Server," later in this chapter.

## Using an AirPort Extreme or Time Capsule firewall

Lion Server has some special features for Apple's wireless Internet routers, Apple's AirPort Extreme Base Station and Time Capsule. If you're going to run the firewall on the AirPort device, the Server app will display it in the sidebar, listed under Hardware. You can use the Server app to configure the firewall on the server or on the Apple router. You can also add another layer of security for users accessing your AirPort wireless network.

In order to use the Server app to configure AirPort devices running firewalls, you first need to configure a few items with AirPort Utility (in the `/Applications/Utilities` folder of any Mac):

✔ Connection Sharing must be set to Share a Public IP Address.

✔ IPv6 Mode (an advanced option) must be set to Tunnel.

✔ Default Host must be set to Off.

By default, the firewall is turned on in AirPort Extreme and Time Capsule. To keep the firewall running on the device, you need to enable port mapping on the device with the AirPort Utility or the Server app, which I describe in the next section. To instead have the firewall run on the server, use AirPort Utility to enable a default host on the device.

### Configuring firewalls on AirPort devices with the Server app

To use the Server app to configure port forwarding on an AirPort Extreme Base Station or Time Capsule, launch the Server app and follow these steps:

1. **Select the AirPort device in the sidebar under Hardware.**

2. **Click the Add (+) button and choose a service (iChat, Mail, and so on) from the pop-up menu.**

   For services not listed, choose Other and enter the service name and port. (Refer to Table 18-1 for port numbers.)

   This setting tells the AirPort device to let traffic for these services through.

3. **To block traffic from listed services, select a service and click the Delete (–) button.**

4. **When you're finished, click the Restart AirPort button and enter a password for the device if prompted.**

   This step interrupts services that the AirPort device may be providing, such as DHCP, access to a Time Machine hard drive, or Internet access.

### RADIUS for extra AirPort security

Lion Server comes with another feature for Apple wireless routers: the Remote Authentication Dial In User Service (RADIUS). It provides an extra layer of security for users accessing your network wirelessly via an AirPort Extreme Base Station or Time Capsule. With RADIUS running, instead of logging on to the network with the wireless password, users log in with their server account usernames and passwords. You can also prevent users from accessing the Wi-Fi network and allow their accounts access only from Ethernet.

You can set up RADIUS with Server Admin:

1. **Click the Settings icon in the toolbar and then click the Services tab.**

2. **Select the RADIUS check box and then click Save.**

3. **Choose RADIUS in the list under your server.**

4. **Click the General icon in the toolbar.**

5. **Click Configure RADIUS Service.**

   The Configuration Assistant takes you through the settings choices.

 A much simpler method (though with fewer configuration choices) is to turn RADIUS on in the Server app. Select the AirPort device under Hardware and then choose Allow User Name and Password login over Wi-Fi. RADIUS will be turned on, and all server user accounts will have access to the wireless network.

## Configuring a firewall on Lion Server

You use Server Admin to configure a firewall on Lion Server. (Remember, Server Admin is a separate download, as part of Apple's Server Administration Tools.) Using Server Admin to configure a firewall is actually easy. You can click to select services to allow through the firewall, as well as add your own services and ports, such as those used by third-party server software. Server Admin also enables you to create new rules for allowing or blocking ports.

When you first turn on and start the firewall, most ports for services are blocked. You have to set which ports to allow. The ports that are opened by default are those needed to allow you to log in and administer the Mac.

## Enabling the firewall

Before you can configure the firewall, you have to enable the firewall service. In Server Admin, the procedure is the same as with other services:

1. **Open Server Admin and select the server in the left column.**
2. **Click the Settings icon in the toolbar and then click the Services tab.**
3. **Select the Firewall check box and then click the Save button.**

As with other services, you also need to start it to get it running:

1. **In Server Admin, click the triangle next to your server in the left column to expand the list of services.**
2. **Select Firewall from the list.**
3. **Click the Start Firewall button in the lower left.**

You can now stop the firewall by clicking the same button, which changes to Stop Firewall. With the firewall stopped, all incoming traffic is allowed.

## Allowing services through the firewall and editing ports

Server Admin lets you set which services you want to allow through the firewall by selecting them from a list. The list of services is much larger in Server Admin. If your service isn't in the list, you can add it to the list. You can also change the port number.

To change the port number in Server Admin:

1. **Click the triangle next to your server in the left column to expand the list of services and select Firewall from the list.**
2. **Click the Settings icon in the toolbar and then click the Services tab.**

   Server Admin looks like Figure 18-1.

3. **Select check boxes next to the services/ports that you want to allow traffic on.**

   The list of ports includes many services not included in Lion Server (such as FTP and WINS), as well as ports for some third-party products that may be on a network. Notice also that the protocol (TCP or UDP) is already set.

4. **To change a port number, service name, or protocol, double-click the service you want to edit.**

   A dialog appears, with fields for the service name and port number.

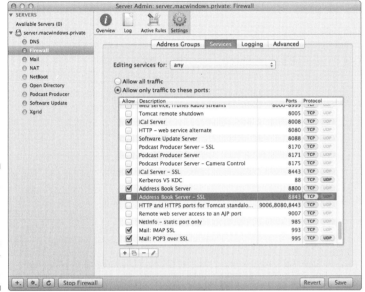

**Figure 18-1:**
The
Services tab
of Firewall
Settings
in Server
Admin.

5. **In the new dialog, type a new service name and/or port number or choose TCP, UDP, or TCP and UDP from the Protocol pop-up menu; click OK.**

   The Port field can contain a range of ports (such as 8000–8999) or a list of port numbers separated by commas (with no spaces).

6. **To add a new port, click the Add (+) button under the list of services.**

7. **When the same dialog from Step 5 appears, type a service name and a port number and choose a protocol from the pop-up menu.**

8. **Click OK and then click the Save button.**

Near the top of the window in Figure 18-1 is a pop-up menu called Editing Services For. In the preceding steps, I assume that Any was chosen in this menu. Any means that the set of ports you selected is applied to all IP addresses that receive traffic. You can also choose an address group, which is a range of addresses that you apply settings to. Lion Server automatically creates two address groups covering the range of private IP addresses: the 10-net range (10.x.x.x) and the 192.168-net range (192.168.x.x). This isn't a choice of one address group or another; you can set different port settings for different address groups.

The next section describes creating your own address groups.

### Creating your own address groups

An address group can be a single IP address, such as for a device or server, and it can also be a range of addresses designated by an address and subnet mask. An address group can have multiple entries. Here are two forms you can use to represent an address group (IP address with a subnet mask):

✔ **Netmask notation:** `192.168.0.0:255.255.255.0`

✔ **CIDR notation:** `192.168.0.0/24`

This web page has a simple explanation of CIDR notation: `www.alexonlinux.com/what-is-cidr-notation`.

To create an address group for use with your firewall, do the following:

1. **In Server Admin, click the triangle next to your server in the left column to expand the list of services and then select Firewall.**

2. **Click the Settings icon and then click the Address Groups tab.**

   Server Admin looks like Figure 18-2, with the two default address groups and Any.

   The name of the address group is the text next to the triangle (such as `192.168-net`). The addresses in a group appear below its name.

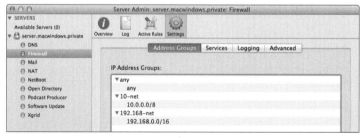

**Figure 18-2:**
The Address Groups tab of Firewall Settings in Server Admin.

3. **Click the Add (+) button, located under the IP Address Groups field.**

4. **In the new dialog, type a name for the address group and then click the Add (+) button to the right of the Addresses in Group field.**

5. **Type an IP address or an IP address with a subnet mask in netmask or CIDR notation.**

6. **Keep using the Add (+) button to add as many IP addresses as you want a rule to affect.**

7. **Click the Delete (–) button to remove any IP addresses if you don't want the rule to apply.**

8. **Click OK in the dialog and then click the Save button.**

### Playing by your own rules

If you want to get into deep firewall-configuration territory, you can use the Advanced tab of Firewall Settings to create your own rules that describe what to do with incoming traffic. You can set a rule to allow or deny traffic, and you can define both the source and the destination of the traffic. You can apply this rule to standard services or services that you create. Here's how:

1. **In Server Admin, click the triangle next to your server in the left column to expand the list of services and then select Firewall.**

2. **Click the Settings icon in the toolbar and click the Advanced tab.**

3. **Click the Add (+) button or duplicate an existing rule by selecting it, clicking the Duplicate button, and double-clicking the rule.**

   The editing dialog, shown in Figure 18-3, appears.

4. **Select choices in the top third of the dialog:**

   • *Action pop-up menu:* You can choose Allow or Deny to define access through the firewall. A third option, Other, lets you type additional (more advanced) commands.

   • *Protocol pop-up menu:* Select TCP, UDP, or Other.

   • *Service pop-up menu:* Choose 1 of more than 100 services, including third-party software. You also have the choice Other.

   • *Log All Packets Matching This Rule check box:* A simple choice.

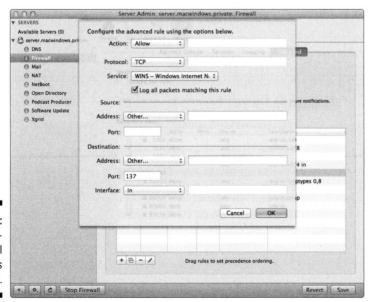

**Figure 18-3:** Create custom firewall rules in this dialog.

5. **Select the source of the traffic to be filtered.**

   The Address pop-up menu contains the address groups that are configured. Choose Other to type a source IP address range you want to filter. (Use CIDR notation.) Type a source port number if you're using a nonstandard service port.

6. **Select the destination for the traffic to be filtered.**

   The Address pop-up menu contains configured address groups, including Any. Or choose Other to type a destination IP address range in CIDR notation. Enter a destination port number if you're using a nonstandard service port.

7. **From the Interface pop-up menu, choose In to apply the rule to incoming traffic; choose Out to apply the rule to packets the server sends; or choose Other to type an interface name (such as en0, en1, or fw1).**

8. **Click OK.**

Be careful with creating and deploying your own firewall rules. You could inadvertently block traffic that your network needs to function properly.

# Hosting NAT on Lion Server

If you're not using network address translation (NAT) on another router device to connect your network to the Internet, you can run it on Lion Server in conjunction with Lion Server's firewall. You use Server Admin and the Gateway Setup Assistant.

To configure NAT with Server Admin, follow these steps:

1. **Open Server Admin and select the server in the left column.**

2. **Click the Settings icon in the toolbar and then click the Services tab.**

3. **Select the NAT check box and then click the Save button.**

To configure NAT with the Gateway Setup Assistant, do the following:

1. **In Server Admin, click the triangle next to your server in the left column to expand the list of services.**

2. **Select NAT from the list.**

3. **Click the Overview icon in the toolbar.**

4. **Click the Gateway Setup Assistant button in the lower right.**

   The assistant takes you through the steps for configuring NAT and related services while providing explanatory text about port forwarding

or just port forwarding without NAT. Here, the assistant configures DHCP and turns on the firewall and DNS, if necessary, as well as VPN, if you desire.

# Working with Secure SSL Certificates

A *Secure Sockets Layer (SSL) certificate* is a small file that enables the server to prove its identity to client computers and other networks and enables encrypted communications. A certificate contains your server's domain name and organization information; it also has a cryptographic key associated with it (a *public key*). You can use SSL certificates with Address Book, Web, e-mail, iCal, and iChat services to encrypt data sent between clients and the server.

You can purchase an SSL certificate from a trusted certificate authority such as VeriSign (www.verisign.com), Thawte (www.thawte.com), and GlobalSign (www.globalsign.com). When you set up the Apple Push Notification service, the Server app guides you through obtaining a push notification certificate from Apple specifically for that service.

You can also create self-signed certificates on Lion Server. A self-signed certificate is created automatically when you install Lion Server. With self-signed certificates, the user's software asks the user whether the certificate should be trusted. With third-party certificates, the user's application accepts certificates without asking the user.

## Using SSL certificates

In Lion Server, you won't see check boxes for SSL in the configuration screens for user services. Instead, you enable SSL for a service simply by assigning an SSL certificate. With the Server app, you can select a certificate to use, create a self-signed certificate, and import a certificate. You can also add and delete certificates and renew a certificate with an updated or signed version.

### Assigning an SSL certificate to a service

Follow these steps to specify a certificate for a service:

1. **In the Server app, select your server in the sidebar under Hardware.**

2. **Click the Settings tab.**

   The SSL Certificate item will have one of these descriptions next to it:

   • The name of the certificate selected for all running services

   • Not Configured, if none of the running services has a certificate

   • Custom, if different services use different certificates

3. **Click the Edit button next to SSL Certificate.**

4. **Choose a certificate from the pop-up menu (see Figure 18-4), or select Custom to change the certificate for specific services.**

**Figure 18-4:** Selecting and creating secure certificates with Server Preferences.

At least one certificate is listed: the self-signed certificate created by the server, named after the server.

If you choose Custom, the dialog expands (see Figure 18-5).

5. **If you chose Custom in Step 4, select a certificate (or none) for a service by clicking the double arrows next to the service to display a list of certificates to choose among.**

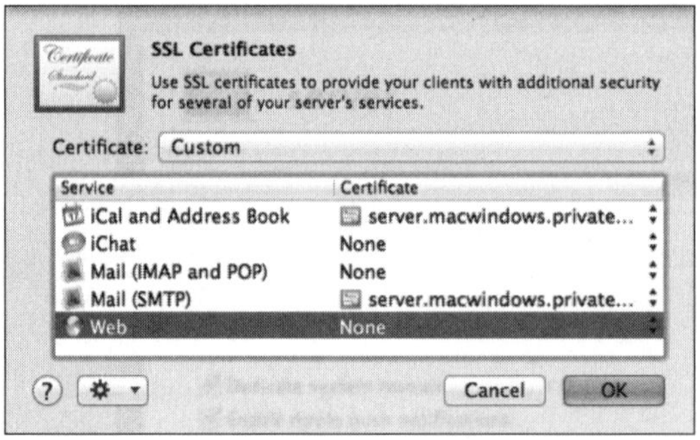

**Figure 18-5:** Selecting different certificates for individual services.

6. **Click the OK button when you're finished selecting certificates.**

### Creating a self-signed certificate

If you don't see any certificates or want to create another, you can create a self-signed certificate:

1. **In the Information pane, click the Edit button to the right of SSL Certificate.**

2. **Select the Use SSL Certificate check box.**

3. **In the pop-up menu, choose Certificate Import⇨Create Self-Signed Certificate.**

   The Certificate Assistant opens.

4. **Type a fully qualified DNS name for the server, and click Continue.**

   Don't change the other default settings: Identity Type = Self Signed Root; Certificate Type = SSL Server; Let Me Override Defaults is deselected.

### Creating a request to a certificate authority

You can use the Server app to create a certificate signing request (CSR) to send to a certificate authority. The authority *signs,* or authorizes, a certificate you've created and supplies a public key. After the certificate is created, you can create a CSR file in Server Admin. Follow these steps in the Server app:

1. **Select the server in the left column under Hardware and click the Settings tab.**

2. **Click the Edit button next to SSL Certificate.**

3. **Click the Actions menu (gear icon) below the list of services and choose Manage Certificates.**

4. **Click the Actions menu in the dialog that appears and choose Generate Certificate Signing Request (CSR).**

   A signing request is generated and displayed in a new dialog.

5. **Click the Save button.**

   A Save As dialog asks you to pick a location on the hard drive.

You can send this file (which ends in .csr) to a certificate authority, such as Comodo Group, Inc. (www.comodo.com), Thawte, Inc. (www.thawte.com), or VeriSign, Inc. (www.verisign.com). Just upload the file or copy and paste into the authority's website. The certificate authority sends you a signed certificate. To use it, replace the certificate you used to generate the CSR, as I describe in the following section.

### Importing a certificate

To import a certificate, such as one purchased from a certificate authority or created by another server, do the following:

1. **Locate the files containing the certificate and the matching private key in the Finder and then position the folder's window in a place where you can get to it.**

2. **In the Server app, select your server in the left column, select the Settings tab, and click the Edit button next to SSL Certificate.**

3. **Click the Actions menu and choose Manage Certificates.**

   A new dialog slides down (see Figure 18-6).

4. **Click the Add (+) button and select Import a Certificate Identity from the Actions menu.**

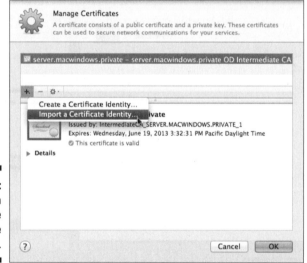

**Figure 18-6:**
Importing a
certificate
with the
Server app.

5. **Drag the certificate and private-key files from the Finder to the dialog and then click the Import button.**

6. **Choose your imported certificate from the pop-up menu.**

### Renewing/replacing an existing certificate

The process for renewing an expired certificate and replacing a self-signed certificate with a signed version is the same. Here's how to do it:

1. **In the Server app, select your server in the left column, select the Settings tab, and click the Edit button next to SSL Certificate.**

2. **Click the Certificates pop-up menu and then select the certificate that you want to replace.**

If you're using different certificates for individual services, select Manage Certificates from the gear menu and then perform Step 2.

3. **Click the gear icon below the list of certificates and choose Replace Certificate with Signed or Renewed Certificate.**

4. **Drag the certificate file you received from the certificate authority and the private-key file to the dialog that slides down.**

5. **Click the Replace Certificate button.**

You must also replace certificates if you change the DNS name of the server or virtual hosts.

## *Becoming a certificate authority*

You may want to act as a certificate authority, with the ability to sign certificates created elsewhere in the organization. Use the Keychain Access to create a certificate authority and to sign certificates.

To create a certificate authority, do the following:

1. **Launch Keychain Access (in /Applications/Utilities).**

2. **In the Keychain Access menu, choose Certificate Assistant⇨Create a Certificate Authority.**

   The Certificate Assistant launches.

3. **Choose to create a Self Signed Root CA and then click through the screens, providing information as needed.**

   The process is much shorter if you choose not to override the defaults.

You can also use the Keychain Access to create a signed certificate for someone who's sent you a certificate signing request file. Here's how:

1. **Launch Keychain Access.**

2. **In the Keychain Access menu, choose Certificate Assistant⇨Create a Certificate for Someone Else as a Certificate Authority.**

   The Certificate Assistant launches.

3. **When asked, drag the CSR file you received from the Finder into Certificate Assistant.**

4. **Click through the screens, following the directions.**

At the end of the process, the Mail application launches and creates a new e-mail message with the new signed certificate file attached.

# Using Virtual Private Networks

A *virtual private network (VPN)* is a secure encrypted connection to a local network from outside it, typically made over the Internet. Remote users connected through a VPN see the local network, including servers and printers, as though they're connected directly to it. You can also connect two remote local networks through a virtual private network.

If you set up Lion Server as a private server (with a `.private` domain name), not serving to the Internet, a VPN is one way for users outside the building to privately connect to your hosted websites, wikis, and other services.

In Lion Server, you create virtual private network connections with the Server app. Veteran Mac administrators, take note that you can no longer set up VPN with Server Admin, as in previous versions of Mac OS X Server. You also have fewer options than in the past unless you go to the command line.

If you're setting up NAT on your server Mac and you're using the Mac server as an Internet gateway, the Gateway Setup Assistant is another choice for setting up VPN service. I describe how to use the Gateway Setup Assistant in the section "Hosting NAT on Lion Server," earlier in this chapter.

## VPN protocols: L2TP/IPSec and PPTP

Lion Server supports two alternative protocols for transporting encrypted data. The one you see in the Server app is *Layer Two Tunneling Protocol/ Secure Internet Protocol (L2TP/IPSec,* or *L2TP over IPSec).* Lion Server, however, no longer has any way to turn on the second protocol, *Point-to-Point Tunneling Protocol (PPTP),* except to use the command line.

PPTP is a Microsoft technology that's long been used in Windows networks. Only older clients, before Windows XP and before Mac OS X 10.3, require PPTP. L2TP/IPSec is newer, with bits coming from Cisco and Microsoft. L2TP/IPSec is the preferred VPN protocol in Lion Server for various reasons, including the fact that it supports Kerberos authentication.

## The shared secret

IPSec uses a *shared secret,* a password stored on the server and clients. The shared secret is *not* used for authentication or login, and it doesn't play a role in encryption. The shared secret is a token that's exchanged between computers to establish trust. If a client doesn't have the shared secret, it can't connect. Users don't type a shared secret; it's stored on the computers.

The shared secret must be at least 8 characters, but 12 or more is better, and it can include letters, numbers, and punctuation but no spaces. The shared secret shouldn't be easy to remember; it should be a random string of characters.

The Server app's VPN pane generates a shared secret for you or lets you use your own.

## Getting your network ready for VPN

To access the local network from outside through a virtual private network, you may need to configure some other aspects of your network first:

- ✔ **DHCP IP address range:** When you configure VPN service, you set a range of IP addresses that is assigned to the remote VPN users. These addresses are on the server's network. This range must not contain static IP addresses used on the network and must not overlap ranges provided by a DHCP server, an Internet router, or an AirPort Base Station. Make sure that these devices aren't assigning IP addresses from ranges that overlap with those that the VPN service is providing to remote users.

  The IP address that the VPN service assigns to a remote computer for its VPN connection is *in addition* to the IP address that the remote computer is already using to connect to the Internet. The VPN IP address is released back to the server when the VPN session concludes.

- ✔ **Port forwarding:** If you have an Internet router, including a DSL or cable router, you need to set it up to use port forwarding (also known as port mapping) so as to forward traffic to your server's IP address.

- ✔ **Firewall VPN ports:** If you have a firewall running on the server or on a separate device, the administrator needs to open ports on the firewall to allow VPN traffic. These are TCP port 1723; UDP ports 500, 1701, and 4500; and IP protocol 50. (For PPTP, use TCP port 1723.)

- ✔ **Firewall ports for services:** If the only way you're allowing access from remote users is through an encrypted VPN connection, you don't have a reason to open the firewall ports for specific services; all the traffic goes through the VPN instead of the firewall. This means you could set the firewall to block those ports for increased security.

  You could also have a mixture: Keep open web and e-mail ports on the firewall, but close file sharing and iCal to restrict those types of access to a VPN connection. If you have a firewall between your workgroup and the rest of your organization, you may also want to keep ports open for people in your organization who are outside the workgroup.

# Configuring VPN in Lion Server

The Server app automates the configuration of a VPN service, but doesn't give you many options. The Server app allows you to easily do four things:

- ✔ Turn VPN service on or off.
- ✔ Set a VPN shared secret.
- ✔ Edit the IP address range for VPN users.
- ✔ Export a VPN client configuration file for automating VPN setup of Mac OS X clients.

The Server app also automatically adds the client information to Profile Manager (see Chapter 16).

Turning on VPN service in Server Preferences enables L2TP/IPSec only. To enable PPTP, you'll need to use the Unix command line in Terminal.

To turn on and configure VPN, do the following:

1. **In the Server app, click the VPN icon to get to the VPN pane (see Figure 18-7).**

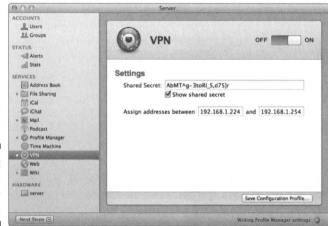

**Figure 18-7:**
The VPN pane in the Server app.

2. **Select the Show Shared Secret check box to view or edit the shared secret that the Server app generated for you.**

3. **Make any required changes to the IP address range fields.**

This is the range the server reserves for users connected through the VPN service. You may want to make the range larger to allow more simultaneous VPN users or to prevent a conflict. (See the preceding section for more about the VPN IP address range and conflicts.) You can change the *first* address, which is the beginning of the range, or the *second* address, which is the end of the range, or both.

4. **Click the big switch to the On position and click the Save Configuration Profile button.**

## Configuring VPN clients

Mac, Windows, Linux, and iOS devices can all connect to your network through Lion Server's VPN. Mac OS X clients and iOS devices can take advantage of Profile Manager for getting VPN configuration information; the Server app automatically includes the VPN setup in Profile Manager (described in Chapter 16).

For Macs, particularly older ones, the Server app also creates a VPN configuration file. In the Server app's VPN pane, click the Save Configuration Profile button to create and save a file that you can distribute to Macs. On the Mac OS X client, open System Preferences, click the Network icon, and add a VPN interface. With the VPN interface selected, choose Import Configurations from the gear icon's pop-up menu and then select the VPN configuration file you created.

For Windows and Linux clients, you need to manually configure VPN configuration. You need the following information:

- ✔ **Account name:** This is the user account's short name on the Mac server.
- ✔ **User password:** This is the user's account password on the Mac server.
- ✔ **VPN server or host:** This is your server's DNS name or IP address.
- ✔ **VPN type:** This is L2TP over IPSec or PPTP.
- ✔ **Shared secret:** This is visible in the VPN pane of Server Preferences (click the Edit button and select the Show Shared Secret check box).
- ✔ **Firewall ports:** If users are running firewalls on their computers or on a remote network, that firewall must be configured to allow VPN traffic on TCP port 1723; UDP ports 500, 1701, and 4500; and on IP protocol 50. For PPTP, use TCP port 1723.

These firewall-port settings apply to Mac clients as well.

# Part VI
# The Part of Tens

# In this part . . .

Steve Jobs's keynote addresses (known as *Stevenotes*) at Macworld Expo and Apple's developers' conferences often ended with a simple statement: "There's just one more thing."

He'd then go on to make another product announcement, often something big. Things like the MacBook Pro, the iPod touch, and the AirPort Base Station.

Well, here I am at the end of this book, and I have more to tell you. Nothing as big as the MacBook Pro, but I make up for it in quantity.

I have just 20 more things.

In Chapter 19, I present ten things you can add to Lion Server. These are mostly products from developers other than Apple, from free widgets to enterprise-level servers that add new capabilities.

Chapter 20 is my desperate attempt to get more articles into this book — ten more, to be exact. Here you find condensed how-to's for additional cool things to do with Lion Server, as well as some handy tips and some references to other information.

# Chapter 19

# Ten Things You Can Add to Lion Server

*L*ion Server comes with so many different services and features for your users and your administrators that it's hard to imagine that you need to add anything extra. Although you may not *need* to run additional server software, you can enhance Lion Server with new functionality. And if you want to manage your server from your iPad, iPhone, or iPod touch, you can find an app for that.

## Antivirus for Your Server

Mac viruses and malware are fairly uncommon. Virus programmers tend to focus mostly on the several hundred million Windows PCs in the world. This doesn't let Mac OS X off the hook. Mac malware has been appearing during the past few years, and one of these days, a big Mac-focused virus wave may hit. Servers in particular are important computers to protect.

Intego's VirusBarrier Server (www.intego.com) automatically checks files located on a Mac server and files that are launched from the server. VirusBarrier Server quarantines infected files it finds and sends an e-mail message to an administrator. It can also repair files that have been quarantined. Like all good virus packages, VirusBarrier Server automatically checks for and downloads updates of the latest virus definitions.

Lion Server's e-mail service already comes with well-respected open source antivirus software, ClamAV. But if you want another layer of protection, VirusBarrier Server comes with VirusBarrier Mail Gateway, which automatically checks all e-mail messages when running Lion Server's built-in mail server.

VirusBarrier Server can detect a variety of malware, including *scareware,* which is software that tells users that their Mac is infected, often to trick them into downloading more malware or buying something. VirusBarrier Server also detects spyware that monitors keystrokes, dialer viruses that dial your modem access number, and other sneaky invaders.

# Kerio MailServer

If you want an even more cross-platform groupware server with even more features, try adding Kerio Connect to Lion Server. Kerio Connect (www. kerio.com) is considered by some to be an alternative to Microsoft Exchange for small to midsize businesses, and it syncs with Active Directory and Open Directory. The big advantage over the built-in groupware of Lion Server is that Kerio Connect supplies e-mail, calendar, contacts, notes, and tasks to just about any client: Outlook for Windows and Mac, Entourage, Apple Mail, iCal, and Address Book.

Like Lion Server's services, Kerio supports iPhone, but it also supports BlackBerry, Android, Windows Mobile, Symbian, and Palm Treo. The remote console is cross-platform, too: You can manage Kerio Connect from Windows, Linux, and Mac OS X. And the server is also available for Windows and Linux.

Kerio MailServer has some expanded features, too. Although Lion Server lets users delegate calendars to other iCal users, Kerio Connect lets users delegate calendars to Outlook, Entourage, and iCal users. Another thing that Kerio has that Lion Server doesn't is integrated, automatic server backup.

# Network Backup

With Time Machine, Lion Server does some great backup for all your clients — as long as they're running Mac OS X 10.5 or later. For backing up older Mac OSes or Windows or Linux clients and servers, you can add third-party software to Lion Server. Here are three that also come in versions for Windows clients:

✔ **Roxio Retrospect Single-Server** or Multi-Server (www.roxio.com) is for small to medium-size shops. Retrospect Server comes in several configurations, from a single server to multiple servers. Modules are used for your Mac, Windows, and Linux clients.

✔ **Tolis Group's BRU Server for Mac OS X** (www.tolisgroup.com) comes in packages from workgroup to enterprise levels. BRU Server can run concurrently with other services and includes error recovery for restoring from damaged media.

✔ **Quest NetVault: Backup for Ma**c (www.quest.com/netvault-backup) is a full-blown enterprise-level backup system for big, complex networks. Quest NetVault: Backup for Mac supports Apple's Xsan, features modular scalability, and is optimized for virtual machine backup. You can apply policy management tools to individuals and groups.

All these can back up to tape libraries.

# Media Asset Management and Workflow

Asset managers take thousands of photo, image, video, and audio files sitting in a pile on your server and organize them. They keep track of the assets that are part of a workflow and what final projects they're used in. Asset managers tell you which version of a project is the current version, and they let you return to older versions. They also automate workflow, performing routine tasks such as assembling pieces into a whole and converting files to different file formats. Lots of server-based asset manager products are available. The following list provides just a sampling of different types:

✔ **Adobe InDesign Server** (www.adobe.com/products/indesignserver) is aimed at automating InDesign-based print publishing, design, typography, and page layout. Because InDesign Server is highly customizable with an InDesign markup language, third parties sell premade workflow systems based on your type of publishing.

✔ **Canto Cumulus** (www.canto.com) was designed for photos and graphics but now also handles audio and video. Because it's a sophisticated workflow product, you can send Cumulus an e-mail to place an attached file in a catalog. Cumulus tracks users' actions and lets you see what's being used. It also has a built-in photo editor.

# General-Purpose Database Server

If you want to create a custom multiuser database with a graphics user interface, you have several choices. Here are two:

✔ **FileMaker Server** (www.filemaker.com) can do invoicing, labeling, tracking inventory, or managing contacts with maps and video. For the user, you can create simple data entry forms or use sophisticated graphical interfaces. FileMaker is also a software development platform, so lots of prebuilt FileMaker-based applications are available.

✔ **Panorama Enterprise Server** (www.provue.com) focuses on speed as a RAM-based database. Data fetchers are thousands of times faster than disk-based data retrieval. This server can also distribute the database to clients, automatically syncing changes with all users. This reduces the server load. And the software comes with powerful data analysis tools.

# Apple Remote Desktop

Apple Remote Desktop (www.apple.com/remotedesktop) is a remote adminstration tool for Mac clients and servers. You can use this tool to manage any Mac with Mac OS X v10.4.11 or later, including Lion Server. You can use this tool to distribute, install, and upgrade software on hundreds of Macs at the same time.

You use Apple Remote Desktop to generate reports about what applications are being used, what versions of Mac OS X are installed, and who is logging into the computers. Apple Remote Desktop is also a remote-control program that lets you see and control what's going on with any Mac from your Mac. You can use this feature to give tech support to a user or fix a problem remotely. You can also perform remote Spotlight searches on the other Macs. You can even copy any files you find to your Mac or delete them.

You have to set up each Mac that you're going to administer with Apple Remote Desktop. But you can partly automate that procedure with Apple Remote Desktop itself.

# InterMapper, a Network Monitor

Dartware's InterMapper (www.intermapper.com) is a tool for your entire network; at its base, it provides maps of your network. You can create a map to show the location of servers, clients, switches, and routers. And InterMapper shows the existence of notebook computers on your maps. You can create schematic maps and maps superimposed on a building floor plan or on a map of a city or school district. InterMapper even interacts with Google Earth for long-distance mapping. Other maps get you back into a building.

But InterMapper is also a problem-solving tool: It can point out problems before they manifest themselves in downtime or slowdowns. You can check router utilization and traffic at various points on the network. InterMapper can perform tests that target an area or a device. A traffic analyzer can show you exactly who (or what) is generating a large amount of network traffic. InterMapper stores its data in an SQL database, which lets you generate various types of reports.

You can receive alerts by e-mail and other methods. You can use InterMapper from a web browser or from an iPhone. InterMapper runs on Mac OS X, Windows, and several flavors of Linux and Unix.

# TechTool Pro

If something goes wrong with your server hardware, MicroMat's TechTool Pro (www.micromat.com) is good to have on hand for its hardware checking, troubleshooting, and repair and data recovery functions. TechTool Pro can check your Mac's system memory, which, when it goes bad, can cause all sorts of mysterious problems; it also checks the memory on your graphics card. TechTool Pro scans disks for bad blocks and directory corruption, scans files for problems, and performs a number of other tests.

The tests are also useful to run before you have problems. You can run individual tests or the entire suite. TechTool Pro can detect a potential problem with a piece of hardware and recommend a way to proceed. You can run tests while your server does its thing because the software doesn't require a lot of resources.

The eDrive feature creates a bootable drive partition with every TechTool Pro tool installed. You don't have to erase the drive to create this partition, which you can use when your Mac refuses to boot.

TechTool Pro can also fix drive problems. The Volume Rebuild feature recreates disk directories, even on damaged drives, to bring a drive back to life or to improve performance with optimization. TechTool Pro includes several types of data recovery to pull important files off damaged drives; it can even recover deleted files.

# iOS Apps to Manage Servers

Who needs a notebook when you have an iPad or iPhone? Well, I do, but a growing number of apps lets you manage and monitor Lion Server from an iPad or iPhone. Here's just a sampling, which you can buy at the App Store in iTunes and from your iOS device:

✔ **Server Admin Remote** (www.harlekins.org) is not from Apple, but it can be more convenient to use than Server Admin on a Mac for certain tasks. You can start and stop services, monitor the running status of services, and view server logs. You can also check on server CPU usage and network traffic. It works over EDGE, Wi-Fi, and 3G connections.

- ✔ **iTeleport** (www.iteleportmobile.com), from the company of the same name, lets you remotely view and control Mac, Windows, and Linux PCs, including Lion Server; just enable sharing on the computer. iTeleport lets you use Apple's server tools running on a Mac. iTeleport has great use of iOS gestures and a smooth typing implementation. The zoom also works well.

- ✔ **iNag Nagios Viewer** (http://idevelop.fullnet.com/iapps) is an iOS interface to the open source Nagios network monitoring system, described in the next section. iNag lets you monitor multiple servers through Nagious and issue commands to Nagios. You can't do everything that you can from a computer, but some prefer iNag to Nagio's native web interface. If you're using Nagios, John Fullington's iNag is a must.

# Nagios for Network Monitoring

Keeping tabs of multiple servers and services on a larger network can be a challenge, especially with mixed operating systems. Nagios (www.nagios. org) from Nagios Enterprises is a set of open source network monitoring software that runs on Mac OS X Server as well as Windows and Linux servers. Via e-mail or SMS, Nagios can tell you about software problems with services and hardware, enabling you to attend to issues before they become major mishaps. Nagios can also automatically fix certain software problems, such as restarting services or applications that have crashed.

Nagios uses a plug-in architecture that lets you add features from the Nagios project or from third parties. Your IT group can write its own plug-ins and scripts. Nagios is serious enterprise software and requires technical expertise, but help is available through conferences and a large online library that includes videos and tutorials.

# Chapter 20

# Ten Cool Things That Didn't Make It into the Book

*O*ne of the difficult things about writing this book was deciding which of Lion Server's many aspects didn't fit in the 400-plus pages. Some features are cool but obscure; others just don't fit in with the other topics. So in this chapter, I want to squeeze in a few more useful bits, in no particular order. This chapter gives you a bird's-eye view of the how-tos. Some tips are simple things that anyone can use, and others are pretty technical, but they're all pretty cool.

## Using Gateway Setup Assistant to Share an Internet Connection

I mention in several places throughout the book that you can use your Mac OS X Server to share an Internet connection with your local network. I also describe how to set a static IP address for your server, configure VPN, configure a firewall, and enable DNS service. You'll also need to enable DHCP and network address translation (NAT) to share your Internet connection.

There is one place in Lion Server you can do all these tasks and more. The Gateway Setup Assistant takes you on a guided tour of the settings, asking you questions about what you want to do with your network. It can set up

the services you need to share your Internet connection. You can then use
Server Admin to tweak your settings. Here's how to get started:

1. **Launch Server Admin and connect to the server.**

2. **If you haven't enabled the NAT service, click the Settings icon in the
   toolbar and then click Services.**

3. **Select the NAT check box and then click Save.**

4. **In the left column, click the triangle next to your server to expand the
   list of services.**

5. **Select NAT from the list of services and click the Overview tab.**

6. **Click the Gateway Setup Assistant button.**

7. **Click through the various setup screens, answering Gateway Setup
   Assistant's questions along the way.**

   Be sure to read all the help offered.

8. **In the final screen, review the settings to make sure that you've made
   the right choices.**

   To have a record of what you did, take a screen shot by pressing
   ⌘-Option-3. An image file appears on the Desktop.

9. **Click the Configure button.**

   The Gateway Setup Assistant turns on and configures any services
   needed to do what you told it to do.

# Hosting User Start-Up Disks on the Server

In Chapter 17, I describe putting users' home folders on the server — a great
convenience for users on multiple Macs — but what about Macs with multiple users? For example, in a school library or lab, you want the same system
configuration on multiple machines and an easy way to reinstall systems that
get out of whack by an anonymous user.

The answer is to host not just the home folder but also the entire start-up
drive on the server, using the NetBoot service in Lion Server. The Mac clients
actually boot from the same disk image of a start-up drive on the server.
Every time a Mac starts up, it boots from the pristine image, which includes
applications.

To host the entire start-up drive on the server, you first must enable NetBoot
in Server Admin:

1. **Select your server, click the Settings icon in the toolbar, and then click the Services tab.**

2. **Select a disk to store the images and client data by clicking NetBoot in the left column, clicking the Settings icon in the toolbar, and then clicking the General tab.**

3. **While you're in this screen, select one or more of the server's Ethernet ports to use and click Save.**

   NetBoot creates the required folders on the server.

4. **Create a NetBoot image with System Image Utility.**

   If you're not sure how, see the section "Creating Installation Images with System Image Utility," later in this chapter. A folder with a name ending in .nbi appears.

5. **Upload this folder to the server's NetBootSP0 folder, a share point that NetBoot created.**

6. **Back in Server Admin, click the Images tab, select your image, click Save, and then start NetBoot.**

7. **On the client Macs, go to the Startup Disk pane in System Preferences and select the NetBoot volume as the start-up disk, or start up while holding the N key.**

# Installing Mac OS X and Updates from the Server

When you're upgrading a bunch of Snow Leopard clients to Lion, downloading from the App Store on every Mac isn't the most effective use of your time or your network bandwidth. Two more Lion Server features, NetInstall and Software Update Server, let you deploy client installations of Mac OS X from the Server, as well as provide Apple's updates from your server. NetInstall uses the NetBoot service (see the preceding section) but uses a different image created with the System Image Utility. Where a NetBoot image is a server-based boot drive, a NetInstall image acts as a server-based installation DVD. The client Mac boots from it and launches the Mac OS X installer. You need a volume license from Apple to install multiple copies of the OS on all your Mac clients.

The Software Update Server downloads Apple's software updates to your server, providing them to users. This feature lets you control the software versions on users' Macs and prevents them from installing updates that your organization may not be ready for.

1. **First, enable Software Update Server: Select your server, click the Settings icon in the toolbar, and then click the Services tab.**

2. **Click Software Update under your server, and select the Settings icon in the toolbar.**

3. **Change any settings you like.**

   You can change the location of where the downloads are stored. It's a good idea to use a volume other than the start-up drive. You can select Automatically Enable Copied Updates to begin serving all updates or keep it unchecked to manually select updates. Lion Server contacts Apple's server to get a list of updates, displayed in the Updates pane.

The Mac clients must be bound to a network directory and set up using Managed Preferences, described in Chapter 16.

# Creating Installation Images with System Image Utility

System Image Utility is part of the Server Administration Tools download that includes Server Admin and Workgroup Manager. You use it to create images for NetBoot and NetInstall (see the two preceding sections). You can also use System Image Utility to create a third type: NetRestore images, which enable you to restore a volume over the network. A NetRestore image is a clone of a user's volume and is used to restore that user's boot volume by using the NetBoot service.

The System Image Utility is easy to use. When you launch it, it lists volumes or installers that it can create images from. (It can't create an image of the drive you are booted from.) The first screen lists the Mac OS X 10.7 Lion installer that you downloaded from the App Store, if you have it on a drive. You then choose whether to create a NetBoot, NetInstall, or NetRestore image. From within System Image Utility, you can save the image to the NetBoot share that Server Admin created when you started the NetBoot service.

# Running Lion from the Command Line

One of the things that I try to do in this book is spare you from typing commands when possible. But the fact remains that you can do just about everything in this book — and much more —with commands in a Unix shell, Terminal, which you can find in /Applications/Utilities.

Apple offers a 300-page *Command-Line Administration* PDF reference here:

```
www.apple.com/server/macosx/resources/documentation.html
```

If you know your way around a Unix shell, you'll find it all in Apple's PDF.

# Clustering Mail Services

You can distribute the load of a mail server by creating a mail cluster. A *mail cluster* is a group of mail servers sharing the mail data store with Apple's network-based storage solution, Xsan software (`www.apple.com/xsan`), and the storage area network (SA) hardware that Xsan requires. If one server fails, the other servers pick up the slack.

With your hardware in place, set up Xsan on the network with Xsan Admin, which comes with Lion Server, in the `/Applications/Utilities` folder. Then create the cluster's first member, open Server Admin, select your server, and select Mail. Click the Settings icon, click the Advanced tab, click the Clustering tab, and then click the Change button. A setup assistant appears to guide you through the procedure.

After a mail server is part of the cluster, when you make changes to its mail settings (POP, IMAP, SMTP, and others), these changes are made automatically to all the servers in the cluster.

# Researching Ruby on Rails

If mail clusters aren't geeky enough for you (see the preceding section), try this tip: Lion Server comes with built-in support for Ruby on Rails (`www.rubyonrails.org`), an open source language and framework for creating web-based applications. Mac OS X Server comes with several Ruby on Rails component packages (called *gems* in Ruby-speak), one of which is the Mongrel web server.

Apple has information about developing Ruby on Rails applications here:

```
http://developer.apple.com/tools/developonrailsleopard.html
```

Apple also has some information about deploying Ruby on Rails and the Mongrel web server in the *Web Technologies Administration* PDF document, available here:

```
www.apple.com/server/macosx/resources/documentation.html
```

# Grouping Servers in Server Admin

If you think about it, Server Admin looks a little like iTunes. You have a list of servers in a left column. Click one, and you see stuff on the right. The comparison is a stretch, but when you have a lot of Mac servers on the network, you can create the equivalent of iTunes playlists. You can even create the equivalent of smart playlists.

With Server Admin, the "playlist" is called a *group,* and the "songs" are *servers.* The group lives in the left column and, when you expand it, displays the servers in that group. You can group servers by function, geography, or anything you like. As with iTunes playlists, servers can be in more than one server group. You even have the equivalent of smart playlists: smart groups.

To create a server group, click the Add (+) button at the bottom left of the window, select Add Group, and give the group a name. The group appears in the left column. Now you can drag servers into the new group.

To create a smart group, click the Add (+) button and select Add Smart Group. Give the smart group a name and then add the criteria that decides which servers are added to the smart-group list. Click OK, and the group appears in the left column, with a list of servers that meet your criteria.

# Setting the Server to Autorestart

If you want your server to get back up and running after a power failure or a system freeze, you can tell Mac OS X Server to start up automatically:

1. **While logged on to the server Mac as an administrator, open System Preferences.**

2. **Click the Energy Saver icon and then select the Restart Automatically After a Power Failure check box and/or the Restart Automatically If the Computer Freezes check box.**

   For the latter setting, the power management hardware restarts five minutes after a kernel panic or a freeze.

# Finding Help at Apple.com

Apple has quite a bit of information about Mac OS X Server on its website. Unfortunately, finding what you want can take some time. Here's a list of several different ways you can enter Apple.com that might provide a quicker route to what you need regarding Mac OS X Server:

✔ **Recently updated tech-support articles:** This page lists the newest and most recently modified troubleshooting and how-to articles. This is a good page to check a few days after Apple releases a software update.

```
http://support.apple.com/kb/index?page=articles
```

✔ **Mac OS X Server support:** Here, you can find links to support pages for individual Mac OS X Server services, such as file sharing, iCal Server, and the rest. It also has links to popular how-to and troubleshooting articles and to recent software updates related to Mac OS X Server.

```
www.apple.com/support/macosxserver
```

✔ **Apple Discussions pages:** Here, you can post a question or search the forum for an answer to a question that someone else may have asked. This first page lists forums for everything Apple, but the Server Product category has areas for Mac OS X Server, Xserve, and other IT topics. To post a question, log in with an Apple ID, such as your iTunes account.

```
http://discussions.apple.com
```

# Index

• N •

# Notes

## Apple & Macs

iPad For Dummies
978-0-470-58027-1

iPhone For Dummies,
4th Edition
978-0-470-87870-5

MacBook For Dummies, 3rd
Edition
978-0-470-76918-8

Mac OS X Snow Leopard For
Dummies
978-0-470-43543-4

## Business

Bookkeeping For Dummies
978-0-7645-9848-7

Job Interviews
For Dummies,
3rd Edition
978-0-470-17748-8

Resumes For Dummies,
5th Edition
978-0-470-08037-5

Starting an
Online Business
For Dummies,
6th Edition
978-0-470-60210-2

Stock Investing
For Dummies,
3rd Edition
978-0-470-40114-9

Successful
Time Management
For Dummies
978-0-470-29034-7

## Computer Hardware

BlackBerry
For Dummies,
4th Edition
978-0-470-60700-8

Computers For Seniors
For Dummies,
2nd Edition
978-0-470-53483-0

PCs For Dummies,
Windows
7 Edition
978-0-470-46542-4

Laptops For Dummies,
4th Edition
978-0-470-57829-2

## Cooking & Entertaining

Cooking Basics
For Dummies,
3rd Edition
978-0-7645-7206-7

Wine For Dummies,
4th Edition
978-0-470-04579-4

## Diet & Nutrition

Dieting For Dummies,
2nd Edition
978-0-7645-4149-0

Nutrition For Dummies,
4th Edition
978-0-471-79868-2

Weight Training
For Dummies,
3rd Edition
978-0-471-76845-6

## Digital Photography

Digital SLR Cameras &
Photography For Dummies,
3rd Edition
978-0-470-46606-3

Photoshop Elements 8
For Dummies
978-0-470-52967-6

## Gardening

Gardening Basics
For Dummies
978-0-470-03749-2

Organic Gardening
For Dummies,
2nd Edition
978-0-470-43067-5

## Green/Sustainable

Raising Chickens
For Dummies
978-0-470-46544-8

Green Cleaning
For Dummies
978-0-470-39106-8

## Health

Diabetes For Dummies,
3rd Edition
978-0-470-27086-8

Food Allergies
For Dummies
978-0-470-09584-3

Living Gluten-Free
For Dummies,
2nd Edition
978-0-470-58589-4

## Hobbies/General

Chess For Dummies,
2nd Edition
978-0-7645-8404-6

Drawing
Cartoons & Comics
For Dummies
978-0-470-42683-8

Knitting For Dummies,
2nd Edition
978-0-470-28747-7

Organizing
For Dummies
978-0-7645-5300-4

Su Doku For Dummies
978-0-470-01892-7

## Home Improvement

Home Maintenance
For Dummies,
2nd Edition
978-0-470-43063-7

Home Theater
For Dummies,
3rd Edition
978-0-470-41189-6

Living the
Country Lifestyle
All-in-One
For Dummies
978-0-470-43061-3

Solar Power Your Home
For Dummies,
2nd Edition
978-0-470-59678-4

## Internet

Blogging For Dummies,
3rd Edition
978-0-470-61996-4

eBay For Dummies,
6th Edition
978-0-470-49741-8

Facebook For Dummies,
3rd Edition
978-0-470-87804-0

Web Marketing
For Dummies,
2nd Edition
978-0-470-37181-7

WordPress
For Dummies,
3rd Edition
978-0-470-59274-8

## Language & Foreign
## Language

French For Dummies
978-0-7645-5193-2

Italian Phrases
For Dummies
978-0-7645-7203-6

Spanish For Dummies,
2nd Edition
978-0-470-87855-2

Spanish
For Dummies,
Audio Set
978-0-470-09585-0

## Math & Science

Algebra I
For Dummies,
2nd Edition
978-0-470-55964-2

Biology For Dummies,
2nd Edition
978-0-470-59875-7

Calculus For Dummies
978-0-7645-2498-1

Chemistry For Dummies
978-0-7645-5430-8

## Microsoft Office

Excel 2010 For Dummies
978-0-470-48953-6

Office 2010 All-in-One
For Dummies
978-0-470-49748-7

Office 2010 For Dummies,
Book + DVD Bundle
978-0-470-62698-6

Word 2010 For Dummies
978-0-470-48772-3

## Music

Guitar For Dummies,
2nd Edition
978-0-7645-9904-0

iPod & iTunes For
Dummies, 8th Edition
978-0-470-87871-2

Piano Exercises
For Dummies
978-0-470-38765-8

## Parenting & Education

Parenting For Dummies,
2nd Edition
978-0-7645-5418-6

Type 1 Diabetes
For Dummies
978-0-470-17811-9

## Pets

Cats For Dummies,
2nd Edition
978-0-7645-5275-5

Dog Training For Dummies,
3rd Edition
978-0-470-60029-0

Puppies For Dummies,
2nd Edition
978-0-470-03717-1

## Religion & Inspiration

The Bible For Dummies
978-0-7645-5296-0

Catholicism For Dummies
978-0-7645-5391-2

Women in the Bible
For Dummies
978-0-7645-8475-6

## Self-Help & Relationship

Anger Management
For Dummies
978-0-470-03715-7

Overcoming Anxiety
For Dummies,
2nd Edition
978-0-470-57441-6

## Sports

Baseball
For Dummies,
3rd Edition
978-0-7645-7537-2

Basketball
For Dummies,
2nd Edition
978-0-7645-5248-9

Golf For Dummies,
3rd Edition
978-0-471-76871-5

## Web Development

Web Design
All-in-One
For Dummies
978-0-470-41796-6

Web Sites
Do-It-Yourself
For Dummies,
2nd Edition
978-0-470-56520-9

## Windows 7

Windows 7
For Dummies
978-0-470-49743-2

Windows 7
For Dummies,
Book + DVD Bundle
978-0-470-52398-8

Windows 7 All-in-One
For Dummies
978-0-470-48763-1

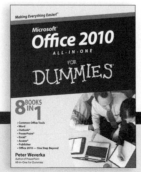

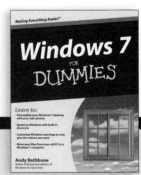

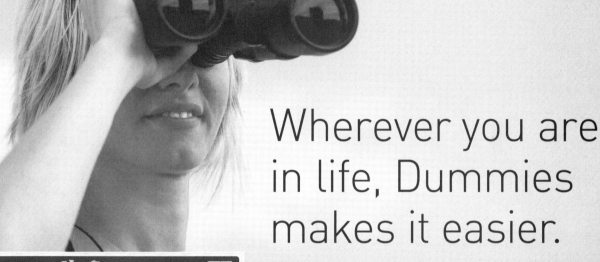

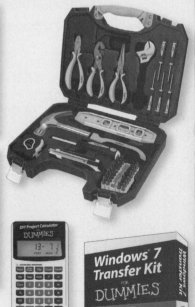